W9-BNH-610

THE HUXLEYS

BOOKS BY

RONALD W. CLARK

Non-Fiction

The Birth of the Bomb

The Rise of the Boffins

Tizard

'Living Biographies' of *Sir Julian Huxley*, *Sir John Cockcroft* and *Sir Mortimer Wheeler*

The Victorian Mountaineers

An Eccentric in the Alps

Six Great Mountaineers

The Picture History of Mountaineering

The Day the Rope Broke

The Huxleys

Fiction

Queen Victoria's Bomb

Ronald W. Clark

THE HUXLEYS

McGRAW-HILL BOOK COMPANY
NEW YORK TORONTO

Library of Congress Catalog Card Number: 68–17745

First Edition 1968
Reprinted 1969

11134
Printed and Bound in Great Britain by
Cox & Wyman Ltd., London, Fakenham and Reading

CONTENTS

ILLUSTRATIONS

ACKNOWLEDGEMENTS

The author wishes to thank:

Many members of the Huxley family for their help and co-operation, but particularly Sir Julian and Lady Huxley, Sir Laurence Collier, Mrs Rosalind Huxley, Mr Gervas Huxley, Mrs Renée Tickell, Mrs Joyce Kilburn, Mrs Joan Buzzard, Mrs Oriana Haynes, Mr Rupert Crawshay-Williams, and Mrs Laura Huxley.

Sir Gavin de Beer for writing the Preface.

Mrs J. Pingree, archivist of the Imperial College of Science and Technology, for her constant help in connection with the Huxley Papers.

President K. S. Pitzer of Rice University for much help and for photostats of letters concerning Julian Huxley's work at Rice.

Mrs Rosalind Huxley and Mrs Geoffrey Cooke for the generous loan of photographs.

Mr C. M. Berkeley, formerly of Unesco, for his great personal help.

Mr Jake Zeitlin and Mr G. R. Doubleday for help and advice.

Metro-Goldwyn-Mayer for the loan of the Aldous Huxley treatment of *Madame Curie*.

Methuen & Co. Ltd for the letter from *The Life of John Middleton Murry*; the Cambridge University Press for the extracts from *The Individual in the Animal Kingdom* by Julian Huxley; Mrs Laura Huxley, Chatto and Windus Ltd and Harper & Row, for extracts from *Along the Road*, *The Art of Seeing*, *Antic Hay*, *Jesting Pilate* and *What Are You Going to Do About It?*; Laurence Pollinger Ltd, the Estate of the late Mrs Frieda Lawrence, William Heinemann Ltd and The Viking Press, Inc., for extracts from *The Collected Letters of D. H. Lawrence* edited by Harry T. Moore (copyright 1932 by the Estate of D. H. Lawrence, 1960 by Angelo Ravagli and C. Montague Weekley); Sir Osbert Sitwell and Macmillan & Co. for the extract from *Laughter in the Next Room*; the late Roy Campbell and Hollis and Carter Ltd for *Light on a Dark Horse;* Mr Gerald Heard and *The Kenyon Review*;

the Executors of the Cecil Gray Estate and Jonathan Cape Ltd for the extract from the biography of Peter Warlock by Cecil Gray; Sampson Low for the extract from *The BBC and All That* by Roger Eckersley; A. D. Peters for the extract from *Africa View* by Julian Huxley.

Sir Laurence Collier for permission to use etrxacts from his unpublished manuscript, *North House;* and, for other copyright material, Sir Julian Huxley, Lady Huxley, Mr Gervas Huxley, Mrs Rosalind Huxley, Mrs Renée Tickell, Mrs Laura Huxley, Mr Kingsley Martin, *The Observer*, Mr Ronald Lockley, Dr Humphry Osmond, Mr Warren R. Dawson, Miss Anita Loos, the Executors of H. G. Wells, and the editor of *Nature*.

He also wishes to acknowledge the gracious permission of Her Majesty the Queen to print the letter from Lord Knollys on pages 123 and 124.

AUTHOR'S NOTE

At first glance the Huxleys present a tidy family appearance, seeming to consist solely of the direct descendants of Thomas Henry Huxley. Flourishing almost exactly a century ago, he might well be expected to present the biographer with a clean-cut array of children, grandchildren and great-grandchildren, so that successive generations could be neatly fitted into successive chapters. In fact, the position is more involved. TH's brothers and sisters impinged on his life in a variety of ways. The clean division into generations is complicated by the twenty years separating the birth of his first son and his last daughter; and also, in later years, by his eldest surviving son's two marriages, which produced half-brothers born some thirty years apart. And while it is easy to believe, as TH himself believed, that the particular Huxley spirit sprang from the union of his mother and his father, yet the main family tree is complemented, in mid-twentieth-century, by the usual collaterals.

There are also the Huxleys-in-law. Mrs TH; Leonard Huxley's two wives; the present Lady Huxley; Elspeth; and the two wives of Aldous – these are only the more obvious of the women who have played significant parts in the family fortunes, while the same is certainly true, among the husbands, of Alfred Eckersley, the Hon. John Collier and E. S. P. Haynes.

All this tends to produce a complicated background to the distinctive mixture of scientific curiosity and artistic perception which is the family's most continuing characteristic and which can be traced through more than a century. It tends, also, towards a concentration on some members whose modesty can easily be disturbed and to the giving of little more than passing glances at others whose activities lie outside the main Huxley stream. The author therefore wishes to stress that while he has received help and co-operation from many members of the family, as well as from those who are specifically thanked in the acknowledgements, he alone is responsible for the balance of the following pages, the accuracy of the facts and the opinions expressed.

'That man, I think, has had a liberal education who has been so trained in youth that his body is the ready servant of his will, and does with ease and pleasure all the work that, as a mechanism, it is capable of; whose intellect is a clear, cold, logic engine, with all its parts of equal strength, and in smooth working order; ready like a steam engine, to be turned to any kind of work, and spin the gossamers as well as forge the anchors of the mind; whose mind is stored with knowledge of the great and fundamental truths of Nature, and of the laws of her operations; and who, no stunted ascetic, is full of life and fire, but whose passions are trained to come to heel by a vigorous will, the servant of a tender conscience; who has learned to love all beauty, whether of Nature or of art, to hate all vileness, and to respect others as himself.'

T. H. HUXLEY

('A Liberal Education and Where to Find It')

PREFACE

Not a dynasty, nor a clan, but an *élite*

There has been much argument about whether the hundred and fifty nine members of the Bach family who were musicians owed their bent to the genes that they inherited, or to the possibility that if you were born into the Bach family and drenched with music from morning to night, you could not avoid becoming a musician. Such a view makes no allowance for the possibility that contra-suggestion might fill some with nausea, as children brought up by Jesuits may become communists. With the Huxleys, there is something more nearly approaching a controlled experiment, for they excel not in one, but in almost every line of human endeavour, and this chiefly by means of a quality of character, inculcation of which would not be expected during the formative years of childhood: non-conformity and individuality. This is borne out by TH's splendid remark about Julian: 'I like that chap. I like the way he looks you straight in the face and disobeys you.'

Francis Galton and the genes have it, and this leads me to the only point on which I disagree with the author, where he says that the great-great-grandchildren of TH have only one-sixteenth of his genes. His children could, of course, not have had more than half his genes, but many of them may have been linked, and his later descendants may have more of them than their degree of descent would have allowed on the old discarded view of blending inheritance.

It is disconcerting to find that nearly twenty years after theological prejudice had been overcome sufficiently to allow Darwin to be buried in Westminster Abbey, Albert Edward, Prince of Wales, found it politic to decline chairmanship of the Huxley Memorial Committee. He did, however, unveil the statue of TH in the Natural History Museum, and the event provided an episode which is well in character. Mrs Huxley bent down and whispered urgently, 'Julian, give Aldous your top hat.' 'Shan't.' 'You must.' 'Why?' 'Because Aldous is going to be sick.' *Antic Hay* reflects the anecdote.

There can be few men more religious, in the proper sense of the word, than TH, Julian, and Aldous, devoting all their energies and gifts to improving the sorry lot of men, without mummery, petitionary prayer, or superstition. Their views are interesting to compare with those of the Swiss pastor Charles Rittmeyer, who shows, quite satisfactorily to the unprejudiced, that Christ's disciples constantly misunderstood Him (He told them so repeatedly); that the evangelists made matters worse by ignorantly crystallizing the legends of physical miracles and superstitions that had, perhaps inevitably, grown up around Him, for people will believe anything; and that the real nigger in the woodpile was Paul, who not only invented a deadly disease, original sin (which would have been that non-starter, the inheritance of an acquired character), but convinced all members of his sect that they suffered from it, and, masterstroke, persuaded them that he had the only remedy for their distemper. One of Rittmeyer's most important conclusions is that Christ's God has nothing whatever to do with that 'revengeful tyrant', which was how Darwin described the god of the Old Testament. It is in a sense to prevent the tragedy of the real Christ baby (and what He really stood for) from being thrown out of the window with the bathwater of theology that the Huxleys are in the forefront of the humanist movement, to free mankind from exploitation by a system that does much good but depends for its power and money on the fear of death, and to protect them in time from the horrors of the otherwise inevitable explosion of the bomb that threatens them most, by exposing the criminal folly of those who believe in big battalions and oppose practical methods of population-control.

It has rightly been said that Darwin changed the whole direction of human thought by establishing the fact and the method of evolution. To the dissemination of this truth, the Huxleys have contributed more than any, not only to elucidate the past and show that evolution is an opportunistic, unprogrammed process, but also to point out the potential benefits of the future, unhampered by any fantasies of built-in disharmonies which would, in any case, have been weeded out millions of years ago by natural selection. The Huxleys have been remarkably conciliatory in their approach to this and kindred problems. They could, for instance, have pointed out that if the Virgin Birth were true, Christ would have been haploid and half-size; that Eve could not have been made from Adam because her chromosomes were different; or that when man-like apes were turning into ape-like men, forty thousand generations ago, they were not a single pair, but a population which can reasonably be estimated at not less than a hundred and twenty-five thousand, which would have provided a sufficient supply of heritable variations by recombination of genes for natural selection to have effected the evolutionary changes which it has during that time. (It is strange to see how ill-informed many people still are about the relative importance of natural selection and mutation, which latter process does not direct evolution at all.)

But the Huxleys have made no less a contribution of their own to human understanding, collectively and individually, by showing that there is no real cleavage in western culture. TH: 'Science and literature are not two things, but two sides of the same thing'; Julian: "No sensible man of science imagines for a moment that the scientific point of view is the only one. Art and literature, religion and human studies, are other ways of exploring and describing the world'; Aldous: 'The great truth that art and literature and science are one.' This is completely in line with Descartes's teaching, that there is a uniformity of method in the healthy human mind which remains fundamentally the same, whatever the object or the field to which it directs its attention. It only shows how misguided, ill-founded, and unfortunate is the glib journalistic slogan of 'two cultures', which mistakes what is a temporary dichotomy of educational policy and practice for a sort of schizophrenia of western civilization.

The creative process of the mind is the same in the arts and the sciences, and the Huxleys, possessing imagination, have ideas; and whether they be poetic (*poiëtēs* means 'he who makes'), literary, philosophical or scientific, they illustrate the truth pointed out a hundred and fifty years ago by Coleridge, and not improved upon, that 'The imagination, true inward creatrix, instantly and out of the chaos of elements or shattered fragments of memory, puts together some form to fit it.' The 'form', in the Huxleys' case, has grace.

Western culture is so rich that it contains many streams, and the Huxleys have done more than any to weave them together. The sorry fact remains, however, that few men are so much as half educated. When this is remedied, they may see that the universe is not constructed on a plan that admits of written revelations by personal gods in national languages (which constantly change their meaning) to chosen peoples (enough has been seen of these with Hitler); long-term specific prophecies based on tendentious false translations, 'verified' *post hoc*, on purpose to 'prove' their 'truth'; or interference with the laws of nature (which George III wanted to do with Benjamin Franklin's lightning-conductors). What people do not seem to realize is that such a concept leaves, not less, but more scope for the exercise of loving kindness, the most important principle in the world, by whatever name it be called.

Living as I do, in the Alps with their innumerable human associations, from Petrarch to Albrecht von Haller, Shelley and Byron, John Addington Symonds and Conan Doyle, D. H. Lawrence and Katherine Mansfield, my thoughts often turn to Huxleys. I think of TH riding across the Grimsel Pass on a penny-farthing bicycle, falling off, and bleeding so profusely that the blood had to be staunched with cobwebs; or sitting in the Grands Mulets Hut on Mont Blanc, 'on a pinnacle like St Simon Stylites, and nearly as dirty as that worthy saint must have been'; or at the Kurhaus, Maloja, going downstairs and running into the Duchess of Teck, Queen Mary's mother, who walked with difficulty, so he gave her his arm and helped her into the room that had been prepared for her tea. By the side of the lovely Lake of Sils, a granite block has been erected and inscribed to TH. I think of the combined Huxley families taking an entire hotel at Mürren; of Trev's 'great day' when he started from Rosenlaui at six to cross the Grosse Scheidegg and make geography 'concrete'; and of Julian writing, 'I expect that the mountains can give the climber more than climbing, and will do so if he but keep his eyes open. From them there will come to him flashes of beauty and of grandeur, light in dark places, sudden glimpses of the age, the glory, and the greatness of the earth.' And I remember that these Alps belong to the admirable and adorable Juliette. But I must no longer stand between the reader and this magnificent book.

November 1967 Gavin de Beer

Retrospect

The Reverend Aelfric Hudson was ushering his parishioners from the porch of St Nicholas, parish church of Compton, Surrey: a building more growth of history than work of human hands. The Saxon tower held pink fragments of Roman brick, built in by men who had used the material nearest to hand; the wooden screen had been zealously carved from a tree which had been growing in Alfred's day; Norman pillars still carried small *graffiti*, the masons' personal comments on the French conquerors of nine hundred years ago; neat notices in polished brass holders on the pews showed where more modern Christians had reserved their place with God. How very lasting, these signs that as time's ever-moving stream passed through the church at least some of its sons had left their marks and were not forgotten!

As Mr Hudson bade farewell to the last of the baptismal party, the mechanism of the church clock echoed down its relentless 'toc' from the darkness above – the personal metronome of St Nicholas counting the future into the past.

It was then that Mr Hudson saw his visitors.

He recognized the elder of the two tall men immediately. And beside Sir Julian Huxley, nimbly alert in his seventies, already framing in his mind the many testing questions he wished to ask about the church, there stood the taller and almost wraith-like figure of his brother.

Mr Hudson elucidated as he led his visitors up the nave. Sir Julian, recalling how sixty years ago the surrounding countryside of hammer-pond and common, of chalk ridge and sandstone height, had been the Huxley home territory, remembered how it had awakened them to the natural beauties and to the mysteries of life and death. Their home had been Prior's Field, and from Prior's Field they had walked to St Nicholas's across the fields on an afternoon more than fifty Decembers past, mourners at their mother's funeral.

Now Aldous, already under sentence from the disease which was soon to kill him, approaching the end of a lifetime of near-blindness, had returned 6,000 miles from his adopted home across the Atlantic. He had returned to nearby Laleham, the house on the hill where he had been born, and had lingered for a while to consider the view from what had once been his nursery windows. He had returned to Hillside where, like more than one Huxley relative, he had received his first lessons from Mr Gidley Robinson. He had returned to Prior's Field itself, where at the turn of the century the Huxley children had played together; and he was now completing his own private survey of the past.

Yet deference to the past had always been overlaid in the family tradition with a determination to look fearlessly towards the future – a Victorian confidence which had persisted past the middle of the twentieth century. There were still great things to be accomplished. Could any of them lie beyond the limits of a family which had travelled so far in such little time? When Aldous Huxley had been born in 1894 his grandfather Thomas Henry still carried the banner almost alone. Now, less than seventy years later, brothers and half-brothers, first cousins and second cousins, sprigs from an ancestral tree whose branches spread widely across the page, all bore witness to the transformation.

The proliferation was impressively apparent to Aldous on this visit to Britain in the early 1960s. During the late spring evenings he would sit in the garden of his brother's Hampstead home, lath-thin, rather tired but still speaking in a wonderfully melodious voice, touching rather than seeing the relatives and friends whom his sister-in-law Juliette had conjured up by letter or by telephone. They came to meet him once again, perhaps for the last time, this angular cerebrotonic, the hot young man of the 1920s matured into kindly mystic, a gentle man partly obscured by his crisp public image, kindly, helpful and among the most equable and least neurotic of the Huxleys.

They were indeed a remarkable intellectual crop, a fascinating collection sprung from Thomas Henry Huxley and his wife Henrietta Heathorn. There was his own brother Julian, leader among the neo-Darwinists, zoologist extraordinary, dedicated upholder of scientific humanism, the first Director-General of Unesco; a man whose diverse interests were reflected in the African carvings, the modern paintings, the biological prints, the multitudinous items collected on a score of journeys across the world which overflowed from walls and shelves of his study on to the stairs and hallways of his house. There was Andrew Huxley, a half-brother thirty years younger than Julian, physiologist and Nobel Prize-winner. There were the three Eckersley brothers, grandsons of T. H. Huxley, who between them had helped to usher the radio age into Britain. There were the two separate Collier families, provided by daughters of TH who, in succession, had married the Hon. John Collier, Edwardian portrait-painter *de luxe*.

All knew this Hampstead home of the Huxleys, its garden later ornamented with blanched elephant and rhino skulls, which had for long been the family headquarters. To it there came Gervas, six-foot-four in the Huxley fashion, and his wife Elspeth, whose *White Man's Country; Lord Delamere and the Making of Kenya* had first revealed her intuitive understanding of Africa and its peoples. Here had lived Julian's sons, one botanist, the other anthropologist, grandsons of Julia Arnold, that link with another great Victorian family, and a woman whose ethereal mother-figure still shimmered out in memory through Aldous's novels after more than half a century.

And here had come cousins and nephews and nieces, Huxleys who had been attracted like Aldous by that borderland where mind and matter meet, men and women drawn to the study of social medicine, of industrial psychology; to conservation of wildlife and of the human habitat; to the exposition, in language for ordinary people, of the multiple problems raised by that question of questions, man's place in nature. Their individual personalities stood up sharp from the surroundings; yet most bore the family imprint, being physically tall, spare, and slightly avian in appearance; mentally vigorous, mercurial, independent and, at their best, merciless in their devotion to truth.

But history must have a start. For the Huxleys it had begun little more than a century earlier, as Britain was flexing her muscles astride the world and a young surgeon sailed east on a voyage that was to change his life and open the way for the Huxley dynasty.

PART ONE

The Founding of a Family

Chapter I

Voyage of Discovery

(*i*)

On the morning of 11 December 1846, as the 28-gun frigate H.M.S. *Rattlesnake* chopped westwards down the Channel from Plymouth Sound, the world had spun in its orbit for some 4,500 million years, give or take the odd few hundred million. On its surface there dwelt nearly 1,000 million human beings, divided from one another by biological inequality, colour of skin, ignorance of mind, and beliefs of varying plausibility. No less than 400 million of them lived among the crumpled brown folds of China, ancient and isolated peoples whose Empire had only recently signed a humiliating peace with the British. Another 180 million of differing faiths swarmed on the sub-continent of India where their destinies were firmly ruled by a small handful of white conquerors. Some 70 million were spread across the plains of the Russian Empire, whose monolithic rule reached for 5,000 miles across two continents from Baltic Sea to Bering Straits. In the dark continent of Africa, a population as great as India's was steadily, by Bible and by bludgeon, being made aware of the white man's existence. The remaining sixth of human life was stretched across the globe, uneven both in distribution and in influence. Less than one-fifth of a million lived in the huge sub-continent of Australia for which the *Rattlesnake* was bound. The United States, across whose interior great herds of bison and buffalo still thundered in natural splendour, harboured a mere 12 million white men, some unnumbered thousands of 'red'-skinned native inhabitants, and 2 million African Negroes whose bodies, or whose ancestors, had been snatched into slavery. From Britain, a small island off the north-west coast of Europe, fewer than 28 million people ruled one-sixth of the world.

On board the *Rattlesnake* as she turned westwards past the red rocks of Eddystone there served as assistant-surgeon Thomas Henry Huxley, now voyaging into fame; a man whose work was to help transform the human view of the world so that its wonders no longer appeared as disconnected fragments but as related parts of one evolving organism. Huxley, aged twenty-one as the *Rattlesnake* left England for her four-and-a-half year survey of the reefs which lay between Australia and the uncharted waters of Borneo, was a striking example of the extraordinary 'sports' which nature can produce; an illustration of the casual way in which geniuses are thrown up from the deep genetic recesses of the past.

Nothing unusual might have been expected of him when he was born, the seventh child of George and Rachel Huxley, in what was then the small village of Ealing on the western outskirts of London. The Huxleys were a Cheshire family, and could trace their name back to the days of Richard I, when it was linked with the manor of Hodesleia, some eight miles south-west of Chester. From Hodesleia, or the hamlet of Huxley as it later became, the family spread to surrounding villages such as Eccleston, where they were represented by a flourishing yeoman family in the late eighteenth century; to Macclesfield, where they ran a prosperous business as silk merchants; and across the border into Wales, where they became first Ap-Huxleys and then Puxleys. They also spread southwards into the Midlands, and at the beginning of the nineteenth century there was living in Coventry a George Huxley, tall, dark, rather quick-tempered, one of the numerous surviving sons of a Thomas Huxley who according to family tradition had moved to the city from Lichfield.

In 1810 George Huxley married Rachel Withers, a slender, dark-haired, dark-eyed woman of great charm who had dutifully borne him eight children, of whom six survived. Eliza, Ellen, George Knight, William Thomas and James Edmund were to lead unremarkable lives, and only with the appearance of Thomas Henry, born on 4 May 1825, did the union of Rachel Withers with the Huxley stock act as a catalyst and produce in her son a combination of rare qualities which were to be transmitted, through him, to successive generations.

It is ironic that the name of Huxley might never have rung like a battle-cry had it not been for Rachel Withers.

> Physically [TH later wrote in a fragment of autobiography] I am the son of my mother so completely – even down to peculiar movements of the hands, which made their appearance in me as I reached the age she had when I noticed them – that I can hardly find any trace of my father in myself except an inborn faculty for drawing, which, unfortunately, in my case, has never been cultivated, a hot

temper, and that amount of tenacity of purpose which unfriendly observers sometimes call obstinacy.

Throughout his youth it became increasingly clear that Thomas Henry was no ordinary boy. Yet if the chances of nature had endowed him well, the accidents of nurture did much to counter them, making his early life frustrating and his eventual success the more remarkable. At the time of TH's birth, his father was senior assistant master at Great Ealing School, then run by a Dr George Nicholas. The establishment had a great reputation and was attended by John Henry Newman and his two brothers, the Newman parents comparing it favourably with Eton. Soon after leaving Ealing for Oxford in 1817, the future Cardinal wrote to George Huxley. In his reply, only a torn portion of which has survived, Huxley asked Newman not to

> be surprised if I express myself very proud if I have been instrumental in paving the way towards the necessary requirements your prospects demand. I must not [for]get to name the unbroken line of good conduct [and] attention during the whole of your residence [her]e – these I shall remember, and in anticipating [you]r future success I am persuaded I do so on [r]ational grounds....

Later pupils included Sir Henry Lawrence, Captain Marryat, W. S. Gilbert, Thackeray, and Hicks Pasha.

Nevertheless, Great Ealing School also had a reputation of a different sort. Converted from an ancient rectory, its dormitories consisted of an old brewery and a former washhouse; the best part of the school estate appears to have been the twelve acres which Nicholas had converted for cricket, fives and tennis, and there seems little doubt that the pupils lived rough even judging by the rough standards of the day. According to George Macfarren – later Sir George Macfarren, principal of the Royal Academy of Music – life there was 'the very hardest ship that sails the ocean of existence'. T. H. Huxley's memories were even more damning.

> My regular school training was of the briefest, perhaps fortunately [he later wrote], for although my way of life has made me acquainted with all sorts and conditions of men, from the highest to the lowest, I deliberately affirm that the society I fell into at school was the worst I have ever seen. We boys were average lads, with much the same inherent capacity for good and evil as any others; but the people who were set over us cared about as much for our intellectual and moral welfare as if they were baby-farmers. We were left to the

> operation of the struggle for existence among ourselves; bullying was the least of the ill practices current among us.

This miserable existence was to last only a short while. Dr Nicholas died in 1835. George Huxley left in the reorganization that followed and returned to his native Coventry as manager of a local savings bank. His son, Thomas Henry, concluded the two years of formal education that were all he was ever to receive.

Few details of Huxley's youth have been recorded. The only clues are provided by passing references in his brief autobiographical note written in old age, a fragmentary journal kept between the ages of fifteen and seventeen, and the occasional references to boyhood made from time to time in his massive correspondence. Yet from this slender evidence it is possible to build up the picture of a youth notable for the vigour with which he tackled the business of self-education. At the age of twelve he was reading Hutton's *Geology* in bed by candlelight. Shortly afterwards he was mastering Hamilton's *Logic*, while before reaching the age of sixteen he had been led on by the thundering sentences of Carlyle to teach himself German. 'It is not so hard as it seems,' he advised a student many years later. 'Don't bother much about the grammar to begin with, but go straight to the book you want to read, translate the first ten lines with the aid of a dictionary, and learn all the words. Do this day by day and it will not be long before you only need to use the dictionary now and then.' The young Huxley was remembered as the youth who went haymaking in the fields then still surrounding Coventry with a hay-fork in one hand and a book in the other. His books might be hidden by his companions, but the companions remained his friends; for in spite of his taste for high thought, he displayed, in youth as in later life, an ability to rub along with the rest of mankind.

At the age of sixteen he was a tall, dark-haired, and strikingly handsome youth. He had first hoped to become a mechanical engineer but, as he put it, 'the fates were against' him, a reference to the straitened circumstances into which the family appears to have fallen after the move from Ealing. Instead, he was drawn into medicine. Both his sisters had married doctors and Ellen had come with her husband to live in Coventry. It was this husband, a Dr Cooke, who gave the young Huxley some elementary instruction in medicine while he was in his early teens; and it was probably Cooke who encouraged him to attend a post-mortem at the age of fourteen, an event which was to have a great effect on the boy's life.

> I did not cut myself, and none of the ordinary symptoms of dissec-

> tion-poison supervened, but poisoned I was somehow, and I remember sinking into a strange state of apathy [he subsequently wrote]. By way of a last chance, I was sent to the care of some good, kind people, friends of my father's who lived in a farmhouse in the heart of Warwickshire. I remember staggering from my bed to the window on the bright spring morning after my arrival, and throwing open the casement. Life seemed to come back on the wings of the breeze, and to this day the faint odour of wood-smoke, like that which floats across the farmyard in the early morning, is as good to me as the 'sweet south upon a bed of violets'.

Huxley soon recovered. But there was a curious sequel. When, years later, he began to suffer from the long series of dyspeptic attacks which were to burden his life, TH attributed them to the youthful poisoning – an attitude which may well have prevented him from seeking an alternative, and possibly more likely, explanation.

Instruction from Dr Cooke no doubt guided Huxley into a medical career.

> I am now occasionally horrified to think how very little I ever knew or cared about medicine as the art of healing [he wrote in old age]. The only part of my professional course which really and deeply interested me was physiology, which is the mechanical engineering of living machines . . . what I cared for was the architectural and engineering part of the business, the working out the wonderful unity of plan in the thousands and thousands of diverse living constructions, and the modifications of similar apparatuses to serve diverse ends.

In January 1841 he travelled from Coventry to Rotherhithe to start work as assistant to a Dr Chandler; and he thus served his apprenticeship in a London dock area of concentrated squalor. The experience left its mark so that in later years it was unnecessary to talk to Huxley of the condition of mankind, of the way the poor lived, or of the problems posed by poverty; he had felt and touched and smelt it all at close range.

After a short while he moved from Rotherhithe to North London, following his elder brother James Edmund as apprentice to the doctor husband of his other, and favourite, sister Eliza. This was Dr John Salt, of whom little is known but who spoke of a colourful youth during which he had fought with Byron's Legion in Greece, been captured by the Turks, and swum the Hellespont twice.

The move to the Salt home in the Regent's Park area gave Huxley more time for study. He began to prepare for matriculation at London

University and attended lectures at Sydenham College, where he made his entry into the scientific arena.

> My first public competition, small as it was, was an epoch in my life [he wrote in his autobiography]. I had been attending (it was my first summer session) the botanical lectures at Chelsea. One morning I observed a notice stuck up – a notice of a public competition for medals etc. to take place on the 1st August (if I recollect right). It was then the end of May or thereabouts. I remember looking longingly at the notice, and someone said to me, 'Why don't you go in and try for it?' I laughed at the idea, for I was very young, and my knowledge somewhat of the vaguest. Nevertheless I mentioned the matter to S. when I returned home. He likewise advised me to try, and so I determined I would.

He was soon studying from eight or nine in the morning until midnight, and two or three times a week walked from North London to Chelsea to hear special lectures. He frequently worked through the night, illustrating even at the age of seventeen the extraordinary capacity for knuckling down to hard work which was to become a family characteristic. The result was success – the Silver Medal of the Apothecaries' Society for botany, and examination marks high enough to win a coveted Free Scholarship. And in the Charing Cross Hospital minutes for 2 September 1842 it was recorded that:

> Applications from the following gentlemen (including the two sons of Mr. George Huxley, late senior assistant master in Ealing School), were laid before the meeting, and their testimonials being approved of, it was decided that those gentlemen should be admitted as free scholars, if their classical attainments should be found upon examination to be satisfactory.

TH started his course in the hospital on 1 October 1842 together with his brother James. From this date he began to be singled out from his companions although his own later account is almost misleadingly modest:

> I worked extremely hard when it pleased me, and when it did not, which was a very frequent case, I was extremely idle (unless making caricatures of one's pastors and masters is to be called a branch of industry), or else wasted my energies in wrong directions. I read everything I could lay hands upon, including novels, and took up all sorts of pursuits to drop them again quite as speedily. No doubt it was very largely my own fault, but the only instruction from

which I obtained the proper effect of education was that which I received from Mr Wharton Jones, who was the lecturer on physiology at the Charing Cross School of Medicine.

Yet the following year, 1843, he was winning prizes in chemistry and anatomy and physiology. Two years later he took his first M.B. at London University and, at the age of twenty, he published his first scientific paper, 'On a Hitherto Undescribed Structure in the Human Hair Sheath', which appeared in the *Medical Gazette.* It was, he later wrote, both suggested and corrected by Wharton Jones, 'for at that time, and for many years afterwards, I detested the trouble of writing, and would take no pains over it'. Huxley, the young man so frequently bent behind a window over a microscope that his silhouette became known to companions as 'The Sign of the Head and Microscope', had made a brilliant start. He now had to look for a career.

He was rising twenty-one, had passed his first examinations at London University, and knew that he would soon have to set about earning a living. He might have turned towards general practice even though he 'knew and cared very little about medicine as the art of healing'. Yet he was a deeply sensitive human being; and it seems likely that he, who was to shrink from so little, yet shrank from too intimate a day-to-day contact with poverty and squalor. He might have turned to research – although, as he was later to find, the rewards of research in early Victorian Britain were grotesquely slight. Instead, he was turned by chance towards the Royal Navy, towards the path that was to lead to the *Rattlesnake* and all that sprang from it.

Sitting next to Huxley in the medical school at Charing Cross was Joseph Fayrer, son of a naval commander and later to become famous as Sir Joseph Fayrer, Surgeon-General. Why not, Fayrer suggested to Huxley, write to Sir William Burnett, Director-General of the naval medical services? 'Rather a strong thing to do,' was how Huxley regarded this approach to the top. And yet there was a lot to favour the idea. In the navy a man might earn his keep, follow his own line of country, and might see something of the exciting and unknown world. During long days at sea he might have time to think for himself, and in uncharted waters he might discover fresh facts which would help him to understand the mysteries of the natural world. When one came to think about it, the Royal Navy offered enticing prospects.

Huxley returned to his lodgings, took a two-page sheet of foolscap, and sat down to write what he later called 'the best letter he could devise':

Sir, Having a great desire to enter the Medical Department of Her

> Majesty's Naval Service and being at the same time totally unprovided with any friendly influence by which the attainment of my object might be accelerated, I take the liberty of addressing myself to you as the Head of the Department to inquire whether (supposing I can produce the requisite qualifications) any application from myself simply will have any chance of success.

He went on to outline his experience, noted his awards, and drew attention to his paper in the *Medical Gazette*. Then he sealed the letter, delivered it himself and awaited results.

A few days later official acknowledgement arrived, and at the foot of the formal note there was a hand-written invitation to call on Sir William at a certain hour. Huxley duly arrived, sent in his card, and shortly afterwards found himself facing a tall, shrewd-looking old gentleman with a broad Scots accent. 'I see him now as he entered with my card in his hand,' he wrote nearly half a century later. 'The first thing he did was to return it, with the frugal reminder that I should probably find it useful on some other occasion.'

It is possible that Fayrer had pulled strings. It is more likely that Burnett was struck, as others were to be, by the extraordinary air of calm confidence which was radiated by this handsome young man. For Sir William asked only a few formal questions before telling Huxley to hold himself in readiness for an examination; and within two months the young man was passing through the gates of Portsmouth Naval Dockyard, having been posted to H.M.S. *Victory* for duty in the nearby Haslar Hospital.

Before this, however, he was to be engaged in one curious exploit whose details still remain unknown. Huxley was due to present himself at Charing Cross Hospital on Thursday, 19 February, before being passed on to the College of Surgeons and formally enrolled in the navy. The preceding day saw him, however, crossing the Channel to Antwerp with a small party that included his sister Eliza. During the following days he wrote to her as 'Miss Knight'; there are suggestions that the correspondence might be tampered with in transit; and when Huxley was finally installed at Haslar, he at once wrote to his sister, saying: 'I think you had better not send any more letters to me in case of accidents.'

This was three weeks after the sudden journey across the Channel, recorded in a letter which Huxley wrote on 20 February from Agar Street, facing Charing Cross Hospital:

> My dear Lizzie, You will be glad to hear that I got over here safe and sound and without sea-sickness by a quarter to eight on Thurs-

day morning. I presented my certificate in person before eleven and everything being found satisfactory I received today the order to go for examination before the College of Surgeons. This exam will occur either next Friday or the Friday after – two or three days after that I shall go before Sir W. Burnett and the day after that I shall begin to receive pay; all the rest is a matter of indifference. So you see all the prophets' noses are rubbed the wrong way.

Another of the strange coincidences occurred to me on the voyage back. [Huxley then explains how he got into conversation with a man who turned out to be the pilot of the vessel.] He asked me, if I knew who it was that came over in the vessel who wanted private lodgings? Inasmuch as somebody had been inquiring at the house in which he was – whether a gentleman, two ladies, their maid, and two children could be accommodated – of course I did not know who it was. Is it not odd? I make no question that he was in the house of the Englishman to whom I first applied. I should advise you to keep to yourself and the children as much as possible out of the way of the people belonging to the Victoria – which lies not very far from you – and Elizabeth should be particularly careful not to pick up any English acquaintance – she would not be a difficult person for anyone to pump, I imagine. . . . Keep your spirits up my dear Liza and believe me for better or worse your affectionate brother THH.

Lizzie was joined by her husband. The couple moved on to Germany – as Dr and Mrs Scott, and it was in that name that they emigrated to the United States in the late 1840s. No reasons for the sudden journey across the Channel, or for the change of name have come to light, although most things from debt to body-snatching have been rumoured. They must have been compelling ones.

Less than a month after this journey, and TH's act of family goodwill that appears to have endangered his chance of joining the Royal Navy, the young doctor had become Lieutenant Huxley, waiting at Haslar for whatever service abroad the navy might offer. His commanding officer was the redoubtable Sir John Richardson, naturalist and surgeon, one of those born Arctic explorers who had taken part in the search for the North-West Passage. 'I always look upon him as the founder of my fortunes,' Huxley wrote.

Richardson, dour man that he was, at first ignored the young surgeon. It was only when Huxley had been at the hospital some weeks that he was suddenly stopped by Sir John who said that he had unfortunately been unable to get Huxley one of the coveted postings abroad.

'However,' he added, 'I mean to keep you here until I can get you something you will like.'

There followed another spell of silence. Then Richardson again stopped Huxley. The Admiralty, he explained, was fitting out the frigate H.M.S. *Rattlesnake* for exploration of the waters between Northern Australia and New Guinea, and those of New Guinea itself. The commander-designate, Captain Owen Stanley, had asked Richardson to suggest an assistant surgeon who knew something of science. Was Huxley interested?

When TH clasped the offer with both hands he was given leave of absence, visited Stanley in London, and subsequently explained in a long letter to his sister Eliza the reason for his enthusiasm. The object in New Guinea, he said, was

> to bring back a full account of its Geography, Geology and Natural History. In the latter department with which I shall have (in addition to my medical functions) somewhat to do, we shall form one grand collection of specimens and deposit it in the British Museum or some other public place, and this main object always being kept in view, we are at liberty to collect and work for ourselves as we please. Depend upon it, unless some sudden attack of laziness supervenes, such an opportunity shall not slip unused out of my hands.

Other visits to London followed, and Huxley was introduced by Captain Stanley to more than one naturalist who was to affect his career – notably Edward Forbes of King's College, London.

Preparations for the voyage went ahead, but one delay followed another. Sailing date was postponed from September to October, then to December. At the end of November all was ready. James Huxley organized a special dinner party for his brother and at it TH appeared for the first time in his uniform as assistant-surgeon, bravely wearing his badges of rank.

The following day he joined his ship at Spithead. Within twenty-four hours she was making her way to Portsmouth where she was inspected on the afternoon of 3 December and her crew mustered by Admiral Sir Charles Ogle. The same evening she weighed anchor and beat westwards down the Channel.

(ii)

The orders of the *Rattlesnake*'s commander were to base himself on

Sydney, to explore northwards up the east coast of Australia, and then to chart the approaches to the Torres Straits which run between Australia and New Guinea, and were normally used by vessels sailing from the South Seas to India. If possible he was to find a second passage through the Barrier Reef leading to the Straits. It was generally understood that he would explore the hinterland of northern Australia and of New Guinea itself as opportunity offered. In addition he would send to the Admiralty's hydrographer 'tracings of all charts and plans that [he might] have completed, accompanied by sailing directions, and with notices of any facts or discoveries which may be of interest to navigation'.

A naturalist was to accompany the expedition and Captain Stanley was instructed that 'every reasonable facility is to be given him in making and preserving his collections'. This naturalist was John MacGillivray, sound man and good ornithologist, a scientist of no outstanding genius but a companion with whom Huxley was to work at ease. As assistant-surgeon, Huxley himself would handle the routine of ship's doctoring, but unless much went amiss this would not be too arduous a task; he was to help MacGillivray in the collection of specimens, but it was clear that he would have considerable time for whatever study he chose. Here was the great opportunity, and as the *Rattlesnake* beat down the Channel on her seven-and-a-half-months' voyage to Sydney, having picked up £65,000 of specie in Plymouth for delivery to the Cape, Huxley noted in his diary how he intended to seize it:

> I must keep two points in view. 1st. that I *am* simply a student. 2nd. from the peculiar circumstances in which I am placed, care and caution in observation may enable me to *become* a teacher with regard to particular points. And on my success in this latter matter my future prospects and usefulness in this appointment clearly depend. Not only my previous habits and tastes but the nature of the accommodation and opportunities afforded by the ship, clearly point to the study and structure of the more perishable or rare marine productions as that most likely to be profitable. Naturalising for systematic purposes is not *à mon gré*. My memory is not sufficiently selective of these facts to give me any hope of attaining profound systematic knowledge – and furthermore all the nameing and determining of place is far better done by those who sit in museums at home. But what I *can* and they *cannot* and where therefore the chief value of my position: I can observe 1. the 'habits' of living bodies, 2. their mode of development and generation, 3. their anatomy by

dissection of fresh specimens, 4. their histology by microscopic observation.

These general principles, which were followed by a list of the specific tasks which Huxley hoped to accomplish, foreshadowed much of his working life, especially the clear acceptance of factors which conditioned his brief and the emphasis on personal observation. In the *Rattlesnake* they were to be implemented for nearly four years – on the voyage to and from Sydney and during the four cruises of varying length which the vessel made from her base; and they were to be carried out in conditions of great discomfort and limited resources.

The *Rattlesnake* was a 113-foot frigate of only 503 tons. Her timbers leaked from the start of the voyage, and although plans had been made to adapt her for Captain Stanley's special tasks of survey and exploration, little of the work had been carried out. The quarters were still those of Nelson's day, and the lower deck on which Huxley's cabin lay had headroom of only four foot six. The cabin itself was seven feet by six with a height of only five foot six – Huxley stood five foot eleven. It was badly lit, at times ankle deep in water, and from beneath it came, throughout the voyage, the sound of water slopping back and forth on the deck below. Here, lacking space and light, with microscope lashed to the improvised laboratory bench, Huxley worked on the specimens which he and MacGillivray so laboriously collected: dissecting, peering, thinking, and trying to understand the significance of the minute structures he was seeing for the first time. There were no scientific books, the Admiralty having either ignored or forgotten the captain's request for them. Equipment was equally scarce. On one occasion specimens were collected in a gauze meat-cover trailed through the sea from a small boat manned by natives, the *Rattlesnake*'s crew being on other duties; a machine for cleaning rice was sometimes used and, on one occasion, nothing was available but bare hands. As for the tow-net, this was improvised from a two-foot length of ship's bunting attached to a fourteen-inch wooden hoop.

It was in such conditions that Huxley worried away at the details of the work he had set himself. Yet the difficulties made him; the difficulties, the need to think for himself without leaning back on even the most casual observations of others, the excitement of stepping into a new field of knowledge. As he studied the structural organization of the Molluscs or the Coelenterates, these combined to encourage the discipline of scientific approach which was to be his most formidable weapon down the years. The difficulties refined in him a process valuable not only in itself but in its bearing on his work; for Huxley, in the words of his friend Michael Foster, believed that 'the clearer the sight, the sharper the hearing, and the readier the touch, the greater the firmness with which the student can lay hold of the phenomena of nature, the more surely he can gain the basis needed for exactitude of thought and judgement'.

The long days at sea, the sight of strange lands, animals and peoples, the contact with the heady bustling life of what was still colonial Australia, were to do more. For Huxley's comradeship with the other young officers nourished his feeling for people. When he joined the *Rattlesnake* his attitude was epitomized by one entry in his diary:

> What a precious pack have I to deal with in these delightful messmates of mine, as might have been expected. I have five years of silence (that is to say of speaking from the mouth outwards only) to look forward to. Save the necessary courtesies of life, I shall make it my business to have very little to do with them . . .

Yet he later added in pencil: 'Unjust – they turned out very good fellows.' In fact, it seems quite clear that during the voyage Huxley learned to rub along with the rest: he might still be regarded as a rather curious character by ordinary folk, yet he was no longer perpetually standing alone. Naval life educated him in other ways. As he wrote later in his diary:

> It was good to live under sharp discipline, to be down on the realities of existence by living on bare necessities; to find how extremely well worth living life seemed to be when one woke up from a night's rest on a soft plank, with the sky for canopy, and cocoa and weevily biscuit the sole prospect for breakfast; and, more especially, to learn to work for the sake of what I got for myself out of it, even if it all went to the bottom and I along with it.

As the ship passed through the tropical waters with their swarming life; as Huxley caught his first glimpse of fairy seas, of splendid scenery; as he experienced the clean dawns and marvelled at the kaleidoscopic colours of the strange life around him, a three-fold development took place. A sense of wonder at the natural world was awakened in him. He began to look at these marvels not only with the inquiring mind of the scientist but with the intuitive eye of the artist: and he began to write, in his diary and in his notes, in his correspondence with friends and relatives, with the care and craftsmanship which was to make Leslie Stephen describe him as in the front rank not only of scientists but of men of letters.

This mixture of scientific observation and transforming artistry, which was to become almost a family tradition, first became clear in Huxley's accounts of the voyage. He remembered how he would wake up 'in the bright dawn of a tropical morning, when my comrades were yet asleep, when every sound was hushed, except the little lap-lap of the ripples against the sides of the boat, and the distant twitter of the sea-bird on the reef'. His comment on the albatrosses which swung back and forth in the ship's wake was not merely scientific but added that nothing could 'be more easy and beautiful than the flight of these birds'. When the *Rattlesnake* sailed through a colony of phosphorescent tunicates,

> a more beautiful sight [he later told the Royal Society] could hardly be imagined than that presented from the decks of the ship as she drifted hour after hour, through the shoal of miniature pillars of fire gleaming out of the dark sea, with an ever-waning, ever-brightening, soft bluish light, as far as the eye could reach on every side.

And his last sight of Australia as the ship headed for home in 1850 was of 'a dark grey line along the horizon backed up by as splendid a sky as ever the setting sun had lighted up'. All these words suggested, as was later to be spelt out plain, that for Huxley at least there were not two cultures but one.

This sensitivity, which increased his stature as a natural scientist, developed throughout the four years of the voyage. He grew in other ways as well. With the help of a dictionary he worried out the necessary knowledge of Italian to read Dante in the original; he later noted that Carlyle's '*Sartor Resartus* and the *Miscellanies* were among the few books devoured partly by myself and partly by the mighty hordes of cockroaches in my cabin'. And long before the voyage was over, before the serious work of the expedition had really started, there took place the meeting which was to lay the foundations of the Huxley dynasty.

On the night of 15 July 1847, the *Rattlesnake*'s look-out reported the revolving light on the South Head of Port Jackson; by the following morning the ship had passed through the narrows into Sydney Harbour and had anchored at Farm Cove.

In 1847 the city of Sydney was a rapidly-expanding State capital of some 50,000 inhabitants. Here the *Rattlesnake* stayed for nearly three months, her crew surveying the harbour to discover whether it would take battleships and whether a dry dock could be built as planned on Cockatoo Island. Meanwhile the schooner *Castlereagh*, which had been awaiting the *Rattlesnake*'s arrival, was found unfit for survey work and sold back to her owners; the *Bramble*, which had been waiting with her, was recommissioned; and ten additional crew had to be found, while the *Rattlesnake* and the *Bramble* were to be refitted for the work ahead. The ships and their crews quickly became the centre of attention.

> In this corner of the universe, where men-o'war are rather scarce, even the old *Rattlesnake* is rather a lion, and her officers are esteemed accordingly [Huxley wrote to his sister Lizzie]. Besides, to tell you the truth, we are rather agreeable people than otherwise, and can manage to get up a very decent turn-out on board on occasion.

Huxley found that his commission in the navy opened the doors of Sydney society. He gained the entrée to many houses where he would be received whenever he wished. He struck up a friendship with William Macleay the naturalist. And he was invited, only a few weeks after the arrival of the *Rattlesnake*, to a small private party at the home of a Mrs Campbell, a colonial-style white stone house standing in its garden of tropical plants, a comfortable-looking home whose photograph Huxley kept throughout his life inscribed with the words 'Where we first met, 1847'. For it was here that he was introduced to Miss Henrietta Heathorn, a shortish girl of twenty-two with Saxon yellow hair and blue eyes, interested in German poetry and dancing.

The Heathorns were a Kentish family of yeoman stock which had lived for centuries near Maidstone. Henry Heathorn, the head of the family in 1847, had married Sarah Richardson, a widow whose people were planters in the West Indies, and their daughter Henrietta had been born in 1825, the same year as T. H. Huxley. She had been brought up largely by her aunt, Kate Heathorn, a resolute woman who lived an active life until well past her ninetieth year, gave up gardening only at ninety-four, and who died at the age of 104. Henrietta had spent two years finishing her education at Neuwied on the Rhine. And in 1842 she had bidden good-bye to her father, who had sailed to Australia hoping to set up in business before bringing out his family.

Henry Heathorn was an ambitious man. A family legend has remained that on one occasion, expecting Sydney to become an important railway terminus, he had bought the famous harbour, subsequently selling it – at a loss – when the railway by-passed the town. However, within four months of arrival in Australia, he had set up a small sawmill and brewery in the outback some ninety miles from Sydney. He established himself, and early in August 1843 his wife Sarah, his daughter Henrietta, and one of his step-daughters, Oriana, sailed for Sydney, where they arrived on 15 December.

The life of the young Henrietta was tough and demanding. As she later described it in an article in the *Cornhill Magazine*:

From sheer necessity I learned to make my own and my mother's dresses and her caps, since Sydney, the nearest place where such things could be made, was ninety miles off. The way I set about the business was to buy a bit of stuff at the stores attached to the mills. Then I would unpick a dress bought in England – which went to my heart, as I had afterwards to put it together again. Each piece I laid upon a linen lining and pricked the shape off with a pin; upon this the new material was placed, tacked and joined to it, and fitted on myself until it satisfied me. . . . . For amusement I took charge of the dairy, hitherto managed by our cook, Henry, a ticket-of-leave man. Twice a week before breakfast, I churned twelve pounds of butter. I also made all the bread for the household, the cook heating the brick oven with wood, and then when the oven was hot enough he swept out the embers, then pushed in the loaves with a long-handled flat wooden spade. I think I can still smell the scent of hot baked bread. On a Friday there was cake-making, when I would invent new combinations of ingredients, and with curiosity await the result.

In 1844 Oriana Heathorn married William Fanning, a Sydney merchant who settled in a house on Cook's River, and it was here that Henrietta was living, keeping house for her half-sister, when the *Rattlesnake* sailed into Sydney Harbour. As an item in the social round, the Fannings were invited to the Campbells, and a few young officers from the *Rattlesnake* were also invited.

Of her first brief meeting with TH Miss Heathorn later wrote: 'We . . . only exchanged a few words, he asking me for a dance and my brother-in-law who stood by declaring it impossible as his wife, my sister, had already gone to put on her wraps and the horses could not be kept waiting.'

The Huxley response was significant. 'Never mind,' he said; 'we shall meet again and then remember you are engaged for the first dance.'

The next occasion was one of the small balls at Government House. Here Henrietta suddenly saw, through the crowd, the dark-haired young assistant-surgeon dancing with her half-sister. Huxley caught up with her in the refreshment room where, as she later put it, 'we met and chatted so long that the man who brought me there had gone away.'

This was the beginning. Huxley was soon invited to the Fannings and discovered an unexpected common interest with Miss Heathorn, who was eager to discuss the German language and its literature. She was, however, the antithesis of the blue-stocking, riding, swimming, taking vigorous exercise in the open and on at least one occasion joining a 'boat-picnic' which involved the male members of the party in rowing thirty-six miles.

The couple were quickly in love 'after seeing one another – I will not tell you how many times, lest you should laugh', Huxley wrote to his sister Lizzie. They had met only four times when both attended a large ball, held in honour of the visit by a French frigate. Here Huxley proposed and was accepted; and the engagement was formally announced before the *Rattlesnake* got under way for her first northern voyage in mid-October.

The engagement might not have been accepted so readily by the Heathorns and the Fannings had its future appeared more certain. It was true that the young Huxley had a curious flashing magnetism, the product perhaps of clear mind and direct blunt confidence; he was extraordinarily good-looking and carried himself well. Yet an assistant-surgeon of distinctly unorthodox and scientific leanings was no great match. This one had, in addition, a markedly 'irreligious' attitude, appearing to question many of those accepted views which might not be thought about too seriously but did good service in buttressing society. And even to his emotions he brought an observing intelligence that somehow succeeded in being clinical though humane. Describing to a brother officer how Miss Heathorn had handled a young niece, he confided that he could already form a perfect judgement about what sort of mother his future wife would make:

> I told him that I had had the opportunity of watching a most interesting series of experiments on that very point and that while I laughed at Nettie for her attachment to a child, I was in truth anxiously watching how she managed it, how she made it at once love and obey her, and how I *knew* from what I had seen, that all my requirements would be satisfied....

By the time that the *Rattlesnake* sailed from Sydney, Huxley's position was radically different from what it had been a mere three months earlier. Then he had given himself unreservedly to science; now this resolution had to be measured against the prospects of position and hard cash that science held out. Now it was even more essential to succeed, and he brought to his work both a keener cutting edge and a worry about any failure to squeeze the most from his opportunities. And, tantalizingly, the opportunities were on far waters and kept him separated from Henrietta Heathorn.

From mid-October 1847 until mid-January 1848 the *Rattlesnake* and her crew surveyed the southern stretches of the Inshore Passage, which lies within the Great Barrier Reef and was a route taken by ships sailing from India to the Southern Seas. They had a spell of about three weeks back in Sydney and then, since the season was not yet right for further work up north, spent five weeks visiting Bass Strait, where they inspected the lighthouses between Tasmania and Australia. There was another spell of some weeks in Sydney, and on 20 April 1848 they set off for their longest single voyage – up past the northern end of the Great Barrier Reef and into the Torres Straits, before turning back to Sydney, which they did not reach until the end of January 1849. There followed about three months of refitting before they set out for the Torres Straits once again, this time travelling down the south-eastern coast of New Guinea to the Louisiade Archipelago and returning to Sydney only in mid-February 1850.

During the two and a half years that followed Huxley's engagement to Miss Heathorn there was thus a total of less than six months during which they could meet. While the *Rattlesnake* was at Sydney, Huxley would send almost daily messages to her, 'miniature letters' which he entrusted to anyone who was going ashore. But the exigencies of the Service were great, meetings were rare, fresh voyages were always in preparation, and at the end of the *Rattlesnake*'s expedition there loomed merely the prospect of an extended separation which would end only when an assistant-surgeon had climbed sufficiently high up the ladder to support a wife. The Heathorns, therefore, attracted though they undoubtedly were to the young Huxley, may well have thought that here was one engagement which would almost certainly fall by the wayside.

For Huxley, meanwhile, work was the thing; work among the extraordinary living material which he was now seeing for the first time; work which would lighten the tedium of long days at sea, and which would enable him to break open the door to a scientific career. Whatever the attraction of the work, it was carried on in conditions that were frequently appalling.

> Rain! Rain, *encore et toujours* – I wonder if it is possible for the mind of man to conceive anything more degradingly offensive than the condition of us 150 men, shut up in this wooden box, and being watered with hot water, as we are now [Huxley later wrote in a thinly-disguised personal comment when reviewing in the *Westminster Review* MacGillivray's official account of the voyage]. It is no exaggeration to say *hot*, for the temperature is that at which people at home commonly take a hot bath. It rains so hard that we have caught seven tons of water in one day, and it is therefore impossible

to go on deck; though, if one did, one's condition would not be much improved. A *hot* Scotch mist covers the sea and hides the land, so that no surveying can be done; moving about in the slightest degree causes a flood of perspiration to pour out; all energy is completely gone, and if I could help it, I would not think even: it's too hot. The rain awnings are spread and we can have no wind sails up; if we could there is not a breath of wind to fill them; and, consequently, the lower and main decks are utterly unventilated; a sort of solution of man in steam fills them from end to end, and surrounds the lights with a lurid halo. It's too hot to sleep, and my sole amusement consists in watching the cockroaches, which are in a state of intense excitement and happiness.

It was in such circumstances that Huxley carried out the work which was to set his feet on the first rungs of the ladder. His labours ranged across a wide sector of biological research and investigation but it was concentrated on the animals which float in the sea's upper layers. Their perishability meant that they had never been carefully investigated as fresh specimens; their extreme transparency meant that the main features of their anatomy could be examined on ship without elaborate equipment. These two factors combined to help Huxley establish a new classification of such creatures on anatomical grounds. Thus he was able, while still in his early twenties, to make an original contribution to knowledge: to show that in this particular sphere living organisms were not arranged as men supposed.

This contribution was of significance not only in itself but as illustrating the way in which Huxley's mind worked. When he set sail in the *Rattlesnake*, most investigation of animal forms had followed one of two lines. There had been the mere accumulation of facts – an accumulation which was not followed by any attempt to make the facts lead on to a theory. Or there had been a theory, frequently a fantastic one, and then a search for facts which might, with luck, buttress the theory. Huxley's method was different from both. He marshalled the facts of the creatures he investigated under the laws as he knew them, and then used observation and experiment to develop the known laws. Following dissection, following note-taking, following study, there came the careful description of the results, written out in the chart-room and illustrated by neat pen-and-ink drawings that would have been models of work from a tidy town laboratory, let alone from the rolling body of a ship. The first of the papers which thus came from the *Rattlesnake* dealt with *Physalia*, the creatures popularly known as Portuguese men-of-war, which float with their brightly coloured bladders on the seas and trail their long tentacles, animals 'whose structure and affinities had never been properly worked out'. It was followed in 1848 by observations upon the anatomy of the *Diphydiae*, and by many other papers, which were sent via Captain Stanley to Edward Forbes, then President of the Linnean Society.

Publication was the main yardstick of success, a possibility never far from Huxley's thoughts. Years later Henrietta described how TH, sailing into harbour after the months-long cruises, would tell her of the papers that had been dispatched to England. 'I had only the dimmest idea, if any,' she wrote, 'of how a description of a marine creature should win for him fame, or help in any way to bring about his obtaining a position that would enable us to marry....'

Huxley received no news of his papers and became very depressed. He had, as he wrote, 'sent home communication after communication to the Linnean Society with the same result as that obtained by Noah when he sent the raven out of his ark'. Yet in spite of efforts by his brother George – who told him that their sister Lizzie and her husband were now trying to start life anew in Bonn – no news of the precious papers was forthcoming. Then, before the ship's second voyage north, Huxley determined on something more ambitious. On 9 March 1848 he was finishing his drawings for a paper on the *Medusae* when Captain Stanley came into the chart-room where he was working. The captain asked Huxley what he was engaged on. When told, he suggested that the paper might be sent to Stanley's father, the Bishop of Norwich. The good Bishop would, as he said, 'if it were on account of the ship merely, push it to the utmost in the proper quarters'. Huxley suggested the Royal Society, completed the paper, and duly handed it over for dispatch. This paper illustrated three traits not only of TH himself but of many of his descendants. It showed a reluctance to accept current ideas without a cautious and critical consideration of the evidence. It showed a highly developed ability to observe the facts of nature. And it showed the native ability to draw which could have provided many a Huxley to come with a second profession.

The paper on the *Medusae* was, Huxley wrote, 'my dove, if I had only known it'. But he did not know it. All he knew as the *Rattlesnake* voyaged north for a second and then for a third time, was that his work appeared to have been greeted with silence; that he was but a mere assistant-surgeon. 'Have I the capabilities for a scientific life or only the desire and wish for it, springing from a flattered vanity and self-deceiving blindness?' he asked himself in his diary. 'Have my dreams been follies or prophecies?' For a while he neglected science. Instead he read *Candide*, and struggled through the *Divine Comedy* in the original. He speculated dismally on the fate of his papers. He doubted whether he should have proposed marriage. He was, in fact, deep in one of those ominous seas of depression which seem at times to flood even higher round the Huxleys than they do round most young men. TH, unlike some, survived the ordeal.

He survived not only the psychological ordeal of doubt but the physical chances of exploration on the mainland where the sight of tribes which had never before seen a white man aroused his interest in anthropology. He made a foray into the Queensland bush with the ill-fated Lieutenant Kennedy from whose subsequent expedition only two men came back alive. And he worked on at his investigations and his note-books, ignoring the silence from England, hoping for the best.

There appears to have been no hard-and-fast limit to the *Rattlesnake*'s plans, and she might have continued voyaging for another year or so had not Captain Stanley been struck down by disease, dying in Huxley's arms. Back in Sydney in the early spring of 1850, the crew learned that they would now be sailing home.

In May, Huxley said good-bye to his Henrietta. He would send for her when he was able. But both must have realized, as the ship sailed out into the Tasman Sea for the long journey home, that prospects of marriage were as bleak as ever. He wrote to her from his cabin:

> I have been thinking much of what my plans are to be when we arrive in England. I shall go first to Sir William Burnett. I shall tell him that it is my wish to remain in England and if possible in London for a twelvemonth, for the purpose of publishing my papers, but I shall tell him that I cannot afford to lose a year's time and a year's pay. Therefore can he or will he manage the matter so that I may be nominally attached to some naval hospital or wards for that time. I on my side only ask this on condition that I can obtain from Owen, Herschel, Forbes and others, favourable opinions as to the value of my papers.
>
> If he will do this for me I shall work up my book, and at the same time prepare for my second examination at the University of London, so as to take my M.B. there.
>
> Perhaps I may go in for honours, and then there is a chance of £50 a year for two years.
>
> Perhaps living in London may be a *poser* – but I think at any rate I can continue to be attached to a hospital – Armstrong managed that. If my plan of living in London succeeds I shall make use of my privilege as a member of the Service to see the practice of the best hospitals. And I shall take three or four months' dissection. This will

> bring me to the end of 1851. And what is to be done then? That is not so clear, but I hope *s'éclaircira* as we go along. At any rate, my dearest, we are no further off than we always expected to be at the end of 1851 (supposing Captain Stanley had lived). And my position will be infinitely improved to what it would have been had I only then just returned.

The *Rattlesnake* rounded the Horn with snow falling and the ice forming great stalactites on her bows, reached Plymouth on 23 October, and was paid off at Chatham a month later.

Huxley, eager for promotion, soon found that there were 150 officers of his rank above him in seniority. Prospects seemed slim, although, as he wrote,

> The Admiralty have quite recently published a distinct declaration that they will consider scientific attainments as a claim to their notice, and I expect to be the first to remind them of their promises, and I will take care to have the reminder so backed that they must and shall take note of it.

It was clear that Thomas Huxley, assistant-surgeon, would keep the Lords Commissioners of the Admiralty up to the mark.

Chapter II

A Man Finds his Work

(*i*)

Huxley arrived back in London in 1850 with few prospects but great ambitions. In many ways it must have been a dispiriting homecoming. Lizzie, he now learned, had already left Germany and had emigrated to the United States with her children and her husband, who now called himself Dr John Godwin Scott. His brother George was apparently finding it difficult to make ends meet, while an argument between TH and his eldest brother William concerning George's marriage produced a rupture that lasted for nearly forty years.

Only brother James had prospered. He had been caught up in the contemporary movement towards a more humane treatment of the mentally ill, and in the year that the *Rattlesnake* sailed from England, only twelve months or so after returning to his former post at Gloucester, had been appointed Medical Superintendent of the Kent County Asylum at Barming Heath outside Maidstone. A founder-member of what was to become the Royal Medico-Psychological Association, James took what would now be regarded as a modern view of mental treatment, asking 'whether restraining is *ever* a true, eligible, indispensable remedy in the treatment of insanity', and insisting that spring locks should be fitted to the doors at Barming to spare patients the nightly sound of keys being turned on them. Yet to offset the position of James, well started on a specialist medical ladder on which there were few older men to bar progress, there were the Huxley parents, who had left Coventry to be near him; a mother already in precarious health and a father deep in increasing senility.

As Thomas looked glumly around for lodgings, London was busily preparing for the magnificence of the Great Exhibition. Being unsuccessful, he eventually found a temporary home with his brother George near Regent's Park. Here the young officer, settling down to put his

Rattlesnake papers in order, quickly found himself caught between lack of prospects and totally unexpected scientific success.

For on reporting to the Admiralty he had learned that his paper on the *Medusae*, sent back with Captain Stanley's blessing from Sydney nearly three years previously, had been read before the Royal Society and published in their *Philosophical Transactions*. A second paper had been published in their *Zoological Transactions*, while another was being considered by the Linnean; furthermore, some of his notes and drawings might be required by the Royal. The latter's influential secretary, Professor Bell, quickly invited him to dine and, as Huxley put it in a letter to Lizzie, 'meet a lot of the nobs'. Edward Forbes, now reaching the height of his fame, was eager to support the young man. 'I take all these things quite as a matter of course, but am all the while considerably astonished,' TH confided to his sister: 'The other day I dined at the Geological Club and met Lyell, Murchison, de la B[eche], Horner and a lot more, and last evening I dined with a whole lot of literary and scientific people.'

Huxley's star was rising more quickly than he knew. The Royal Society was electing each year a number of men whose names were put forward solely on the merit of their work; publication of a paper in the *Philosophical Transactions* was one qualification, and Forbes now submitted Huxley's name for consideration by the Council, who were to select thirty-five from among thirty-eight candidates. TH was not yet twenty-six years old; he was probably the least known of all the candidates; and he was therefore genuinely surprised when, calling on Forbes at the Museum of Practical Geology, he was greeted with the news: 'I am glad to be able to tell you that you are all right for the Royal Society. The selection was made on Friday night, and I hear that you are one of the selected.'

This was not all. A few months after his election Huxley barely missed being awarded the Royal Society's Medal, a circumstance which sparked off another letter to his sister:

> . . . I have at last tasted what it is to mingle with my fellows – to take my place in that society for which nature has fitted me, and whether the draught has been a poison which has heated my veins or true nectar from the gods, life-giving, I know not, but I can no longer rest where I once could have rested. If I could find within myself that mere personal ambition, the desire of fame, present or posthumous, had anything to do with this restlessness, I would root it out. But in those moments of self-questioning, when one does not lie even to one's self, I feel that I can say it is not so – that the real pleasure,

the true sphere, lies in the feeling of self-development – in the sense of power and of growing *oneness* with the great spirit of abstract truth.

Here was an omen of attitudes to come. Here, also, was a confidence that in a lesser man would have smacked of arrogance; in Huxley's case it was confidence well justified. The following year he was not only awarded the Royal Medal but was elected a member of the Society's Council – at the age of twenty-seven. 'When I last wrote, I was but at the edge of the crush at the pit-door of this great fools' theatre,' he said in a letter to his old biologist friend in Sydney, William Macleay, '– now I have worked my way into it and through it, and am, I hope, not far from the check-takers.'

In one respect, therefore, the months that followed the return of the *Rattlesnake* saw Huxley on the crest of a swelling wave. His confidence, moreover, might well have been bolstered by the striking similarity between his own position and that of two scientific near-contemporaries. Charles Darwin had circumnavigated the world in the *Beagle* and was even now ruminating on the vast collection of facts with which he was to change man's ideas of the world; Joseph Hooker had sailed with Ross on his voyage of discovery to the Antarctic, and was busy publishing his massive botanical results. Yet when it came to developing their work, both men had advantages denied to Huxley – Darwin had the comfortable wealth which allowed him to generate and mature his theory at leisure; Hooker had the reputation of his great father, since 1841 Director of Kew, the post in which his son was to succeed him. Huxley, self-schooled, self-scanned, and with his betrothed waiting on the far side of the world, had no such benefits and it is clear from a letter written to Lizzie after the British Association meeting which he attended at Ipswich in 1851, that he was fully aware of the fact:

> How I envied Hooker. He has long been engaged to a daughter of Professor Henslow's, and at this very meeting, he sat by her side. He is going to be married in a day or two. His father is director of Kew Gardens, and there is little doubt of his succeeding him.

The young Huxley was thus half in and half out of what would now be called the Establishment. He was an F.R.S.; he had the ear of those who mattered; yet at this stage he still had to fight harder than his equals for each move up the ladder. Luckily, he was under no illusions as to what was necessary, and his very presence at the British Association meeting was evidence of this. 'Anyone who conceives that I went down from any especial interest in the progress of science makes a great mistake,' he told his sister. 'My journey was altogether a matter of policy, partly for the purpose of doing a little necessary trumpeting, and partly to get the assistance of the Association in influencing the Government.'

Huxley's description of events at this Ipswich meeting gives a vivid impression of the young man assiduously concentrating on his *Rattlesnake* notes, establishing himself in the capital's scientific society, and persistently scanning the scene for any opening which would improve his standing, raise his stipend, and enable him to summon Miss Henrietta Heathorn from Sydney.

He travelled to Ipswich with John Tyndall, the young Irishman five years his senior who was just girding his loins as a free-lance scientist, and both men joined the Red Lions Club, an institution devoted to attack on dons and donnishness in science.

> With this object [wrote Huxley years later in an obituary notice of Tyndall] the 'Red Lions' made a point of holding a feast of Spartan simplicity and anarchic constitution, with rites of a Pantagruelistic aspect, intermingled with extremely unconventional orations and queer songs, such as only Forbes could indite, by way of official counterblast to the official banquets of the Association, with their high tables and what we irreverently termed 'butter-boat' speeches.

At the meeting Huxley had his first experience of public speaking. He was put on the Sectional Committee which dealt with Natural History, and then found himself forced to fill a gap produced by the non-delivery of papers. 'I was considerably surprised to find that when I had once made the plunge, my tongue went glibly enough,' he noted. The response was satisfactory, for by this date Huxley had learned to speak with the direct blunt fluency for which he later became famous. He was also, already, a striking figure: of only middle stature and slender build, he more than redeemed these commonplace features with his raven hair, worn rather long even for the period, with his grave, earnest expression, his dark, almost Svengali-like eyes and his full mobile lips, 'grim and resolute in repose but capable of relaxation into a smile of almost feminine charm'.

His experience at Ipswich was useful. He carried out some successful lobbying. But in spite of his Fellowship of the Royal Society, in spite of the fact that he was already being talked about, his duties were still mainly and frustratingly limited to work on the *Rattlesnake* material. And that, he realized, might never see the light of day.

As soon as the ship had touched at Plymouth, Huxley had written to his former commander, Sir John Richardson, asking that he should be given the chance of publishing his zoological notes and illustrations – 'over 180 sheets of drawings' – together with various papers. The

H.M.S. *Rattlesnake (National Maritime Museum)*

T. H. Huxley and his wife at the time of their visit to the United States in 1876

THE DAILY GRAPHIC

AN ILLUSTRATED EVENING NEWSPAPER.

39 & 41 PARK PLACE.

VOL. XI. | All the News. Four Editions Daily. | NEW YORK, WEDNESDAY, SEPTEMBER 27, 1876. | $12 Per Year in Advance. Single Copies, Five Cents. | NO. 1104.

HUXLEY EIKONOKLASTES.

Grand in the light the sacred records throw
Old Moses stands, a hero of all time—
Lawgiver, prophet; on his form sublime
Wrought with his art great Michael Angelo
And Milton, whose blind eyes with clearer ray
Grand visions saw, and fixed with mighty pen,
Unwielded yet by hands of newer men,
The vision of Creation's primal day!
Stands ever, and shall stand while Time shall be,
A shadow of that God of whom he spake.
Not thou, O Huxley! though thy frame should break,
Can st harm these giants, hew thou mightily.
Hold off! hold off! and go thy chosen way,
Nor Moses with thy fictious Milton seek to slay.

Front page of the New York *Daily Graphic* following T. H. Huxley's visit to the United States

Lords Commissioners of the Admiralty, giving with one hand and taking back with the other, had granted a six months' appointment to H.M.S. *Fishguard* at Woolwich, practically leave of absence on half pay, so that the material might be set in order. Yet they refused to make arrangements for publication. However, Huxley had settled down to the task, at first in his brother-in-law's home. He soon felt the need for surroundings with fewer distractions, and again trudged the streets, searching for rooms, finding that the coming Great Exhibition had sent prices rocketing, and that a junior naval officer who wished to use dissecting instruments and microscope had no particular attraction as a lodger. Eventually he found a succession of temporary rooms, and in these worked steadily away at his *Rattlesnake* material throughout 1852 and the following year. He gave the occasional public lecture. He wrote on science for such journals as the *Westminster Review*. He contributed to a number of scientific publications and was soon estimating that writing was earning him £250 a year – more than his naval pay.

This might have been encouraging to a different man. To Huxley it was not enough.

> The worst of it is, I have no ambition, except as means to an end, and that end is the possession of a sufficient income to marry upon [he wrote to his sister]. I assure you I would not give two straws for all the honours and titles in the world. A worker I must always be – it is my nature – but if I had £400 a year I would never let my name appear to anything I did or shall ever do.

And the chances of earning enough money to marry on remained infinitely remote. He wrote to his sister:

> To attempt to live by any scientific pursuit is a farce. Nothing but what is absolutely practical will go down in England. A man of science may earn great distinction but not bread. He will get invitations to all sorts of dinners and conversaziones, but not enough income to pay his cab fare.

His ambitions were soundly hit on the head, time after time, with a regularity that steadily, throughout the early 1850s, began to drive him down into depression. It had been suggested that the new Sydney University should endow a Chair of Anatomy and Physiology, and Huxley rightly believed that with the support of his old friend Macleay, his chances of gaining it were good. Then the project fell through. There was a vacancy in Toronto, but the Chair went to a well-connected local man. There were other vacancies – in Aberdeen, in Cork and in King's College, London, but Huxley failed in his applications for all.

Reasons are difficult to pin down; but science was only now beginning to break through the veils of prejudice which had long kept it the preserve of gentlemen-amateurs. Those at the top, men such as Forbes or de la Beche, knew Huxley's worth; but, as always, there was the need to convince lesser men. And to many in 1850 it must have seemed strange that a naval assistant-surgeon, with no experience outside the navy, or university background, should even be considered for such posts.

And to the series of professional rebuffs there was now added deep personal distress. In 1852 his beloved mother died, a blow made even heavier by the circumstances outlined in a letter to his sister; for he had to tell her of his 'father's increasing infirmities (he is now completely imbecile – and very feeble)'. Deep depression, which had flickered for a while during the *Rattlesnake* voyage and which was down the years to provide a mirror image of the volatile Huxley spirit, began to take over. As would so often happen, a bout of hard walking – in this case with his brother George in the Pyrenees – dispersed the gloom for a while. But gloom returned in the end – returned and remained; perhaps naturally enough, since Huxley was suffering from a double frustration.

As he saw it, his naval position reduced his chances of being offered any satisfactory scientific appointment. Yet as the months passed the one result which he knew would justify his labours appeared less and less likely. This outcome was publication, the financial responsibility for which had been skilfully handed to the Treasury by the Admiralty; the Treasury, with equal skill, had taken successful evasive action so that by the end of 1853 the authorities were faced with Assistant-Surgeon Huxley still on leave of absence at half pay, and still working on a project which so far as they were concerned would never see the light of day. And in January 1854 his request for yet further leave was met by orders, not unreasonable from the naval point of view, to join ship – the *Illustrious* at Portsmouth.

Here the Lords Commissioners failed to allow for the streak of Huxley stubbornness. Far from joining ship, TH now wrote to the Secretary of the Admiralty, recalling the promise of publishing aid, or promotion, as an inducement to original research in the navy. He had had neither. And he concluded his letter by commenting that 'Considering the distinct pledge given in the minute to which I have referred, then granting it would seem as nearly to concern their Lordships' honour as my advantage'. This almost unparalleled thrust by a junior officer at their Lordships' good name was followed by what appears to have been a month's hushed silence. Then three brief letters were written in quick succession.

On 2 March Huxley received a letter marked 'Immediate' which informed him that the Lords Commissioners 'signify their direction to you to report *immediately* the reasons for your neglecting to obey the orders you have received to join the Illustrious'. On the following day their Lordships received a letter from their assistant-surgeon:

> I beg respectfully to state for the information of My Lords Commissioners of the Admiralty that it is impossible for me to join any ship so long as the question of a grant for the publication of my researches is still undecided by the Lords Commissioners of the Treasury. It would be obviously impossible for me to carry out the object of the Grant while occupied with other duties.

To which he received the reply that unless he joined his ship and submitted himself to the Orders of the Board his name would 'be removed from the List of the Navy'.

Both the Admiralty and Huxley stuck to their guns and he was duly struck from the Navy List, thus being brought in the spring of 1854 to the very nadir of his hopes. He had no post or appointment. By standing up to the Lords Commissioners, he had apparently struck away the last possibility that the *Rattlesnake* papers would ever be published. His Fellowship of the Royal Society appeared to count for nothing. Desperately depressed, he was yet intent on marriage. 'I may give up the farce altogether,' he wrote to sister Lizzie, '– burn my books, bury my rod, take to practice in Australia. It is no use to go on kicking against the pricks . . .'

Yet somehow he held on, reluctant to admit failure, reluctant to cut adrift from the ambitious possibilities of London, to wade out into the stream of Colonial life which he knew was no place for a man like him. Moreover, he could not really believe that in this age of progress there was no place in London for a man of his talents. Somehow he held on.

Then, within a mere ten weeks, his entire position was almost miraculously changed, not by one chance happening but by a number. The series of events which were to transform Huxley's prospects began with the death of Professor E. Jamieson. Jamieson's Chair of Natural History at Edinburgh University was given to Huxley's old friend Edward Forbes. Forbes had only recently started a series of lectures at the Royal School of Mines in Jermyn Street, but was obliged to take up his Edinburgh duties at once; and Forbes, having given only the first two of his twice-weekly lectures, called upon Huxley to give the remaining twenty-four.

This, however, was only the beginning. Within a few weeks, the £100-a-year lectureship was augmented by a second similar appointment, previously held by Forbes and initially given to another man who had at first accepted it and who then declined. All this was in July. In August Huxley was offered first a part-time appointment with the

Geological Survey and then a lectureship in Comparative Anatomy at St Thomas's Hospital, while the appointment at the Royal School of Mines was now formalized into the Professorship of Natural History that he was to hold for more than thirty years. As if this was not enough, September brought a final request – would he be willing to give a course of lectures for the Government's recently created Science and Art Department?

What is more, tenacity now appeared to have earned not only rewards but dividends as well. For while the Royal Society had felt unable to support publication of Huxley's work while he had been an officer in Her Majesty's navy, the position was reversed now that he had been dismissed. And a few months later he was informed that the Society was assigning £300 to the costs of publication. The Ray Society underwrote the rest, and in 1859 there at last appeared *The Oceanic Hydrozoa: a Description of the Calycophoridae and Physophoridae observed during the Voyage of the Rattlesnake, in the years 1846–1850.* As Huxley himself commented, the book should have appeared eight years earlier, and subsequent researches had, as he put it, 'made sad havoc with my novelties'. But by this time he himself had moved on and up in the hierarchy.

(ii)

Even before the change in Huxley's fortunes, the Heathorns had decided to return to Britain. Now their decision chimed in with his good news and as he set to work on his multiple tasks he also began preparations for marriage the following summer.

First, however, there was a grave shock. For when Huxley met the Heathorns on their arrival in London in May 1855 he was dismayed at the appearance of his bride-to-be. He knew that she had visited the newly opened mining camp at Bathurst the previous year; he knew that she had caught a chill, been wrongly treated on her return to Sydney, and had gone through months of ill-health. But her appearance alarmed him and he insisted on taking her to one of London's leading doctors.

Having concealed his personal interest, he was solemnly told: 'I give her six months of life.' To the consternation of the specialist, he replied: 'Six months or not, she is going to be my wife.'

Henrietta Heathorn, mother of the long line of Huxleys which stretches from left to right along the top of the family tree, was to be racked throughout life by many ailments. She was resigned to them all, as to the regular succession of child-births, with the feminine resignation of her age. She might pour out her troubles in page after page to her sister-in-law, Lizzie, in the United States, but in the family circle she rarely complained, did her duty as wife and mother, and yet succeeded in acting as the censor and critic to whom so many of her husband's papers were read before the evening fire.

They were married at All Saints', Maida Vale, London, on 21 July 1855, 'an ideal midsummer day', as Mrs Huxley later called it, remembering all her life how, 'as we knelt at the altar, he holding my hand to his lips, a great beam of jewelled light fell upon us from the coloured window'. The service over, they went into the vestry, where they signed the register. The new Mrs Huxley looked at her name in 'a mist of amazement'. Her husband's sister Ellen asked if she was nervous. 'No,' she replied. 'I feel I have got home at last.'

They drove to the home of the George Huxleys, where a quick wedding breakfast was given to an assembly that included Hooker and Tyndall as well as a number of other young men waiting to grow into Victorian giants. Charles Darwin – 'I hope your marriage will not make you idle; happiness, I fear, is not good for work,' he wrote a few days later – was unavoidably absent. Darwin need not have worried. Henrietta recorded how 'after we were married, during his sleepless nights [he] mastered Kant and Hegel'. She remembered how one evening 'he brought home a Dutch scientific pamphlet and a Dutch dictionary. "I've got to know what this means tonight," he said.' And while their honeymoon journey was by easy coach stages, through Oxford, Warwick and Stratford, their destination was Tenby, where they stayed at first with Dr Dyster, a scientific colleague of TH, and where a full programme of work had apparently been arranged. Huxley continued with this work after they had moved to lodgings. And when Dr Dyster looked in one sunny morning, Henrietta later recorded, he 'found us on the back verandah, my husband, coat off, and shirt sleeves tucked up, dissecting a big fish, while I wrote down its description'. They were later joined by another colleague, George Busk, and remained at Tenby throughout August and September, Huxley taking his wife down to the beach every day and then going off with Busk, dredging for specimens for his own work and taking notes for the Geological Survey.

The Huxleys returned to London in the autumn, moving in to 14 Waverley Place, Maida Vale, a narrow, three-storeyed, stucco-fronted house lying in a quiet cul-de-sac, long since destroyed to make way for London's Underground. Here, during the following years, TH steadily built up for himself the first of the secure home bases from which he could sally out to fight the battles of the mid-Victorian age, scientific, theological and ethical. It was a base whose safety was assured by Henrietta. A young woman almost entirely innocent of science, she provided an admirable audience for her husband's papers designed for the popular lecture-room. Of simple but unyielding religious beliefs, she was for TH a good illustration of what cultivated English men and women were thinking, a useful example to have at hand in the stormy days ahead. And as a pioneer from the outback she was not one to be deterred from the difficulties of keeping house on an income that always lagged a little behind the rising tide of demand:

> My bush life in Australia had taught me to turn my hand to anything so that I could cook, paper a room, polish a floor, make a dress, and make myself generally useful [she later wrote]. Owing to this I was able to get on quite comfortably with two maid-servants, and many a pleasant club dinner with just two guests I held in my dining-room.

Huxley was now becoming known. In 1855 he was made a regular officer of the Geological Survey, 'with a commission to work out the natural history of the Survey'. He was lecturing at the Royal Institution and was much in demand elsewhere. The results of his zoological research were being published regularly in the learned journals, while he was much sought-after as a contributor by the editors of the quarterly and similar journals. First had come Chapman with the *Westminster*, for which Huxley had written a long critical review of MacGillivray's book on the *Rattlesnake* voyage. The *Saturday Review* and *Macmillan's* soon followed. So, in later years, did *Fraser's*, the *Fortnightly* and the *Contemporary Review*. Some of this work, carried out 'after hours' at home, was the result of Huxley's inextinguishable enthusiasm for pushing out into print all new knowledge that came his way, all the views he wished to expound. Yet much of it was dictated by need, and as Henrietta commented years later, if he 'had not had the wits to write regularly for the *Saturday Review* and magazines, we should have been in a sore plight'.

From 1855 onwards, the Huxley home became a familiar rendezvous for those resolute scientists and philosophers who stood unknowingly on the verge of the Darwinian revolution – particularly Tyndall and Hooker, who with Huxley himself were to play such prominent parts in the coming battles. Tyndall had been the first – 'in a short time we were Brother John, Brother Hal and Sister Nettie to one another', Henrietta wrote. Hooker soon followed, although it was the bachelors among the scientists who came most frequently, and three of them – Tyndall, Herbert Spencer and Thomas Hirst – were among those with no homes of their own who were regularly invited for the New Year's dinner. During it, afterwards, and on such regular occasions as Huxley's Sunday afternoon walk with Herbert Spencer, the talk would range over the latest scientific theories, the politics of recent scientific appointments and the fate of the world in general. Work continually flowed over into private life. Friends were colleagues. In fact it was difficult to think of dividing life into such separate compartments as work and play; Instead, each twenty-four hours was a day to be experienced with as much thought and action as could be crammed into it. This may have been partly the spirit of the age but it was certainly one foundation of the Huxley ethos, soundly laid during the later 1850s in 14 Waverley Place.

This continuous integration of public and private life, of work and pleasure, was an important factor in the growth of Victorian mountaineering, and Huxley himself by chance played a part in the development of Tyndall as a leading exponent of the craft. Tyndall had been investigating the problem of dia-magnetism and on 10 June 1856 delivered a lecture at the Royal Institution. Huxley was present, felt that Tyndall's theories might have some bearing on the laminated structure of glacier ice which had been discussed in J. D. Forbes's *Travels in the Alps* and advised his friend to read the book. Tyndall did so, was dissatisfied with the explanations which Forbes gave, and shortly afterwards suggested that he and the Huxleys should pay a summer visit to the Alps where the two men could investigate the glacier problem at first hand.

They met at Basle on 16 August and either then or soon afterwards all three climbed the steps of a cathedral tower to get a view of the Alps.

> Whether it was in the belfry of Berne or Basle I know not [Mrs Huxley wrote later], but in the great bell of one or other of them each of us wrote a rhyming line with a stiletto on my watch-chain.' The biggest bell, Twixt Heaven and Hell, This tongue can tell'. Dr. Tyndall's was the first, Mr. Huxley's the second and the last was mine – how I wish I knew if they were still to be seen.

Soon afterwards, and quite fortuitously, Hooker and his wife appeared on the scene, and the party of five travelled on together to Interlaken, where they hired two donkeys and continued up to the Wengern Alp. Mrs Huxley rode one animal, while Huxley and Tyndall disdained the help of the second one – presumably given over to the Hookers – and carried their packs to toughen themselves for the work ahead. Tyndall noted in his diary:

> Huxley looked tenderly after his wife; I called her *Sancta Maria* and him *der heilige Joseph*. His affection for his wife is a manly feeling,

founded on an appreciation of her superior qualities, on which he sometimes likes to dwell. Her sincerity, courage, freedom from conventionalism are among the chief qualities on which he dwells. Lifting her off her donkey in the presence of the Jungfrau, he said. 'You are worth all the other Jungfraus put together.' 'Dear Hal,' was her reply.

They spent the night at the Wengern Alp, and the following morning, after inspecting the Guggi Glacier, made their way over the Little Scheidegg and down to Grindelwald, with the magnificent spectacle of the Wetterhorn before them. A few days later Huxley and Tyndall went on alone to inspect the Rhône Glacier and then walked up to the little inn on the Furka. Tyndall wrote:

> The valley was full of vapours when we arrived, and standing on a mountain ridge, with the sun behind us, each of us suddenly observed his head surrounded by a coloured halo, and his shadow projected on the vapour mass in front. We raised our hands, the gigantic spectres before us did the same, and imitated all our actions; we had, in fact, the 'spectre of the Brocken' in all its splendour. We closed this day of wonders over a chop and a bottle of wine in the Furka Hotel, whence I descended to see Huxley on his way to the Rhône *auberge*. The marmots were piping on the rocks as we bade each other good-bye, and I was soon on my way back to my lonely lodging.

Tyndall had made one previous visit to the Alps, but it was from this journey with the Huxleys that there appears to have sprung his interest in mountaineering as a sport. From it, also, there came an intensification of Huxley's feeling for natural scenery, and much of his belief that hard exercise in the open air provided a panacea for many troubles. Both were to be transmitted down the family line.

The holiday had been so enjoyable, the work so interesting, that a similar trip was made the following year, although this time Mrs Huxley remained in England. Tyndall was soon deep in a long series of geological investigations and Huxley, writing of his friend forty years later, remembered how on one occasion the party had come upon

> a perpendicular cliff of ice of considerable height, formed on the flank of the glacier, which seemed to present a good opportunity for the examination of the structure of the interior. A hot sun loosening them, the stones on the surfaces of the glacier every now and then rattled down the face of the cliff. As no persuasion of ours could prevent Tyndall from ascending the cliff, by cutting steps with his

> axe, in order to get a very close view of the ice, we had to content ourselves with the post assigned to us, of looking out for stones. Whenever any of these seemed likely to shoot too close, we shouted, and Tyndall flattened himself against the cliff. Happily, no harm ensued . . .

This tour of 1857 was not all work, however, and soon after Huxley had arrived from London he joined his friends in an expedition from the Montanvert which it was hoped would reach the summit of Mont Blanc. By this date the ascent presented no great difficulties under good conditions but it was soon clear that Huxley was hardly up to the expedition. At one point, while the guides fetched a ladder with which to bridge a crevasse, he 'sat down upon the ice' (according to Tyndall) 'with an expression of fatigue stamped upon his countenance: the spirit and the muscle were evidently at war, and the resolute will mixed itself strangely with the sense of peril and feeling of exhaustion'. As they crossed the ladder above the blue depths, Tyndall noted that 'the exhausting journey over the boulders and debris had been too much for his London limbs. Converting my waterproof haversack into a cushion,' he continues, 'I made him sit down upon it at intervals, and by thus breaking the steep ascent into short stages we reached the cabin of the Grands Mulets together.'

Huxley knew his own limitations and, after lighting a succession of wax matches by whose gleams his companions drank their cold breakfast tea, he watched them, at 2.20 a.m., scramble down the steep rocks on to the ice. Later, in a letter to Dyster, he described his situation.

> It was as well that I stopped behind, for my two friends and the guide met with unusually deep snow and were seventeen hours away from the Grands Mulets, . . . on which solitary peak in the snowfields, two thousand feet up, I, alone all day, 'sate like a Cormorant'. Don't misread it 'ate like a Cormorant' for there was hardly anything to eat – the guide having stowed away the chief stores in a place I knew not of. Imagine my perplexity when, at sunset, my friends had not come back and I was divided between the conviction of the necessity of trying to get down to Chamonix to get help for them and the equally strong conviction that I should break my neck in the attempt! However, just as it grew dark they returned – Altogether I spent six and thirty hours on the Grands Mulets and as the weather was glorious you may imagine what sunrises and sunsets I had.

Huxley, unlike Tyndall, had as keen an eye for a sunset as for a useful fact.

From Chamonix, to which he now returned with his companions, Huxley made the Tour of Mont Blanc, across the Col de Géant down to Courmayeur and then back home. He wrote to Dyster:

> The only sad thing was to see the Cretins – in that beautiful valley of Aosta they swarm – flat-headed, blubber-lipped – deformed senseless wretches who are far worse caricatures of humanity than a respectable baboon. I should think a twentieth of the people I saw were cretins and of the rest fully half had goitre.
>
> They tell me the habits of the people are beastly in the extreme and justify any retribution on the part of Providence . . .

Like many Victorians, Huxley travelled hard. He wrote to Tyndall after his return:

> My financial calculations were perfect in theory, but nearly broke down in practice, inasmuch as I was twice obliged to travel first class when I calculated on second. The result was that my personal expenses between Paris and London amounted to 1.50!! [fr.] and I arrived at my own house hungry and with remainder of a few centimes.

He was still – as he was to remain for most of his life – hard-pressed financially, a situation kept constant as his responsibilities increased with the regular additions to his family. His first son, Noel, was born on New Year's Day 1857, 'a lovely child with large blue eyes, golden curls, a clear firm skin and regular features,' as he proudly described him. 'He looks out on the world with bold confident eyes and open brow, as if he were its master. We shall try to make him a better man than his father.' Jessie Oriana was born in the spring of the following year, the second name being, as Huxley explained to his sister, 'a family name of my wife's and not, as you might suppose, taken from Tennyson.' He was an enthusiastic family man, revelling in his children, the third of whom, Marian, was born in the spring of 1859.

But it was the firstborn, Noel, on whom he lavished most love – 'the apple of his father's eye and chief deity of his mother's pantheon', as he told his sister Lizzie. 'He is the great comfort and solace in the troubles of this weary world and is my domestic chaplain, though he doesn't know it,' he wrote to Dyster, adding a year later from Broadstairs that 'the chicks are wonderful to behold – and my yellow-haired boy riots in the luxury of unlimited sand and a spade to dig withal'. And Herbert Spencer later wrote to Huxley recalling 'your having told me how his existence had disclosed to you a new side of your nature, previously dormant'. This immensely human concern with his children's doings continued and grew throughout the years so that Huxley quickly became the example of the Victorian paterfamilias, counselling, guiding, understanding, and ever aware of human frailty. This is in contrast to the popular picture that was to develop, and the contrast itself an early illustration of a difference between the Huxleys' public image and the reality that waxes and wanes throughout the years but never entirely disappears.

As TH's family increased, so did his star rise steadily in that dark firmament from which there were already sparkling such names as Lyell and Owen, Tyndall and Hooker. Yet from the first, one Huxley tendency was to make him very different from most of his contemporaries. For in an age when science was still predominantly the business of the professional classes, Huxley realized that a basic knowledge of its principles could he understood by at least some of the masses, and that this knowledge alone would help them to develop whatever native ability they possessed. It would, moreover, enable the poor fellows to live happier lives. His first fame, it is apt to be forgotten, was not as the controversialist but as the humane professor bringing the light of science into places where no one had previously taken the trouble to shine the lamp.

Huxley's favourite medium was 'the people's lecture' – '*Popular* lectures I hold to be an abomination unto the Lord', he wrote to Dyster – and his success here was an example of the way in which he triumphed over natural difficulties. His first important lecture, on 'Animal Individuality', read at the Royal Institution in 1852, had not repeated the success of his impromptu speeches at Ipswich. Perhaps it was not only that he was speaking to one of the most critical audiences in London. He may, like others, have been affected by the concentric semi-circles of listeners, ranged on steeply-rising tiers so that the audience looked down in one focused stare at the speaker. Whatever the reason, 'at that time I disliked public speaking, and had a firm conviction that I should break down every time I opened my mouth,' he admitted. 'I believe I had every fault a speaker could have (except talking at random or indulging in rhetoric) . . .' However, he persevered – and carefully filed letters of criticism under 'Good Advice'.

By 1855, when he prepared to give six lectures at the Royal School of Mines for working men only, he had begun to learn the tricks of the craft. His view of his audience is well shown in a letter to Dyster:

> I want the working classes to understand that Science and her ways are great facts for them – that physical virtue is the base of all other, and that they are to be clean and temperate and all the rest – not because fellows in black with white ties tell them so, but because

these are plain and patent laws of nature which they must obey 'under penalties'.

I am sick of the *dilettante* middle class, and mean to try what I can do with these hard-handed fellows who live among facts.

He did a great deal, speaking on each of the six evenings to a theatre crammed with an audience of 600. The lectures were the first of many to be held during succeeding years for similar audiences, and while other professors also took part, few had Huxley's genius – and it was nothing less – for presenting the facts of the natural world; for explaining them in terms that ordinary men could understand; and for impressing on his listeners that when he put forward awkward, unpleasant, or unpopular facts or theories, he did so after due study and with honest belief. This was in some respects a two-way traffic.

I found [he later wrote] that the task of putting truths learned in the field, the laboratory and the museum, into language which, without bating a jot of scientific accuracy, shall be generally intelligible, taxed such scientific and literary faculty as I possess to the uttermost; indeed my experience has furnished me with no better corrective to the tendency to scholastic pedantry which besets all those who are absorbed in pursuits remote from the common ways of men, and become habituated to think and speak in the technical dialect of their own little world, as if there were no other.

To be right yet to be comprehensible: that was the yardstick and its use was to become almost a standing order for subsequent Huxleys.

From these beginnings in Jermyn Street, Huxley's reputation as a public speaker steadily grew. His clarity, and his command of every subject on which he spoke, first caught attention; his sincerity held it; and the results showed that among the inarticulate proletariat of Victorian cabbies, journeymen and waiters there lurked more than the occasional man ready to grasp at the intellectual lifeline unexpectedly thrown to him. Among one group at least, Huxley earned early fame. 'Will you give me the envelope, sir,' asked a working man who one day brought a note from Huxley to a colleague. '. . . it's got Professor Huxley's signature, and it will be something for me to show my mates and keep for my children. He have done me and my like a lot of good; no man more.' One cabby refused his fare from Huxley with the words: 'Oh, no, Professor. I have had too much pleasure and profit from hearing you lecture to take any money from your pocket – proud to have driven you, sir.'

Huxley's reputation as a man eager and able to take science into unlikely places spread quickly following the lectures of 1855. It was an illustration of the influence and the popularity that he was acquiring while only just in his thirties, and it may well have helped produce the personal storm which was to play a significant part in his life and whose first rustlings were heard in 1857.

The storm was between Huxley and Owen, later Sir Richard Owen, K.C.B., President of the Royal Society, more than twenty years Huxley's senior and in 1857 already heavy with fame. The two men had first met in 1846, being introduced by Captain Stanley during preparations for the voyage of the *Rattlesnake*. Huxley had then noted of Owen that 'he is the superior of most of his contemporaries and does not conceal that he knows it', a remark that reveals perception and suggests that antagonism between the two men may have been instinctive. It was certainly lasting, and of a quality which shows that for bitter quarrels the scientist can equal even the mountaineer.

Late in 1856 Owen received permission to use the Jermyn Street lecture-theatre for a palaeontological course. No exception could be taken to this, but early in January 1857 Churchill's the publishers produced a new edition of their *Medical Directory*. A few days later they received a letter from Huxley:

> In your valuable *Medical Directory* I observe after the name 'Owen, Richard', the title Professor of Comparative Anatomy and Palaeontology, Government School of Mines. Mr Owen holds no appointment whatever at the Government School of Mines and as I am the Professor of General Natural History (which includes Comparative Anatomy and Palaeontology) in that Institution you will observe that the statement referred to is calculated to do me injury.

Huxley's feelings cannot have been assuaged when, two days afterwards, he received a polite note from Churchill's pointing out that the details were, in fact, those sent to them by Mr Owen.

Huxley had neither time nor inclination for malice. He believed that personalities should be kept on a lower level than the grand arguments of science. Yet he was human, and he must have felt a good deal of satisfaction when the opportunity came, the following year, to deliver the Croonian Lecture. His subject was the theory of the vertebrate skull, and he started by outlining the proposition first made by Lorenz Oken, the German naturalist. The skull, according to this, was but a gradually developed elaboration of a part of the backbone in which it was, even now, possible to distinguish the parts of separate vertebrae. This proposition was supported by Owen, one of the most distinguished leaders of British science, and it was one which Huxley, aged thirty-two, now coolly and efficiently demolished. Showing calmly, and with his usual wealth of assembled detail, that the skull was in fact an independent growth, he cut away Oken's foundations and at the same time brought to the ground the structure which Owen had erected upon it. The debate which ensued was conducted on the most gentlemanly lines and with Owen fighting a skilful rear-guard action. Yet the controversy was to have two important results. One was that it encouraged Huxley into an even more vigorous investigation of any possible similarities between man and the apes. Another was its effect on Owen. For Owen, also, was but human, and two years later he involved himself, with great expectations no doubt, in events which were to fling Huxley into the harsh limelight of public controversy.

At the time of the Croonian lecture, Huxley was willing enough to push his beliefs forward into the scientific arena. Apart from anything else, this was a duty. But he had no wish to swim out into the deeper waters of public controversy. He was a happy man immersed in the multiple duties of work for the Geological Survey and the Royal School of Mines, in lecturing and research and writing, in unravelling more mysteries of the natural world which were so often solved merely to reveal yet fresh mysteries beyond. He had, after all, every reason to be content. By his early thirties he had successfully struggled through the first prickly barriers which chance had placed across his path. His intellect had soared up and over the limitations of a negligible education. He had, moreover, begun to establish his position in that scientific society which in the 1850s stood on the threshold of such great things. 'I shall take pleasure in working the place into what I think it ought to be,' he wrote of the Royal School of Mines to Dyster in August 1858. 'I have had a hard fight of it but as things go I must count myself singularly fortunate. The man should be thankful who has found his work and has only got to do it...'

It might have all stayed there. The way ahead stretched rewardingly and almost comfortably clear. For Huxley a life of science, unimplicated with exterior controversies, was the really worth-while thing. To be involved in the public debate was not only unnecessary but faintly distasteful. How very thankful, in fact, should a man be who had found his work and had only got to do it.

Then, in December, 1859, a parcel arrived on Huxley's desk in the comfortably cluttered study of 14 Waverley Place. Inside was a letter asking him if he would review for *The Times*, at length, the enclosed book by Charles Darwin, *The Origin of Species by Means of Natural Selection, or the Preservation of Favoured Races in the Struggle for Life.*

Chapter III

Battle for *The Origin*

(*i*)

The Origin of Species, and the revolution in thought which it started, had much in common with the release of nuclear energy some eighty years later. Both probed deeply down into man's knowledge of the natural world and his beliefs about it. Both upset apple-carts, raised problems, made the world a more intellectually stimulating place. Both in their own ways began by affecting the thin upper intellectual layer of society and seeped down only later to play their roles among ordinary people. Yet in one way these two expressions of mankind's intellectual advance were very different. The release of nuclear energy would, whatever its context, whatever the circumstances surrounding it, have impinged quickly and relentlessly on human activity. With *The Origin* things might have been otherwise. Close-reasoned as its argument was, fully supported by massed facts as were its theories, it might yet have remained for decades on the margin of history, pushed there by Victorian reluctance to face up to the awkward problems it raised. Without the master gunner to set the sights and select the fuse, Darwin's masterpiece might, in spite of everything, have been a powerful book which misfired. Huxley himself was to see that this did not happen, doing more than any other man to ensure that it arrived on target, and then defending, explaining, augmenting the results that the impact had produced. Moreover, as Huxley battled for a rational study of *The Origin* he found that the battle helped to firm up his own conception of the task which he felt that he could and should do. *The Origin* made Darwin; its defence made Huxley.

The first contact between the two men had come soon after Huxley's return to England on the *Rattlesnake*, when he sent Darwin a technical report on a number of specimens. Darwin in turn supported Huxley's candidature for the post in Toronto when he was adrift in the bleak wilderness of the early 1850s, looking for work, recognition, and the few hundred a year which would make marriage possible. Acquaintance developed into friendship, and by 1854 Huxley, whose mind Darwin found 'as quick as a flash of lightning and as sharp as a razor', had become Darwin's expert on zoology. Two years later TH and his wife were invited to Downe and were driven to Down House where Darwin was already sorting and re-sorting his voluminous notes, cogitating on their implications, pouring in from his own mind and transforming thought which would eventually produce from the amorphous mass of facts the hard diamond of evolutionary theory.

It must have been an intriguing meeting, with the deeply religious Mrs Darwin possibly confiding her fears to Henrietta – for it is one of the quirks of history that the two men who were to push evolution through the Church barricades had married women who were sincere, obstinate and devout Christians.

In these late 1850s one of two beliefs was still strongly held by a majority in the western world. The first was that the earth had been created almost within historical times. James Ussher, the Archbishop of Armagh who had pin-pointed the moment as nine o'clock on the morning of 23 October 4004 B.C., might not be entirely correct, but it was widely held that the earth's life was of this order. And if the world had been created thus, then the multitudes of living things had surely been created in the same way, by a stroke of omnipotent genius which produced fishes and men, snakes, birds, and the most minute insects, perhaps not exactly in the seven days and nights of the Bible but at least in some comparable period. The alternative belief was that even if the seven days and seven nights were purely allegorical, yet creation had still been a matter of separate events.

> It was gravely maintained and taught [as Huxley said, speaking in 1886 to the Royal Institution on 'The Coming of Age of the *Origin of Species*'] that the end of each geological epoch was signalized by a cataclysm, by which every living being on the globe was swept away, to be replaced by a brand new creation when the world returned to quiescence.

And he noted that:

> A scheme of nature which appeared to be modelled on the likeness of a succession of rubbers of whist, at the end of which the players upset the table and called for a new pack, did not seem to shock anybody.

These beliefs were, it is true, already being eroded. Sir Charles Lyell had shown in his *Principles of Geology* that the form of the earth as man knew it could have been – and quite probably had been – produced over vast periods against which Ussher's 6,000 years were a mere flicker in time. Boucher de Perthes, persistently prodding in the gravel-pits of the Somme Valley near his home at Abbeville, had discovered flints which were certainly fashioned by man, and whose positions in the strata dated them far back beyond Archbishop Ussher's creation. As Huxley was so neatly to put it years later, 'the abyss of time began to loom as large as the abyss of space'. And might the time not be long enough to make credible tentative beliefs in an evolutionary process; might not all have been developed 'by natural laws from a primitive unformed material', as had been held by the Greeks, the Romans and even by the early Christian Fathers? Buffon, Erasmus Darwin – the grandfather of Charles – and Lamarck had all during the previous century believed it possible that the various kinds of life had not been created independently but had arisen from other species. Yet all had failed to explain successfully how this could have happened. And they had left their successors with the problems that had hung, unresolved and challenging, as a background to much scientific thought; a question from which most men turned away towards less difficult, less disturbing and less dangerous matters.

Huxley's position was clear, although at a superficial glance misleading. On the *Rattlesnake* his work on the molluscs had shown him that all the varieties shared a similar basic or archetypal structure. All, he deduced, must have been derived by modifications from a single original type, and for the process he even used the word 'evolution'. Yet this was not the evolution whose existence Darwin was to make plain. Huxley believed that within any particular group of living organisms, gradual change through the centuries might produce different varieties; but he believed also that the changes were circumscribed by the limits of the group – even his argument with Owen involved nothing more, since man and the apes both belonged to the same group and might well therefore have shared the same original structure. Beyond that he could not go.

> I remember [he wrote in 'On the Reception of *The Origin of Species*', contributed to *The Life and Letters of Charles Darwin*] in the course of my first interview with Mr Darwin, expressing my belief in the sharpness of the lines of demarcation between natural groups and in the absence of transitional forms, with all the confidence of youth and imperfect knowledge. I was not aware, at that time, that he had then been many years brooding over the

species-question; and the humourous smile which accompanied his gentle answer, that such was not altogether his view, long haunted and puzzled me.

In Huxley's view the whole complex question of evolution was one which merged into the unknowable. All his life he was to keep clear the distinction between those problems which were, from their very nature, capable of solution and those whose solution lay beyond the realm of human experience. His view, before the arrival of *The Origin* of the place that evolution occupied in this division of things is shown by one statement. He usually, he wrote,

> defended the tenability of the received doctrines when I had to do with the transmutationists; and stood up for the possibility of transmutation among the orthodox. I imagine that most of those of my contemporaries who thought seriously about the matter were very much in my own state of mind – inclined to say to both Mosaists and Evolutionists, 'a plague on both your houses!' and disposed to turn aside from an interminable and apparently fruitless discussion, to labour in the fields of ascertainable fact.

Then came Darwin. His interest in the origin of species had been aroused almost three decades earlier during the five-year voyage of the *Beagle* around the world. It increased following his return to England in 1836, and for years the major part of his work had been the compilation of notes on the problem – notes immensely aided by his own observations at Down where conservatories, fowls, pigeons and garden, the raw material of a country gentleman's life, all added grist to his scientific mill. In 1844 he briefly sketched out his conclusions, but with characteristic caution kept them unpublished. And it was not until fourteen years later that the receipt from the explorer Alfred Russell Wallace of a memoir outlining similar conclusions led Darwin to produce a paper that was read with Wallace's at a meeting of the Linnean Society on 1 July 1858.

This paper stimulated Huxley as it stimulated many others. But it was only an *hors d'œuvre* to the dish that Darwin began to prepare during the following months. He was still hesitant about writing more than a paper or series of papers for the learned journals, and only towards the end of December did he realize that his manuscript would run to 400 pages or more and would have to emerge as a book. Lyell mentioned the matter to John Murray, who objected only to Darwin's suggestion that the title page should read 'An Abstract of an Essay on the Origin . . .' and who agreed to issue a cautious 1,250 copies. Even so, publication was not yet certain. Darwin had been worried about Murray's reaction to the more unorthodox conclusions of the manuscript and early in 1859 wrote that: 'If you feel bound for your sake and my own to say in clearest terms that if after looking over parts of my MS you do not think it likely to have a remunerative sale, I completely and explicitly free you from your offer to publish.' Murray, in his wisdom, decided that *The Origin of Species* was a fair gamble, and the book appeared on 24 November 1859.

Darwin had decided that the opinion of three men, Lyell, Hooker and Huxley, would provide the acid test of the book's scientific worth. Huxley's immediate reactions are revealed in the chapter which he contributed many years later to Darwin's *Life and Letters*. The book, together with the earlier Linnean Society lecture, had, he said, the effect 'of the flash of light which, to a man who has lost himself on a dark night, suddenly reveals a road which, whether it takes him straight home or not, certainly goes his way'. Huxley, like many others at the time, intuitively wanted to reject the 'creation hypothesis' but had so far seen no feasible alternative.

> That which we were looking for, and could not find, was a hypothesis respecting the origin of known organic forms which assumed the operation of no causes but such as could be proved to be actually at work. We wanted, not to pin our faith to that of any other speculation, but to get hold of clear and definite conceptions which could be brought face to face with facts and have their validity tested. The *Origin* provided us with the working hypothesis we sought.

It was also to provide them with a battlefield. For although Darwin had carefully avoided bringing the ancestry of man directly into the hypothesis, those who believed in man's divine creation could see clearly enough that he had outflanked their positions. Huxley, with the insight of a born fighter, knew what was coming and warned Darwin:

> I trust you will not allow yourself to be in any way disgusted or annoyed by the considerable abuse and misrepresentation which, unless I am greatly mistaken, is in store for you [he wrote on 23 November]. Depend upon it you have earned the lasting gratitude of all thoughtful men. And as to the curs which will bark and yelp, you must recollect that some of your friends, at any rate, are endowed with an amount of combativeness which (though you have often and justly rebuked it) may stand you in good stead.
>
> I am sharpening up my claws and beak in readiness.

He was doing more. He was, in fact, preparing to play his self-styled role as 'Darwin's bulldog'. From Jermyn Street he could exert his influence. In the Royal Society, in the Linnean, in the British Association, in the multiplicity of scientific organizations where his reputation was already beginning to make men turn and look back as he passed – in all these he would be able to speak, to defend, to explain, to turn away the wrath of all but unreasonable men. Yet here he would be speaking if not to the converted at least to the convertible. What surely mattered as much, if in another way, was opinion in that greater, more rumbustious and more uninformed world that lay beyond the scientific establishment, the world where public opinion was made; opinion which, in its consideration of new ideas, was apt to be conservative, critical and contemptuous.

The ideal opportunity was provided by Mr Lucas, a staff writer on *The Times*, who was handed *The Origin* and told to prepare a review. Lucas, '. . . as innocent of any knowledge of science as a babe . . . bewailed himself to an acquaintance on having to deal with such a book', Huxley later wrote. The acquaintance suggested that Professor Huxley might help out, and Lucas wrote asking if he would do so, adding only that he would – apparently to keep the record straight – have to lead off the review with two or three paragraphs of his own.

> I was too anxious [Huxley wrote in *The Life and Letters of Charles Darwin*] to seize upon the opportunity thus offered of giving the book a fair chance with the multitudinous readers of *The Times*, to make any difficulty about conditions, and being then very full of the subject, I wrote the article faster, I think, than I ever wrote anything in my life, and sent it to Mr Lucas who duly prefixed his opening sentences.

The review was written, as was so much of his work, with Henrietta reading the sheets as they came from his pen, each covered with the long and rather scrawny writing that developed through the years into the almost undecipherable undulations of the man whose pen can hardly keep pace with his brain. There were a good many sheets and the review, which appeared on 26 December, ran to some five thousand words – three and a half columns. 'The old fogies will think the world will come to an end,' commented Darwin. The opening of the review by Lucas had, oddly enough, an almost Huxleyan ring about it – "There is a growing immensity in the speculations of science to which no human thing or thought at this day is comparable.' Then followed an account of the book and the opinion, the nub of the review, that Darwin's theory of the origin of species, this 'ingenious hypothesis' as

Huxley called it, 'enables us to give a reason for many apparent anomalies in the distribution of living beings in space and time, and it is not contradicted by the main phenomena of life and organization.'

He had expected the review to cause reflection among 'some of the educated mob, who derive their ideas from *The Times*'. This it certainly did, pushing the book on to the notice of those who could no longer avoid discussing it, passing opinions, making up their minds, attacking or defending what steadily became the most controversial topic of the scientific world and a debating point among thousadns of ordinary men and women. More important, the review was an avowal that Huxley had now firmly nailed his colours to the Darwin mast. It was not an open avowal, since at first only Hooker knew that the author was Huxley. Yet the chance opportunity of writing the review, and of pushing the book out into wider non-specialist seas, showed Huxley just what a strong weapon he could wield in the scientific battle.

He naturally enough went on with his normal routine, lecturing and carrying out research in Jermyn Street, preparing his papers for the learned journals, reviewing and writing. Yet, increasingly throughout 1860, everything tended to revolve round *The Origin*. Like all able commanders, Huxley was quick to discover correctly the really vital part of the battlefield. If science was to press on with its task, evolution was the subject on which the obscurantist forces had to be beaten.

The Times review – which was reprinted in full by the *Gardeners Chronicle*, much to Darwin's delight – was therefore merely the opening of a campaign which Huxley began to wage, in private conversation, in journals of opinion such as the *Westminster Review*, and in scientific forums.

On 10 February 1860 he spoke at the Royal Institution 'On Species and Races, and their Origin'.

In this Royal Institution lecture he raised, apparently for the first time in public, the subject which he was to take further than Darwin, and the one which was to provide a central core for his beliefs. In *The Origin* Darwin had taken care not to underline too strongly the fact that man himself was but part of evolving life. 'Light will be thrown on the origin of man and his history,' he had claimed; but he had gone no further. Now Huxley was to harden up slowly throughout the months the inevitable conclusion to which acceptance of Darwinism led. At the Royal Institution his shot across the bows of contemporary opinion was a warning of things to come and an example of the fine style which his lecturing was developing. He said that people took fright at the logical corollary of Darwinism – the belief that Man himself must have risen in the same way as the rest of life:

> But to those whose life is spent, to use Newton's noble words, in picking up here a pebble and there a pebble on the shores of the great ocean of truth – who watch, day by day, the slow but sure advance of that mighty tide, bearing on its bosom the thousand treasures wherewith a man ennobles and beautifies his life – it would be laughable, if it were not so sad, to see the little Canutes of the hour enthroned in solemn state, bidding that great wave to stay, and threatening to check its beneficent progress. The wave rises and they fly; but unlike the brave old Dane, they learn no lesson of humility: the throne is pitched at what seems a safe distance, and the folly is repeated.

Huxley continued in the same vein throughout the spring and early summer. More than one scientist must have wondered how the simmering question of evolution would be handled at the meeting of the British Association to be held at Oxford that summer.

The meeting began on Wednesday, 27 June, with the usual formal reception. The controversy began the very next day when, at the first session of Section 'D', Dr Daubeny spoke 'On the final causes of the sexuality of plants, with particular reference to Mr Darwin's work on the "Origin of Species"'. Daubeny, then sixty-five, drew heavily on his own experiences in botany and geology, and strongly supported Darwin's theory. When the debate was thrown open Huxley, a known protagonist, was called upon to speak but tried to avoid discussion, feeling that 'a general audience, in which sentiment would unduly interfere with intellect', was not the right public. Owen had other views – the Owen, by this time a past President of the Association, whose opinions had steadily diverged from those of Huxley during the previous few years and who was now taking up generalship of the armies massing against Darwin. Owen rose to his feet, a formidable and confident figure, and began to discredit *The Origin* with what he stated to be facts. One of these was that the brain of the gorilla 'presented more differences, as compared with the brain of man, than it did when compared with the brains of the very lowest and most problematical of the Quadrumana'.

Now this was just the assumption which, three years earlier, had set Huxley off on his complete reinvestigation of the whole question. Fresh dissections, rereading of the earlier authorities, even work on the specimens at the Hunterian Museum under Owen's care, had all driven him inexorably to an exactly opposite conclusion. He rose and contradicted Owen – and added that he would later support his contradiction. Thus he underlined his position opposite the forces which were, as yet unknown to him, being marshalled for battle.

These forces were very powerful and were to be led by Samuel Wilberforce, Bishop of Oxford. His part was to be played two days later and it was to be a dramatic one.

Wilberforce was in 1860 at the height of his fame. Social gifts; the ability to speak on platform, from pulpit, and in Parliament; calm enthusiasm and not too much intellect – these qualities had combined to make this son of the great abolitionist a model of the new English Churchman struggling against the drift to Rome, a drift which had already swept along his three brothers, his only daughter and his son-in-law. Wilberforce – who would smiling explain away his soubriquet of 'Soapy Sam' with the remark that he was always in hot water and always came out of it with clean hands – was a formidable opponent. At Cuddesdon Palace, the Bishop's seat six miles outside the city, he had during the previous few days been coached by Owen in the minutiae of what the latter believed to be the defects in the Darwinian theory. The facts, it was planned, would be deployed by the Bishop when he attended, on the Saturday afternoon, the session of Section D at which an American, Dr Draper, was to speak on 'The Intellectual Development of Europe considered with reference to the Views of Mr Darwin.'

This was to be the first major confrontation of the opposing forces; it was also to be an appointment with history that Huxley nearly missed. He was already tired and overworked; to the actual business of the meeting there had inevitably been added a certain minimum of social junketing, a good deal of behind-the-scenes policy making, much investigatory gossiping. Huxley had had enough of it all; he had planned to tie up the loose ends of his business on the Friday, and on Saturday join his wife at her brother-in-law's house outside Reading. He had heard that Wilberforce would be speaking on the Saturday afternoon but had little faith in the kind of audience that would be assembled – the Bishop 'had the reputation of being a first-class controversialist', he wrote many years later, 'and I was quite aware that if he played his cards properly, we should have little chance, with such an audience, of making an efficient defence.'

Chance decided otherwise. On Friday Huxley fortuitously met Robert Chambers, the author of *Vestiges of Creation*, whom he had visited in Edinburgh five years previously. Huxley mentioned that he would not be attending the following afternoon's session – since he 'did not see the good of giving up peace and quietness to be episcopally pounded'. Chambers was astounded that Huxley should, as he put it, be deserting them.

'Oh!' TH replied, 'if you are going to take it that way, I'll come and have my share of what is going on.'

He was therefore among those who on the following afternoon crowded into the University museum, a building opened only five years earlier, with piers and columns illustrating the rocks of the British Isles, and capitals and pediments showing the plants and animals of the country in their natural orders.

The bush-telegraph had been beating through Oxford. There was a sense of battle in the air on this Saturday afternoon, and so great were the numbers that the plan for holding the meeting in the lecture-room had to be abandoned. Instead, the long west room was chosen and into it there moved more than seven hundred men and women, finding places where they could, crowding the gangways and the aisles and sitting in silhouette on the window-seats above which the afternoon sun streamed in. Opposite them, ranged along the east side of the room, was the platform. On to it there first came J. S. Henslow, the president of Section D, black-clothed and clerical-looking, a man who gave only qualified support to Darwin but who had insisted, throughout the discussion of the preceding months, in holding the ring fairly for the rival forces. On his right sat the Bishop, coming late, and in the words of one onlooker, 'trampling his way through the dense crowd to his place upon the platform, his face no longer refined and spiritual as in the early Richmond portrait; coarsened somewhat, even plebeianized, by advancing years, but resourceful, pugnacious, impregnable, not a little arrogant.' To his right sat Dr Draper of New York. On Henslow's left sat Hooker; Sir John Lubbock, later Lord Avebury; and Sir Benjamin Brodie, sergeant-surgeon to the Queen and President of the Royal Society. Beside Brodie sat Huxley, 'hair jet black and thick, slight whiskers, pale full fleshy face, the two strong lines of later years already marked, an ominous quiver in his mouth, and an arrow ready to come out of it.'

The proceedings began with Dr Draper reading his paper. He droned on for more than an hour, no doubt making some of those present feel that the afternoon was to be less exciting than rumour had suggested. Then Henslow threw open the discussion, adding that only those who had valid arguments to put forward would be allowed to speak.

It is here that the clear-cut picture of the proceedings begins to shimmer, as though affected by the heat of the summer afternoon and the press of expectant men and women. For while Dr Draper's paper is on record, no verbatim account was taken of the debate that followed. J. R. Green, then a young undergraduate, later gave his version. Hooker gave his, in a letter to Darwin a few days afterwards. Huxley himself outlined the events in a letter to his old friend Dyster; others later recalled the occasion, while a little-known book of reminiscences by the Reverend W. Tuckwell, a spectator, paints a detailed picture. All accounts agree in general terms; all disagree on, or fail to mention, the exact words used by Wilberforce and Huxley. However, the main course of events is clear.

There first came a number of disjointed comments from the body of the hall. There was the Reverend Richard Cresswell, Tutor of Worcester, 'who with great eyes, vast white neckcloth, luminous bald head and spectacles, rising and falling rhythmically on his toes, opined that all theories as to the ascent of man were vitiated by the fact, undoubted but irrelevant, that, in the words of Pope, Great Homer died three thousand years ago.' There was the canon of Durham who 'let off his theological venom', and the grey-haired, Roman-nosed Admiral Fitzroy, captain of the *Beagle* thirty years before, who said that Darwin's book had given him the acutest pain. Another voice came from the end of the hall:

> a stout man waved and slapped a blue-book; told us he was no naturalist but a statistician, and that if you could prove Darwin's theories you could prove anything [wrote Tuckwell]. A roar of displeasure proclaimed the meeting's inaptitude at that moment for statistics, and the stout man made his exit with a defiant remonstrance. Now, we thought, for business; but no, there was another act of comedy. From the back of the platform emerged a clerical gentleman, asking for a blackboard. It was produced, and amid dead silence, he chalked two crosses at its opposite corners, and stood pointing at them as if admiring his achievement. We gazed at him, and he at us, but nothing came of it, till suddenly the absurdity of the situation seemed to strike the whole assembly simultaneously.

The clerical gentleman was laughed into oblivion. There came a pause and, according to Tuckwell, 'an appeal from the chairman to Huxley, his sarcastic response that he certainly held a brief for science, but had not yet heard it assailed.'

There were now loud calls for the Bishop. Wilberforce rose, square-faced, broad-nosed, prod-chinned, a resolute figure, and mildly said that his friend Professor Beale had something to say. Beale, providing the perfect foil for the Bishop, said that while the theory of *The Origin* ought to be fairly discussed, he lacked enough knowledge to do so adequately.

Wilberforce felt no such inhibitions. He looked confidently across the room to the silhouette of ladies outlined against the windows and started off, florid and fluent. He ruminated round the facts, retrod common ground, distinguished between 'a working and a causal hypothesis' and then flung out a compliment to Huxley who, he commented cheerfully, 'is about to demolish me.' And he expressed, as he put it, the disquietude he should feel were 'a venerable ape' in the Zoo to be shown to him as an ancestress.

It was clear to those who knew what the argument was about, that the Bishop was entirely dependent on a briefing that had almost certainly come from Owen. He provided no scientific kernel to his argument, and according to Hooker 'spouted for half an hour with inimitable spirit, ugliness and emptiness and unfairness'. Yet it was a speech well-tuned to a great deal of the audience – eloquent, ignorant and persuasive. Replying to it would be like punching cotton-wool.

It seems likely that Wilberforce sensed the audience going his way and that it was over-confidence that pulled him on towards a fatal error. He may now, as we shall see, have remembered an earlier encounter. He turned towards Huxley. Exactly what he said we do not know. One version is that 'he begged to know whether it was through his grandfather or his grandmother that he claimed his descent from a monkey'. Another, and slightly more likely version is that he asked, with what must have been only a sly glance at Huxley, 'if anyone were to be willing to trace his descent through an ape as his *grandfather*, would he be willing to trace his descent through an ape on the side of his *grandmother*?'

Whatever the exact words, Huxley turned to Brodie, slapped hand on knee and exclaimed, 'The Lord hath delivered him into mine hands!'

Such was to be the case. It was permissible for the Bishop to muddle the scientific facts. It was permissible for him to float along to victory on a mixture of oratorical expertise, good intentions and empty argument. But in an assembly of this sort one did not descend to personalities; and one did not, in any case, bring ladies into the argument. In his search for ammunition, Wilberforce had for the moment forgotten both unwritten laws.

Huxley rose to reply: cool, quiet, dispassionate. It seems that at the start he did not carry the audience with him. He was unable, according to Hooker, to throw his voice successfully over so large an assembly, and it was only as he turned to exploit the Bishop's false step that the tide began to turn. He explained that when one talked of descent one meant descent through thousands of generations. And he then went on to explode his demolition charge.

The details of what Huxley said differ as much as do those of Wilberforce's speech. But in Huxley's case there does exist his own account, given in a letter to Dyster only a few months later. The letter is of interest not merely in itself but in suggesting that there may have been an earlier exchange between the two men:

> It was great fun. I had said that I could not see what difference it would make to my moral responsibility if I *had* had an ape for a grandfather, and saponaceous Samuel thought it was a fine opportunity for chaffing a savan.

Now there is no record that Huxley had spoken before the Bishop at the meeting; but the implication of Huxley's 'had said' is that an earlier remark had been made in the Bishop's presence, and it seems at least possible that by this famous Saturday the two men had already crossed swords – conceivably at one of the Association's social functions – an act which would help to explain an error of tactics on the part of Wilberforce, a man not used to making errors.

> However [Huxley continued to Dyster], he performed the operation vulgarly and I determined to punish him – partly on that account and partly because he talked pretentious nonsense, and when I got up I spoke pretty much to the speech – that I had listened with great attention to the Lord Bishop's speech but had been unable to discover either a new fact or a new argument in it – except, indeed, the question raised as to my personal predilections in the matter of ancestry – That it would not have occurred to me to bring forward such a topic as that for discussion myself, but that I was quite ready to meet the Rt Rev. prelate even on that ground – If, then, said I, the question is put to me, 'would I rather have a miserable ape for a grandfather, or a man highly endowed by nature and possessed of great means and influence, and yet who employs these faculties and that influence for the mere purpose of introducing ridicule into a grave scientific discussion' – I unhesitatingly affirm my preference for the ape. Whereupon there was unextinguishable laughter among the people – and they listened to the rest of my argument with the greatest of attention. Lubbock and Hooker spoke after me with great force and among us we shut up the bishop and his party. I happened to be in very good condition and said my say with perfect good temper and politeness – I assure you of this because all sorts of reports were spread about, e.g. that I had said that I would rather be an ape than a bishop.
>
> All the Oxford Dons were there & several hundred people in the room – so that I think Samuel will think twice before he tries a fall with men of science again.

> If he had dealt with the subject fairly and modestly I would not have treated him in this way — But the round-mouthed, oily, special pleading of the man who, ignorant of the subject, presumed on his position & his larger faculty, gave me a most unmitigated contempt for him. You can't think how pleased all his confrères were. I believe I was the most popular man in Oxford for full four & twenty hours afterwards.

One account claims that Huxley concluded with some such words as . . . were to discredit and crush humble seekers after truth, then I hesitate what answer to make'. But the precise words were drowned by the great burst of applause from what should be called the audience but might be described as the spectators. This was, after all, what they had come to see.

Lady Brewster, wife of Sir David, the inventor of the kaleidoscope, fainted at the enormity of a bishop being called to order in his own diocese, and all was ready for the *coup de grâce*.

It was administered by Hooker, and one would give much to know just what he said; it must have been strong enough for he wrote to Darwin:

> I swore to myself that I would smite that Amalekite, Sam, hip and thigh if my heart jumped out of my mouth . . . I hit him in the wind at the first shot in ten words taken from his own ugly mouth; and then proceeded to demonstrate in as few more: (1) that he could never have read your book, and (2) that he was absolutely ignorant of the rudiments of Bot. Science.

Most accounts suggest that Wilberforce disdained to reply. Tuckwell, however, comments that 'The Bishop radiantly purged himself. He did not mean to hurt the Professor's feelings; it was our fault – we had laughed, and that made him pursue the joke. We laughed again and Huxley was not appeased'. The discussion now ended, whether or not after a belated apology from Wilberforce remains unclear.

One point should be made in fairness to Hooker. Although accounts differ in emphasis and sometimes contradict in detail, Hooker's importance is clear. Huxley had marshalled his facts, used them for attack, and was casting about with the decision still in the balance. Hooker, coming up at the decisive moment, played Blücher to Huxley's Wellington and should be remembered in the battle-honours.

The debate had lasted four hours. Its effects were considerable. In one way they were unfortunate since they tended to imply that the debate was only between Darwinism and the Church, between religion and science – over-simplifications which were to produce ruts from which the controversy later found it difficult to escape. Yet the mere spectacle of a bishop being successfully confronted – and this Bishop in particular – gave an adventitious publicity to what might still have been an almost private argument. Perhaps the British Association was the ideal forum for such a spectacle, providing the authority of science yet listened to by far wider numbers than the older and more restricted learned societies. Darwin wrote to Huxley the following month:

> From all that I hear from several quarters, it seems that Oxford ... did the subject great good. It is of enormous importance to show the world that a few first-class men are not afraid of expressing their opinion. I see daily more and more plainly that my unaided Book would have done *absolutely* nothing.

More important still was the effect on Huxley of that moment when he realized he had helped to turn the tables before an audience of hundreds. Perhaps he had almost expected that. But by this time, and in what was to become a Huxley tradition, he was thinking one or two moves ahead. He had so far detested, and possibly despised, public speaking of this sort – after all, it was not very often that appeal could be made to the reason rather than to the emotion of the mob. Yet to beat the Philistine it might at times be necessary to use his own weapons; at least it would be no bad thing to have them under command. Huxley left the meeting with Hooker and as the two men walked back into the centre of Oxford, he spoke to his friend, whose words had helped to win the day. The experience, he said, had changed his opinion as to the practical value of the art of public speaking: henceforth he would 'carefully cultivate it and try to leave off hating it'.

Henceforth, in addition, he was to show a bulldog unwillingness to let go of an argument. A year later, when he took over editorial responsibility for the *Natural History Review*, Huxley drafted a letter to Wilberforce. Dated 3 June 1861, it read:

> Professor Huxley presents his compliments to the Lord Bishop of Oxford. Believing that his Lordship has as great an interest in the ascertainment of the truth as himself, Professor Huxley ventures to draw the attention of the Bishop to a paper in the accompanying number of the *Natural History Review*, 'On the Zoological Relations of Man with the Lower Animals.'
>
> The Bishop of Oxford will find therein full justification for the diametrical contradiction with which he heard Professor Huxley

meet certain anatomical statements put forth at the first meeting of Section D during the late session of the British Association at Oxford.

(ii)

The battle for acceptance of *The Origin* and all it stood for, made doubly necessary by the retiring nature of Darwin himself, brought Huxley out into the realm of public controversy; it enlarged his interests beyond the purely scientific; it forced him to become a public figure of the seething argumentative mid-Victorian world, just as his voyage on the *Rattlesnake* more than a decade earlier had forced a contemplative young assistant-surgeon into companionship with ordinary people. Furthermore, the search for ammunition which the battle made necessary drew Huxley along a road which was to open up ever broader views. After regarding the theory of evolution he next contemplated man's place in the scene; then the scene as a part of the universe; and, finally, the philosophical rigging which held it all together and enabled man to chart his own short journey through existence. This personal evolution, which was to have great influence on succeeding generations, was quickened by the Oxford debate. But it was challenged, and then hastened, by personal tragedy.

From Oxford, Huxley set off for the Geological Survey upon whose coastal work he was now busily engaged. Henrietta returned to London after her brief stay with the Fannings, and here Huxley joined her in September, towards the end of a long hot summer. On Thursday, 13 September, his son Noel, not yet four years old, was struck down by scarlet fever. The following day two-year-old Jessie was attacked, although not so seriously. The baby, Marian, just a year old, escaped. On Friday the boy worsened. By Saturday night he was dead.

> The four corners of my house are smitten, and I stand face to face with bare patience and resignation [Huxley wrote to Dyster the following day]. It is very bitter. As for my poor brave wife – you can imagine more than I can tell you – she is very good, very patient but broken-hearted . . .

For Mrs Huxley, six months pregnant, the unexpectedness of the event was absolute, the shock appalling. For Huxley himself, the grief was to be lasting and the results of the sudden death tremendous. As he stood by the graveside a few days later, mechanically breaking off the leaves from an oak tree overhead, he heard an officiating minister read, as part of his duty, the words: 'If the dead rise not again, let us eat and drink, for tomorrow we die'. Writing a few days later to Charles Kingsley, to whom he had been introduced by his friend Dyster, and who had written to console him, Huxley commented: 'I cannot tell you how inexpressibly they shocked me . . . Why, the very apes know better, and if you shoot their young, the poor brutes grieve their grief out and do not immediately seek distraction in a gorge.'

This traumatic experience, the brusque and sudden confrontation with the death and disappearance of a dearly loved person, had two important results. The first was that Huxley was now pushed to the brink of belief. Did he, or did he not, believe in the prospect of a life beyond the grave? Here was the most poignant affirmation or denial that any mortal ever has to make. TH, pressed to the uttermost, was forced to answer himself truly and to answer that, however much he wished for the reverse, the answer was 'No'. Almost as important, although on a different level, was the second result of this searing experience. For the words of the minister dissolved any inhibitions which TH might have retained about pushing the Church from its position astride the path of evolution. He himself had never taken its dogmas seriously. But he was the most human of men. He had felt that if the Church, for all its propagandist paraphernalia, did offer bewildered mankind a mite of help and solace during their struggle through the vale of tears, this was at least a weight to be put in the scales. Now he was brought up, personally and brutally, against what the Church did really offer – and 'the very apes knew better'.

Huxley may also have noticed that his wife, abiding Christian that she was – she had, he wrote years later, 'a sneaking love for the old story' – found little solace from her beliefs. Her grief was, however, assuaged by the kindly Darwins who immediately insisted that she come to Down. She accepted, being, as she later wrote, 'almost out of my mind. My head was one . . . patch of pain. My husband would walk me up and down outside the house to let the rain fall upon my burning head. Our little girl and the baby sister were as nothing to me – Tho' I did my duty to them.' From the Darwins she travelled on to stay with friends at Folkestone. Return to 14 Waverley Place, where Noel had been so happily growing up, was now impossible, and TH came back to London alone, intent on finding a new home. After much search, followed by the interchange of numerous letters to Henrietta in which Huxley drew detailed ground plans of the house he had discovered, 26 Abbey Place, only half a mile from their old home, was duly acquired.

Tyndall, seeking about for a home of his own, was glad to move into 14 Waverley Place.

All this was still being settled when on 11 December Henrietta gave birth to a boy, to be christened Leonard since the name contained the letters which make up 'Noel'. Her recovery was slow, and once again she was helped by Mrs Darwin:

> . . . she begged me to come to her and bring the three children and nurse, and I should have the old nurseries at Down [Mrs Huxley wrote many years later]. I first wrote that I was too weak and ill to be out of my home, that I could not get downstairs till 1 o'clock. Her reply was, that that was the usual state of the family at Down, and I should just be following suit.

Meanwhile, after a conspiracy between Tyndall and Mrs Huxley, Huxley himself had been induced to take that never-failing cure for depression and dyspepsia – a sniff of mountain air. With Tyndall and Busk he took train to Bangor, walked up to Bethesda and after crossing the Glyders to Pen-y-Pass ascended Snowdon under the care of the redoubtable local guide, Robert Hughes.

Huxley returned to London from Wales refreshed for the battles ahead. The confrontation with Wilberforce and the death of Noel had combined to end one chapter of his life. Now he could see clearly the path he must follow wherever it might lead. He already knew the quality of his work. As he wrote to Hooker:

> . . . It is no use having any false modesty about the matter. You and I, if we last ten years longer – and you by a long while first – will be the representatives of our respective lines in the country.

Now his duties began to press in upon him from all sides – from the laboratory where problems rose up to demand his attention, from those who wished him to lecture, from the committees of the learned societies which formed the scientific government of the day, from publishers who had interesting projects for Professor Huxley. During the next ten years he was to be Secretary, and then President, of the Geological Society, Hunterian Professor at the Royal College of Surgeons and Fullerian Professor at the Royal Institution. He was to lecture to Working Men's Colleges and to learned societies. Books on comparative anatomy, physiology and the classification of animals, all came from the study of 26 Abbey Place, as well as scientific papers by the score. As the Royal School of Mines developed, Huxley's duties grew likewise, while from 1862 onwards his field-work for the Geological Survey was augmented by service on several Royal Commissions.

The four eldest daughters of T. H. and Henrietta Huxley: Jessie, *top left*, painted by Marian, *top right;* Nettie, *bottom left;* and Rachel

T. H. Huxley in 1895, the year of his death, with his son Leonard and grandson Julian

It was during this period of expanding interests that TH formed the 'X' Club, a body including TH himself, Tyndall, Hooker, Lubbock and Frankland, and whose influence was in inverse proportion to its membership of nine. With a six o'clock dinner held on the first Thursday of all but the three summer months, before the meeting of the Royal Society, it enabled the friendly *élite* of Victorian science to exchange personal pleasantries – and to bring together their wives on an annual week-end excursion known as the 'x's and yv's'. TH always decried the idea that the X Club 'governed scientific affairs'; yet during its twenty-nine years of existence between 1864 and 1893 its nine members provided three successive Presidents of the Royal Society, as well as a Secretary, a Foreign Secretary and a Treasurer, and six Presidents of the British Association.

The multiplicity of demands made on Huxley, and the willingness with which he agreed to so many of them, meant that, as the writer of a profile in *Nature* was to say, he 'lived in London a life of continued and brilliant labour'. Yet it meant also that two aspects of his life tended to be concealed by the overflowing mass of papers and appointments. One was the continuous development of his thought and philosophy. The other was the deep feeling for family life which lay behind the dispassionate figure on the lecture-platform. It is true that the almost clannish reaction of the Huxleys to close ranks and stand together in times of personal crisis has sprung partly from the instinctive response to attack from outside; yet much has flowed from the example of TH, the slayer of bishops of whom Mrs Tait, wife of the Archbishop of Canterbury, once concluded '. . . and yet I hear that he is a devoted husband and affectionate father'.

Before the 1860s were out, this Victorian paterfamilias had surpassed even Darwin in shaking accepted beliefs. For Huxley's progress was along a line suggested by Darwin but made even more congenial by the continuing argument with Owen – that irritation within the oyster-shell which was to have such great results. From the disagreements that followed the Croonian Lecture there had come the brusque pledge made by Huxley at the Oxford meeting to support his claim for the simian ancestry of man's brain, and thenceforward the subject was rarely far from his thoughts.

Yet he did not concentrate only on the detailed comparison of the brains of men and apes. Another point of interest was the relationship between the hand and the foot in both mammals. In fact, the deeper Huxley probed, the greater appeared to be the material which offered itself for dissection, study and thought. He was now seized of the subject and decided to make 'The Relation of Man to the Rest of the

Animal Kingdom' the theme of the lectures he was to give at the Royal Institution, once a week from February to May, 1861. As usual when Huxley was speaking, the lecture-hall was packed. The audiences were attentive, rapt in fascinated interest. 'My working men stick by me wonderfully, the house being fuller than ever last night,' he wrote to his wife after one of them. 'By next Friday evening they will all be convinced that they are monkeys.' The lectures, published in the *Natural History Review*, led to a crisis of the argument with Owen, a cantankerous row that spluttered in the pages of the *Athenaeum* throughout the spring. Then, in mid-April, there came an invitation from an unexpected source. The Philosophical Institute of Edinburgh wrote inquiring whether Professor Huxley would give two lectures the following year on 'The Relation of Man to the Lower Animals', a request that brought from him the comment, 'Fancy unco guid Edinburgh requiring illumination on the subject!'

Huxley agreed to give the lectures in January 1862. But before he travelled north he had been drawn more deeply into certain aspects of the question by Sir Charles Lyell, who had now, thirty years after *The Principles of Geology*, taken the plunge and was preparing his *Antiquity of Man*. Would Huxley, he asked, supply him with anatomical data concerning the ape question? Huxley agreed – and by the end of 1861 had acquired material from a number of fresh sources.

The Philosophical Institute of Edinburgh had been founded only a few years previously, and had thus far confined its invitations to speakers on such safe subjects as history and music, literature and the arts. The invitation to Huxley was therefore something of an innovation, and the organizers must have wondered how many people would buy tickets for the two meetings to be held in the Queen Street Hall on 9 and 10 January. They need have had no worries. The hall was packed on both nights; packed, moreover, with an audience which applauded enthusiastically – a fact which drew from the bitterly critical *Witness* the comment:

> We do not know what Professor Huxley thought of the intelligence of his audience; but it was a somewhat remarkable fact, that when their kindred to the brute creation was most strongly asserted, the applause was the most vigorous.

In the first lecture he described in general terms the process of development among vertebrate animals. In the second he came to the nub of the matter, showing that the differences between man and the higher apes in such things as hand, foot and brain were no greater than those between the higher apes and the lower ones. The conclusion, he suggested, was unavoidable.

For a few days a stunned Edinburgh allowed the message to sink in. Not until the 14th did the storm break when the *Witness* demanded to know why the Institute had asked Huxley – 'the advocate of the vilest and beastliest paradox ever vented in ancient or modern times amongst Pagans or Christians' – to appear on the platform 'and exhibit his anti-scriptural and most debasing theory of the origin and kindred of man'. It asked what conceivable end could be gained by bringing Huxley and 'his ignoble hobby' to Edinburgh. It was shocked that the lecturer had not been chased from the hall, but had actually been applauded. And it was surprising, the writer added, 'that at the end of the lecture, the hearers refrained from forming themselves into a "Gorilla Emancipation Society", and from concerting some prompt measures for humanizing and civilizing their unfortunate brothers . . .'. Even an invitation to an apostle of Mormonism would, the writer protested, have been 'less offensive, mischievous and inexcusable'. About all this there was, so far as Huxley was concerned, one satisfaction: it meant that his views were being ventilated in places which otherwise would have heard nothing of them.

In these Edinburgh lectures, Huxley concentrated on the anatomical and physiological evidence by means of which man's ancestry could be traced back to the brutes. Yet he now had at his finger-tips far more than this; he had also the evidence of the rocks and he used this in a lecture 'On the Fossil Remains of Man', given at the Royal Institution three weeks later. And he now realized, considering the evidence from so many sources, that the total was more than the sum of the parts. The case was overwhelming, and he determined to edit and amalgamate his researches of the previous eighteen months into a single short book. The result was *Evidence as to Man's Place in Nature*, written in defiance of advice from at least one shrewd friend who believed that it would ruin all Huxley's prospects. This friend was Lyell, who feared that some parts of the book would raise a storm. It is significant that he hoped Huxley would 'send none of these *dangerous* sheets to press without Mrs Huxley's imprimatur'. Huxley metaphorically gritted his teeth and pressed on. The book was published in February 1863. By the summer it had appeared in the United States, two German publishers were competing for translation rights, and two separate Russian editions were in preparation.

Fashions change, perhaps more frequently in science than elsewhere; words and phrases quickly acquire an almost palaeolithic ring. Yet even today, a century later, it is difficult not to open *Man's Place in*

Nature, as it soon became known, without feeling some of the excitement that surged into Keats from Chapman's Homer. When the breath comes back there is wonder at the clear, relentless way in which the story is unfolded; there is also admiration for the manner in which the job of transmitting technical information is handled, for the sheer expertise of the work.

There were three sections to the book: 'On the Natural History of the Man-like Apes', 'On the Relation of Man to the Lower Animals', and 'On Some Fossil Remains of Man'. There was also, at the end of part two, what was called 'A History of the Controversy respecting Cerebral Structure of Man and the Apes'. A masterpiece of damaging detail, this was Huxley's own account of his argument with Owen, and while every item in it could be substantiated it was written with extraordinary outspokenness. It speaks of Owen, then at the height of his career, as being 'either in ignorance of these well-known facts or else unjustifiably suppressing them'; it says of Owen's attitude, that 'it would not be credible, if it were not unfortunately true'; and it twists the dagger in the wound with a verve that appears astonishing to modern eyes.

While Huxley dealt in the main body of his text with the evolutionary links between *Homo sapiens* and his ancestors, the sweeping scope of the book is clear in the opening challenge of its second part:

> The question of questions for mankind – the problem which underlies all others, and is more deeply interesting than any other – is the ascertainment of the place which Man occupies in nature and of his relations to the universe of things. Whence our race has come; what are the limits of our power over nature and of nature's power over us; to what goal we are tending; [these] are the problems which present themselves anew and with undiminished interest to every man born into the world.

These words have two points of interest. The first is that they show how TH could rise quite above the level of even the best informed scientific writing. At times, something seized him. He ignored his customary guide-lines and soared not outside but above them, so that while he kept in the general direction they commanded, he yet wrote on an entirely higher, different, and what can only be described as inspired level. The second point is that one hears in them, as clearly as in anything which TH was to write, the rumble of the Huxley drum, an echo of the questions on which so many of his descendants were to expend their labours. The very title of the book, de-capitalized and broadened to include nature from the molecular level to the cosmic, was to lie at the focus of their interests as they tried to discover how man could best live with the rest of the world, how he could control his numbers and his built-in capacity for destruction. TH was in later years to enlarge his interests so that they included the relationship between mind and matter, and the need for man to build an ethical structure which could cope with the odd questions this relationship raised. Yet those interests too, bore directly on the essentials with which, as anthropologists and zoologists, conservators, disseminators of the new gospel which had sprung from *The Origin*, the Huxleys were to be occupied down the years.

Man's Place in Nature was in one way as important as *The Origin* since, in letters which men were to find it increasingly difficult to ignore, it spelt out the lesson at which Darwin had only hinted. It was, moreover, the work of a man very different from the retiring genius of Down, content to spend most of his life thinking and writing, quietly happy among his perpetual ailments and devoting what little spare time he had to the scientific pursuits of a nineteenth-century country gentleman. Huxley not only carried heavier scientific guns but was of the temperament and in the position to deploy them on more important parts of the battlefield. For by the mid-1860s his spare figure, moving through the lecture-halls of London with the presence and confidence of an accomplished actor, was becoming a subject for cartoonists and for the light verses of *Punch*. His name was an assurance of a packed hall, and when his evolution lectures 'On our Knowledge of the Causes of the Phenomena of Organic Nature' were hurriedly brought out as a slim book, it quickly became a best-seller. 'What is the good of my writing a thundering big book, when everything is in this green little book so despicable for its size,' Darwin jokingly complained. 'In the name of all that is good and bad, I may as well shut up shop altogether.'

If Darwin had been an envious man he would have felt envy now. For TH's 'green little book' was merely another example of his still developing facility for giving a simple explanation of complicated facts. He could do more. While Blake could 'see a world in a grain of sand', Huxley had the ability not only to take this conspective view but also to explain it, and its significance, to his listeners. All natural phenomena were related to all others – the newly-revealed scale of the Universe and the minuteness of the atoms, their orbits still hidden within the next century, were but parts of one another: and had man but the instruments he might measure the impact of each sparrow's fall. It was on this level that Huxley spoke to, and not down to, his audiences of working men, possibly the finest example being 'On a Piece of Chalk', a special lecture given during the Norwich meeting of the British Association in 1868.

Like all such careful work it took time – time which was in ever shorter supply as TH's commitments continued to increase. When he did arrive back at Abbey Place in time for dinner the meal was usually followed by an hour or two of work in the study – frequently with the pages of tracery-like writing being passed across to Mrs Huxley for scrutiny and criticism. Years later, George Gissing wrote privately of Huxley that 'the plainest of plain men can read him with instruction; the finest lettered folk can read him with delight'. One explanation lay in the unfailing heed he took of his wife's suggestions – that this point would not be understood by laymen; that this paragraph was unclear; that for a moment the thread of argument had been dropped. Even so these post-prandial sessions were all too rare. Quite as frequently Huxley – 'the lodger' as he would sometimes call himself – would arrive home after a working day which had started more than a dozen hours earlier and had ended with attendance at one of those learned societies where not merely science but the machinery for its dissemination and use had been the subject of the evening's discussion.

While *Man's Place in Nature* was providing fresh ammunition for the Darwinians in what had by this time become a world-wide controversy, Huxley himself was moving on. His interest in the natural world had been illuminated by the 'blinding flash' of *The Origin.* He had fitted man into the unfolding story of living matter. And it now became necessary to pursue the argument still further, to question where the frontiers of life itself merged into those of the non-living, inorganic world; to question and, when the answer had been found, to speculate upon the implications of the answer. The opportunity to do this occurred in 1868.

In the autumn Huxley received, among what had become a voluminous correspondence, a singular, clearly-written, eight-page letter from Edinburgh. It was signed by a Reverend James Cranbrook and, like many others which came Huxley's way, asked if he would give a Sunday evening lecture. Reading the letter today it is easy to see why Huxley agreed. The writer explained that he had recently left the established Church. He was supported by a number of other young clergymen. He was interested in organizing a series of Sunday evening lectures which would help to spread useful knowledge. He stressed that Huxley would have complete freedom to say whatever he wished, quite apart from choosing his own subject; and he openly said that while they had very little money, they would pay as much as they were able. The forthright letter induced Huxley to agree to the long, almost profitless journey and on 7 November he travelled north to speak 'On the Physical Basis of Life'.

Edinburgh's Mission Hall had been booked for the evening of 8 November. However, at three o'clock on the 7th the organizers were suddenly informed that the 'hall could not be granted for the purpose intended', and another meeting-place had to be hurriedly found. Thus it was on to a small platform in the Hopetoun Rooms, enlivened only with a blackboard, that Huxley stepped on Sunday evening.

As props he had merely a bottle of solution of smelling salts and a pinch of one or two other ingredients. These, he was to explain to his audience, represented the elementary substances entering into the composition of every living thing from a jelly-fish to a man. 'Well might the removal of the stopper to that bottle take their breath away,' as one observer later commented.

In many ways, 'On the Physical Basis of Life' was one of the most remarkable lectures which Huxley ever delivered. It challenged, for the first time in terms that most laymen could understand, the validity of the boundaries which were conventionally held to separate living and non-living things; it raised the problems of interaction between mind and matter which were to be investigated with increasing thoroughness in the next century; and it concluded with a broad admission of the limitations confining human inquiry that both raised the lecture to a new level and cut much of the ground from beneath its inevitable critics. Yet it was, in spite of this qualification, a lecture whose delivery demanded much courage – 'the boldest act' of Huxley's life, according to Sir Roderick Murchison. This was perhaps true. For while in his earlier work Huxley had linked man with the apes he now compounded the crime, linking human life not merely with the animal world, but with inanimate matter.

He began by saying that so far as form was concerned, plants and animals were not separable and that it was, in many cases, a matter of convention whether one called a given organism an animal or a plant. He described the *Aethalium septicum*, which appeared on decaying substances as a fungus – in other words, as a plant – but which, in different conditions, took in solid matter upon which it appeared to feed, and was also an actively locomotive creature. 'Is this a plant?' he asked. 'Or is it animal? Is it both; or is it neither?' And he pointed out that protoplasm, the basis of all living matter, was common to both plants and animals. He went on:

> If the properties of water may properly be said to result from the nature and disposition of its component molecules, I can find no

intelligible ground for refusing to say that the properties of protoplasm result from the nature and disposition of its molecules.

But the argument could not be allowed to end there. It went logically on – to the conclusion

> that the thoughts to which I am now giving utterance, and your thoughts regarding them, are the expression of molecular changes in the matter of life which is the source of our other vital phenomena.

Huxley was under no illusion as to the reaction to be expected. He saw it thus and he had to put it this way. But he realized that for most men he would appear as the prophet of despair, implying that at the time of Tennyson's sunset and evening star there would be not merely darkness but also emptiness beyond the Bar. Yet Huxley also knew that this was an over-simplification, and he was honest enough to say so. He realized, he said, how the growing revelations of physiology weighed like a nightmare upon many of the best minds of the times.

> They watch [he said] what they conceive to be the progress of materialism, in such fear and powerless anger as a savage feels, when during an eclipse, the great shadow creeps over the face of the sun.

Yet there need be, he suggested, no great terror or fear about what would no doubt be described as gross and brutal materialism:

> For, after all, what do we know of this terrible 'matter' except as a name for the unknown and hypothetical cause of states of our own consciousness? And what do we know of that 'spirit' over whose threatened extinction by matter a great lamentation is arising, like that which was heard at the death of Pan, except that it is also a name for an unknown and hypothetical cause, or condition, of states of consciousness?

The conclusion was simple: that the fundamental doctrines of materialism, 'like those of spiritualism, and most other "isms", lie outside the limits of philosophical inquiry.'

This proud admission was revealing. For Huxley was one of those who in an age of expanding human knowledge yet saw that there were inherent limitations to the process. He knew that one did not use a balance to measure time, or the best watch in the world to measure pound for pound. He knew, not so much by reasoning but intuitively, that some things were not merely beyond the breadth of human intelligence but were of a nature which put them outside the scope of man's mental measuring instruments. Reading his words today, it is impossible not to be struck by the parallel between these reservations and the current views of the physicists – that even exact physical knowledge is in any case impossible, since the mere act of observation itself alters the knowledge.

This humility runs through a great deal of Huxley's life and thought. On his own ground he was confident, and to his enemies he might appear arrogant. Yet he always realized what a small patch of ground he really commanded. He never ceased feeling the wonder of the universe; his astonishment at its mysteries never grew less, and he always believed that the solution of those mysteries would merely reveal deeper and more difficult problems beyond. Only a man who was something more than a great zoologist could write, as Huxley wrote in his masterpiece on the crayfish, of the problems of Nature as being 'nowhere inaccessible and everywhere unfathomable'. Only an honest man, if he were leading the evolutionary fight, could write of animals that he did 'not know whether the infinite difference between us and them may not be compensated by *their* persistence and *my* cessation after apparent death, just as the humble bulb of an annual lives, whilst the glorious flowers it has put forth die away'.

TH's influence as a scientist, it became clearer as the years passed, lay in the fact that he was very much more than a scientist.

(iii)

As the physiologist, as the educator, as the organizer of victory in the endless battle with the Church, Huxley moved on throughout his central creative years with a confidence remarkable even for a confident age. So sure was his step, so constant was the adulation of the scientific establishment, that it was easy for many to think of Huxley as a man almost unworried by the normal troubles of the human race.

The reality was very different, and in matters of finance few public figures of the age can have been more constantly harassed by the difficulties of making both ends meet. Early in the 1860s he described the situation in a letter to his wife, written while travelling for the Geological Survey. His original work was, he said, 'the whole of my existence, and reputation is as important to me as money. . . .' Yet he must, he pointed out, 'make at least £900 a year.' For there was no escaping the family responsibilities which came crowding in upon him. In 1863 his brother George died. He had badly muddled his affairs and to prise his widow from her difficulties TH had felt bound to help; his own resources were small and he was forced to sell his Royal Society medal for the £50-worth of gold which it contained.

George's widow Anne, whom TH was to help for the rest of her life, was not the only burden, for he was soon bringing up his niece Kate, the daughter of brother James with whom he had studied at Charing Cross medical school. James had sacrificed his health for his patients and had been obliged to retire, at the early age of forty-two, by the growing threat of a breakdown. Thereafter he 'lived the quietest and most secluded of lives', constantly in poor health, and on to TH's broad shoulders was shifted the upbringing of Kate.

Even more constantly worrying than the financial burdens of Anne and Kate was the uncertainty about his sister Ellen. Following the death of her husband, Dr Cooke, she had leaned heavily on TH for support; when the support was not forthcoming in sufficient quantity she took the law into her own hands and appears to have pledged her brother's credit and to have compounded the act by constant demands. 'From time to time we get pathetic letters . . . asking for more money,' Henrietta wrote to Lizzie, 'but as Hal has strictly desired her to confine her requests to his lawyer, who when he sees good increases her allowance, the letters are unnoticed.' The demands continued; so did the worry of what would happen next, and when Ellen died in 1890 TH confided to his younger son that 'the poor woman has been a grievous burden to me (not so much money, of which she would have been very welcome) but with the continual expectations of some awful scandal . . .'

To all such family importunings TH was particularly vulnerable. He was the successful man who had rocketed up in the world. He would be able to advise; to find work for younger nephews or elder sons; to put in a word here or prod a selection board there. And when it came to the delicate question of money, surely a man of such eminence must have a bottomless pocket?

If the popular impression of Huxley as a man of means was well off the mark, so too was the image of the stern unbending scientist divorced from human realities. Huxley relished his family responsibilities even when they imposed stringency if not hardship, as when his youngest daughters had to wait as successive dresses were handed down, part-worn, by their elder sisters. He might write to Dyster that he wished 'a revised edition of the Genus Homo would come out, at any rate as far as the female part of it is concerned – one half of them seem to me doomed to incessant misery so long as they are capable of childbirth . . .' Yet his children continued to grow in numbers through the years. Jessie, Marian and Leonard were followed by two more daughters, Rachel and Nettie, born in 1862 and 1863; by Henry born in 1865; and by the youngest daughter Ethel who was born the following year.

All the Huxley children inherited their father's good looks; most inherited more than any family's fair share of wit and wisdom; and all were beloved of their father who was never happier than when he could snatch time from work to attend to them. 'I dare say it would be a strange picture could you see him with his seven children round him, playing with them as heartily as if he were a child himself,' Mrs Huxley once wrote to a friend. 'Ethel, our youngest, is a special pet, and he teases her by pretending he is going to have "mother all to himself", and then she goes frantic.' Holidays, when the whole family would move *en bloc* to a seaside resort such as Littlehampton, Swanage, or Tenby, provided the few occasions when parents and all seven children could be together for more than the stray half-hour. The effect they created can be judged by a letter from Dr Anton Dohrn, the founder of the Marine Biological Station at Naples, who visited the family on holiday. He mentioned the word 'happiness' and he added:

> If I had to give anybody a definition of this much debated word, I should say: go and see the Huxley family at Swanage; and if you would enjoy the same I enjoyed, you would feel what is happiness, and never more ask for a definition of that sentiment.

This figure of TH surrounded by his brood of children, taking them on Sunday walks through Hampstead, telling them his own brand of story, illustrated by his own sketches in which there was more than a touch of Edward Lear, was one whom few suspected. Each child in turn appears to have reigned as favourite, although his youngest daughter Ethel, blue-eyed and fair-haired, seems to have held the position longest. It was always Ethel to whom the elder children turned when it was necessary to explain to father, to request or to intercede with him and it was invariably to Ethel that Huxley turned when he found his favourite cat sitting in his favourite chair – one of those cats which were, as one visitor described them, 'such a prominent feature' of the Huxley home. 'Ettie,' the great man would say, 'move the cat off the chair.' Then, having avoided the animal's personal wrath, he would sit down.

This affection for cats was acknowledged by TH in one of the letters which he so rarely sent to those asking for personalia:

> A long series of cats has reigned over my household for the last forty years, or thereabouts, but I am sorry to say that I have no pictorial or other record of their physical and moral excellencies. The present occupant of the throne is a large, young, grey Tabby – Oliver by name. Not that he is in any sense a protector, for I doubt

> whether he has the heart to kill a mouse. However, I saw him catch and eat the first butterfly of the season, and trust that this germ of courage, thus manifested, may develop with age into efficient mousing. As to sagacity, I should say that his judgement respecting the warmest place and the softest cushion in a room is infallible; his punctuality at mealtimes is admirable; and his pertinacity in jumping on people's shoulders until they give him some of the best of what is going, indicates great firmness.

The picture of TH and his children, of the happy family home with the cats and the favourite chair, an evocation of the lamplighter atmosphere with drawn-down blinds and muffins for tea, was real. But it represented only one side of the Victorian coin. Work, on the other side, was never very far away.

Work was a part of life. So were the friends, particularly Darwin and Tyndall and Hooker, whose orbits crossed those of the Huxleys most frequently. Of the children, Henry was apparently Darwin's favourite; but it was Leonard who left a vivid picture of the children's visit to Downe when the whole family was invited for a fortnight in 1870 so that Mrs Huxley might accompany her husband to Liverpool for his presidential address to the British Association:

> Well do I remember the visit; the comfortable late Georgian house, with its unpretentious interior, fragrant with a certain unforgettable country smell, ever associated with this memory in the mind of town-bred children.

The two elder sisters were the favourites of Tyndall, who years later would remember how 'both Jessie and Marian . . . used to argue together as to which of them I loved best . . .'. With Tyndall, Huxley continued to take an occasional mountain excursion. A letter from his wife while the two friends were tramping in the Lakes in 1863 describes what each of the children is doing with the loving detail which filled so many hundreds of her letters:

> They are all very quiet, missing dear Papa to prompt them to a romp. I quite rejoice in this lovely day for you, my darling. You will be enjoying it on some mountain-top with that bundle of muscular forces, 'Uncle John'. Would that I had a man's physical strength. It *is* a warring against the spirit to be obliged to sit at home and bear children . . .

Like so many of his contemporaries, Huxley used many of his holidays for work as well as hard exercise. In 1867 he spent a fortnight in

Brittany with Hooker and Lubbock exploring the prehistoric stone monuments. The following Easter they went to Snowdonia, Tyndall being away on the Continent; while in 1870 Hooker, his son Charles and TH all visited the Eifel, Tyndall being hard at work lecturing – 'Damn the lectures,' Huxley wrote to him. 'We dabbled a little in geology, which is most curious,' Hooker wrote subsequently, 'took long walks, ate very heartily, and came back quite as well as we went.'

This picture of Huxley in his prime – he was now forty-five – is superficially very similar to that of the man who on the threshold of a career some sixteen years earlier had made his way with his young wife through Switzerland, climbing towers to scratch rhymes on church bells and watching for the white spume of avalanches on the Jungfrau. Yet in some ways the year 1870 marked a change in the climate in which Huxley worked. Just as it brought a new balance to the Victorian prospect, with a united Germany now starting to flex her muscles on the Continent, so did it herald a subtle difference in Huxley's standing in the world. His influence had been increasing throughout the decade. Now the figure wielding that influence was transformed. Previously it had been the figure of the rising, thrusting, inevitably contentious, scientist; the same outlines remained, but they now became fainter as there was to be discerned, superimposed upon them, those of the established man, a member of two Royal Commissions, President of the British Association and, in addition, an original member of the London School Board, the authority which was to play a decisive role in implementing the new Education Act.

Chapter IV

The Question of Questions

(*i*)

The year 1870 took Huxley across a watershed. There would still be argument about evolution, but by this time reasonable men could be expected to argue reasonably about it, even if they disagreed. Man's place in nature was also becoming a subject for respectable discussion; so here, too, Huxley could feel that an important battle had been won. In a totally different way the transition from the '60s to the '70s marked a change; it was a change of emphasis in Huxley's activities, partly due to success in the battles that lay behind him, partly to the new position which he found himself occupying, partly to his expanding personal interests. But it was also due to the evolution of his interests. His scientific work went on; his scientific papers continued to fascinate the expert by their logical exposition and the layman by the enthusiasm which shone through them; *The Crayfish*, often cited as the perfect example of what a scientific work should be, still lay almost a decade ahead. Yet from 1870 onward more and more of Huxley's time was to be given to two particular subjects. One was education. The other and deeper question concerned the ethical structure which should be erected to serve man's purpose in a world now illuminated by Darwinism and all that sprang from it. For Huxley, the need for this structure was but the natural outcome of a process which had begun with *The Origin*, had continued with the work which linked man firmly to the beasts, and was continued yet further by the apparently irrefutable evidence that the boundary between living and non-living matter was at times merely arbitrary. If this were so, then all the guidelines which men had so far carefully laid to regulate their conduct were falsely laid. Removing them, laying down others, dealing with the question of questions, were therefore the tasks to which he turned his hand during the last third of his life; they merged with his scientific researches and his fight for education which was underlined by election to the London School Board.

Huxley's election was important not only because it reflected the new position that he now occupied but because it illustrated a subtle change of emphasis in the climate of public opinion. He had for more than a decade almost dominated the hierarchy of science; elsewhere, in what would now be called the Establishment, his status was more difficult to define. Like some of his descendants, he was half in, half out, a man whose views might have to be considered on many topics but one whose importance it might be unwise to acknowledge by too formal a recognition, by any suggestion that this linker of man with the apes, this confounder of bishops, should really be admitted to anything beyond the learned societies. Thus Huxley's election on to the Board was something of a precedent. It meant that a belief in evolution, a disbelief in the dogmas of Christianity, no longer barred a scientist from an official position where he could influence the minds of the young.

The appointment, moreover, carried Huxley across a barrier into the Establishment itself, just as a wave only slightly greater than the rest can take a ship across the bar into calmer waters. The brilliant if controversial young scientist was to mature into Secretary and then President of the Royal Society; a governor not only of Owen's College but of Eton; a trustee of the British Museum. And during the last years of his life, he was to become a Privy Councillor – looking up from his kneeling position before the Queen when he was invested, he found that she too had wondered what the strange creature was like and had fixed her beady eyes upon him. 'The Archbishopric of Canterbury is the only object of ambition that remains to me,' he commented to Hooker.

Appointment to the London School Board was the first recognition in these more formal arenas of the times. Huxley's election had, of course, been brought about largely by his work first in Jermyn Street, and then in the South Kensington building to which the Royal School of Mines was moved, and which was eventually to become Imperial College.

The qualities which helped Huxley to wield such influence during his life of educational, as distinct from scientific, work were described after his death by more than one contemporary. They are nowhere so well revealed as in a broadcast by H. G. Wells, who as a student heard Huxley lecture and who more than a quarter of a century later said:

> He had an excellent full voice and spoke in clear completed sentences in words so well chosen that only afterwards did you realize how much that quiet leisurely voice had said and how swiftly it had

covered the ground. Before him, among other objects, was a dead rabbit, and he took up and stroked the little body as he sketched the cycle of its life. Here was something that had just been living. We were going to see in the laboratory how it was made, how its body worked, how it was related to other and similar forms. He pointed out to us some of its chief distinctions from other kindred species and some of its main resemblances to other types. We were going to ask ourselves: What *was*, what *is*, this life? What was it had held this small furry individual together, made it run, eat and play? What animated it? What animated the swarming, eating, burrowing multitude of its race? How was that race related to other living races, that sought the same food, or pursued and preyed upon our rabbit?

That little limp furry body was the key by which we were to make our way towards the understanding of the whole incessant network of life, breeding and dying and changing about the world.

This power to take a view of life which was not only comprehensive but was also both human and humane, was reinforced by the practical changes which Huxley made in the mechanism of teaching. Until the middle of the century biological education had consisted of little more than the lecture. Huxley now linked this with laboratory work, so that each student could do, see and judge for himself. This meant that each might arrive at his own conclusions and then challenge those of his teacher, yet in the long run it made for better teaching, more understanding. Another point was that zoology and botany had both been progressing in relatively watertight compartments, and to give them unity Huxley planned a course in general biology, a course whose original programme was later published in Huxley and Martin's *Elementary Biology*. It was held for the first time in the summer of 1873 and Huxley himself supervised one hour's laboratory work in the morning and two in the afternoon. The lectures, like his campaign of instruction, were more practical and more realistic than was usual at the time – recalling an earlier demonstration during the Jermyn Street days when he had appeared at the lecture-table with plate, oyster and knife. Having explained that the oyster was kept closed by muscular action, he remarked: 'If the cook is a person of any judgement at all, she will insert the knife here' – whereupon he did so and the valves fell apart. 'The quizzical expression and its rhythm,' one spectator commented, 'I knew afterwards to be authentic Huxley.'

His life was packed, not only with the work of what had now become the Royal College of Science – where his eventual appointment as Dean implied that he could be addressed as 'The Very Reverend', a fact which gave him great amusement – but with the other manifold activities which pressed in upon him. A typical day would involve lecturing as well as laboratory and administrative work in South Kensington. He would eat a hurried lunch then take a cab to Whitehall for attendance at one of the Royal Commissions on which he sat. He might return to the College or go straight home – but in the latter case for an hour's work before dinner. And after dinner there would be writing, or reading and careful annotation of books which had to be read however great the pressure might be.

Huxley kept a watchful but kindly eye on his staff, and Frederick Bower, lecturer in botany at the College, has recalled in *Nature* how his first lecture brought a moment of trepidation:

> The day before this event was due, a message came to me: 'The Dean presents his compliments, and will you have any objection to his attending your first lecture?' I replied, perhaps straining the strict truth, that I should be happy to see him. He entered the lecture-room with me, conversing pleasantly. But he sat himself in the middle of the front row, stretched out his legs, buried his chin in his waistcoat, and snorted at intervals. At the close of the lecture he said cryptically that he had been interested, and that I had told him various things that he had never heard before. Then came the reward for this trying ordeal, for he said: 'There is one thing I should like to tell you as a young lecturer: lecture your audience, do not lecture your blackboard.' He went up to the blackboard, took a piece of chalk, and began to draw, then looking over his right shoulder he said: 'Cultivate this attitude.' I have never forgotten that advice, and have passed it on to many other beginners. But why do not all seniors help their junior staff by similar kindly advice?

This, then, was the man who in 1870 became one of the chief architects in building London's new educational structure. He could win the confidence of all manner of students. He could inject the principles of science into the mind with such sweet reasonableness that they had some quality of the humanities, and opposition appeared merely perverse. Thus few men were better able to ensure that in the new organization which was to become an example for the rest of the country, science and its implications would find an honourable place. Yet herein lay a danger. The spread of education made possible by the Act was itself still under fire. The clerics, naturally unwilling to relinquish any part of the hold on instruction which they had acquired down the ages, were breathing down the necks of the authorities, alert to any threat. And for many such men the mere fact of Huxley's election to the

London School Board, was an unhappy augury if not a direct menace to the existing order.

In spite of this Huxley played a successful part in launching the Board. His success was due to two things: his commonsense, undogmatic, down-to-earth assessment of the task that education should do; and his ability to steer an issue between two conflicting parties in a way which satisfied both. His view of what education could, and should, do was a revealing reflection of his own experiences, of his own beliefs – and in many ways of the Huxley philosophy down the generations. He had put it clearly on record two years before being elected to the London School Board in 'A Liberal Education and Where to Find It':

> That man, I think, has had a liberal education who has been so trained in youth that his body is the ready servant of his will, and does with ease and pleasure all the work that, as a mechanism, it is capable of; whose intellect is a clear, cold, logic engine, with all its parts of equal strength, and in smooth working order; ready like a steam engine, to be turned to any kind of work, and spin the gossamers as well as forge the anchors of the mind; whose mind is stored with knowledge of the great and fundamental truths of Nature, and of the laws of her operations; and who, no stunted ascetic, is full of life and fire, but whose passions are trained to come to heel by a vigorous will, the servant of a tender conscience; who has learned to love all beauty, whether of Nature or of art, to hate all vileness, and to respect others as himself.

How were such ideals to be translated into instruction, and in an age when Huxley was merely the main target for those who accused the new Boards of trying to 'cram full of nonsense' the children who never before had been crammed with anything at all? Huxley himself had suggested a rough way, in an article for the *Contemporary Review*, extracts from which were sent to the Press shortly before the School Board elections, and played their part in Huxley's success. In them, he divided education into four parts, physical training and drill; household work or domestic economy, especially for girls; the elementary laws of conduct; and intellectual training which would include reading, writing and arithmetic, as well as elementary science, music and drawing. This broad plan for education cut the ground from beneath many who had been preparing to attack; and attack was made even more difficult when Huxley suggested the hours that might be devoted each week to the subjects covered by intellectual training: ten to ancient languages and literature, ten to modern languages and literature, eight to arithmetic and mathematics, eight to science, two to geography and two to religious instruction.

The London School Board met for the first time on 15 December 1870, and between this date and the end of the following year, Huxley attended no fewer than 170 meetings and chaired the Scheme of Education Committee which for all practical purposes built the structure of London education that was to last for more than half a century. 'Reading through [the] early papers of the London School Board,' writes Cyril Bibby in his impressive account of Huxley's educational work, 'one is repeatedly impressed by the way in which Huxley seems to have dominated the proceedings; and it is clear that he indulged in no idle boast when telling Michael Foster "I . . . bore the brunt of the battles when the policy of the Board was being settled until the beginning of 1872 when as you know I collapsed". Apart from the two major matters of religious instruction and the scheme of education, he seems to have been involved during the first year in every other issue of importance.'

It was in two matters concerning religion that he first surprised opponents by his moderation. When it was proposed that meetings of the Board should always open with prayers, Huxley pointed out that any decision on this was really outside their brief – but quietly recommended that a room should be set aside for those who wished to pray. More important was the question of religious instruction in schools, a subject that might have been expected to produce a major clash. Yet Huxley supported Bible readings in the schools and 'such explanations and such instruction in the principles of religion and morality as are suited to the capacities of children'. The reason for his attitude was simple. He believed that in the climate of the times the best means of encouraging a thoughtful moral approach to life was through 'the great truths of Christian life and conduct' – a quotation from his friend Michael Foster which he had used in his *Contemporary Review* article; and he hoped that the 'explanations and instructions' would avoid theological dogma.

> The persons who agreed to the compromise [he explained years [later did exactly what all sincere men who agree to compromise, do. For the sake of the enormous advantage of giving the rudiments of a decent education to several generations of the people, they accepted what was practically an armistice in respect of certain matters about which the contending parties were absolutely irreconcilable.

It was a statesmanlike action. But it may have helped reinforce the rumour that Huxley's move on to the School Board was but the preliminary to his standing for Parliament, a rumour he immediately denied. He was no doubt wise. Even today, a century on, the difficulties of marrying up the objective approach of the scientist to the realities of political life still appear formidable. They were more so in the 1870s, and TH was shrewd enough to stick to his last.

Quite apart from the range of his duties, health alone ruled out parliamentary life. For throughout 1871, as he carried on with half a dozen working lives, it was clear that the physical strain was telling. In addition, there were the bouts of dyspepsia which nagged him throughout life. He persistently believed that these sprang from the post-mortem he had attended as a youth, although the evidence for this does not appear to be great. One alternative explanation was first put forward by Dr Gould of Philadelphia, more than half a century ago. Gould believed that the root of the trouble was simple astigmatism and eye-strain:

> One of the most fundamental and important of the senses, one of the greatest of physiological functions, the origin and creator of intellect, is vision. Of its physiology Huxley was incurious. Its malfunction in his case wrecked his life, and when he read made every day a day of wretchedness. Whenever he read or wrote he suffered, whenever he stopped reading or writing he was well.

'Wrecked' seems a strong word; 'every day' too sweeping a phrase. Yet the theory is supported by considerable evidence provided by Huxley himself. At the age of thirty-one he wrote: 'You can't think how well I am as long as I walk eight or ten miles a day and don't work too much.' Six years later he wrote from the Aeggishhorn in Switzerland that his health had remained bad during his trip up to the hotel from which he was writing, and until the day after his arrival. 'On that day, however,' he continued, 'I had a very sharp climb involving a good deal of exertion and a most prodigious sweating, and on the next morning I really woke up a new man.' More than two decades later, at the age of sixty-one, he found that walking ten to sixteen miles a day still brought him back to health, noting that 'the only thing my demon can't stand is sharp walking, and I will give him a dose of that remedy when once I get into trim'.

There are many other examples among Huxley's letters, and one can conclude that whenever he travelled he pulled a book from his pocket; then when he holidayed with his family, the games with the children were interspersed with quiet work; and that what really had its effect was Tyndall's 'living for four days on Welsh mutton and mountain air', that life when one plugged steadily uphill or across rough country, and hard physical exercise was combined with the end of eye-strain. 'The incubus of thought,' he once wrote, 'is got rid of if you walk uphill and walk fast.'

Whatever the cause of the dyspepsia, it combined with pressure of work to produce a breakdown towards the end of 1871 and Huxley was forced to resign from the London School Board. Yet he apparently continued to accomplish almost as much from outside the organization as from within it. Above all, he hammered away with proposals for technical education, using them on the City companies, expounding them in the columns of *The Times*. Finally, in the mid-1880s the City guilds, 'swollen with long accumulating cash' as they have been described, agreed to set up two technical colleges, one at Finsbury and the other at South Kensington – the latter eventually becoming part of the Imperial College of Science and Technology.

Huxley's breakdown in 1871 was followed by two efforts at recovery. First he took two months leave of absence and sailed to Egypt, travelled up the Nile to Aswan, and returned overland to Britain via Messina and Naples. The rest from work did him good, but with the exception of an adventurous ascent of Vesuvius while it was in eruption the rest was sedentary. Then in the summer the whole Huxley family moved to a house in Morthoe, near Ilfracombe. '... I propose to take a couple of months' entire rest – and put myself in order for next winter's campaign,' he wrote to Dohrn. But this cure also failed to work, and after little more than six weeks he was back at Abbey Place. He explained to a friend the chemist, Sir Henry Roscoe:

> At last, I could not stand it any longer, and came home for 'change of air', leaving the wife and chicks to follow next week. By dint of living on cocoa and Revalenta, and giving up drink, tobacco, and all other things that make existence pleasant, I am getting better.

Maybe. But the hard work of the winter set him back again. In December 1872, moreover, the Huxley family moved into new quarters. The previous year, while deeply engaged on London School Board work, TH had decided that his growing family of seven required a larger home; he had picked an existing building in near-by Marlborough Place, a deep-eaved, white-painted cottage to which he added a yellow brick, four-storey house – the result being big enough not only to accommodate the family, but also to take the occasional visitor. The whole operation was accompanied by dire warnings from his legal adviser. These turned out to be justified, since a neighbour claimed to be affected by the new buildings. A complicated lawsuit followed, and although Huxley won his case, the litigation proved merely an additional worry during an already worrying period. What he needed, and what his friends realized he needed, was a long break free of the financial burdens that every idle day normally increased.

One possible solution occurred to the wife of TH's old friend Lyell during a visit to the Darwins, who had temporarily taken a house in London. Darwin's daughter later wrote that during a talk with Mrs Darwin Lady Lyell wondered whether a very few of Huxley's 'intimate friends might not quite privately join in making him a gift to enable him to get away'. Charles Darwin, who found that more than one other acquaintance – notably Herbert Spencer – had the same idea, agreed to the suggestion, started the gift with a cheque for £300, and within a few weeks raised £2,100 from a total of eighteen friends. Then Darwin himself had the delicate job of writing to Huxley, describing what had happened, and ensuring that he viewed the matter in the right light:

> We have done this to enable you to get such complete rest as you may require for the re-establishment of your health; and in doing this we are convinced that we act for the public interest, as well as in accordance with our most earnest desires. Let me assure you that we are all your warm personal friends, and that there is not a stranger or mere acquaintance amongst us. If you could have heard what was said, or could have read what was, as I believe, our inmost thoughts, you would know that we all feel towards you, as we should to an honoured and much loved brother. I am sure that you will return this feeling, and will therefore be glad to give us the opportunity of aiding you in some degree, as this will be a happiness to us to the last day of our lives....

This letter is revealing evidence of the deep, personal feelings that Huxley inspired. The reply which Huxley sent to Darwin the following day suggests the reasons for those feelings.

> ... I accept the splendid gift you and my other friends offer, frankly, and in the spirit of the givers; – and by my acceptance, I pledge myself to make the best I can of this cranky frame of mine, and get it in order for the best and highest kind of work of which I am capable. With such a letter as yours before me, I should be the smallest of men, if I allowed even the shadow of an obligation to mingle with the great happiness so signal a demonstration of good-will has given me. And indeed, not a shadow of that feeling exists; or I do not confound with that – and you will not – a sort of impression, more or less morbid perhaps, that for the first time in my life I have been fairly

> beaten – I mean morally beaten. Through all sorts of troubles and difficulties, poverty, illness, bedevilments of all sorts, – have I steered for these 30 years, and never lost heart, or failed to buffet the waves as stoutly as they buffeted me. And now that I am what people call a successful man, better off than I ever was in my life – and in spite of all my misadventures, with no claim upon me but what I could have cleared in a twelvemonth – I have for months been without energy and without hope, and haunted by the constant presence of hypochrondriacal apprehensions, which my reason told me were absurd but which I could not get rid of.

He hoped that he would one day be told the names of all those who had taken part in the gift and he wanted them all to know his feelings – 'feelings fully shared by my wife – whose anxiety for me has, I know, been a heavy burden for many months past. She is not used to see me beaten.' He ended by saying that he would preserve Darwin's letter – 'I shall keep it for my children, that their children may know what manner of man their father's friend was, and why he loved him.'

(ii)

The generous tribute organized by Darwin eased the pressure – as far as anything could ease the pressure on a man towards whom work was drawn as iron filings to a magnet. In the summer he was able to take a long, unworried holiday in the Auvergne with Hooker, 'walking, geologizing, sketching and gradually discarding doctor's orders,' as his elder son later put it.

During 1873 he published no scientific papers, but he continued with his regular lectures, working away on his *Manual of Invertebrate Anatomy* and on other books. He served on the Royal Commission on Scientific Instruction and the Advancement of Science, and devoted much time to working up his address for Aberdeen, of whose university he had been elected Lord Rector. He was soon back, in fact, in the uninterrupted round of work, preparing for the British Association meeting of 1874 one of his most famous addresses, 'On the Hypothesis that Animals are Automata, and its History'; personally involving himself in women's education, and the new Vivisection Bill; keenly lobbying on behalf of Anton Dohrn, whose biological station at Naples was in financial difficulties; and standing in for Professor Wyville Thomson at Edinburgh in 1875 to give a twelve-week course. 'I . . .

polished off the Animal Kingdom in 54 lectures,' he wrote to Henrietta of the Edinburgh work. 'French without a master in twelve lessons is nothing to this feat.'

Huxley was now a national figure, to be parodied as the immortal Mr Storks in Mallock's *New Republic* in which Jowett is cast as Dr Jenkinson, Tyndall as Professor Stockton, Ruskin as Mr Herbert, Matthew Arnold as Mr Luke and Carlyle as Donald Gordon. It was, moreover, not merely throughout Britain that his fame had spread. Huxley and his beliefs were a constant topic of discussion on the Continent, particularly in Germany, while in 1876 there came a significant invitation from the United States.

He had often thought of visiting America and of meeting his 'dearest Lizzie' once again, after a quarter of a century. However, for a man of his many and various interests the problems were considerable. He would have to organize at least a couple of months during which he would not be required – by any of the educational authorities who leaned on his knowledge, by the royal commissions on which he served, by the Royal Society, or by any of the other scientific bodies who were apt, when in doubt, to seek the advice of T. H. Huxley. There was, moreover, the question of money. The combined demands of awkward relations and a growing family still forced him to keep a watchful eye on the bank balance, and a visit to the States needed careful consideration.

But he dearly wanted to see his sister again, and early in 1876 a visit with Henrietta was tentatively arranged for the summer. 'It is just thirty years since I left you at Antwerp, a boy beginning life,' he wrote to Lizzie. 'Now I am a grey old man looking towards the end of it.' He had already been warned by one American that 'we will make infinitely more of [you] than we did of the Prince of Wales and his retinue of lords and dukes', and there now came, quite unexpectedly, a letter from the Johns Hopkins University at Baltimore asking him to deliver the inaugural address and offering £100 for the occasion. 'I . . . don't much like taking money for the performance,' he noted, but finally agreed to do so. Soon a request followed to lecture in New York, and what had originally been conceived largely as a private visit now developed into a royal progress in which the great man was called upon to say a few words to the citizens at every whistle-stop. It was not what Huxley had envisaged, although there was consolation in the fact that he could end his diary for the year with figures for the American visit and the note, 'say £600 profit on the whole transaction' (expenses of £300 for the two-month tour being offset by an income of £900).

Whatever the labour involved – and Huxley had inevitably worked up a formidable list of things to be seen and done – the American tour was in many ways a complete break. The children were left in Britain under the care of a fellow scientist Sir William Armstrong and his wife. Family cares were abandoned for the first time in twenty years, and Huxley later referred to the journey as his second honeymoon. The couple spent a calm ten days crossing the Atlantic in the *Germanic* in a restfulness now largely eliminated by air travel. As the ship steamed into New York Harbour on 5 August Huxley turned to a fellow-passenger, Mr Smalley, the London correspondent of the *New York Tribune*, and asked for details of the tall tower and the building with a cupola, then the two most conspicuous objects on the skyline. These were the *Tribune* and the Western Union Telegraph buildings. 'Ah,' Huxley said, 'that is interesting; that is American. In the Old World the first things you see as you approach a great city are steeples; here you see, first, centres of intelligence.' After these, Smalley added later, it was the tug-boats which attracted Huxley. 'He looked long at them and finally said, "If I were not a man I think I should like to be a tug." They seemed to him the condensation and complete expression of the energy and force in which he delighted.'

Within four days of landing at New York, Henrietta was taken off to Saratoga 'to see what an American summer resort was like', while TH travelled to Yale for a week's work with Professor Marsh and the fossils which the latter had collected from the Far West. 'Breakfast at 8.30,' he wrote in a letter to his wife, 'go over to the Museum with Marsh at 9 or 10 – work till 1.30 – dine – go back to Museum to work till 6.' Then his host would take him for drives through New Haven, beneath the avenues of elm trees which arched to meet overhead, before a return for tea at about 8.30. This week at Yale was important, since March's work upon the North American horse had led him to conclusions quite different from those arrived at by Huxley, who had worked entirely on European specimens. 'With the generosity of true greatness,' Marsh wrote later, 'he gave up his own opinions in the face of new truth, and took my conclusions as the basis of his famous New York lecture on the horse.'

With the visit to Yale behind him, Huxley rejoined his wife and they both travelled first north to the White Mountains, then west to Niagara, where Huxley's favourite pastime was to lie by the river and listen, through the roar of the waters, for the sound of stones being macerated by the forces of Nature at the foot of the falls.

From Niagara they at last went south to meet 'dearest Lizzie', the Eliza Salt who had become Eliza Scott and had emigrated with her doctor husband thirty years previously. The Scotts had first settled in

Tennessee where their eldest surviving son Thomas was born. Life appears to have been hard and unprofitable, and they moved to Pensacola, Florida, where they were living at the time of the Civil War. Following the Battle of Pensacola, Dr Scott served as a surgeon in the Confederate army and his son, aged twelve at the time, long remembered helping his father amputate the limbs of the wounded, holding an ether-soaked rag to their noses while his father did the cutting.

After the end of the Civil War the Scotts moved to Montgomery, Alabama, while their son and his two sisters settled in Nashville, Tennessee; and it was in Nashville that Mrs Scott had arranged to meet her brother, thus shortening the journey for the visitors and sparing them the intense summer heat of the deep South. Here, as the train steamed into the station and up to the waiting crowds, Mrs Huxley was able to recognize the sister-in-law she had never seen – by the piercingly dark eyes, so like those of the mother whom Huxley had often described.

At Nashville, as at all other stopping-places, Huxley was almost startled by his reception. For by now it was not merely professors and publishers who knew his name. It may have been an exaggeration when a manager at the Philadelphia Exhibition told him that 'the very miners of California' read his books over their camp fires; yet among thousands of ordinary men and women he appeared as a liberating influence from the Old World, come to loosen the sectarian bonds of the New. At Nashville, a delegation begged that Huxley 'would either deliver a formal address, or be entertained at a public dinner, or "state his views"' – presumably to an interviewer. He chose the first option and delivered an address on the geology of Tennessee. The following day he left Nashville, after but four days with the sister he had travelled half-way round the world and waited thirty years to see. And now the serious business of the visit was to start.

The Huxleys travelled to Baltimore, where they stayed with the President of the Baltimore and Ohio Railway. They made a day trip to Washington and then Huxley was ready for the opening address at Johns Hopkins, a task after his own heart. One half of the founder's fortune had been spent on the university and the other half on the foundation of a splendid hospital in Baltimore. Huxley was therefore able to discuss at length, in an address on the principles of education, the special subject of medical training, about which he knew much and felt strongly. But with a strange insight he foresaw the coming problems of the country which had emerged only a decade previously from the internecine struggle of the Civil War and saw also, within the context of his own knowledge, how it might develop.

The address at Johns Hopkins was delivered under great difficulties. Huxley had returned to Baltimore from Washington late on the previous afternoon and had expected to spend the evening writing the address. But he then learned that he was expected to attend a formal dinner and reception – news that brought from him an anguished: 'I don't know how I shall stand it!' He went to his room, snatched an hour's sleep, then set to work and completed his notes at a mental run. They were still only notes, but help appeared to be at hand, for he was now confronted with a reporter from one of the New York papers. To him Huxley dictated an 'advance' of the address – and was promised a good long-hand copy the following morning. This took a weight off his mind. The copy did not arrive, however, until he was on his way to the lecture theatre; moreover, as Huxley discovered to his horror, it was written on 'flimsy' from which he would be unable to read. He abandoned the attempt; instead, he delivered the lecture from memory.

He dealt at length with the principles of education, illustrating them with his own great knowledge of medical training, and then came to what was, in effect, his message to America:

> I am not in the slightest degree impressed by your bigness or your material resources, as such. Size is not grandeur; territory does not make a nation. The great issue, about which hangs a true sublimity, and the terror overhanging fate is – 'What are you going to do with all these things?' . . . The one condition of success, your sole safeguard, is the moral worth, and intellectual clearness of the individual citizen.

Americans, he went on, had yet to face the problems of the Old World. And as he outlined what these really were, the audience of 2,000 grew even more silent.

> You are undertaking the greatest political experiment that has ever been performed by any people whatever. You are at this present centenary a nation of 40,000,000 of people. At your next centenary, rational and probable expectation may look to see you 200,000,000, and you have before you the problem whether 200,000,000 of English-speaking, strong-willed people will be able to hold together under the form of republican institutions and under the real despotism of universal suffrage [at which there came a great burst of applause], whether State rights will hold their own against the necessary centralization, or whether centralization will gain the day without breaking down republican institutions.

This foray into political prognostication, as much as his close-reasoned argument for education, won Huxley the respect of his audience, and did something to prepare for his reception a few days later in New York. Here, however, the subject-matter, the audience, and the prospective reception were all to be very different.

He had agreed to give three lectures on Evolution, and he must have known that his audience would consist of men and women drawn not so much by their interest in the subject as by his own fame – or notoriety – in this field, across which contending forces still fought with vigour and venom in America. The lectures were to be given in the Chickering Hall and this was full to overflowing as Huxley arrived for the first of the series on the evening of 18 September. Members of the professions mixed with members of society. The back of the hall was lined with those who had been unable to secure seats but were prepared to stand.

Huxley was greeted by a tremendous burst of applause as he appeared on the platform as punctual as in the university lecture-room. As it died down he approached the reading-desk and laid upon it a copy of Milton's *Paradise Lost.* He carried nothing else; neither manuscript nor notes. He looked across to his audience, leaned forward slightly over the desk and began speaking – quietly and calmly, taking the listeners slowly with him.

How great had been the transformation since the raw young lecturer had stumbled through his early efforts at the Royal Institution; how great had been the effect of that catalytic debate with Wilberforce, after which Huxley had said of public speaking that he would henceforth 'carefully cultivate it, and try to leave off hating it'. Now he was the practised artist, pausing instinctively where useful, emphasizing without conscious emphasis, driving each point home with a sureness that was none the less dramatic for being calm and confident.

The second and third lectures had an equal success, one measure of this being the protests that they brought from the anti-evolutionists. The *New York Tribune* published a special commemorative issue on 23 September, the day the Huxleys sailed for home, but four days later the *Daily Graphic* reflected the opposition attitude with its huge front page completely filled with a cartoon showing the professor attacking Moses with a bauble in the form of Milton's head. Below, under the heading 'Huxley Eikonoklastes', there appeared the following:

> Grand in the light the sacred records throw
> Old Moses stands, a hero of all time –
> Lawgiver, prophet: on his form sublime
> Wrought with his art great Michael Angelo
> And Milton whose blind eyes with clearer ray

Grand visions saw, and fixed with mighty pen
Unwielded yet by hands of newer men

The vision of Creation's primal day –
Stands ever, and shall stand while Time shall be,
A shadow of that God of whom he spake
Not thou, O Huxley! though the frame should break
Cans't harm these giants, hew though mightily.
Hold off! hold off! and go thy chosen way,
Nor Moses with thy fictious Milton seek to slay.

The Huxleys' return voyage was uneventful, and it seems likely that both TH and Henrietta were glad to get back home, to the accustomed much-loved sights and sounds of Marlborough Place. For both were unsophisticated people, surprisingly unlike their public images. Herein, no doubt, lay part of TH's strength. One might disagree with his scientific theories and accuse him of pulling down the pillars of society; yet there was something invulnerable about the man who could write on his return from abroad that one was always 'glad to see one's own dear native mud again. There is no foreign mud to come near it.'

The American visit consolidated Huxley's already great reputation in the United States. This continued to grow, and six years later he received a letter from Alexander Agassiz, asking if he would consider an appointment at Harvard and tentatively suggesting a salary of 10,000 dollars a year. He replied:

At first, I confess, I was greatly tempted by the prospect you offer, not pecuniarily, for I doubt whether taking one thing with another it would be an improvement but because I should like to throw myself into the foundation of a great school.

My pursuits here are more varied than I could wish, and I sometimes groan that my energies are frittered away.

But sober reflection has convinced me that it would never do. It my wife and I were ten years younger it might be another matter. But we both of us have begun to feel the English winters when they are at all sharp, and I do not think she could face a Massachusetts climate, whatever I might do. How should I feel, think you, if my brave and loyal comrade of twenty-seven years began to suffer from the transfer? Besides we have children and grand-children and old friends – not to be replaced, at our time, by new ones.

So that though there is nothing I should have liked better than to work with you as a colleague in making a great biological school at Harvard, you see it cannot be.

Chapter V

A Place in the Establishment

(*i*)

TH had enjoyed America. But his pleasure had been doubled by the fact that Henrietta had been at his side for the whole journey. As he had written when travelling alone on Government business a few years earlier, separation from her was one of the things which brought 'a sort of saturnine humour of half melancholy'. The presence of friends, of other members of the family, made little difference, so that when in old age he travelled to Madeira with his eldest son he could write to his wife:

> 'Catch me going out of reach of letters again. I have been horribly anxious. Nobody – children or anyone else – can be to me what you are. Ulysses preferred his old woman to immortality, and this absence has led me to see that he was as wise in that as in other things.'

The strength of their attachment was merely one of the unerodable links which held the family together and which was to be typical of the dynasty which TH created. Yet it must have been exceptional even in an age which encouraged deep feelings. There is something incongruous – if charming – about a married couple who write poetry to and for one another throughout the passing years. It becomes even more surprising when the husband is T. H. Huxley, that stern seeker after truth. Yet when Mrs Huxley published her own book of poems in 1913 – 'her verses are very good', Matthew Arnold had written years earlier – she included three of her husband's, the first of which, written in 1887 when TH was over sixty, begins 'Dear wife, for more than thirty years . . .'

The wife's poems were even more revealing, recalling the occasion in the 1840s when the young assistant-surgeon had made a way for her through the Australian undergrowth; regretting family bereavements; and including one, simply, 'To My Husband'. In yet another she noted how he would work in his study

> 'In the simplest things perceiving
> Basis for some truth sublime,
> From creation's fair threads weaving
> Hangings for the halls of Time.'

Their affection lacked strong intellectual basis, and it was only late in life that Mrs Huxley could be brought to a genuine personal interest in the shattering truths which her husband was helping to reveal. On religion, moreover, they agreed to differ, Henrietta insisting on having the children baptized, and taking them regularly to church. As TH explained to Lubbock,

> ... my wife likes to have the children christened and she has a right to her own way in such matters. ... I am afraid she is not very orthodox but looks upon the process as a kind of spiritual vaccination without which the youngsters might catch Sin in worse forms as they grow up.

As for the naming of a godfather that went with christening, this was, TH wrote to Hooker when asking him to accept the role, 'the only way of turning the farce into a reality ... by making it an extra bond with one's friends'. If Hooker would consent, TH noted '... the clerk shall tell all the lies for you, and you shall be asked to do nothing else than to help devour the christening feed, and be as good a friend to the boy as you have been to his father'.

At the time of the American journey in 1876 the children were the seven boys and girls ranging from Jessie Oriana, by this time eighteen, down to ten-year-old Ethel. In some ways the upbringing of these Huxley children was more conventional than might have been expected. Yet even their most ordinary experiences were shot through with what TH's grandson Julian later called the Huxley tradition –

> with its fiery implications of hard but high thinking, plain but fiery living, wide intellectual interest and constant intellectual achievement, great outspokenness and moral courage, and, back of all, [the] sense of the ultimateness and supreme value of truth and goodness.

In much the same way, recreations and relaxations were on a different level from those of less lucky children. On Sunday mornings the elder son Leonard and his two eldest sisters might be taken for a walk up the green lanes that then led from Maida Vale towards Hampstead Heath. But there were also Sunday excursions to the Zoo. Here Huxley's standing meant that the children were given lions to pet, or were taken into the inner rooms of the monkey house and allowed to walk hand in hand with chimpanzees too delicate to be exposed to the perils of the open houses.

At night, 'bedtime stories' had a wonderful quality of truth, while many of them were augmented by TH illustrating with pencil or coloured chalks on brown paper such tales as the history of Mr Bull Terrier.

> Curiosity was kept on tenterhooks of fearful expectation [Leonard wrote]; if we clamoured to know what was coming next, there was the invariable warning that the pencil might take control and produce something portentous and unspeakable.

Some remembered incidents have an almost Dickensian quality:

> Dinner on Christmas Day had a joy of its own, for before our eyes he invariably carved wondrous beasts out of orange peel, mostly pigs with crooked legs, but also elephants and well-paunched apes. At the time when Whistler was stirring the Academic pool with his nocturnes and harmonies, one of these masterpieces was solemnly ticketed 'A Piggurne, or a Harmony in Orange and White'.

By 1876 the decade was approaching which was to create the Huxley dynasty, a period during which the members of that long list stretching across the page from left to right began to marry, to provide TH with grandchildren, to push their tentacles out into the non-scientific world and to produce the first lines of what has since been called the Huxley network. At first glance, it must have seemed likely that the children would be circumscribed in their matrimonial choice although the youngest, Ethel, once remarked that the daughter of a famous agnostic did have one advantage: her dancing partners were inevitably forward-looking intelligent young men. The limitations were more imagined than real, and of TH's seven children one was to marry into a family of ecclesiastical architects; another into a wealthy family of Yorkshire landowners; and two others into the aristocracy.

The first to break away was Jessie Oriana who, on TH's birthday, 4 May 1877, married Frederick Waller. His family had been connected with the architectural maintenance of Gloucester Cathedral for fifty years, and he himself was to be architect to the Dean and Chapter, as was his son after him. Jessie's four sisters were bridesmaids. Henrietta, wore a 'rich brocade of golden green and pale blue – the whole

Julia Arnold, first wife of Leonard Huxley

Rosalind Bruce, second wife of Leonard Huxley

Ethel, youngest daughter of T. H. Huxley, painted at North House by her husband, John Collier

Aldous Huxley as a boy

effect being a shimmer of palest blue'; while TH walked up the aisle 'grey in colour from suppressed emotion'. After a short honeymoon Jessie was carried off for a life in the comparative wilds of Gloucester, from which base her husband now combined cathedral maintenance with what was soon an unofficial position as architect-in-chief to the Huxley family.

At Jessie's wedding Henrietta had, as she put it, seized upon an acquaintance to help her in seating the congregation. This acquaintance was John Collier, younger son of Sir Robert Collier, a former Attorney-General soon to become the first Lord Monkswell. 'He is small, fair, has good features and wears glasses,' Henrietta confided to Lizzie of this young man who was to become one of the best-known portrait-painters of the Edwardian era. 'At times he has a stutter but never in making a speech nor whilst acting in a play. Besides being clever in his profession he is also clever otherwise, writes amusing little comedies and holds his own in conversation.' It was probably at the Slade that Collier had first met TH's second daughter Marian, who not only showed her father's flair for drawing, but quickly developed into an artist of distinction. At the age of seventeen she had painted Lecky; the following year she had painted both Burton and Darwin; and the three portraits, as well as two fine drawings of her father, today hang in the National Portrait Gallery. Her sisters were frequently models, and both fair-haired Ethel and dark-haired Nettie are shown in Marian's first Academy picture, accepted when she was aged only twenty. TH's paternal pride was qualified by his strong views on gambling, for the picture, recognizably portraying his own two daughters, in the guise of children playing cards, was entitled 'The Sins of the Fathers'.

Early in 1879 Collier asked TH to approve his marriage to Marian. Huxley readily agreed, since he had great admiration for this thin bearded man.

Collier was one of the few rationalists in the Victorian Establishment and many of his views were strikingly similar to those of his prospective father-in-law.

'My religion is really negative,' he later wrote in *The Religion of an Artist*. 'Most people assume that some kind of religion is necessary. I do not see the necessity; some of the best people that I have ever known have no religion at all.' This was fine stuff so far as Huxley was concerned, and when the two men retired to the study they usually found they had much in common. Years later, Collier would recall how on one occasion TH had listened while he speculated on the strangeness of Egyptian art, and said that it had declined steadily from vigorous realism to life-less formalism and convention under the Ptolemies and the Romans. Huxley replied with a grim smile: 'My boy, it got into the hands of the priests.'

Late in May 1879, a few weeks before the marriage, Collier visited the Huxleys at 4 Marlborough Place with his brother and his sister-in-law. The latter, eventually to become the second Lady Monkswell, recorded in her diary how she found Marian to be 'quite the artist's wife, her hair comes down, she forgot the band to her dress, she is always wanting pins, etc. She is a dear child full of brightness and life . . .' The rest of the Huxleys impressed her as much.

> Mrs Huxley is about 45, she seems to adore her clever husband, & has suffered in a way that made my hair stand on end at the story. Old Huxley is a wonderful looking man, such deep piercing eyes, which peer out from between long hairs in his eyebrows in manner quite uncanny. He took me in to tea & I found him most interesting & pleasant. What I like about the family is the way they all seem to care so much for each other & they are all so very bright.

The marriage took place shortly afterwards, the guests combining the worlds of science and art, and including Hooker and Herbert Spencer, Alma Tadema and his wife, who appeared, again according to the future Lady Monkswell, 'enveloped in a most wonderful garment which looked like a cream-coloured pillow-case.' One result of the marriage was that Collier became Portrait-Painter Extraordinary to the Huxley family much as Frederick Waller became their architect, and was to paint no fewer than thirty-two Huxley portraits during the next half-century.

Six years later there came the marriage of the third daughter Rachel, a dark-haired, quick-witted girl who appears to have been a counterpart of her grandmother, Rachel Withers – inventive, resourceful and determined. Her husband was Alfred Eckersley, a Lancastrian brought up with prospects of being a gentleman of leisure but flung against life while still at Oxford when his father suddenly lost a considerable fortune. He returned home at once, studied civil engineering, quickly made his mark, and by 1884 was due to supervise the building of a railway between Algeciras and Gibraltar. 'In appearance', Henrietta informed Lizzie, 'he is handsome, with the most beautiful blue eyes, brown hair and tawny moustache; not very tall, 5′ 9″ I think, very broad and rather too stout.' He left Britain for Spain a fortnight after his engagement, returned only a few weeks before his marriage and shortly afterwards left the country with his bride to resume work on the railway.

By 1884 three of Huxley's five daughters were thus set up in married life; an eminently satisfactory situation in an age when even for women in the Huxley tradition marriage was still the most rewarding career. Sons, however, were expected to think longer, marry later, and then only when well launched on life. It was with some surprise, therefore, that the family learned from their elder son that he had other plans.

Leonard Huxley had been sent to University College School, London, at the age of ten. He had not, however, followed the customary path from the school to the free-thinking University College. Instead he had gone up to St Andrews, the college of the scarlet gown, where his education had been of a kind rather different from that of an English university.

> Well do I remember [Leonard later wrote in the *Cornhill Magazine*] meeting there the stalwart lad who, till he was fourteen, had never gone so far from his Western islet as to see a train; the budding mathematician who spent the long summer in a clerk's office to win the wherewithal to pay for his keep during the winter session, over and above his slender bursary; the poetically minded scholar who had shepherded his flocks on the Highland pastures.

It is tempting to suppose that TH had chosen St Andrews in preference to either Oxford or Cambridge. This, however, was not the case, and after a year at St Andrews Leonard won a scholarship for Oxford which he took up in the autumn of 1879. TH proposed Balliol and wrote to Jowett – the Master being an old friend – and Jowett wrote to Mrs Huxley of her son that he had 'no doubt that he will succeed'. There was, indeed, no reason to doubt. Leonard was as quick-minded as most of the Huxleys. He was good-looking, hard-working, and his one weakness was an over-eagerness to make himself popular which is immortalized in the Balliol Rhymes:

> I am Huxley, blond and merry,
> Fond of jokes and laughter – very.
> If I laughed at what was witty
> I'd laugh less, and that were pity.

Perhaps he found the family connection a little intimidating, feeling that the name of Huxley provided him with an invisible aura which tended to keep acquaintances at bay. He was popular and he was also original, travelling with a companion in the summer of 1880 across Europe on a penny-farthing, crossing the Simplon on the contraption, and taking it to many places in which its like had never before been seen.

Back at Oxford, his academic life took its predestined course. A

First in Classical Moderations in 1881 was followed by a First in Literae Humaniores two years later. All seemed set for the Bar. And it was now that Mrs Huxley received a letter from Jowett:

> . . . Your son wrote to me the other day about his future. Before advising him I should like to hear what you and Prof. Huxley think, and had intended to talk to you about it; he wants to get married & thinks that the nearest way to obtain that happiness would be to become a schoolmaster; and he doubts whether his health would stand the Bar: he seems to me to be choosing the easier rather than the better course of life. In social qualities he is well fitted for any pursuit: in other respects I think him rather better fitted for the Bar. For he is very ready and clear-headed. He would probably obtain a . . . mastership at Rugby or Haileybury of 3 or 400 a year – would get on to a house & 1200 a year at 36 years of age, but he would never get much further. He would be ending where he would have been beginning at the Bar.

This was disturbing news, although it seems more than likely that the Huxleys already guessed their son's intentions. For Leonard's prospective bride was a relative of Matthew Arnold, with whom TH had been on terms of close friendship for more than a decade. The two men met at the Athenaeum, at the Geological Society's dinners; they exchanged views on religion, education, and the fate of the world; and both TH and Henrietta were present at the last dinner-party held by the Arnolds before they moved from London to Harrow. It is likely that the Huxleys had met Matthew's brother Thomas; it is probable that there was much social, as distinct from academic, intercourse between the two families; and it is almost certain that Leonard had already met Thomas's daughter Julia when both found themselves at Oxford in the early 1880s.

Julia Frances Arnold had been born on 11 December 1862 on the outskirts of Birmingham, the third daughter of Julia Sorell, granddaughter of a former Governor of Tasmania, and the Reverend Thomas Arnold. As a seeker after truth, this Arnold was persistent but indecisive. He left the Anglican Church for Rome not once but twice; was the thinly-disguised parson in Clough's 'The Bothie of Tober na Viaolich'; and a character of whom traces can be discerned in his grandson Aldous Huxley. Julia's grandfather was thus Arnold of Rugby, her uncle was Matthew, and one of her sisters was Mrs Humphry Ward, the novelist whose books, 'all solidly earnest, relieved their readers from any reproach of wasting their time on trifles.' Raised in such an intellectual climate, it was natural that she should wrestle with the spirit, should in later years call religious teaching 'Christian discipleship', insist that it should be non-sectarian, and should stress the matters on which humanity was united rather than divided. To these traits chance added a character in which steely discipline combined with an almost ethereal charm; somehow, for a reason one could not always pin down, one did not forget Julia Arnold.

A tall raven-haired girl with a face which managed to be thin without being angular, she had been one of the group of young Oxford children regularly photographed by Lewis Carroll, who wrote *Sylvie and Bruno* for the three Arnold sisters. She attended Oxford High School; and from being one of the first Home Students, went to Somerville on a Clothworkers Exhibition and in 1882 gained a First in English Literature. And at Oxford she again met Leonard, soon intent on marriage and happy to abandon all thought of the Bar.

The exact course of events is unclear, and as late as 3 September 1883 Henrietta was telling Lizzie that in the autumn Leonard would begin 'to eat his dinners at the Inns of Court'. By the autumn, however, Leonard had in fact returned to the University of St Andrews as assistant to Lewis Campbell, Professor of Greek, undeterred by Jowett's advice, and still determined to marry his Julia. He was forced to wait almost two years. Then he returned south once again, having triumphantly secured a junior mastership at Charterhouse, on the outskirts of the Surrey village of Godalming, for a trial three-month period at a salary of £350 a year. The appointment was confirmed, and in 1885 Leonard and Julia married and set up house in the near-by countryside south of the Hog's Back.

This country which was to become the home territory of so many Huxleys, watered by the River Wey, and bounded on the north by the broad ridge of the North Downs, had already become the retreat of many eminent Victorians. In the south-west, the tangle of heath and coppice rose towards Hindhead where Tyndall built his grotesquely ugly country house, and to Blackdown with its brown bundle of contours from which Tennyson at Aldworth had caught his 'one blue glimpse of sea'. The whole area had been crossed and recrossed on innumerable occasions by Leslie Stephen and his 'Sunday Tramps'; while in 1883 TH had himself rented a house for the summer in near-by Milford, walking on one occasion twenty miles across the sandy heathlands, and, as he said, 'except a blister on one heel, was none the worse'.

Julia's family also had an association with the region; for three years earlier Mrs Humphry Ward had occupied with her husband the rectory at Peper Harow – the Mureswell Rectory of *Robert Elsmere*.

Later they rented Borough Farm, a mile or so away, before building their own house at Grayswood Hill between Godalming and Hindhead.

Leonard Huxley and his bride lived at first on a modest scale, starting their married life and their family in a small house at Godalming.

> It is charming [Henrietta wrote enthusiastically to Lizzie], roses growing up the walls, a small garden back and front, with a fresh bit of land at the back to be added where they intend keeping poultry. They [have] picked up some picturesque old-fashioned furniture & with their heaps of wedding-presents – good silver and fine engravings – their walls and tables are fully adorned.

(ii)

TH, surveying his family, the children whose love, as he wrote, 'warms our old age better than the sun', now found only three of them unattached – Nettie, Ethel and Henry. He was aged sixty and ill-health continued to niggle away. In one major respect he regarded his work as done. That this fact showed through is evident from D'Arcy Thompson's account of the Rede Lecture which Huxley delivered at Cambridge in 1883, the year after Darwin's death, a discourse based on the one hundred species of the *Nautilus*, all but two of which were extinct:

> As he stood there with [the] shell in his hand we young men listened to him with tingling ears. His message was as plain as thought and reasoning could make it, and his words came clear as a bell to unfold and enforce his meaning. He spoke as one having a mission and his theme was in fact a recapitulation of the great effort and purpose of his life, the chief of all his multifarious activities, the defence and advocacy of the Theory of Evolution.

The battle had been won and in 1885 Huxley decided, with great reluctance, upon official retirement – from the presidency of the Royal Society, from his professorship at South Kensington, and from his Government work. There was disagreement about his pension, the Department of Education feeling that his thirty-one years of service warranted retirement on full pay of £1,500. The Treasury cut this to £1,200. But a few months later a new Ministry restored the missing £300 as a Civil List pension.

He was now shedding one kind of work and responsibility but there were others. Having desperately tried one remedy after another for his chronically poor health, he wrote to a friend that 'The only thing I am inclined to do is to write a book on Miracles. I think it might do good and unload my biliary system.'

When in fact he faced up to retirement a few months later, chance thrust forward other literary work. For in November Mr Gladstone, writing in the *Nineteenth Century*, had tried to show that the order of creation as given in Genesis 1 was supported by the evidence of science. 'This article, Huxley used humorously to say,' commented his son, 'so stirred his bile as to set his liver right at once.' It did far more, rousing him to a reply which Gladstone answered in the journal; this in turn was replied to by Huxley – the opening shots in a controversy which spilled over into the columns of *The Times* and kept both sides happily at work for months.

It was natural that Huxley should be lifted out of his gloom by the opportunity for renewed journalistic combat with such an opponent as Gladstone. 'He was born to be a leader of men, and he has debased himself to be a follower of the masses,' Huxley said of him years before; and as TH's vision had broadened, as he had begun to see evolution in an ever-wider context, so had he found himself more frequently ranged against Gladstone, an adversary even more woollily cocksure, more professionally formidable, than 'Soapy Sam'.

Although Huxley had long ago jettisoned the Christian dogmas, he had been married with the Christian trappings. He had been able to jog along with his devout Henrietta, and he had good-humouredly agreed to the baptism of their children. Throughout life, moreover, he would stress not only the magnificence of the Authorized Version's measured prose, but also the fact that

> the Bible has been the Magna Carta of the poor and the oppressed; down to modern times no State has had a constitution in which the interests of the people are so largely taken into account, in which the duties, so much more than the privileges, of rulers are insisted upon, as that drawn up from Israel in Deuteronomy and in Leviticus. . . .

Huxley was more anti-Church than anti-Christian.

Yet as he went about his daily tasks, as the last doubts about man's ancestry were removed, as fresh knowledge of the natural laws shimmered in the sunlight cast by the Victorian evolutionists, the gulf between scientific evidence and religious faith was seen to be opening wider, a dark chasm into which only the courageous dared to peer. This horror hypnotized men of lesser calibre than Huxley. He himself was able to see it in different perspective. For what was this immense gulf but an illustration of those limits which, all thinking men must surely admit, circumscribed metaphysical inquiry. Surely the basic differences between science and religion were, of their nature, insoluble. Surely it was far better to admit the fact and turn to the more important issue raised.

For Huxley, this issue was clear enough. Having helped to nudge man from his position at the centre of the universe, he had turned his inquiry to the current religious dogmas that had propped him there; and having realized that the ethical standards of Christianity, which he did respect, might well go out of the window with the religious dogmas for which he had only contempt, he saw the new requirement. This was nothing less than the construction of a new ethical formula, a new set of beliefs, a new pattern of rules by which humanity might live. For whatever might be the nature of the ultimate mystery, there was little doubt that the dogmatic assertions by which many men had governed their lives were dissolving as surely as Prospero's insubstantial pageant. The compass by which mankind had been plotting its course across the oceans had been found useless and discarded. Huxley, worried about the breakers ahead, was to spend much of his last years in trying to construct another one.

His involvement in the two linked aspects of this one subject, the unsolvable ultimate mystery and the best system of ethical conduct that could be devised in lieu of a solution, was revealed in lectures, in papers, in articles for the monthly reviews which provided the arena wherein the Victorian giants fought to the delight or anger of a half-comprehending readership. It was shown, above all, in the proceedings of the Metaphysical Society, which can easily be considered an epitome of the Victorian spirit, but which TH described as a 'singularly rudderless ship, the stalwart oarsmen of which were mostly engaged in pulling as hard as they could against one another, and which consequently performed only circular voyages all the years it was in commission'.

Founded by TH's old friend Sir James Knowles in 1869 after a casual talk with Tennyson and Charles Pritchard, the society numbered among its members such a heterogeneous collection of deep-thinking personalities that Huxley himself thought it 'would be a case of Kilkenny cats. Hats and coats would be left in the hall, but there would be no owners left to put them on again'. For here, after all, there were to be gathered, for the express purpose of discussion, the Archbishop of York and T. H. Huxley; Cardinal Manning and Tyndall; Gladstone and Frederic Harrison; Froude, Tennyson and that plump apple-cheeked W. G. Ward who 'looked so like a jovial country squire'. In his spirited defence of the Catholic Church, Ward might almost have been Chesterton's Father Brown, and he became, as TH put it, 'the friendliest of foes.'

The Metaphysical Society held its first meeting in April 1869, and its practice remained essentially unaltered until it died in May 1880 – 'of too much love', according to Huxley or because, in Tennyson's words, 'after ten years of strenuous effort no one had succeeded in even defining the term metaphysics'. Even so, discussion was kept satisfactorily a-simmer for more than a decade. A member would write a paper – on the 'Relativity of Knowledge'; on 'What is the Good of Truth?' – which was printed and distributed. A few days later the society would meet and dine in a private room at the Grosvenor Hotel, after which the paper would be discussed. And at the end of the day the members realized, perhaps with surprise, that as Knowles later said, their companions had not 'all got horns & hoofs'. Their discussions delineated the areas of common ground on which the disputing parties could move without fear of attack but they also hardened the boundaries of those areas; thus towards the end of the century there began to develop a situation more akin to that of today, a situation in which those of truly antagonistic beliefs could co-operate in the business of keeping the world moving while yet agreeing to differ, basically and irreconcilably, on the really important matters which they had decided to keep from the arena.

So far as Huxley was concerned, an important result was the constant oiling and improving of the argumentative mechanism which the meetings of the society encouraged. He was already a fine speaker, a compelling lecturer. But it was only now, in the post-prandial clashes with the masters of debate, that his powers of exposition were polished into the gleaming machine which was to operate with such splendid efficiency for the next quarter of a century. This operation was always governed by the one principle in which Huxley had instinctively believed for years – that a descent to personalities or to intolerance was not only bad manners but bad strategy.

Only once, early in the history of the society, did the mounting feeling threaten the explosion which would have transformed the nature of the meetings or even ended them completely. On this occasion it had been suggested that moral disapprobation should be avoided, whatever the members might say, and at first it seemed likely that all present would agree to the proposition. Then W. G. Ward spoke:

> While acquiesing in this condition as a general rule, I think it cannot be expected that Christian thinkers shall give no sign of the

> horror with which they would view the spread of such extreme opinions as those advocated by Mr Huxley.

This, even given the best will in the world, was too much.

> As Dr Ward has spoken [Huxley replied], I must in fairness say that it will be very difficult for me to conceal my feelings as to the intellectual degradation which would come of the general acceptance of such views as Dr Ward holds.

It was a tribute to both men that the dangerous corner was passed without disaster; and it was typical of Huxley that when he came to prepare a paper on miracles he should choose as his subject 'The Evidence of the Miracle of the Resurrection' – since 'as it was a miracle not worked by Christ himself a discussion of its genuineness could not possibly suggest a personal fraud and so inflict gratuitous pain upon believers in it'.

However, a sharpening of Huxley's expository powers was not the only result of the Metaphysical Society. If the meetings increased his ability to expound his own beliefs, they also helped to crystallize them. They confirmed his view that the Roman Catholic Church was the spearhead of the opposition. They confirmed his feeling that while the Church might be staffed by amiable men doing personal good which was to be supported, religious fanaticism was too heavy a price to pay for good deeds. This was also true of many Christian allies, so that Huxley could write of the Salvation Army or 'Corybantic Christianity' as he called it, 'Undoubtedly, harlotry and intemperance are sore evils, and starvation is hard to bear, or even to know of; but the prostitution of the mind, the soddening of the conscience, the dwarfing of manhood are worse calamities.' And it was within the forum of the Metaphysical Society that Huxley brought forth the doctrine of agnosticism from which his grandson Julian was to refine a scientific version of humanism.

In the society every man wore his own 'isms' with pride.

> I, the man without a rag of a label to cover himself with [Huxley wrote in 'Agnosticism', published in the *Nineteenth Century*], could not fail to have some of the uneasy feelings which must have beset the historical fox when, after leaving the trap in which his tail remained, he presented himself to his normally elongated companions. So I took thought, and invented what I conceived to be the appropriate title of 'Agnostic'. It came into my head as suggestively antithetic to the 'Gnostic' of Church history, who professed to know so very much about the very things of which I was ignorant; and I

took the earliest opportunity of parading it at our society to show that I, too, had a tail like the other foxes. To my great satisfaction, the term took; and when the *Spectator* had stood godfather to it, any suspicions in the minds of respectable people that a knowledge of its parentage might have awakened, was, of course, completely lulled.

Just as defence of *The Origin* made Huxley so had the dogmatism of the churchmen added strength to his religious scepticism. The bishops had made agnosticism inevitable.

The agnostic beliefs were strangely modern, acknowledging that while there was more than force and matter in the universe, yet man knew nothing about spiritual existences, divine or human; also admitting, at least by inference, that although discoveries in the border country between chemistry and consciousness might solve some problems, they were just as likely to create fresh ones. Basically the beliefs were simple. Huxley wrote:

> Positively the principle may be expressed, in matters of the intellect, follow your reason as far as it will take you, without any regard to any other consideration. And negatively: in matters of the intellect do not pretend that conclusions are certain which are not demonstrated or demonstrable. That I take to be the agnostic faith, which if a man keep whole and undefiled he shall not be ashamed to look at the universe in the face, whatever the future may have in store for him.

The discussions in the Metaphysical Society were carried on by some of the best brains in the country, and here Huxley quickly emerged as one of the most formidable debaters. What was so surprising, and what no doubt disturbed his adversaries, was that he could successfully carry the metaphysical argument, as he had carried the evolutionary argument, into the columns of the journals and newspapers as well as expounding it on the public platform. He could also carry it to the dinner-table. Here his wry wit helped, as on one occasion when the possibility of an after-life had been linked with premonitions. Huxley commented that he himself had once had just such an experience. He was about to leave England, he related, and had a strong premonition that the ship would sink. He recounted at length how he had gone to Dover and boarded the vessel, which had ploughed out into mid-Channel; at one point it appeared that there might be a collision with a boat coming from France, but the two vessels had finally passed at some distance from one another. There had been a lowering storm on the horizon, but this had come up and disappeared without incident.

He then described how he had landed in France and travelled on. What, his listeners asked, what about the premonition? 'Oh, that!' Huxley airily answered. 'That was wrong.'

The pertinacity with which he kept to the argument brought its own penalties and it was Huxley who throughout the last third of the century acted as the lightning conductor which attracted the most jagged flashes of protest. The continuity of attack was a measure of TH's influence in the metaphysical field, and with his retirement from public life in 1885 there came the chance of devoting even more thought and time to the subject. His main medium now became the *Nineteenth Century*, founded in 1877 by Knowles. Huxley was presumably among the contributors described by Tennyson in his Prefatory Sonnet to the first issue as the

> wilder comrades, sown to seek
> If any golden harbour be for man
> In seas of Death and sunless gulfs of Doubt.

'The Interpreters of Genesis and the Interpreters of Nature', published in the December 1885 issue, was his broadside at Gladstone, and it was followed during the next few years by a steady fire whose character can be judged from the titles of the papers – 'The Evolution of Theology: An Anthropological Study', 'The Value of Witness to the Miraculous', 'The Lights of the Church and the Lights of Science' and 'The Keepers of the Herd of Swine'.

For most practical purposes, the evolutionary battle had been won, as TH himself had already stressed in his evening lecture to the Royal Institution on 'The Coming of Age of *The Origin of Species*'. Man's place in nature was almost accepted. And it was on the repercussions of these advances on religion and ethics that Huxley now concentrated.

(*iii*)

Meanwhile, as the last decade of the century arrived, the Huxleys began to proliferate and the family picture to conform, in this respect at least, to that of the typical Victorian household, constantly filled by visiting uncles and cousins and aunts and nephews and nieces. From Gloucester the Wallers would arrive with TH's eldest granddaughter, born in 1883 and christened Oriana. The Colliers would come from their Chelsea home in Tite Street, built by cousin Fred Waller, where their daughter Joyce had been born in 1884, Leonard and Julia would visit Marlborough Place from Godalming, bringing, after 1887, their son Julian Sorell, the first offspring of the mixed Huxley and Arnold strains.

The three unmarried children, Nettie, Henry and Ethel, were always ready to help welcome all these, or their sister Rachel when she returned from the far corners of the world where Alfred Eckersley was still industriously railway-building. With her came either husband or growing family – accompanying 'an indulgent mother who would, in most things, twist her much less romantic husband round her little finger', according to her eldest son, Roger Huxley Eckersley, born in Algeria in 1885. Her second, Thomas Lydwell, was born the following year. In 1888, the Algeciras contract having been completed, the family left for Mexico, where Eckersley's task was to supervise the construction of the Mexican Grand Southern, a railway linking the interior with the Pacific coast. The father was forced to go on ahead, leaving wife and family to follow. 'My mother,' Roger later wrote, 'afterwards told my brother and myself graphic stories of the journey out to Puebla. She boarded the train at New York with two squalling infants, and, with changes, took a week or more on the journey.' And in Mexico the third Eckersley, Peter, was born in 1892.

Across this essentially happy Huxley picture there was now thrown a deepening shadow. It was cast by Marian, whom Fate had showered with artistic ability and with good looks which were striking even among the Huxleys. But these were not the only Huxley traits which she showed. For the birth of her daughter had been followed by melancholia of the most intractable kind, and TH must have remembered with some distress the trace of mental instability which had flickered through the family. At Tite Street Marian was attended by a nurse and two special maids. It was eighteen months before she showed any sign of improvement; shortly afterwards, for reasons which the doctors were unable to fathom, she lapsed into an even worse mental state. One evening she met her father, and years later TH, making family notes on the unused pages at the end of his *Rattlesnake* diary, wrote of what he described as the horror of that evening 'when she knew she was going mad and I knew it too by her look of melancholia. . .'. In the autumn of 1887 Marian was taken to Paris by her distracted husband in the hope that the specialist Charcot might affect a cure. Charcot was hopeful. But she had, as it was later said, 'strung herself up for the interview and had then relapsed into quiescence'. Before the results of any new treatment could be noted she was struck by pneumonia and died on 18 November 1887.

Her condition at the time can be judged from TH's note to his old friend Dyster. 'Rationally we must admit it is best so – but then . . .

man is not a rational animal – especially in his parental capacity.' And to Hooker he wrote: 'It is well as it is, but it is a bitter blow and my poor wife is utterly broken-hearted as well as physically ill.'

The tragedy was to be curiously ameliorated. For less than two years later TH learned, without much surprise it appears, that John Collier now wished to marry his youngest daughter Ethel – an act made illegal in Britain by the provisions which the rejected Deceased Wife's Sister Bill was designed to remove. Henrietta favoured the engagement despite, as she wrote to Lizzie, 'the social difficulty'. Huxley himself had already entered the lists on behalf of the D.W.S. Bill (as it was usually called), having, as he wrote, done his best 'to aid and abet other people in disregarding the disabilities imposed by the present monstrous state of the law . . .'. To Hooker he wrote that he had always

> been a great advocate for the triumph of common sense and justice in the 'Deceased Wife's Sister' business and only now discover that I had a sneaking hope that all of my own daughters would escape the experiment. They are quite suited to one another, and I would not wish a better match for her. And whatever annoyances and social pinpricks may come in Ethel's way, I know nobody less likely to care about them. We shall have to go to Norway, I believe, to get the business done.

This was to be so, and later that year TH accompanied Collier and Ethel to Christiania – today Oslo where the law allowed the marriage to be legally solemnized. Both bride and bridegroom appreciated the unusualness of the situation and in later life Collier was always pleased when a visitor commented upon his own portrait of TH which hung above his mantelpiece. 'Yes,' he would say, 'I married two of his daughters.'

Ethel also relished the situation and is claimed to have visited Somerset House on one occasion to seek out the highest possible official dealing with income tax, presumably because her income was being assessed with that of her 'husband'. The senior Civil Servant who received her was immediately told: 'I would have you know, young man, that I am not married to the Hon. John Collier.'

However, there were two views on the marriage and on Huxley's action in supporting it. Joseph Chamberlain was in no doubt. 'I have no patience with the bigotry and superstition on which the opposition to a much needed social reform is founded,' he wrote to TH on the latter's return from Norway. 'I congratulate you on the new happiness which your daughter's marriage has brought into your family life, and I hope that Mrs Collier will find time to call on my wife.' The other side of the coin was represented by Collier's sister-in-law who had become the second Lady Monkswell in 1886 on the death of her father-in-law, and who now broke off all contact with her brother-in-law. T. H. Huxley, she noted in her diary on his death a few years later, 'has been the cause of immense trouble, sorrow, expense and estrangement in this family, and has destroyed the faith of many.'

While preparations for the journey to Norway were going ahead, TH learned that Nettie, his remaining unattached daughter, was about to become engaged. Like all the Huxley girls, she was a more than competent amateur artist and had illustrated an extraordinary small book written for children by Henrietta – *My Wife's Relations*, which recounts and illustrates the adventures of a homely family of pigs. Even among the individual Huxleys, Nettie stood apart as an individualist. While travelling in Worcestershire she had met Harold Roller, an unassuming man who with his brother owned and ran a firm of picture restorers. 'A very good fellow, very capable without being remarkably clever & very handsome and tall,' was Henrietta's verdict passed over to Lizzie. 'He has a moderate private income, £640 pr. annum, but intends returning to work again, I think as a mining engineer. Hitherto he has had no motive for continuous work, tho' I believe he did rather well in America.' Whatever the truth of the details, Roller was warned by TH 'that he would be taking on a handful if he married Nettie'. It was not long before he found that the handful was too much for him. Nettie was soon spending much of her time travelling on the Continent with their young daughter and keeping herself mainly by her talent as an amateur singer. Her history was not perhaps totally unexpected, for as she had grown from childhood into adult life she had fitted less and less into the family ménage, and it was Nettie who, one memorable evening, arrived at Marlborough Place with Oscar Wilde. The only recorded outcome of the visit was Huxley's comment after Wilde had left: 'That man never enters my house again.'

The Huxley home had now been the family centre for almost twenty years, but in 1889 TH decided to retire to the country. This, however, was not to be the end of a Huxley headquarters in London, for John Collier now settled with his second Huxley wife on the fringe of what was then the St John's Wood artists' colony, commissioning his brother-in-law Frederick Waller to build him North House. This was a four-square, red-brick, many-storeyed building in Eton Avenue, a few hundred yards from Swiss Cottage. It is a construction on which almost every conceivable architectural style still competes for notice, with above the dining-room fireplace the inscription '*Haec Est Domus Quam Aedificavit*'.

Under Ethel Collier's guidance North House became the main London meeting-place of the Huxleys for almost half a century. To it would come the countless relatives; from it would go, written on the distinctive smoke-grey note-paper by which Ethel was known, the accounts of family affairs which became a regular Huxley progress report.

The year 1890 thus became an important date in family affairs, the significant event being the departure of TH and Henrietta from London. As soon as he had talked of moving, Huxley had been badgered by his friends. Tyndall had suggested that he should settle, as he and his wife had done, on the Surrey heights at Hindhead; Hooker, now Director of the Royal Botanic Gardens, proposed the riverside delights of Kew. Finally, on the advice of his old friend Sir John Donnelly, Huxley investigated Eastbourne, taking a house there for the winter. He found himself invigorated by the great sweep of Beachy Head and the rolling Downs behind it. 'So long as I am at Eastbourne (where I am setting up a cottage), walking six or seven miles a day over the Downs and living the life of a hermit, I get along very well,' he wrote to Agassiz in February 1890. He soon made up his mind, chose a plot near the foot of Beachy Head, and commissioned his son-in-law Frederick Waller, already busy with North House, to prepare plans for what he euphemistically called his cottage. This was in fact 'Hodeslea' – taken from the surname of Hodesleia from which 'Huxley' had developed centuries earlier – a comfortable house whose main rooms lay at the back looking towards the Downs.

It was while impatiently awaiting the completion of Hodeslea that TH and Henrietta heard of their younger son's proposed marriage. Henry, born in 1865, was a child of good looks and considerable precocity now finishing his training at St Bartholomew's Hospital, London.

> I wish you would look at him with a medical eye and tell me what I ought to do with him [Huxley had written to Michael Foster when the boy was nine]. I think he has a good constitution but an excitable brain. As a baby . . . he had an imagination which knew no bounds between fiction and fact, and by injudicious treatment he might have been converted into a liar of the first magnitude. He is wonderfully affectionate and sensitive and has all the faculties which lead people to love and spoil the boy – Women will play the devil with him and he with them as he gets older if he doesn't alter. . . .

TH's fears were no doubt exaggerated. Yet in some ways his younger son departed from the family pattern. He had an interest in robust outdoor exercise, but this tended towards riding and shooting rather than mountaineering. And while he was drawn to medicine, like his father, the attraction was less in the mysteries which lay behind the human frame and its functionings than the direct chance of lessening humanity's sufferings. 'Whenever Dr Huxley comes into the room,' the saying went, 'you felt you were going to recover.'

Henry Huxley had become attracted to a young nurse working in the same hospital. She was still only 'Sister Stobart' when they became engaged, and family legend has it that the engagement was nearly broken off when he discovered her name was Sophy. TH – who once commented to Agassiz that daughters-in-law were 'delightful inventions, just daughters with a difference' – was more than happy. 'I am prepared to be the young lady's slave,' he told his son. 'Pray tell her that I am a model father-in-law, with my love (By the way, you might mention her name; it is a miserable detail, I know, but would be interesting).'

On the Stobart side there appears to have been some reservation. Henry's prospective father-in-law was the head of a rich Yorkshire land-owning family. He was, as he put it, 'never able to understand how a girl who had a good hunter in the stables should want to go nursing'. And this same daughter was now proposing to compound the act by marrying – of all people – a son of the Professor Huxley whose name still sent a shudder across the shires and down the High Streets of the cathedral cities. For the Stobarts, with strong Church connections, harboured suspicions that lingered in the backwoods almost until the turn of the century. Henry also was to receive a shock. Early in 1890 he visited for the first time what he had expected to be his fiancée's modest home. He long remembered the massive iron gates of the Stobart estate and the mile-long drive to the house.

During the family meetings that followed, all reservations dissolved, as they usually did when TH was intent on making them dissolve. The two worlds amicably merged, and Henry was successfully set up in a London practice. Thus by the early 1890s five Huxley families were flourishing. Jessie and the Wallers in Gloucester; Leonard with his wife and sons at Charterhouse; Rachel, for ever on the move with Alfred Eckersley and their three children; the Collier ménage at North House, and the Henry Huxleys in Bayswater.

To the grandchildren, 'Hodeslea' became a minor paradise. There was the immense collection of mechanical toys, the children's books and the marbles normally kept by Mrs Huxley in one of the large attics but brought out when occasion demanded. And there was, more exciting than anything else, TH himself – a man who would break the ice with children by asking: 'Would you like me to make a funny face like a parrot?'

To Eastbourne there came Joyce Collier, Marian's daughter for whom TH would pull the hair over his face to provide the mane for a game of 'lions' on the floor. He would teach her the principles of astronomy by drawing the heavens on a paper laid on the carpet and use her rubber ball to simulate the spinning earth. In the garden he would explain the flowers and the soil in which they grew, transforming what might have been mere book-knowledge into a thrilling story that she never forgot. She was, TH wrote to Henry,

> a continual entertainment. I give her scientific instruction through the medium of the Arabian Nights – every evening. She has a rare character and intelligence – and won't she be a handful for somebody some day. *He* won't have much initiative.

To Eastbourne there also came the eldest of the Huxley grandchildren, Oriana Waller, whose golden hair, curling down over her shoulders, caused TH to christen her King Charles. And here came Julian, Leonard's eldest son, a strong-willed precocious boy who, when painted by his uncle John Collier, had been 'so difficult he said he'd never again paint any child'.

From the first there was a good deal of sympathy between Julian and his grandfather, augmented rather than damped by a flicker of arrogance which both could show if they wished. From his earliest days the boy displayed a certain intractable determination, revealed in a letter written by one of his elder cousins, Janet Ward, when he was four:

> Julian has been so fiendish lately that the other day Uncle Leonard had to thrash him. He was drinking some milk in bed and spilt a lot of it on to the sheet; whereupon, being told he was a pig, he promptly emptied all the rest of the milk on to the bed on purpose. Then, when he was told he wasn't to have any jam for breakfast, he seized the loose knob of a bedpost and flung it with all his force within a hairsbreadth of Aunt Judy's face. Then he went into the nursery and scratched Baby till he bled, so that, with all these sins combined, Uncle Leonard had to give him a hearty thrashing. Nurse asked him afterwards if he cried, and he said, 'No, I beared it.' He had to have his hands in gloves all the morning to prevent him scratching so hard again.

Despite the tantrums, TH always bore with him. 'I like that chap,' he said on one occasion, when the four-year-old Julian had been watching his grandfather water the flowers. 'I like the way he looks you straight in the face and disobeys you. I told him not to go on the wet grass again. He just looked up boldly, straight at me, as much as to say, "What do *you* mean by ordering me about?" and deliberately walked on to the grass.'

These anecdotes were chronicled in great detail by Julian's mother in letters to her sister, Mrs Humphry Ward, and it was Julian who became the original of Sandy in Mrs Ward's *David Grieve.* 'Your stories of Julian have been killing,' she wrote to her sister from Naples in 1891. 'I was sorry one of them arrived too late for "David".' When the book appeared TH wrote to Mrs Ward congratulating her on his grandson's appearance in disguise, noting that the same grandson's 'conviction that people who interfere with his freedom are certainly foolish, probably wicked, is quite Gladstonian'.

From TH, Julian took both his interest in the living world around him and his quickness in picking up errors, however august those who made them. On one visit to Hodeslea the conversation turned to parental care in animals. TH remarked that one didn't find that among fish. 'What about the stickleback, Gran'pater?' piped up Julian, aged about seven, irritatingly but correctly noting one of the rare exceptions.

'Like the old Greek sage and statesman, my father might have declared that old age found him ever learning,' wrote Leonard.

> Not indeed with the fiery earnestness of his young days of stress and storm; but with the steady advance of a practised worker who cannot be unoccupied. History and philosophy, especially biblical criticism, composed his chief reading in these later years.
>
> Fortune had ceased her buffets; broken health was restored; and from his resting-place among his books and his plants he watched keenly the struggle which had now passed into other hands, still ready to strike a blow if need be, or even, on rare occasions, to return to the fighting line, as when he became a leader in the movement for London University reform.
>
> His days at Eastbourne, then, were full of occupation, if not the occupation of former days. The day began as early; he never relaxed from the rule of the eight o'clock breakfast. Then a pipe and an hour and a half of letter-writing or working at an essay. Then a short expedition round the garden, to inspect the creepers, tend the saxifrages, or see how the more exposed shrubs could best be sheltered from the shrivelling winds. . . .
>
> Then would follow another spell of work till near one o'clock; the weather might tempt him out again before lunch; but afterwards he was certain to be out for an hour or two from half-past two.

However hard it blew, and Eastbourne is seldom still, the tiled walk along the sea-wall always offered the possibility of a constitutional. But the high expanse of the Downs was his favourite walk. The air of Beachy Head, 560 feet up, was an unfailing tonic. In the summer he used to keep a look-out for the little flowers of the short, close turf of the chalk which could remind him of his Alpine favourites, in particular the curious phyteuma; and later on, in the folds of the hills where he had marked them, the English gentians.

After his walk, a cup of tea was followed by more reading or writing till seven; after dinner another pipe, and then he would return to my mother in the drawing-room, and settle down in his particular armchair, with some tough volume of history or theology to read, every now and again scoring a passage for future reference, or jotting a brief note on the margin. At ten he would migrate to the study for a final smoke before going to bed.

He could still be coaxed out of this haven at the foot of Beachy Head. One such occasion came in the summer of 1891 when he drove up to visit Tyndall at Hindhead, only a few miles from Godalming and a growing literary centre where Conan Doyle lived in a house which was to have a Huxley connection and Richard le Gallienne occupied a near-by cottage as tenant. Later in the same year he and Henrietta stayed with Darwin's widow at Down. And he made more than one visit to North House, whose walls were already becoming covered with Collier canvases. Among them was a portrait which was to remain there for half a century, and which showed Ethel asleep in a chair. A book had fallen from her hands, and on seeing the portrait for the first time, TH pointed to the book with a single comment: 'I expect it's one of Herbert Spencer's.' His son-in-law drew him closer – so that he could distinguish the lettering on the spine. It read: 'T. H. Huxley'.

Too frequently, now that he was in his mid-sixties, he attended the funerals of old friends. Tennyson died in 1892 and TH immediately suggested to Sir Michael Foster, Secretary of the Royal Society, that the Society should be represented at the funeral in Westminster Abbey. His respect for the Poet Laureate had grown through the years, and was equally shared by his wife, who throughout her life kept a small packet labelled 'Tennyson's cab fare' – containing the coppers given to TH by the poet when they had travelled together. Huxley came up to London in mid-October for the funeral and sent an impressive description of it to Tyndall:

Bright sunshine streamed through the windows of the nave while the choir was half in gloom, and as each shaft of light illuminated the flower-covered bier as it slowly travelled on, one thought of the bright succession of his works between the darkness before and the darkness after. I am glad to say that the Royal Society was represented by four of its chief officers, and nine of the commonalty, including myself. Tennyson has a right to that, as the first poet since Lucretius who has understood the drift of science.

Within little more than another year he had lost three more old friends – Andrew Clark, a companion of his days at Haslar who had become a physician of renown and TH's own personal doctor; Jowett of Balliol; and, most tragic of all, his old friend Tyndall, whose accidental death was caused by a dose of poison inadvertently given by his devoted wife.

As his old friends began to fall away TH continued, as resilient as ever, racked by minor ailments but always springing back to the work that never ceased. And in 1893 he was persuaded to give the second Romanes Lecture at Oxford. There was a piquancy about the invitation since Huxley had not spoken in the city since the confrontation with Wilberforce a third of a century earlier. The Bishop had died in a riding accident in 1873. 'His end has been all too tragic for his life,' commented Huxley on hearing the news. 'For once, reality and his brains came into contact and the result was fatal.' Now, in the very city where the battle of 1860 had taken place, Huxley was to occupy the centre of the field. He decided to speak on 'Evolution and Ethics'.

The lecture which Huxley gave in the Sheldonian Theatre on the afternoon of 19 May explained how in the history of philosophy the development of ethical and evolutionary theory had been inter-related. It stated the position as he then saw it. And it laid down, as it were, the guide-lines for mankind as Huxley had come to visualize them after his long searching years of hard thought. As he stepped on to the platform, a rugged determined figure with his silver hair swept back in one leonine mass, most of his audience must have expected to receive the final words of wisdom from a man who had sought them long and earnestly.

Yet the Romanes Lecture was not entirely successful – and not only because this standard-bearer of the Darwinian revolution spoke more reasonably, less like the iconoclast who represented the Huxley image even among some academics. There were other reasons for doubt. Henrietta, that sober touchstone of opinion, revealed years later that she had been sensitive about the contradiction that appeared to lie at the heart of the lecture. Herbert Spencer protested that Huxley's argument went 'practically . . . back to the old theological notions, which put Man and Nature in antithesis . . .', while the nub of the lecture was to be described some fifty years later with a qualification – 'justly celebrated and now out-moded'. The last word gives the clue to much of the criticism. For Huxley's Romanes Lecture was, as it has been described by A. O. J. Cockshut in *The Unbelievers*, 'the last articulate sound made by the old guard of English agnosticism, those strong, simple, immensely energetic, confident moralistic men who [had] never heard of Freud, and ignored Marx and Kierkegaard and Nietzsche, the makers of the world we know'.

What was it that Huxley said to trigger off so much discussion? 'Of moral purposes I see no trace in Nature,' he had already said. 'That is an article of exclusive human manufacture – and very much to our credit.' But how should man react to his predicament? Both the Indian philosophers and the ancient Greeks had started by accepting the burden that personality imposed; and they had ended by finding solace in contesting the very nature of reality itself – by believing that 'personality is a metaphysical fancy; and in very truth, not only we, but all things, in the worlds without end of the cosmic phantasmagoria, are such stuff as dreams are made of.' Both attempts ended, as Huxley now put it, 'in flight from the battlefield' – that battlefield on to which moral men had been drawn by the evolution of a non-moral cosmos. His answer was straightforward and homespun: 'Let us understand, once for all, that the ethical progress of society depends, not on imitating the cosmic process, still less in running away from it, but in combating it.' So although man formed the apex of the evolutionary pyramid, he was now to fight against the system which had created him – an attitude which according to Spencer involved 'the assumption that there exists something in us which is not a product of the cosmic process . . .'.

Spencer's opinion was hardly unbiased since he and Huxley had for some years been irreconcilable on other matters, but his criticism found a chink in the argument which later exegesis has failed to close. However, the outcome of this minor brush was a happy one, for he gave his views in the *Athenaeum* and Huxley now replied to them. There followed an exchange of letters between the two men, the result being that TH finally wrote: 'We are old men and ought to be old friends. Our estrangement has always been painful to me. Let there be an end to it. For my part, I am sorry if anything I have said or done has been, or has seemed, unjust.'

The Romanes Lecture was not to be Huxley's swan-song. The following year he was persuaded to make another visit to Oxford – this time to attend the meeting of the British Association and to second the vote of thanks to the presidential address by Lord Salisbury. It was only thirty-four years after the great debate; yet while Salisbury had been badly briefed in some ways he could yet state that the doctrine of evolution was now 'enunciated as a matter of course – disputed by no reasonable man'. What thoughts must have flowed through Huxley's mind as he listened! Well may he have felt that his long day's work was done; and he must have returned to Hodeslea content.

The long cold winter nibbled away at his small reserve of health. When influenza struck at the beginning of March 1895 he was badly equipped to deal with it or with the complications that followed. He had been busy writing a major two-part reply to *Foundations of Belief*, A. J. Balfour's attack on agnosticism, and had safely dispatched the first part to the *Nineteenth Century* before being struck down. Thenceforward he worked as best he could, worrying about the completion of what he regarded as a necessary task, but only settling down to it as he slowly recovered and was once more able to sun himself in a chair on the lawn.

In June the weakening effect of the influenza bout became apparent. He now had to be carried from his room to a tent erected in the garden, which gave him protection but allowed him fresh air. He was still confident, writing to Hooker that he thought he was 'slowly getting the better of it – thanks to my constitutional toughness and careful nursing and dieting'. He jokingly warned one of his doctors not to argue with him on the physiological aspects of his case unless he wanted to be 'floored'. He considered his case objectively, and when visited by Michael Foster on 15 June commented:

> I have been astonished at the accuracy and the care and the certainty with which my attendants have treated me, and when I compare that with what the profession was in the early days I feel proud of the progress which has taken place.

His daughter-in-law Sophy was among those who tended him. Another was his daughter Ethel, who remembered for years how one of her chief tasks was to intercept, and prevent from reaching Mrs Huxley, who was also ill, letters written by the more virulent of Huxley's religious opponents. 'Some of them, of an almost incredible malignity, arrived from the religious of all denominations, saying how glad they were to learn that he was dying and how happy to think that he was going to Hell,' her son later recalled.

However, Huxley held on. Each day he was taken out to the veranda; each day he forced the mind to drag from the reluctant body just that extra pulse of effort. On 26 June he wrote to Hooker:

> The pessimistic reports of my condition which have got into the papers may be giving you unnecessary alarm for the condition of your old comrade. . . . At present I don't feel at all like 'sending in my checks', and without being over sanguine I rather incline to think that my native toughness will get the best of it – albuminuria or otherwise . . .

an account, Hooker later wrote, that 'precluded my accepting it'. Confident to the last, Huxley was over-optimistic. After two days of slight improvement the heart began to fail and he died quietly on the afternoon of the 29th.

It was as he would have wished. Forty years earlier he had written to Tyndall of a man who had 'vanished in the midst of an unfinished article', and had commented: 'this is the way to die, better a thousand times than drivelling off into eternity betwixt awake and asleep in a fatuous old age'.

He was buried five days later at Finchley beside his first son Noel, beneath the shade of a tall oak, once the sapling from which he had meditatively twisted the leaves as he watched the boy committed to the grave thirty-five years earlier. There was no official ceremony, but the service was read by an old friend, the Reverend Llewellyn Davies, with whom Huxley had forged many links – those of the Alps, of Frederick Maurice's band of social workers, and of the London School Board in its pioneer days.

On the headstone there were inscribed, by his special wish, the following three lines:

> Be not afraid, ye waiting hearts that weep;
> For still He giveth His beloved sleep,
> And if an endless sleep He wills, so best.

No author was given for them, and their next appearance was sixteen years later in H. G. Wells's *The New Machiavelli* – the end of a five-line verse which began:

> And if there be no meeting past the grave,
> If all is darkness, silence, yet 'tis rest.

In the novel, they were found among the mother's papers by the hero who comments: 'I do not know whose lines they are, nor how she came upon them.' They were Henrietta Huxley's.

(*iv*)

In two self-contained and highly specialized fields, Huxley's achievements had been immense. For as biologist and physiologist he had increased man's knowledge of the physical basis of life to an extent which would have seemed unbelievable at the time of his birth; and as an educational administrator he had so guided affairs that men were at last beginning to understand the role that science could play in producing that Elizabethan ideal, the 'compleat man'. For Huxley never saw science as one culture, always at war with the humanities; he saw it, instead, as one half of any civilized man's mental equipment – and it is significant that of two brief biographies which appeared shortly after his death one was published in a 'Men of Science' series, the other among 'Men of Letters'. Yet this success, achieved by long, conscientious hours of unremitting work in laboratory or committee-room, was overshadowed by three others less capable of simple definition, although perhaps of greater significance. These had, moreover, been achieved not so much by hard work as by the flashes of intuitive genius which lit Huxley's life with sudden bursts of light.

There was first his defence of *The Origin*. Today, the non-recognition of Darwin's masterpiece appears almost unthinkable. Yet the upsurge of controversy which it sparked off might well have been doused by the buckets of Christian cold water which were immediately poured on it. The idea of evolution had, it is true, been struggling forward in men's minds for many decades and there is little doubt that it would have continued to struggle; yet without Huxley's pugnacious defence, a defence which at first held the thin intellectual line and then carried the battle into the enemy's camp, the whole basis of evolution for which Darwin provided so much chapter and verse might have remained for decades little more than a scientific curiosity. Second, and just as important, all the implications that an acceptance of evolution held for the human race might have been shuffled aside but for Huxley. Here it was he who forced men to face the facts, to recognize that if evolution were proven beyond all reasonable doubt then society must reconsider man's place in the natural world; must reconsider its moral obligations; must look critically at the huge edifices of belief which now barred the way ahead.

Finally, and of immeasurable importance to the future, Huxley had mellowed the passionate arguments with sweet reasonableness. After the bitter Oxford debate of 1860 he had met Bishop Wilberforce more than once, and the two men had conversed face to face, not backs to the wall. In the Metaphysical Society he had shown that adult men could disagree on the very fundamentals of existence yet keep their daggers sheathed. Although he would never trim his principles to the wind, he yet realized that in an imperfect world men must still live together – just as in the *Rattlesnake* so long ago a diverse company had been forced to make the best of one another in a wooden ship a few score feet in length. Thus Huxley helped the last third of the nineteenth century to face the intellectual challenge with vigour and yet to survive it without too much bloody strife. Both sides stood their ground – although the ground changed continually if imperceptibly beneath their feet. But they kept to the civilized rules of combat; they believed that it was possible 'to honour, while you strike him down'. And while their struggles could have an almost medieval ferocity while the fight was on, both sides shared an almost medieval courtesy when they afterwards went home to tea. The middle classes had enabled Britain to avoid the excesses of the French Revolution; Huxley's leadership at a different level, on a different field, prevented the late Victorian age from tearing itself to pieces in unreasoning fury over the disputes between science and religion, or the balance to be kept between science and the humanities.

The tributes which followed his death were impressive; yet this was to be expected, for even in an age of giants he had been head and shoulders above the rest. More impressive still was the Huxley Memorial Committee. This originated from a letter in *The Times* in which Professor W. H. Flower had suggested that since a statue of Owen would soon be standing in the Natural History Museum, it might well be accompanied by one of Huxley; then the two of them, 'often divided in their lives, would have come together in the most appropriate surroundings . . .'. Flower's letter was followed by meetings in the Royal Society's rooms, and by the formation of a general committee for a national memorial. The small handful of professors from the learned societies was quickly joined by other men. Doctors and lords, bishops and senior statesman, the higher and drier pundits of the Civil Service and the more important members of the literary world stood up to be counted until the general committee had swollen from dozens to scores. Still it mustered. Within a few weeks it included more than 800 names as the heavy artillery of the Victorian Establishment was limbered up and wheeled into line, a formidable force filling the horizon. At its head there rode, as Honorary President of the Huxley Memorial Committee, no less a person than His Royal Highness, Albert Edward, Prince of Wales, Lord of the Isles, heir apparent.

For five years the committee worked on its task. As the money for the memorial flowed in there was great discussion as to the form it should take. A monument to Huxley and Tyndall, 'like that to Goethe and Schiller at Weimar', was proposed. So were a memorial edition of his works, a travelling studentship, a professorship of anthropology. A tablet in Westminster Abbey was suggested and then quietly forgotten when it was hinted that Dean Bradley might object. 'It will no doubt be borne in mind,' added one kindly realist, 'that Mrs Huxley will not be well off.' Finally the original idea of a memorial in the Natural History Museum was decided upon, together with a medal to be awarded by the Royal College of Science, any money left over being devoted to furthering biology. Onslow Ford was commissioned for the statue, and at 1.15 on Saturday, 28 April 1900, it was duly unveiled by the Prince of Wales in the main hall of the museum before a crowd of between seven and eight hundred which included Mrs Huxley's party of thirty-two relatives and personal friends.

Huxley, metaphorically looking down from whatever Elysian fields he was occupying, must have smiled at one incident in the record of the committee's activities. It had come soon after its formation, when the Prince of Wales had been asked to chair the first meeting. It seems certain that he would have been willing to do so but for one thing. The Bishops of Durham and Peterborough had refused to join the committee, and Edward's private secretary, Francis Knollys, wrote explaining the position to Professor Foster:

> The Prince of Wales has given his attentive consideration to the request which you and Sir John Donnelly have made to him. There undoubtedly exists in the minds of many excellent people (evidently the liberal-minded Bishops of Durham and Peterborough among the number) a feeling that Professor Huxley's writings on all questions relating to Christianity constituted an attack against the Christian Religion. His Royal Highness is afraid that these people, whether justly or not he will not say, would be much shocked by the Heir Apparent going rather out of his way to do special Honour to a man who held these views, and he thinks it would be a mistake on his part were he needlessly to offend them.
>
> Under the circumstances he regrets that he will be unable to preside on the occasion in question. It would have afforded him much pleasure had he felt himself at liberty to have done so but he feels sure you will understand his position.

Professor Foster understood – particularly as the Prince found an able substitute in his great friend, the Duke of Devonshire.

The memorial in South Kensington produced an echo in Ealing, where it was decided that a record of Huxley's birthplace should be erected. Among those who replied to the appeal for funds was a dock labourer. He was, he wrote, 'living from hand to mouth and often hardly able to make both ends meet'. But he sent a postal order for a shilling.

TH would have liked that.

PART TWO

Development of a Dynasty

Chapter VI

Interval for Assessment

(*i*)

The death of T. H. Huxley raised a number of questions. His extraordinary genius had forced the Victorian world to turn and consider its own ancestors and then prepare itself for the twentieth century. Now, in less than a decade, the age that stretched back to pre-Darwinian beliefs began to fade from the picture with the memories of the old Queen. The traumatic effects of the war in South Africa, and the sudden end to the traditions of sixty glorious years, were merely two of the events which made the transition to the 1900s more real and more important than the usual change of numbers as one century slips into another.

How were the Huxleys to deal with the future? Were they, in fact, to deal with it at all? Or would TH be seen in perspective as an isolated giant, produced by a chance concatenation of genes which did their job and then dispersed their several ways, so diluted that Darwin's bulldog would be regarded, as he himself had regarded Newton, as a mere sport of Nature? Each branch of the family was to answer the questions in its own way, to bow with its own mixture of respect and caution to the name in the argumentative annals of their youth, the father-figure whose stern but kindly look was for ever upon them as they went forward on the road he flagged out, a path through the minefields of the new century. Family pride acts at times like the grit within the oyster-shell and the memory of TH would always be more than a memory.

At the start of the 1900s, it would not have been easy to forecast how each branch of the family would provide its own clue to the Huxleys' place in Nature. Most of the children who had played with Darwin and Tyndall in what already seemed like the distant historical past were now showing, in adult life, at least a trace of the family penchant for independent thought. But it was, as yet, thought on a different level from that of TH. There was to be an interlude before his grandchildren transformed his individual traits into a new pattern of intellectual vigour, a family delight in swinging heroically into battle, argument between teeth, from one metaphysical chandelier to another above dark ethical mysteries.

At the head of the family hierarchy there remained Henrietta Huxley, still keeping, in the rambling Eastbourne house, the large collection of German mechanical toys which she would bring out for the delectation of her numerous grandchildren. She had many foibles, among them a distrust of hansoms; preferred the four-wheeler in spite of its funereal pace; and used her knowledge of distant Australian days to select a vehicle from the long line on the Eastbourne parade that had the most likely-looking horse. She had also a great passion for punctuality which sometimes caused her to catch the train before the one she had intended to take.

More remarkable than any such minor eccentricities was the way in which she had by this time become intrigued by the sciences. Throughout her husband's life she had been the ideal critic, scanning his spidery drafts of papers and lectures with the eye of the questioning lay reader; but just as her faith appears to have remained unshaken by his rationalist reasoning, so did her interest in his work remain that of the external observer. Now, approaching her eighties, she plunged into the scientific stream, striking out from the bank with confidence, commanding the aid of friends and relations to keep her intellectually afloat and to guide her across the deep water she was reaching so late in life. She would question her doctor minutely about medicine; she would cross-examine her grandson Julian on biology, and another grandson, Thomas Eckersley, about the mysteries of wireless, the infant science in which he was to achieve fame.

Of her daughters, the eldest still remained almost immured in Gloucester and had by the early 1900s become part of the tightly knit society of a cathedral city. In this atmosphere of mitre and close, of cope and chasuble, where the originals of Barchester Towers lingered on into the twentieth-century, Jessie Waller became impressed by one thing – that few of the countrywomen in the surrounding countryside knew how to cook properly. Carrying the assumption further, she theorized that bad food produced bad temper as well as indigestion, and that this in itself could lead to family dissension and broken homes. It was therefore almost as an after-marriage bureau that she helped organize a local service of cookery instruction, brought to the smaller villages by a horse-drawn van from which she explained to the local women how to make the best of the food available.

Julian *(back row, centre)* at Eton

Aldous

Trev

Leonard Huxley with his sons by his second marriage, Andrew and David, on Loch Etive in the 1920s

Andrew Huxley

By the early 1900s this eldest branch of the family had produced two children – Noel, named after TH's first-born, who was to succeed his father as diocesan architect; and Oriana, by the turn of the century a strikingly beautiful young woman who was to marry the eccentric E. S. P. Haynes, the free-thinking reformist solicitor whose reverence for regular hours could be used to check the clocks.

The second eldest of TH's surviving daughters, Rachel Eckersley, was by 1900 back in England, widowed, and faced with the task of bringing up her three remarkable sons. In 1895 Alfred Eckersley had been offered an important engineering contract in Peru which would have lasted for several years. But before he started the work there was one more job to be done: a contract in San Salvador, left unfinished by another engineer, had to be completed. And in San Salvador, in the summer of 1895, Alfred Eckersley died of yellow fever. 'Rachel and her three children have but the slenderest provision,' TH noted at the time. He would do what he could – but he himself died a few days later and his daughter was left to fend for herself. Faced with the responsibility of providing for her family, she entered business in a way that for a Huxley has a touch of the grotesque. For Rachel Eckersley now bought a laundry business in Ravenscourt Park on the western outskirts of London, and ran it successfully until she was found there, and quickly married, by Harold Shawcross, a distant cousin of her former husband, a master cotton spinner, owner of the Townhead Mills in Rochdale, and a man who some twenty years previously had been one of Eckersley's rivals for her hand. Meanwhile her sons, at first put in the care of their uncle Leonard at Godalming, were preparing to take their places in the charmed Huxley circle.

Huxley's fourth daughter, Nettie, 'the handful' as he had described her to her prospective husband, continued her travelling abroad with her daughter Marian, cutting the links with her family for long periods, and showing a vague eccentricity which grew with the years. In the family they thought of her, when they did so at all, as poor Aunt Nettie, or dear Aunt Nettie, with a slightly apologetic stress on the adjective.

This almost total withdrawal of one Huxley daughter from the world in which TH had flourished was more than balanced by the achievement of her younger sister. This was Ethel who had by this time produced Laurence, and his younger sister Joan, half-brother and half-sister respectively to Joyce, the daughter of Collier's first marriage. In becoming the second Hon. Mrs John Collier Ethel had acted not only with love but with faith; both had been vindicated. She and her husband shared the same artistic abilities, the same taste in friends, and the same rationalist-humanist beliefs – their home, says their son,

F

'harboured no fanatical believers in religion or socialism or nationalism, or anything else; and no one there assumed that his opinion on any subject, however important it might seem to him, could possibly entitle him to persecute those who did not share it.' They even shared the same taste in pets – TH's weakness for cats, four of whom would often occupy their home at the same time. One of Collier's portraits of his wife, 'The Autocrat of the Breakfast Table,' shows a sight familiar to their friends – Ethel Collier sitting in a chair along the arms of which are stretched two of her favourites, Cyrus and Mark. And one of the lasting memories of all who visited North House was of the tall windows, always slightly open, so that the cats could come in from the quiet garden, across which there came the distant hum of London's traffic.

Of TH's two sons, Henry had quickly established himself in what was to be one of London's most fashionable practices, and here he brought up his five children, Marjorie, Gervas, Michael, Christopher and Anne.

Yet it was Leonard, quietly schoolmastering away among the Surrey woods beneath the Hog's Back, whose children were to provide the main head of Huxley steam. Indeed, they had no alternative. Resolute and kind, retaining schoolboy enthusiasms past middle life, Leonard was, genealogically speaking, the man who held the pass. Knowing that he would never achieve the brilliance of his father he looked forward to the product of the Huxley and the Arnold blood. If only judgement could be suspended until TH's grandchildren were deployed upon the world, then the world would understand. Julia Arnold, as confident of the Arnold blood as Leonard of the Huxley, thought much the same way. Nothing would be allowed to block the prospects of the children, for whom nothing but the best was suitable – and from whom nothing but the best would be tolerated.

Julian had been followed by Trevenen – Trev – in 1889, Aldous in 1894 and Margaret in 1899. Aldous, delicate, with poor heart and a head so big that he was unable to walk before the age of two, was sent first to near-by St Bruno's, a school for very young children started by the daughter of a Charterhouse master. All three boys eventually went to Hillside, almost on the edge of the Charterhouse grounds and run by Dr Gidley Robinson, a former master who had set up on his own after inheriting money.

With the hallmark of its black, red-striped round caps, Hillside was to find its way into more than one of Aldous's novels. Here Trev followed Julian; then Aldous followed Trev, coming to the school in the same term as his cousin Gervas, so that for five years the two boys were inevitably 'Huxley Major and Minor'. At Hillside the Huxley boys stoically passed through the necessary educational hoops. Here they created their worlds of make-believe or prejudice, and gleefully discovering that one boy's father was the unspeakable of unspeakables, an ordinary brewer. Here Julian and his companions would chant with others

> 'Trev's in love with Sylvia Parry
> She's the girl he's going to marry'.

From Hillside they would walk or ride or cycle across the sandy heathlands of west Surrey, criss-crossed by the minor tributaries of the Wey, to such intriguing places as Frensham Ponds. There on one occasion Aldous and Trev – the latter by this time on holiday from Eton – watched the descent of an early balloon flown by Charles Rolls and a companion, and helped pack it into a waiting dog-cart. They travelled through a countryside unmarred by the motor-car, teeming with wildlife, rich with the possibilities of excitement. On one occasion Julian was given special leave from Oxford so that with his father and Mr Latter, the Charterhouse biologist, he could visit Frensham Little Pond to see a flamingo.

Hillside left its mark on all of them. Yet this was a conventional stamp on a unique product reared in the astringent moral afterglow of TH and the Arnolds. Julian later wrote in *Religion Without Revelation*:

> Any education we had which could be called directly religious was of the slightest. Very simple prayers introduced us to the mysterious word *God.* We were told the history of Jesus. I vividly remember being shown the pictures in Tissot's *Vie de Jésus* and puzzling my small brains over them and the imaginations they raised. Otherwise we were encouraged to read whatever we liked (I recollect reading most of *Sartor Resartus* at the age of eight, and, though comprehending little, being fascinated by the grandeur and sense of mystery), and had our youthful curiosity encouraged rather than repressed. Moral ideas, particularly of truth and unselfishness, were strongly impressed on us; and not only that, but I certainly acquired from my early years a sense that certain ideas were, in some not fully understood way, sacred. I do not subscribe to Matthew Arnold's definition of religion as 'morality tinged with emotion'; but that certainly formed part of the atmosphere of my upbringing.

Leonard's life at Charterhouse was placid enough. He had moved soon after his marriage to a new neat house built by Fred Waller on the height where Charterhouse stands – a house named after Matthew

Arnold's 'Laleham' on the Thames. Here Leonard gardened, taking particular pride in the Alpines which he brought back from his holidays abroad. He skated, being a fine performer in the old English style; knew the fact, and enjoyed the hard winters when he could exercise his skill on Cutmill and other local ponds. He was a good scholar, a competent teacher, but his scholarship lit few flames among his pupils. He was vaguely dissatisfied; perhaps he wished occasionally that he had taken Jowett's advice and risked all at the Bar. After fifteen years there seemed as little chance as ever of promotion – not entirely due to the slightly schoolboyish air of over-exuberance which he failed to throw off. His prospects were also blocked by four young masters who had joined Charterhouse shortly before him in 1885, and who made succession to a house unlikely. There were also his religious beliefs, of debatable utility in an institution which has been described as a 'masterpiece of Protestant English charity'.

However, by 1900 a new profession was already being swept within Leonard's reach. It had first appeared on the horizon soon after the death of TH in 1895 with the decision that his son should prepare the official biography. This was an undertaking whose magnitude and complexity is hinted at by Warren Dawson, who almost half a century later had the task of cataloguing the Huxley papers and who wrote of TH:

> He scarcely ever headed, docketed, or dated his papers, and even when he did date them, the dates were generally expressed by a single sprawling ligature in which the month and the figures of the day and year formed a continuous scribble that might mean almost anything. Many of his notes and drafts are well-nigh illegible and only a long acquaintance with the peculiarities of his script has enabled me to decipher them. Huxley's handwriting was a frequent source of complaint by his correspondents and it was at times, as he had confessed, a severe trial even to himself. He was also equally careless with the filing of his papers, for from nearly all his manuscripts sheets are missing or transposed and the pages are often incorrectly numbered.

From the extensive quarry which this material comprised Leonard hewed a massive two-volume biography that was in some ways a masterpiece of its kind. However, many of those with whom his father corresponded were still alive, and questions of taste and tact caused him to censor some of the material. So did a dislike of bringing to public notice the background and fate of the occasional Huxley ancestor. Yet the book was not only a great success, but a well-merited one. As

Leonard regarded this success in the first years of the new century, he could at last consider the pipe-dream of many a schoolmaster down the ages – the dream of cutting loose from dependence and sailing out into the literary world. With a growing family to support, he now found a happy compromise.

Leonard's sister-in-law, Mrs Humphry Ward, was at this date deep in her endeavour to provide what her uncle Matthew Arnold had called a 'criticism of life'; she achieved this through the medium of her novels, which succeeded in being both well-written and well-intentioned; both deeply serious and gratifyingly popular. They were published by Smith, Elder and it was the most natural thing in the world that Leonard, searching round for a change of occupation, should be offered a vacancy in the firm. This was the post of reader and literary adviser rolled into one; with it, there went a hand in the editing of the *Cornhill* – and, Leonard no doubt hoped, enough spare time to mature those literary plans which had been locked away while he had lived, on the perimeter of Charterhouse, the life of a man tied to his job.

This change might easily have meant an end to the country life which formed a background for the Huxley children and which was to influence their careers so fruitfully. It might have brought them back to London, to the life from which Henry's sons and daughters were only too eager to escape. Instead, the reaction of their mother created a new and stimulating environment. For Julia Huxley, about to be released from the inescapable duties of a master's wife, decided that her husband's departure from Charterhouse gave her the chance, as she put it, of 'doing what I've always wanted to do'. She decided to found, and run, her own girls' school.

(*ii*)

Julia Huxley had two qualities of the great teacher. She had the ability to transmit to others her own inquiring eagerness, her pepetual interest in the world and its beauties. She had also a transcendent honesty – 'you felt', her son Aldous was to write in a thinly disguised fictional portrait, 'the active radiance of her goodness when you were near her....' These characteristics were to give Julia Huxley's new school a peculiarly personal status. So was the well-oiled machinery which drove it to success year by year.

She had been laying her plans for some while and now, in the autumn of 1901, these were put into operation with speed and expertise. Some way beyond the perimeter of the Charterhouse grounds, northwards and uphill towards the ridge of the Hog's Back, lay Prior's Field, an estate which had once belonged to Newark Priory, whose ruins still stand above the River Wey near Ripley. Prior's Field was being sold in five-acre lots and Julia Huxley first bought a plot that included a moderate-sized house; then, since she had ambitious ideas for expansion, four more plots. And in the house there assembled, on the morning of 23 January 1902, six girls aged between seven and a half and sixteen; Aldous Huxley aged seven and a half who, after St Bruno's, was a pupil at Prior's Field until he went to the neighbouring Hillside preparatory school; and Julia Huxley with her staff of two, later to be augmented by visiting teachers for such subjects as drawing, modelling, drill, music and singing.

At first glance it must have seemed a school like many others spread across the country, informal in character, teaching the womanly virtues but not over-occupied with the hard core of academic education. In fact, it was very different. It was different in the attitude adopted towards pupils, who were normally credited with a measure of adult common sense; it resisted the urge to make education the mere accumulation of facts, and it insisted that if literature, history or any other 'subject' were to be worth teaching, it should make students more aware, more alive to the endlessly changing, infinitely exciting world around them. The pupils at Prior's Field not only 'did' Shakespeare but were brought to London to see the plays acted – an almost revolutionary idea at that time. They were taught of the Ancient World not merely from text-books but also by visits to the British Museum, where Julia would expound on the exhibits. Even when it came to the mechanics of school life, there were differences. 'The freedom given to us at Prior's Field from the earliest days was very exceptional in girls' schools at that time,' Joan Buzzard, Ethel Collier's daughter and an early pupil, has written. 'When most schools still walked out in "crocodiles", at Prior's Field we could go for walks and bicycle rides and even sketching parties, provided that not less than three of us were together.' The reputation of the school soon spread, and in 1906 Julia Huxley increased its capacity by taking into partnership a Mrs Burton-Brown. Gilbert Murray's daughter was an early pupil; so was Maurice Hewlett's, while another was Henry Huxley's eldest daughter, Marjorie. The numbers doubled in the first year, doubled again, continued to rise, were more than eighty by 1913 and nearly one hundred by the outbreak of the first world war.

From the beginning, Leonard's children played a part in the life of Prior's Field. Margaret became a pupil when she was old enough; her three brothers, who followed one another to Eton, frequently came home at week-ends. Six months after the school opened Julia held a garden party at which the pupils acted a number of scenes from *A Midsummer Night's Dream.* On the appointed day, bad weather made much of the speech inaudible although, as Mrs Huxley later put it,

> Margaret, who was not quite three years old, made a very engaging fairy, but created some amusement by talking volubly, and singing to herself, whenever she was on the stage, and by entirely refusing to go off the stage when her presence was not required. Trev, who did Puck, had in the end to carry her off, kicking and scratching lustily.

For the younger Huxleys, one of the highlights of life at Prior's Field came with the construction of the new wing. This, according to Joan Buzzard, 'lent itself to roof climbing, which was as popular in the early days at Prior's Field as it still is at Oxford'. The building of this addition, Margaret later wrote,

> stands out in my mind for excursions by the boys at week-ends, up and down the ladders, along scaffolding, over beams – culminating in a Sunday afternoon just before the tiling began, when my poor mother, while taking parents round the garden, happened to look up and see all her brood perched astride the roof-tree in great glee.

In the surrounding woods and fields Leonard's eldest son Julian first learned to watch and study birds systematically. Here Trev first learned to look out over landscape with the eye of a topographer. And Aldous recounted half a century later that 'We knew our countryside by heart for an eight-mile radius round the house. We knew precisely where to find this flower or that bird.'

In good weather, all the children's spare time would be spent exploring the countryside on foot or on bike. On wet days they would congregate in the kitchen where Margaret – for whose doll's house Julian once made a rug from a caterpillar-skin – would produce peppermint creams or wheedle one of her brothers into giving her rides across the floor in the big copper preserving pan. And then there would be nursery tea at which she 'watched delightedly while (I regret to say) one of my large brothers flipped butter-pats from a hot knife and then tried to catch them on a plate, or competed for halving penny buns (in those days as big as a tea plate) with one stroke of the bread knife, like Saladin with his cushion'.

It was during the holidays that the Huxley clan gathered in the greatest numbers. Leonard, Julia and Margaret would set out from Prior's Field in the dog-cart, with the three boys on bicycles acting as outriders until they reached Ferncombe Station. Here they would catch the early morning train – one of those trains whose voice Aldous recorded years later as repeating indefinitely, 'To Lancashire, to Lancashire, to fetch a pocket handkercher'. And eventually they would arrive to meet their relatives in the Lakes, in the Isle of Wight, at one of the still unspoilt villages on the Cardigan coast or, in later years, at a Swiss mountain resort.

It was during these first years of the century that the Huxleys' own version of the poetry game evolved. In this, each participant had to add a line to what had gone before. One vintage specimen, placed by memory as a few years before the first world war, ran as follows:

> 'For consumption's prevention you're prayed not to spit.'
> This I spied on a bus as I rode to the Zoo,
> But the llama he cares for these laws not a bit,
> 'What's a fiver to me!' (and he does it well, too).
> As I watched him thus bravely commit the offence
> I swore that I'd not be outdone by the beast,
> And, espying a keeper, with malice prepense,
> A long-distance one near his face I released.
> Said the judge on the bench 'Your conduct you'll rue,
> What's free for the llama is five pounds to you.'

At times more than a score of Huxley cousins mustered, although in later years it was always Leonard's four children who were remembered as 'the Huxleys'. In the year that Prior's Field opened, Julian was a King's Scholar; Trev was also at Eton; Aldous was still at Hillside while Margaret was a child of three. Laurence Collier, who went to Bedales the next year, was twelve, while his half-sister Joyce was a glowing eighteen and his young sister Joan just nine. Of Henry's children Marjorie was ten, Gervas eight and Michael three. The three Eckersley boys – Roger now eighteen, Thomas seventeen and Peter, another Bedalian, a mere eleven – provided other companions for holidays that can rarely have been dull and must frequently have been uproarious.

> The Huxley boys had tempers [Roger later wrote in *The BBC and All That*]. I can recall one of these furies which broke loose when we were staying with them at Seaview, Isle of Wight. I suppose we must have quarrelled badly over something – but I must have thought it was all over, as I was sitting peacefully at the bottom of a stone balustrade leading up to the front door – when I heard a rumble like thunder

behind me. I turned round to see that one of them had loosened one of those big round stone balls which stand as ornaments at the top of the stonework, and it was practically on top of me before I got out of its way. Table knives were occasionally aimed at one, too, and this habit was reciprocated.

The Huxleys also contrived their own sports of a less potentially lethal kind. Thus they would sometimes play the role of godlike geographers, altering the seashore landscape and, as Trev remembered later in *Oxford Mountaineering Essays*, spending

as much of the day as the day left possible in altering in every conceivable manner, by dams, diversions or channels, the geography of a wet strip of sand, which the tide in its next advance would restore to its old configuration. Sometimes operations, more ambitious in the durability of their materials, were begun in a stream inland; pools were made, and the stream diverted into a new, or perhaps a long disused, channel. Sometimes, too, a part of us would explore along a stream to its source, which we rarely reached, since even small streams are apt to extend farther than childish zeal will endure, though fired by the ambition of finding a real spring, entrancing to the dwellers among sluggish south-country rivers.

To holidays in Britain there were soon added holidays abroad. The family was drawn to the mountains by a tradition dating back to Tyndall, TH and the Hookers, all helping to lay the foundations of Alpinism as they prodded at the everlasting glacier controversy.

The prototype of these summer gatherings was held in 1903 at Rosenlaui, then a peaceful cluster of chalets on the track that leads up from Meiringen past the Reichenbach Falls towards the Scheidegg. Here, where the Swiss now run their training courses for guides, came Leonard, his wife and his four children. They had often planned to visit this ideal resort, slung at just the right height among the Oberland giants, but had been deterred by one thing. The Monkswells stayed regularly at Rosenlaui, whose surroundings had provided the subjects for many of the first Lord Monkswell's Academy pictures, and the breach that followed John Collier's second marriage still made close contact embarrassing. However, in 1903 the Monkswells were forsaking Rosenlaui; the Huxleys, replacing them, could be safely joined by Ethel, John Collier and their children. Other cousins came too, including Oriana 'Ria' Waller, now twenty-six, with her red-gold hair so long that she could sit on it. She helped with the children – and with the eternal re-patching that became necessary as the boys discovered enough snow on the surrounding slopes to allow tobogganing without toboggans.

At Rosenlaui the Huxleys invented a splendid variant on the old game of geography for, as Trev has recorded in *Oxford Mountaineering Essays*, there

> were streams without number, small enough to follow during the course of a long picnicking day, up to real authentic springs, which bubbled clear and cold from the ground at our feet. Geography could be made and altered; our dams made pools where none were before, or caused the paths and water-courses of the neighbourhood to exchange their functions, so that the inhabitants of lonely chalets found their water supply miraculously curtailed, and visited the culprits up above with guttural wrath.

There was the day when they started at six in the morning with a couple of mules, breasted the Great Scheidegg to see a new world before them, dropped down to Grindelwald and returned in the cool of the evening – finding on the top of the pass that the milk in the donkey-panniers had turned to butter and needed Oriana's long hat-pins to disengage it. There was the day when Julian was taken on his first climb, an ascent of the near-by Dossenhorn, by his father, John Collier and a guide. And there were the days, as some of the children later remembered, when Leonard would stand and speculate, gazing at the mountains with reminiscent eye and thinking aloud of things past. He enjoyed his soliloquies, and among some of his nephews 'doing an Uncle Leonard' became a recognized diversion when the holidays were over.

The two elder Huxley brothers responded well, at least outwardly, to Leonard's Alpine homilies.

> Aldous, however [writes Laurence Collier today in his 'North House', an unpublished memoir], seemed, even at the early age of nine, aloof and secretly critical on these occasions: he said nothing, but looked at something else or gazed abstractedly into the distance with a fixed and enigmatic smile, and I began to think that he liked neither Switzerland nor his father – a suspicion amply confirmed when I read in *Eyeless in Gaza* the account of the misbehaviour of a goat at an Alpine picnic, an account founded on fact and given with the sardonic relish of a man 'getting his own back' after many years, and noted that in the same book he makes the hero resent bitterly his father's decision to take him to Rosenlaui for a summer holiday.

Five years later, when at the age of fourteen Aldous was taken to

Argentière, his feelings were mixed, as is clear from a letter to his cousin Gervas:

> This is a most splendid place, . . . we had a vast walk yesterday up to a loathsome mountain called Le Buet. The day before we went on the glacier and father pulled me about on a rope and we had great fun. This place has a splendid air which makes me eat and sleep enormously.

The reactions of Leonard's three sons to mountains were revealingly different. So were their writings on the subject, and it is intriguing to note that with the exception of a specialist book on the animal kingdom by Julian, the first literary efforts of all three Huxley brothers dealt with mountains or mountaineering. Trev's and Aldous's appeared in the *Climbers' Club Journal*; Julian's in *Oxford Mountaineering Essays*, which contained a philosophical essay hung on his Dossenhorn ascent and an account of Oxford roof-climbing – the latter contributed anonymously since its author was by this time a don.

Aldous could feel himself aesthetically involved but later became either aloof or slightly disturbed by the enthusiasms which mountains aroused, a feeling strong enough to draw a protest in later years from Arnold Lunn, that paladin of the world above the snowline. Aldous's view can be inferred from the opening lines of his first published prose – 'A Lunndon Mountaineering Essay' printed in the *Climbers' Club Journal* when he was just twenty. It began:

> Many there are who write the glory of mountains – mountains of youth, health, wealth, happiness, mountains of grandeur, mountains of truth, no doubt; yet who remains but I, a voice crying in the wilderness, a blind stay-at-home mole, to proclaim the glory of the staircase?

Trev's reaction epitomized the synthesis of apparent opposites that is so frequent among the Huxleys, a synthesis that could merge more than science and art, more than the doubt of the scientist and the faith of the believer. Trev's response to the Alps combined the hearty athleticism which reacted to the physical challenge of the mountains and the aesthetic response which could provide prose good enough to pass through the narrow doorway into Arnold Lunn's anthology, *The Englishman in The Alps*.

Julian's response was perhaps the most revealing of all. For to him the mountains represented not one but a dozen different yardsticks with which to measure man's place in nature. Their age, and their slow denudation through the years, were both illuminated by the chance rock-dislodgements of a wandering chamois. The mountains had 'their being, in a different and vaster cycle than man's, their life only another fragment of that change which is the single fixed reality'. Yet the almost perfect mountain prospects in which foreground, mid-scene and peak each formed visual stepping-stones, 'making it possible for the whole grandeur of the peak to slip down, as it were, and find place within the narrow limits of the brain waiting at the other end', awakened a non-scientific, purely aesthetic response. Mountains induced men both to think and to wonder.

> The chief moral is, I expect [Julian wrote], that the mountains can give the climber more than climbing, and will do so if he but keep his eyes open. From them there will come to him flashes of beauty and of grandeur, light in dark places, sudden glimpses of the age, the glory, and the greatness of the earth.

Thus in more than one way these Swiss holidays of the 1900s provided formes from which the Huxley future would be printed. Rosenlaui was visited twice, then Champex, then Argentière, while visits for winter sports began to supplement summer holidays, and in 1911 eight families, all of whom knew one another well, and including the combined Huxleys, took over an entire hotel at Murren.

Yet by this date the Huxley family had already been brutally transformed. Three years earlier, in the summer of 1908, Julia Arnold's world must have been suffused with a pleasant glow. Her school, one of the great joys of her life, was flourishing. She had been right; Prior's Field was a success. Of her sons, Julian had gone up to Balliol as a Brackenbury Scholar and appeared to be on the threshold of a brilliant career. Trev, about to go up to Balliol, showed equal promise; while Aldous, so different from the rest, so curiously adult, so like an Arnold – what might not be expected from him? As for her husband, now happily engaged with his books, he too seemed at last to have found his niche. Now, at the end of the summer of 1908, she had everything to live for. The only trouble was her health, about which the doctors had been worried. But health always did seem to improve, and no doubt it would do so again.

This time it did not improve. It was discovered that Julia had cancer. Her desperate condition was concealed from her for many weeks. Neither Leonard, nor Mrs Burton-Brown, could bring themselves to break the news to her. There was, after all, some flicker of reason to support them. Even half a century ago inexplicable things happened, and the word 'incurable' was often found to be inaccurate. As autumn continued, her condition worsened and at last Mrs Burton-Brown told her the truth.

Julia's sons came to see her for the last time, from Oxford and from Eton. The oldest remembered all his life the anguish of hearing her say: 'I don't want to die – so young. . . .' The youngest, for whom his mother's death was to be the first of three traumatic experiences, thinly disguised the experience in fiction:

> He hadn't known that she was going to die, but when he entered her room, when he saw her lying so weakly in the bed, he had suddenly begun to cry, uncontrollably [he wrote fourteen years later in *Antic Hay*]. All the fortitude, the laughter even, had been hers. And she had spoken to him. A few words only; but they had contained all the wisdom he needed to live by. She had told him what he was, and what he should try to be, and how to be it. And crying, still crying, he had promised that he would try.

She died on 29 November and that evening Leonard Huxley called together the pupils of Prior's Field. First he announced to them that their headmistress was dead. But that was not all. He had something prepared for the occasion. And he now recited to the assembled girls the poem he had a few hours earlier written on his wife's death. It was an occasion which some of them were never to forget.

Chapter VII

The Three Brothers

(*i*)

In the spring of 1913 it might have appeared to the casual observer that there were at times no less than four Huxley brothers treading the trim gravel Balliol paths. One of them, it is true, did look somewhat older than the others, but it was difficult to believe that the handsome ramrod figure was that of Leonard Huxley, now aged fifty-three, and father of the three brothers who had followed one another along the path from Eton. Physically there existed a good deal of similarity between Julian, Trev and Aldous, not only in height, with Aldous topping 6 ft 4 in. by the time he was fifteen, but also in the Huxley nose, the expression of discriminating curiosity which so frequently illuminated their faces, and the darting impatient movements of the hands which they had inherited, at three removes, from Rachel Withers. In their separate ways, from their own separate viewpoints, each son was already concerning himself with that question of questions, the riddle of man's destiny in the natural world. Just what part each of the three brothers might play in unravelling it was still unclear; yet by 1913 any percipient observer might have confidently made one prophecy – that in future the Huxleys' place in nature would not be assessed only by the achievements of TH.

In approaching the central problem with which they were to concern themselves, each of the three brothers revealed in differing strengths their Huxley and Arnold backgrounds.

Julian, just twenty-five, until recently Balliol's Lecturer in Biology and University Demonstrator in Zoology, now planning to emigrate with a young bride to the United States, where an exciting appointment had been offered, showed to formidable degree the traits of TH: he demanded scientific proof, admitted that proof itself might be revealed as chimerical, denied the absolute. Trev, happy to recite that

'One Huxley brother Is as good as another. That is the view Of Number Two', was fine scholar and fine athlete, showing the Arnold trait by putting the speculations of metaphysics on a level with the facts of science. Regarded by as penetrating an observer as Geoffrey Young as 'the most gifted of the three omniscient brothers', and according to Sir Arnold Lunn 'by far the most likeable' – judgements possibly influenced by use of a mountaineering yardstick – Trev had been drawn to the Indian Civil Service. But he was now contemplating postgraduate work at Oxford which would enable him to continue helping his younger brother. For Aldous, in whom the Huxley and the Arnold inheritances were already locked in a battle that was to last a lifetime, needed help. Already encyclopaedic in knowledge and catholic in taste he was about to come up to Balliol despite what had been complete blindness and was still intractable near-blindness. All three brothers were already becoming distinguished in their separate ways, and all had trodden paths that had crossed and recrossed since the death of their mother five years previously.

This tragedy in 1908 had meant the break-up of the family home, for Mrs Burton-Brown had taken over the school. Leonard Huxley had moved to London, leasing a house in Bayswater which he was to occupy for many years. Margaret, aged nine, remained a pupil at Prior's Field but found a new home at Hindhead where one of Julia's married sisters now lived in Undershaw, Conan Doyle's old house that still stands a few hundred yards from Tyndall's home, looking down the Golden Valley to the distant nick of Butser Hill on the horizon. Aldous was brought under the sheltering wing of Mrs Humphry Ward, whose country home at Stocks, the comfortable eighteenth-century house near Berkhamsted, once owned by Sir Edward Grey and bought by Mrs Humphry Ward when she uprooted herself from the Haslemere area, became a second home for the Huxley boys. And Trev was about to leave Eton for Oxford, where in 1908 Julian had one more year to run.

This eldest of the Huxley sons was already on the threshold of a career. At the turn of the century he had sat for a scholarship at Eton and shortly afterwards entered as a King's Scholar. At first it was thought he would join the Civil Service or become a writer, and he embarked on what he later described as a fairly rigorous classical education. However, Julian soon became an enthusiastic biologist, winning the biology prize four years running – a fact inscribed in the red morocco volume of the college records together with the note that he was in 1906 'Keeper of College Grace Card'. At the age of sixteen, there came the choice of German or zoology as an extra subject. His parents ordained that he could always learn German abroad, so Julian took zoology. He was, moreover, induced by one of the masters, 'Piggy' Hill, to work for a while in the biological laboratory which TH had caused to be set up when a governor, and which had been known for years as 'Huxley's Folly'.

'By an irony of fate it provided me', says Huxley, 'with the first taste of real biology, which promptly decided my future career.' All at once the Civil Service appeared a grey occupation, and writing merely a tool for explaining the extraordinary things which might be discovered in the laboratory, in the field, or even by just sitting down and using one's brains. Julian was perpetually grateful to Hill – who like TH quickly put his finger on a salient point in the boy's character, writing of his pupil that 'his one failing is an invariable belief in his own infallibility'.

Julian's interest in the raw material of biology had been roused in the Surrey countryside, and it had been confirmed and sharpened at the age of fourteen during a visit to Stocks.

> I saw a green woodpecker on the grass only a few yards from me [he said in a talk on the B.B.C.]. I had just time to take in the sight of it before the bird was off to the wood beyond the hedge. The green woodpecker is a common bird enough; but I had never seen one close. Here I saw every striking detail; the rich green of the wings, the flash of bright yellow on the back when he flew, the pale glittering eye, the scarlet nape, the strange moustache of black and red; and the effect was as if I had seen a bird of paradise, even a phoenix. I was thrilled with the sudden realization that here, under my nose, in the familiar woods and fields, lived strange and beautiful creatures of whose strangeness and beauty I had been lamentably unaware.

The wonder lasted. And both the wonder and the excitement come through the accounts which he later gave of his early adventures in the Surrey woods and fields on holidays from Eton:

> I can recall today with extreme vividness the pleasure of discovering the detailed loveliness of a cock bullfinch busy on a fruit tree – glossy black of head, soft but vivid brick-red of breast, delicate white of rump, exquisite bluish grey of back – or watching for the first time the mottled brown creeper mousily climbing a tree and prying into the crevices with its long curved beak, and realizing that here was a new kind of existence I had not previously suspected.
>
> I can recall with equal vividness the excitement of coming over the crest of a heathery common (not forty miles from London) and

seeing an enormous bird of prey get up fifteen or twenty yards away, leaving half a pheasant carcass on the ground; and of discovering that this was no less a personage among birds than a young white-tailed eagle. That was my first experience of a thrill of rarity; and it set me off deliberately trying to collect glimpses of rare birds as the philatelist collects rare postage stamps. I could take a map and mark down just where I saw my first Dartford warbler, my first smew, Montague's harrier, and so on.

Thus by the time Julian came to leave Eton, his mind was made up. He had lived up to his promise, and Leonard decided that he should sit for the Brackenbury Scholarship in Science. Candidates had to write an essay on 'What I would do if I had a million pounds to spend', and Julian, half a century ahead of the National Trust's 'Operation Neptune', explained how and why he would buy up large tracts of the British coastline and preserve them from the wrong kind of development. He won his scholarship, and in 1906 went up to Balliol with great things in prospect.

From the first it had been clear that however strongly he might be drawn towards science, his science would be grounded in the Humanities. 'I could and did read Homer and Horace and Catullus for pleasure, sometimes writing verse in Latin and Greek,' he later said. The so-called dead languages served, moreover, a practical purpose since he had constantly to cope with the 1,250,000 Latin names that describe the species of animals and plants. And there was therefore less surprise than might have been expected when in 1908 the budding zoologist won the Newdigate Prize for poetry. Significantly, foreshadowing the future course of his thoughts, his prize poem on Holyroodhouse told how it was

> . . . useful too to dream
> Visions of beauty for mankind – to see
> The Present's place in the Eternal scheme,
> And point which way to turn Life's undeciding stream . . .

Just as significantly, the £50 prize for the poem was spent on a binocular microscope.

At Oxford, Julian did not only work. He was a roof-climber, or stegophilist, in what was still the prehistoric era of the sport, and later wrote – anonymously, being then a don – a tingling account of those night-climbers who can say, as he did, that, 'by our own act we are cut off from men; the thickness of a single wall, if but it be the outer house-wall, dispossesses us of our humanity, and gives back our lost kinship with the stars'. He indulged in equally exciting but less esoteric occupations, becoming at Kingham a frequent guest of Warde Fowler, the historian and ornithologist who could discourse equally on the evolution of birds or on the field systems which man had developed through the centuries.

It was in Wales, during the Long Vacation, that Julian Huxley made his first contribution to original research. With his brother Trev he was one of a reading party based on a lonely farmhouse in Caernarvonshire, and a near-by landlocked sheet of water provided a magnificent display of estuarial birds, particularly redshanks.

> At one side of the head was a low ridge of grass-covered dune, about five feet high and thirty or forty feet long, with level ground behind them [Julian later wrote in the *Proceedings* of the Zoological Society]. Thus, by crawling over the flat, I could get up on to the dunes into an excellent position for viewing the whole top of the bay; every bird was easily seen against the wet mud. So I kept watch with the naked eye until some disturbance or unusual behaviour attracted attention; then, being armed with a telescope magnifying 30 diameters (for the loan of which I have to thank my brother, Mr. N. T. Huxley), I focused this on the spot and could see the minutest details of attitude and behaviour in the nearer birds, and even in those on the far side of the bay and could quite well interpret what I saw. I made a number of notes on the spot, and usually within twenty-four hours embodied what I had seen the day before in a letter to an ornithological friend.

Back among libraries a few weeks later, he realized that little had so far been written of the courtship activities of the redshank which he had been noting so carefully. Almost unexpectedly he found that he had been not only contributing to original research but also thoroughly enjoying himself.

It was now 1909 and Julian found to his satisfaction that he had not only gained a First in Natural Science (zoology) but also the Naples Biological Scholarship, an annual award tenable for a year and taken up when the 'scholar states his readiness to proceed forthwith to use the table rented by the University at the Zoological Station, Naples' – the Station for which TH had given such tireless assistance to Dohrn a third of a century earlier. Julian duly proceeded in the autumn, and the following spring visited his aunt Mrs Humphry Ward, then staying in Florence. A letter he wrote to her following his return to Naples gives an indication of his intermingling attitudes to science and art which were to inform so much of his work:

My dear Aunt Mary,

Back again, sad to say, in dirty old Naples, alias Cesspool, alias Sink of Iniquity! But after a most lovely journey. The first part was extremely hot and rather full, but full also of lovely views. Halfway to Pontassieve, on the left, is a wood like a wood of a dream – on a small round hill, showing a fairly dense growth of Umbrella pines with Cypresses shooting up among them: it deserves to be classed with the towers of the Palazzo Vecchio as something obviously out of Fairyland – or if not that as having been planned and carried out by someone in a state of 'inspiration' – when he was not quite himself, but more, as Wordsworth when he wrote The Ode on &c., or Coleridge in Kubla Khan. Many pleasant towns 'congesta manu', and a lovely bright green Trasimene with snow behind on high mountains. At last, very dirty and heated, to Orvieto, and up by funicular – which as how [or] why it didn't break down, I know not, with such a thin cable to such a full car. I had tea and perambulated the town, getting to the south-west gate just in time for the brilliantest yellow windy sunset over transparent purple Etruscan hills. The cheerful swifts were making an excellent screaming over the houses, and later there was a moon.

Today, up betimes, and 'did' the Cathedral. I think what I liked best were the reliefs on the façade, of early XIVth. century work – Adam and Eve in the midst of absurd little Umbrian ribbed hills crowned with oak-trees boasting (proportionally) gigantic leaves and acorns and a most awful and gruesome scene of Hell. Inside is finer than Florence by far, I thought, though the restorer has been at it a bit. In a hedge I saw Honeysuckle blooming, and the wind carried a nightingale's song up out of a stream-bed in the valley: altogether, it was very well worth doing.

The journey after Rome was almost more striking for the contrast with what it looked like before. All the oaks were out now – none when I travelled up: the mountains were many green up to the top, and everything was in full feather of springtime.

Vesuvius looked very grand – grown while I have been away – and all the vines, here you know strung in curtains from poplar to poplar, were beginning to bud, giving the whole Terra del Lavoro, so ugly in winter, the look of a great bower of greenery. And now here, I confess I am very sorry! It felt just like going back to School used to in early days, leaving the Villa Pazzi – made one quite melancholious.

I enclose my 'pome' – at present my *opus magnum*! That's not saying very much, though. I should very much like to know what you think of it. . . .

Well, after all this I haven't properly thanked you for the week and everything else. I feel much physically set up, and mentally, for I was a little stodgy and unenergetic before I came. What is more, I learnt twice as much in Florence as I should have done alone – that book of Mrs Ady's and you all to show me round combined to make me really understand something about the growth of Italian art, which I had never grasped at all before and so to make me much more interested than merely for the intrinsic beauty's sake (you see my mind is scientific rather than 'Arty' even with Art!) And, last but not least, all you told me about your work and your life made me understand you much more than I had ever before and gave me another ideal to help me along through the mush of 'ordinaries'.

Back in Naples, Julian took up his work once again, much of it an investigation of the ways in which sponges re-form and continue growth after separation into individual cells or fragments – one foundation of his later important work on experimental embryology. Before he completed his year at the Zoological Station there had come a suggestion that he might accompany Captain Scott, then fitting out the *Terra Nova* for his journey to the South Pole. But poor health more than counterbalanced his qualifications as a biologist and in his place there went Apsley Cherry-Garrard, who immortalized the expedition in *The Worst Journey in the World.*

In the autumn of 1910 Julian therefore returned to Oxford in a dual capacity as Balliol's Lecturer in Biology and University Demonstrator in Zoology. Here Trev was already revealing that mental ambidexterity which enabled him to isolate mathematical capacity from his feeling for the Humanities; and here, also, he had already become a confident figure among that gay company of scholar-mountaineers which included Hugh Rose Pope, Arnold Lunn and H. E. G. Tyndale.

Like his two brothers, Trev had much of the brilliance which caused more than one close relative to write as did Roger Eckersley: 'The Huxley connection has always been an embarrassment to me as I was always expected to be so much cleverer than I was. My cousins raked in scholarships as a matter of course wherever they went.' It was Trev who as a boy, deprived of Latin so that he should concentrate on other subjects, had taught himself the language. At Eton he had worked beyond his strength and at one point the matron had written to his parents suggesting he should be removed since his health was unable to stand the pace. Leonard and his wife, keeping their children's sights high, decided he should remain.

In 1907 Trev sat through what he later called 'the long horrors of the

Certificate Examination' that was to provide his passport to Balliol. Then he had escaped, out of London, out of England, along a night-sleeper route that led to Martigny and the long carriage-drive to the upper reaches of the Val de Bagnes.

> Here I was first initiated as a climber, and taken up the Ruinette [he later wrote], and for two lazy hours on the top I watched the Italian mountains raise themselves up from the ever-thickening screen of mist with which the Lombard plains seemed to be hiding their secret.

It was natural that he should become one of the founder-members of the Oxford Roof-Climbing Club, a member of Geoffrey Young's legendary Pen-y-Pass parties in Wales, and should return again and again to the Alps. It was not only that he excelled in the co-ordination of mind and muscle so essential to the rock-climber; in addition, he brought to mountaineering, as he brought to his other interests, a panache which made him remembered long after most other men had been forgotten; and in Young's words 'he excelled as humanist, scientist and naturalist, with artistic, athletic and social talents superadded, and above all a deep sensitive human kindness'.

It was in June 1909 that Trev Huxley first showed the qualities which could have made him, had he wished, one of the finest rock-climbers of his generation. With Claude Elliott, later Provost of Eton, Hugh Rose Pope and Nigel Madan, he paid his first visit to the Lake District. Elliott and Huxley had made a few easy climbs in the Alps, but none of the party had done any serious mountaineering, and as they walked up Wasdale to Burnthwaite they carried in a knapsack the heavy illustrated edition of O. G. Jones's *Rock-Climbing in the English Lake District*, the contemporary climbers' bible. On their first day they made for the Pillar, the great bastion which thrusts out from Pillar Mountain into Ennerdale like the prow of a huge rock ship. They ascended the North Climb, descended Central Jordan – an ambitious enough programme for beginners – and then lunched in Jordan Gap, the sally port which rests between Pisgah and High Man, the true summit of the Pillar. Here Trev suddenly got up and climbed the wall from the Gap to the top of Pisgah, unroped and without hesitation.

> I was struck [Elliott remembers more than half a century later] by the neatness of his movements and his beautiful balance. We ended the day with him leading up Pisgah Buttress from the West, of which the first ascent had recently been made, I think. Next day he led us up the Arrowhead Direct, which was remarkable for his second day on rocks, but he did not do any more leading.

Two years later, the same four formed an Easter party at Ogwen in North Wales, making a minor first ascent on Creigiaui Gleision, spending an icy six hours in the Great Gully of Craig-yr-Ysfa, and one evening meeting Geoffrey Young and George Trevelyan who had walked over the Glyders from Pen-y-Pass, where Young was at the height of his fame. Of the quartet it was Pope who developed as the leader *par excellence*. Trev, interested in all things, felt no need for that deep concentration on difficult rock-problems which is the hallmark of the dedicated cragsman. 'Certainly he did not, like the other three of us in those early days,' writes Elliott, 'tend to consider that a day not spent on the rocks was a day wasted.'

Yet Trev's interest in the mountains clung on, and it was as editor of the *Climbers' Club Journal* a few years later that he produced a *tour de force* of indexing that was an intriguing reflection of the Huxley wit and is still spoken of in climbing circles. Lunn had a little to do with it, but Trev was the man mainly responsible. In the first volume of the New Series Elliott had described an incident during a camping holiday in the Pyrenees. The party had been awakened one night by a scream, produced by someone who had espied a bear; the bear had fled, but they had lain still in their sleeping-bags before crawling out to decide exactly what had happened. And to the single paragraph of description involved, Trev produced more than twenty index entries. They included: 'Absence of Bears from Pyrenees Disputed'; 'Englishmen, Calmness of, Under Difficulties'; 'Intelligence in Lower Animals'; 'Nightmare, Unusual Strength of'; 'Rabbits, Magnified Appearance of, By Night'; 'Daniel Out-Danielled'; and 'Valour, Better Part of'.

The Trev whom Julian found at Oxford in the autumn of 1910 was a man who sparkled. His slight diffidence, accentuated by a mild stammer, seemed to attract rather than to caution off potential friends, and his cousin, Laurence Collier, up at Balliol for the same years, recalls that throughout a long life he has never known a man more widely liked – 'if ever it could be said of anyone that he had not an enemy in the world it could have been said of him'. It was in Trev's rooms that there assembled on Sunday nights – just as there had in Julian's rooms three years earlier – a large group whose kernel was provided by the Amphisboenic Society.

> They met [says Collier in *North House*] to enact, or to watch us enact, 'Nebuchadnezzars,' i.e. dumb-crambo charades, often of a lively, not to say profane nature. This group included in later years John Bell, afterwards High Master of St Paul's School; Tom Lindsay, the younger brother of the future Lord Lindsay of Birker; Denis

Mackail, Angela Thirkell's brother; once or twice Carnegie Brown, now Ivor Brown, the dramatic critic; Robin Barrington-Ward, afterwards editor of *The Times*; Bernstein who became Sir L. B. Namier; and even on occasion the austere Arnold Toynbee. Not all its members liked each other, but they all liked Trev, and in his rooms there was always peace and good fellowship between them.

Trev's letters of this period are revealing. They show what his father was later to call 'brilliant promise ... on the verge of more brilliant performance'. But they suggest, also, that he made an error in choosing Greats for his Finals. In 1909 he had taken a First in mathematics in Moderations; then he switched to Literae Humaniores. In a long letter to Jelly d'Aranyi, the violinist, a friend of the family, he concludes by deploring the fact that he must start an essay on Kant and his ethical philosophy. 'I hate him,' he adds. 'He clearly', his brother Julian was later to comment, 'got fed up with the metaphysicians, just as I would.' Yet Trev was in many ways on the crest of the wave, filled with the pleasure of personal friendships and the excitements of the new mountain world he had discovered.

His brother Aldous was in a very different state. Possibly because of the extra care which had been given him as a child; possibly because his predilections ran back through his mother to the self-questioning Arnolds more naturally than through his father to TH; possibly because his father tended to dehumanize scholarship and to arouse in his son a faint distaste – for whatever reasons, it was Julia Arnold who had occupied the centre of his world. Her death had not only cut down more deeply than it had cut into her other sons; it had also heightened Aldous's sensitivity, increased his awareness, added to the differences which already tended to set him apart from his companions.

Like his brothers, Aldous had cycled along the dusty Surrey roads, had jumped streams, climbed hills, swum in hammer ponds, soaked-in the feeling of that triangle of country through which the Wey twists between the chalk and the last upthrow of the sandstone. But he was still, in some ways, totally dissimilar from the rest of the family. 'From early boyhood,' Julian later wrote, 'I knew in some intuitive way that Aldous possessed some innate superiority and moved on a different level from us other children.' He was aged four when one of his aunts, venturing to break into his reverie with the question: 'What are you thinking about, Aldous dear?' was silenced by the simple reply: 'Skin.' And years later when Prior's Field was flourishing, more than one young pupil, sitting round the almost family table on Sundays when the Huxley boys came on leave from Eton, was nonplussed by the cool questioning glance, the monosyllabic inquiry and the kindly, over-mature attitude of 'The Ogre' – 'Ogie' for short – as he was called by many of his friends.

His preoccupation with words was notable by the time he reached his teens.

> Sometimes indeed [writes his cousin Laurence of one family holiday at Montana], Aldous seemed to cherish words as things in themselves and almost regardless of their meaning . . .; having just discovered, for example, an eighteenth-century poem about 'the lush meadow and the plashy stream', he would introduce the words 'lush' and 'plashy' wherever possible, rolling them off his tongue as if their utterance gave him a physical satisfaction; and when he found on the hotel dining-table a bottle with a label declaring that it 'imparted a zest to fish, game, etc.', he began to compose burlesque sentences and little comic poems to include the words 'imparting a zest' in every possible context.

He already had a rich flow of conversation, well fed from a reservoir which he filled from almost any printed matter he could obtain; he positively enjoyed erudition, and at times Julian, seven years his senior, would quote to him the remark of the gentleman who had listened to an hour of Macaulay's table-talk: 'Sir, his information is greater than society requires.'

At Eton, where Aldous had followed his two elder brothers, he was more popular, less purely aesthetic, than the subsequent image might suggest. He played the Wall Game as his brother Julian had done. And the fact that it was, as more than one of his later companions put it, 'impossible to have a row with Aldous', was a sign not of weakness but of an ability to retreat into his own private world whenever he wished, an ability which made life at Eton possible when it might otherwise have been unbearable.

It was not the ends but the means of 'the fantastic place' which distressed him. 'One of the earliest recollections of the present writer [he was to say], is of having been asked to translate the statement: "Lo, cows (insert epithet) carry distended udders" into a Latin hexameter; while one of the most painful of his later memories is connected with an examination in which he was required to turn Shakespeare's "Shall I compare thee" into a French sonnet.' He long remembered how 'the whole of every Tuesday, from seven in the morning until ten at night, was devoted to the exhausting and preposterous task of translating thirty or forty lines of English poetry into Latin or, on great occasions, Greek verse'. 'For those who were most successful in producing pastiches of Ovid or Horace or Euripides, there were handsome prizes,' he wrote in *Doodles in the Dictionary*. 'I still have a Matthew Arnold in crimson morocco, a Shelley in half-calf, to testify to my one-time prowess in these odd fields of endeavour.' Forty years later he remembered only the intense boredom that the work had involved:

> Even today, the sight of Dr Smith's *Shorter Latin Dictionary*, or of Liddell and Scott's *Greek Lexicon*, has power to recall that ancient ennui. What dreary hours I have spent frantically turning those pages in search of a word for 'cow' that could be scanned as a dactyl, or to make sure that my memory of the irregular verbs and the Greek accents are not at fault! I hate to think of all that wasted time.

Yet nothing could stifle his surprise at a world which contained such fantastic eccentricities of nature; unexpected and almost incredible nonconformities; white-walled cities; splendid prospects; minds of the most extraordinary complexity; limitless vistas; possibilities without number. What a life it could be – just observing and reporting on these things and speculating how the human animal might deal with the splendours and the sufferings that they offered! In the spring of 1910 great futures opened out, even at Eton.

Then, without warning, darkness fell. A persistent story has it that the initial cause was an explosion in the Eton laboratory. In fact, Aldous was suddenly afflicted by a violent attack of what was finally diagnosed as *keratitis punctata*, an inflammation of the corneas. At first, coming down from Eton to North House, he told his aunt, Ethel Collier, that he merely had a touch of pink-eye. A few weeks later he had become so blind that while staying with another aunt he walked into a four-poster bed. The awful possibility had to be faced. He could distinguish between night and day, between strong light and near-darkness, but he could distinguish little else. There were operations, but by 1911 he was faced with what appeared to be, for all practical purposes, a life of blindness, and he was removed from Eton.

Aldous needed constant care and supervision, and little could be done for him at Leonard's widower establishment in London. He went to the Aldershot home of his cousin Joan Collier, recently married to an Army officer, Captain Buzzard, who was distressed to see his condition; then back to North House; and then on again to the Arnolds' relatives by marriage, the Trevelyans in Northumberland.

Finally he came to Hindhead where his sister Margaret was being given a home with the Selwyns at Undershaw. He knew the place well, lying as it did only a few uphill miles from Prior's Field, and here he began a new life. First he taught himself Braille – and it is a measure of his capacity for friendship that one of his Eton companions, Lewis Gielgud, himself learned Braille so that he could write to him regularly. He taught himself to use a typewriter, and then to play the piano by Braille, reading the raised print with the left hand and playing with the right; then reading with the right and playing with the left; and finally, note perfect, putting both parts together.

Even so, even with the kindness of the Selwyns, even with the help of Trev who made the care of Aldous his special task, the experience was a searing one. Nevertheless, his unquenchable spirit found compensations. Being able to read Braille, he told his cousin Gervas, meant that one could read in bed with the book beneath the blankets, thus keeping one's hands warm on even the coldest winter night. There were other unexpected advantages, he would recall. His misfortune, he wrote, prevented him

> from becoming a complete public-school English gentleman. Providence is sometimes kind even when it seems to be harsh. My temporary blindness also preserved me from becoming a doctor, for which I am also grateful. For seeing that I nearly died of overwork as a journalist, I should infallibly have killed myself in the much more strenuous profession of medicine.

His closed world did, moreover, allow him to sharpen his already extraordinary memory. He worked out for himself 'a philosophy of more than Berkeleyan subjectivity'. He completed an eighty-thousand-word novel whose manuscript was lost and has apparently disappeared for ever. He struggled on until, after eighteen months and four operations, the affliction began to clear. One eye was now capable of distinguishing light from dark; the other provided enough vision for him to detect 'the 200-ft. letter' on the Snellen Chart at a distance of ten feet.

> For the first few years [Aldous later wrote in *The Art of Seeing*], my doctors advised me to do my reading with the aid of a powerful hand magnifying glass. But later on I was promoted to spectacles. With the aid of these I was able to recognise the seventy-foot line at ten feet and to read tolerably well – provided always that I kept my better pupil dilated with atropine, so that I might see round a particularly heavy patch of opacity at the centre of the cornea. True, a measure of strain and fatigue was always present, and there were occasions when I was overcome by that sense of complete physical and mental exhaustion which only eye-strain can produce. Still, I was grateful to be able to see as well as I could.

The prospects of the youngest Huxley brother now looked uncertain. Yet as compensation for near-blindness there was something of intangible importance. For with his move from Eton, Aldous had been saved, temporarily at least, from the intense pressure exerted on all three brothers to maintain the Huxley record. He might reach the position at the top of the tree which his father so dearly desired, but he would do so by his own route, feeling free to remark, as he did so, upon the extraordinariness of the whole business.

Thus in the autumn of 1910, some two years after their mother's death, the three brothers had made varied progress. Aldous appeared to have been almost withdrawn by circumstance from the race. Trev was doing well. Julian had already been launched by a brilliant record on to what was to be a brilliant career. He was, moreover, already thinking of leaving England for a post in the United States.

(ii)

To the Naples Biological Station there came, in the natural order of things, a regular stream of visiting scientists. Among them, in the summer of 1910, was Professor Conklin, Director of the biological laboratory of Princeton University. Conklin was not visiting Europe solely on behalf of Princeton, however; in addition he had from the Rice Institute of Houston, Texas, a roving brief to sound out for appointment at Rice the best of the Continent's natural scientists.

The Rice Institute had been inaugurated nineteen years earlier, the brain-child of William Marsh Rice, a resident of Houston who had made a considerable fortune from timber. In 1891 Rice set up, under a Board of Trustees, the William M. Rice Institute for the Advance of Literature, Science and Art, an institute which was to become operational after his death and which was to utilize his money. Rice died in 1901 but in mysterious circumstances which involved a valet, an unscrupulous lawyer, chloroform and numbers of forged cheques. The so-called 'Patrick case' which resulted dragged on for years as a *cause célèbre*, and when at last the trustees came into possession of the estate, it amounted to some ten million dollars. They then decided that the money should not be expended, as it easily might have been, on a practical institution of purely parochial nature, but on the foundation of what should become a genuine university.

On his last night at Naples in the summer of 1910, Professor Conklin talked with great enthusiasm to the young Julian Huxley of the prospects held out by Rice in Texas, this State as large as the whole German

Empire, where single ranches were the size of Yorkshire. Here a great liberal institution, set in the rolling prairies some fifty miles from the Gulf, was to be built from the foundations up and served by the best brains of the world. Perhaps in the future, Professor Conklin suggested, the young man about to take up his appointment among the grey stones of Oxford might be tempted to the New World. The young man decided to think it over.

The following November, already immersed in his new duties, Huxley wrote to Conklin, wondering on paper whether the Rice project was still moving forward. He would have hesitated to write but for one special reason. 'That reason', he explained, 'is that I am informally engaged to be married, and want to become formally so, and this I cannot very well do until I can tell my fiancée's father something more definite about my future prospects.' The father was Sir Herbert Fordham, one of Europe's leading writers on cartography; the fiancée, his daughter Kathleen, whom Julian had known some years earlier as a pupil at Prior's Field.

A tentative offer came from Rice early the following year, but the basic structure of the organization was still being worked out, and it was only towards the end of 1911 that Edgar Lovett, President-designate of the institute, which was to be inaugurated in 1912, visited Europe to engage the staff. In mid-January 1912, Lovett dined at Leonard Huxley's home in Westbourne Square with the Huxleys and Julian's fiancée, who would be an important member of the Rice community. The next month Julian formally accepted a post as head of the Institute's biology department, and it was subsequently agreed that he should attend the inauguration ceremonies in the autumn of 1912, 'spying out the land' for his future wife, as it was described; would return to Europe to acquire further experience in Germany; and would marry and sail to the United States with his wife in the spring of 1913.

Meanwhile Huxley returned, almost as a relaxation, to a specialized ornithological task. He spent a fortnight visiting the Tring Reservoirs in Hertfordshire, thirty miles from London, investigating the courtship habits of the Great Crested Grebe. His observations, published in the *Proceedings* of the Zoological Society, formed a genuine landmark both in the study of birds and, owing to the effectiveness of their presentation, in ornithological writing. Huxley's paper – 'the classical paper (which) gave the first descriptive analysis of mutual display and introduced the notion of mutual selection', in the words of Sir Cyril Hinshelwood half a century later – gave an almost hour-by-hour account of his observations. From bank, boathouse or screened punt, he had watched the birds with both scientific detachment and fascination so that his description is both a learned paper and an invitation to come into the open air and watch. Accurate observation could not be replaced, even by the camera, he noted; while a good glass, a note-book and some patience were the sole main essentials for discovering fresh facts even about familiar birds. Here, the acute reader may have noticed, was not only the expert but the proselytizer.

While Huxley was making his investigations in what was really a new field of ornithology, discussions were continuing in Rice, both on the detailed minutiae of laboratories and laboratory equipment and, more importantly, on the structure and content of the courses to be given. Thus in mid-June Julian sent Lovett a long letter setting forth his views:

> I should like to have a course (which should entitle a man to a degree) which should be a course intended to make people understand the *principles* of a science, the practical instruction being abundant and varied, but intended only to get at the underlying ideas without the thought of getting necessarily very accurate results every time. (This, you may say, would induce a slipshod habit of mind, but one could well have a short course on method alone in each Science, showing the way in which reliable results are to be obtained; the 'science of method' is certainly an extremely valuable one.) Several chemists tell me that here *more than half the time* spent in practical work in the Laboratories is spent in taking precautions.
>
> This, it seems to me, is not real education.

This was significant of things to come. So was Julian Huxley's comment on the Science course itself:

> Besides this, I would have an English course, of literature & Composition, absolutely compulsory on all Science (and I think also all others!) first-year men. It is deplorable to me to see many men of science make their writings ridiculous or forbidding to the general world, and unintelligible to their fellow-workers, by an ignorance of and contempt for all the elements of English composition.

Three months remained before Huxley was due to attend the opening ceremonies in Houston and he made good use of them. He first worked, as he put it, 'as a mere novice and labourer' at the John Innes Horticultural Institution then south of London, and run by William Bateson, founder of the experimental study of heredity and variation which he himself named 'genetics' – 'mostly picking & checking-off peas & such-like,' Julian noted, 'but one can pick up a good deal about the methods & general atmosphere if one keeps one's eyes open'. He joined

Professor (later Sir William) Herdman on his yacht to practise dredging and tow-netting, and then visited the professor's private marine laboratory. He found time to join a family party at Abersoch, on the shores of Cardigan Bay, that included Aldous – slowly recovering and now optimistic of going up to Balliol the following year – Trev, who had just taken a second in Greats; an assorted collection of Huxley cousins; and the Fordhams. Then, in the last week of September, he set sail for the United States.

He broke his journey in New York, where the family name, as much as personal reputation, produced a newspaper headline announcing: 'Huxley, Zoologist, Here'. He met in New York some distant connections of Lizzie Scott who, 'while they thought him exceedingly English "doncher know" . . . thought him a very nice fellow.' He spent some time at Columbia University in whose famous fly room Morgan and his team – including the future Nobel Prize-winner, H. J. Muller, whom Huxley later enrolled as his assistant – were already preparing to postulate the gene as the particulate bearer of inherited characteristics. And he then took train south to Houston, on whose outskirts a notable collection of celebrities had been assembled to take part in the Rice inaugural ceremonies.

Huxley arrived in Houston on an October morning in an era when the eleven-storey Bender Hotel was still the great glory of the town. In the *Cornhill* he has described himself as the stranger

> gazing first at the outer walls of deep red, picked out with facings and mouldings and cornices of cream; then entering and finding himself, as is the way in American hotels, in a wide lobby, garnished with desk and obliging clerk, with many arm-chairs, with many spittoons; with two sides of plate-glass windows, and inside these a brass rail, on which, visible to all passers-by, rest many pairs of commercial feet, belonging to commercial bodies in the chairs, whose commercial big-faced heads, under undoffed hats, are puffing contentedly at large cigars. From this he is whisked by a negro lift-boy to the topmost region, and ushered into the *Banqueting Hall*, whose windows look upon a far-fading prospect of tree-sheltered city and girdling plain. But he has no eyes for prospects today; the room is crowded with people; and the first group that catches his eye holds it. Sir William Ramsay is one, Professor Hugo de Vries another – the Transformation of Elements from England chatting away, here in Texas, with the Transmutation of Species from Amsterdam.

Professors, doctors and scientists travelled out from the city to the site of the new institute which was reached by a tramway through the pinewoods. Only half of the route was served by a good road and the rest became almost impassable in bad weather. Beyond the woods the trams emerged by a ramshackle wooden farmhouse. Near it there stood, miraculously, as though a figment of imagination, the administration building.

> The brown grass with trailing dewberry brambles reached to the very walls of the building, which rose, complete and magnificent, to face the setting sun [Huxley wrote in the *Cornhill*]. Pale granite and soft pinkish brick received a warmth from the rays: a series of slender white marble columns extended along the whole face of the building, rising from the level of the first storey, and supporting the white balustrade. Coloured marble and inlet diamonds of red and blue tile lent brilliance. Below was a cloister, the capitals of whose pillars were curiously carved with heads of scientists, modern and ancient, with grotesques of American footballers and women students, with strange beasts in foliage. Between the two wings a low tower, pierced by a tall central arch almost Moorish in feeling. The high rounded windows, the lavishness of colour and decoration, conspired with the simple and modern form to produce an effect of something entirely original, something as new and real as a new species of Bird-of-Paradise lit on in a New Guinea jungle. Here it stood, brilliant, astounding, enduring: rising out of the barren brown prairie which extended, unbroken save for a belt of trees, to the horizon and far beyond the horizon.

To this outpost there had come, for the four days of ceremonies, Benedetto Croce and Professor Vito Volterra from Italy, Emile Borel from Paris, Sir William Ramsay and Sir Henry Jones from Britain, as well as many others. Julian Huxley watched and listened, attracted even more than before by the vigour of the New World which could draw to such a distant place the dozen learned men who were giving inaugural lectures, and the several hundred scholars and scientists who had assembled from the five continents.

Huxley himself now had one root planted firmly down in this new and exciting community. For the title-page of his first book, a copy of which he had brought across the Atlantic for Lovett, carried his new status – 'Research Associate of the Rice Institute, Houston, Texas, Late Lecturer of Balliol College, Oxford'.

The book was *The Individual in the Animal Kingdom*, and in it Huxley had tried to 'frame a general definition of the Individual, sufficiently objective to permit of its application by the man of science, while at the same time admitted as accurate (though perhaps regarded as incomplete) by the philosopher'; and also 'to show in what ways Individuality, *as thus defined by me* manifests itself in the Animal Kingdom'. A further aim of the book, he added, was 'to decrease still further the gap (today happily lessening) between Science, Philosophy, and the ideas and interests of everyday life'. If it is easy to see in these phrases the shape of things to come, the shape becomes even more clear in many pages of the book. And at least four of the beliefs which Huxley was to expound in detail in later years can be discerned in broad outline.

There was first an emphasizing of the fact that man himself was utilizing an additional evolutionary mechanism quite different from the biological mechanism which had so far sufficed for the rest of the living world:

> By speech first, but far more by writing, and more again by printing, man has been able to put something of himself beyond death. In tradition and in books an integral part of the individual persists, and a part which still works and is active, for it can influence the minds and actions of other individuals in different places and at different times: a row of black marks on a page can move a man to tears, though the bones of him that wrote it are long ago crumbled to dust.

There was also the suggestion that there might be personalities which had got rid of substance altogether, the 'disembodied spirits' postulated by the theologian and felt by the mystic – a hint of Huxley's later belief that the allegedly paranormal might be susceptible to scientific explanation. There was the biologist's insistence, comparable to the metaphysician's, that 'no man is an island, entire of itself'; for each individual is but a system and 'the systems are never quite cut off, for each must take its origin in one or more pieces of the previous system'. Finally there was the concluding paragraph, in which Huxley pointed out that animal individuality could throw light on human problems:

> The ideals of active harmony and mutual aid as the best means to power and progress; the hope that springs from life's power of transforming the old or of casting it from her in favour of the new; and the spur to effort in the knowledge that she does nothing lightly or without long struggle; these cannot but help to support and direct those men upon whom devolves the task of moulding and inspiring that unwieldiest individual – formless and blind today, but huge with possibility – the State.

Here, Lovett must have felt, was a promising first book from a man

Aldous and Maria Huxley with their son Matthew in the early 1930s

Gervas Huxley

P. P. Eckersley

T. L. Eckersley

only twenty-five; and here also, he may have felt, was an echo of the rolling phrase, with which TH had sent his scientific moralities on their way.

The ceremonies at Rice duly ended and Huxley made a leisurely journey northwards, calling at Johns Hopkins and Harvard Universities; then sailed for England, where he stayed a short while with the Fordhams before leaving for Heidelberg and Munich.

He was already devoting almost all thought and energy to preparation for the coming work, concentrating into every minute, in the Huxley way, the full 'sixty seconds' worth of distance run'. He was searching for the European journals that Rice would need, suggesting men from England who could come out as laboratory staff, advising on laboratory equipment, and ceaselessly questioning whether he might not fit himself even more adequately for the tasks ahead. From Munich he wrote to Lovett:

> By March I believe I shall have seen enough of German methods and Universities, and want to get back to England; special methods I can learn here, but I want a general advanced training in Physiology and in the physio-chemical side – that sort of thing is better done in England; and also I could take more advantage of it. Also, after seeing a little of American and German ways I want to get some time at home to look at English Universities with new eyes.

He was also anxious to know how the staff at Rice were to be accommodated, 'as Kathleen in her housewifely heart wants to have an idea of what to be prepared for.' However, all would soon be settled. 'I am looking forward,' he wrote to Lovett at the end of March 1913, 'not to leaving England, I admit! – but to settling down to a (relatively) permanent job.'

A fortnight later Lovett received the first hint of trouble: a note from Julian saying that he had been ill – 'effect of rushing about and German hospitality combined'. He can hardly have been prepared for the letter he received from Leonard Huxley in mid-June:

> Since his return from Germany [Leonard wrote of his son], he has had a very bad nervous breakdown, with insomnia. We imagined this must be the result of overwork, till it came out that for a very long time he and his fiancée had somehow got keyed wrongly and worried over their efforts to readjust 'the little more' or 'the little less', including the hope that all troubles might vanish if once the two got married. It was this that made him quite knock up, and now, to clear the horizon all round, they have formally broken off their

engagement and no definite tie exists between them. What may or may not happen a year hence, I can't say; the main fact for the present is that Julian is in the doctor's hands having a 'rest cure'.

Julian might not, Leonard continued, be able to start for Rice at the end of August as anticipated.

In fact, recovery took longer than expected, and it was the end of October before Julian was able to report to Lovett that things were now going better. He had, moreover, 'come to realize that I am coming out of this a much better person, mentally, morally, and physically than I ever dreamt of becoming before – it has really been worth it, I believe!' The complete nervous breakdown had been traumatic; it was typical that a Huxley could emerge augmented rather than diminished from the far side of the experience.

Early in January 1914, Julian sailed once again for the United States. He reached Rice without incident and during the next few months began to put the new biology department on its feet. At first he shared a two-room apartment, on the upper floors of the tower of the students' 'First Residential Hall', with Dr Griffith Evans, also an assistant professor, a distinguished mathematician who had come to Rice from Harvard. 'Along with other assistant professors we were young enough in appearance so that incoming freshmen could ask us what courses we were planning, not to give, but to take,' Evans commented later. 'The faculty was small in the beginning, and even the more famous oldsters were hardly of middle age.'

From the start, Huxley made a success of the department. What is more, he quickly realized, he was also making a success of himself.

His lecture courses were very large, and he used to take his students in groups out along the *bayous* to collect specimens, watching out of course for water-mocassins [Evans says]. He was a great favourite in Houston and throughout Texas, continually being called on to lecture, partly at first, of course, on account of his grandfather; in fact on one such occasion he was introduced by a flustered toastmaster as 'the famous grandsire of his famous grandfather'. But his wit and knowledge carried him everywhere.

There was still much to do, staff to find, laboratory equipment to collect, a library to be built up – all tasks into which he threw himself with his usual uninhibited enthusiasm.

In the summer of 1914 he returned to England, partly on Rice business, partly to see his family. Aldous was now up at Balliol, having surmounted the handicaps of his near-blindness by the combination of

Braille, magnifying glasses and iron will. He had, moreover, succeeded Trev as the Huxley attraction at Balliol, since it was, as his cousin Gervas has written,

> Aldous's room overlooking the Broad [which] became the centre where the *élite* of our year gathered, drawn by the magnet of his mind, the curiosity of his catholic tastes, and his unassuming friendliness. Over the fireplace was pinned a picture very unlike the 'classical' reproductions generally favoured by undergraduates – a striking French poster of a group of bare-breasted nubile girls by the sea-shore. Against one wall stood a piano. The room seemed always to be full of people talking and laughing and discussing every subject under the sun, serious and frivolous. Among the frivolities was the recent arrival of syncopation, which held a special fascination for Aldous, and on the piano he would strum such novelties of early jazz as 'He'd have to get under, get out or get under', or 'The Wedding Glide'.

Trev had stayed on in Oxford on postgraduate work, helping Aldous to adjust to the initial problems of University life when he had come up in October 1913. Thus it was not until this autumn of 1913 that Trev sat for the Civil Service examination. His father later wrote of Trevenen's 'brilliant promise . . . on the verge of more brilliant performance'; the 'Number 2' Huxley as he had called himself, had every reason to expect a high place. He was bitterly disappointed at the result. From the peak he went to the valley. Throughout the first months of 1914 he was attacked by desperate fits of melancholia, and by the time of Julian's return to England had been living for some weeks at the Hermitage, a small private nursing home in Surrey.

Trev had been over-working and over-worrying when the hopes which had kept his spirits high had been so unexpectedly quenched by the Civil Service results. Yet this was not his only trouble. Over-scrupulous, over-honest, over-sensitive, he submitted his personal relationships to the closest critical scrutiny, and about one he was unhappy. More than one member of the family knew the story, but his younger brother Aldous was thought to be unaware of it; yet he also, it later appeared, knew how Trev feared that he might have compromised one of his women friends. This worry, grotesquely exaggerated, had combined with disappointment to produce its own kind of nervous breakdown 'from too much work and nerve strain, carrying other people's worries as well as his own', according to his father. Yet throughout the summer Trev had responded to treatment at Dr Abbott's Surrey nursing home. He accepted an appointment in a

Labour Bureau, and arranged to leave Surrey for London on the morning of Monday, 17 August 1914. On the afternoon of the 15th he exchanged a few words with one of the nurses at the Hermitage. He seemed to be cheerful and set off for a walk along the surrounding Downs. When he failed to return, the police were informed, but no trace of him could be found, either that evening or on the Sunday.

Leonard came south from Scotland where the family was holidaying on the shores of Loch Etive. The search was continued, without success, for seven days. It was not until the following week-end that a telegram went north with the words: 'Worst fears realized.' Trev had been found in a wood only a few hundred yards from the Hermitage. He had apparently jumped from a tree, fourteen feet up, having tied a rope round his neck. The rope had snapped but his neck was broken. A letter and a postcard found in a coat lying about a yard away 'disclosed no reason', according to the coroner, 'why the deceased should do away with himself'. Dr Abbott, giving evidence in the coroner's court, said that the patient had never at any time hinted that he was likely to take his life. Nevertheless, the coroner brought in the only conceivable verdict – suicide while temporarily insane.

> There is – apart from the sheer grief of the loss – an added pain in the cynicism of the situation [Aldous wrote to his cousin Gervas]. It is just the highest and best in Trev – his ideals – which have driven him to his death, while there are thousands who shelter their weakness from the same fate by a cynical, unidealistic outlook on life. Trev was not strong, but he had the courage to face life with ideals – and his ideals were too much for him.

Chapter VII

The First World War

For the Huxleys the outbreak of the First World War emphasized the break with the previous century which had come earlier in the year when Henrietta, TH's widow, had died in her Eastbourne home. To the end she combined a bird-like gaiety with an intellectual curiosity and an undiminished interest in the arts; by coincidence *The English Review* published one of her last poems almost on the day of her death. She was small and confident, and knew how steadfast support of her husband half a century previously had helped to change man's knowledge of the world in which he lived. The picture of her that remained with many of the family was of a small silhouette against the blue sea which so reminded her of life in Australia sixty years earlier.

Of her six surviving children the eldest, Jessie Waller, still remained in Gloucester. Rachel Eckersley was now settled in Lancashire. Nettie was still roving about the Continent and was to find herself caught in Prague by the outbreak of war; while Ethel Collier, mistress of North House for nearly a quarter of a century, 'The Dragon' who was 'The Grand-Dragon' to the younger generation, had become by general acceptance the one Huxley to whom all went for advice, for help, for consolation.

Of the two sons, Henry had by now established himself as one of London's favourite and most fashionable general practitioners, the epitome of the family doctor; Leonard, about to provide Balliol with a £160 endowment for a N. T. Huxley Fund in memory of Trev, was soon to become sole editor of the *Cornhill*. In 1910 he had met at a dance a young friend of the family, Rosalind Bruce, aged twenty-three, the daughter of William Wallace Bruce, a man who could trace back his ancestry to Robert Bruce and who had, as chairman of the London County Council's Housing and Financial Committee, been largely responsible for the demolition of the notorious Seven Dials slums and the building of the Aldwych that followed. Miss Bruce had met Leonard Huxley again. Their friendship had flourished and they had married in 1912.

After 1914 most of the Huxley grandchildren who had swelled the holiday numbers during the first years of the century, were quickly drawn into war work, Service or civilian. On the left of the line there was Noel Waller, the eldest son of TH's eldest daughter Jessie, who had succeeded his father as diocesan architect of Gloucester Cathedral and who was soon serving in the 5th Gloucesters.

In the Foreign Office were John Collier, his son Laurence, who had been recruited into the service after coming down from Balliol, and Roger Eckersley, the man 'with more charm than any human has a right to deserve', who had been left with a leg made useless by infantile paralysis. Both the elder Collier and Roger Eckersley worked in the deciphering department, where he later became, by picking up the right telegram at the right moment, the first man in Britain to hear of the Russian Revolution.

Of Roger Eckersley's brothers, Thomas was quickly in the army. He had been fascinated by wireless while still at Bedales and had filled the playroom of his London home with, as his brother Peter put it, 'lovely and exciting instruments. There were induction coils to make fat sparks, Leyden jars, long black rods of ebonite wound with green silk-covered wire, X-ray tubes and galvanometers.' Thomas had left Bedales for University College, London, and then Trinity College, Cambridge; had drifted naturally into the National Physical Laboratory, and after a short spell of survey work with the Egyptian Government had joined the Royal Engineers on the outbreak of war.

It was with the Engineers that the foundations of his fame were laid. He first helped to raise and train in England the No. 6 Pack Wireless Section, R.E., equipped with sets which were designed for use with horses or mules. Early in 1916, however, Eckersley and the unit were posted to Egypt and by May he had achieved esoteric fame, as commander of what is believed to have been the first camel-borne wireless section in the world. His spell with the Western Frontier Force of the Egyptian Expeditionary Force was brief and in July he was brought back to G.H.Q. As a specialist wireless officer he was then sent to Salonika, where his duties lay in wireless intelligence work, in attempting to pluck from the ether the garbled or coded messages transmitted by the Central Powers and if possible to locate their source. And it was during the course of this work that he noted two important phenomena – noting them, one feels, much as TH might have done, as interesting aspects of nature which might be investigated in detail when more leisure was available. One of these phenomena involved the deviation of radio waves when they passed from land to sea at a coastal boundary, an effect somewhat analogous to the refraction of light when it leaves one medium for another. This was interesting, but it was of far less significance to the future than Eckersley's second observation. This arose from his work on direction-finding, on attempting to pin down the source of intercepted radio-waves. Some results appeared incompatible with the known causes, and Eckersley 'invoked the existence of an upper ionized layer giving rise to a reflected wave with variable polarization characteristics'. He was thus, as *Nature* put it on his death, 'among the first to obtain evidence of the presence of the ionosphere by the reflection of radio-waves'.

While Thomas was thus beginning what was to be his life's work, his younger brother Peter was also entering the world of wireless. At Bedales, where he had followed Thomas, he was to be remembered as a boy of remarkable energy and individuality, 'the most casual, unpunctual, and untidy pupil of the school,' as one contemporary put it. 'He took pride in the fact that no other boy, before or since, received as many beatings, and it was part of his *panache* that he never cried.' He quickly became infected with his brother's enthusiasm for wireless, formed with another boy what the two called 'The Bedales Wireless Telegraphy Syndicate', and in Wavy Lodge, a hut built at the end of the hockey pitch, started a primitive transmitting station with the aid of 'a coil that would hardly shock a maiden aunt, and a slightly inebriated coherer'. On leaving Bedales Peter Eckersley was apprenticed to a firm of electrical engineers and was studying at Manchester University when war broke out.

He quickly joined the Royal Flying Corps as a Wireless Equipment Officer and for nearly four years helped to install, calibrate and maintain the primitive equipment then used in early aircraft. He was, moreover, to be the eye-witness of one historic event when, at Brooklands, he listened to a brother officer, Major C. E. Prince, speaking into a microphone as a simple plane of struts and wire flew above the track.

'Hullo, Furnival,' Prince called to the pilot. 'If you can hear me now it will be the first time speech has ever been communicated to an aeroplane in flight. Dip if you are hearing me.'

The aeroplane, lumbering along at fifty miles an hour, gave an obedient lurch.

Of Henry's three sons, only Gervas was old enough to join up on the outbreak of war. Aged just twenty, he travelled from his Yorkshire home to Hull, joined the East Yorkshires and by Christmas Eve 1914, was taking a draft to Flanders, having been sustained during his last day in London by Aldous, who had turned up unexpectedly to make himself useful in any way required. Gervas became battalion bombing officer, was brought to England for an eight months' spell of training, and returned to France for the years' agony of mud and blood that the Western Front became. Like his two brothers Michael and Christopher, who also joined the army, he was to survive; and on the first day of Passchendaele he earned a hard-won Military Cross by capturing prisoners whose presence showed that a freshly-arrived German Guards Division was facing that particular sector of the front.

Of Leonard's two surviving sons, Aldous was clearly barred from any form of military service by his poor sight, even though he for some while persistently refused to admit the fact. He returned to Balliol in the autumn of 1914 with the loss of Trev superimposed upon the death of his mother and on the descent of blindness which was lifting only partially, and with further threats. Not even the sympathy of his aunt, Mrs Humphry Ward, could staunch this latest wound. Most of his companions had departed for the war and had left him, for perhaps the first time in his life, with the feeling of being in the wrong place, a feeling only intensified as his peering lighthouse-shaped figure was rejected for military service at first one, then another and then another of the recruiting offices to which he applied.

He was left alone, on the rim of the sea. He 'never attended more than, at the outside, two lectures a week'. And he now began to search inward with a more critical and inquiring light.

> I have been interested in mysticism ever since I was an undergraduate [he wrote a quarter of a century later]. For some time the interest was predominantly negative; that is to say, I read a good deal of Western and Eastern writing, always with intense interest, but always with a wish to 'debunk' them. Later the interest became positive.

But the conscious development of this interest was to come only later still. When Aldous found himself ejected on to the world in 1916 with a First in English he was merely a box of heterogenous ideas, pushed this way and that by external circumstances. Subconsciously, he was already directed by a deeply felt need to understand and to explain, the longing to discern the total nature of reality which was subsequently to govern so much of his writing. Years later he recalled how he had tapped out his eighty thousand-word novel at the age of seventeen. 'After that,' he added, 'I think I decided that's what I wanted to do.' Oxford confirmed the decision.

On coming down in 1916 Aldous worked for a few months on the farm at Lady Ottoline Morrell's home, Garsington Manor. It was here that he first met Osbert Sitwell, who in *Laughter in the Next Room* describes how Aldous visited him in hospital.

Versed in every modern theory of science, politics, painting, literature and psychology, he was qualified by his disposition to deal in ideas and play with them. Nor would gossip or any matter of the day be beneath his notice: though even these lesser things would be treated as by a philosopher, with detachment and an utter want of prejudice. But he preferred to discourse on more erudite and impersonal scandals, such as the incestuous mating of melons, the elaborate love-making of lepidoptera, or the curious amorous habits of cuttle-fish. He would speak with obvious enjoyment, in a voice of great charm, unhurried, clear, without being loud, and utterly indifferent to any sensation he was making. Thus the most surprising statements would hover languidly in air heavy with hospital disinfectants. 'From his usual conduct,' I remember his announcing on one occasion, 'one must presume that every Octopus has read Ovid on Love.'

The attitude of Aldous Huxley during the war years was complex and can only be understood by those able and willing to think back to the context of the times. At first, like so many men, he had been eager to follow the example of such friends as Lewis Gielgud and relatives such as Gervas, who were soon serving on the Western Front. Slowly, as he began to appreciate the reality, as the influence of Garsington began to make itself felt, the glitter rubbed off and he began to view the war with much of the hatred which those in the fighting services felt for it. He was appalled by the casualty lists which named so many he had known at Oxford. He wrote to his brother Julian in the United States urging that he should not return to Britain to join up. Yet he did not – as those who knew him only two decades later might have expected – leap into the pacifist camp without reservations. As his future sister-in-law, Juliette, who knew him well at the time, was later to write, 'though he hated the war, Aldous felt he must do more for his country.'

Playing at agriculture was a mere half-pastime and he applied for Government work in London. At first he was offered a £2-a-week job in the Ministry of Munitions. He hung on for something better and eventually found his way into the War Office where, in his brother Julian's words, he got 'a good secretaryship' with the Air Board, then still under khaki control pending the formation of the Air Ministry. But his eyes were unable to stand the strain of close paperwork, and soon he took to schoolmastering. He went briefly to Repton and for a while was the colleague of Victor Gollancz and D. C. Somervell. Then he passed on to Eton, and spent the rest of the war trying to handle classes that included the future Lord David Cecil, Harold Acton and Christopher Hollis. It was here that Huxley became the original of Gumbril Junior who, in the first paragraph of *Antic Hay*,

> sat in his oaken stall on the north side of the School Chapel and wondered, as he listened through the uneasy silence of half a thousand schoolboys to the First Lesson, pondered, as he looked up at the vast window opposite, all blue and jaundiced and bloody with nineteenth-century glass, speculated in his rapid and rambling way about the existence and the nature of God.

Eton, revisited after seven years, was as dispiriting as ever. His sight, moreover, was so poor – although he cycled with relentless abandon through the streets of Windsor to the Great Park – that he still required a magnifying glass to read print, and his helplessness was eagerly seized upon by some of the boys. 'School-mastering,' as he wrote to his future sister-in-law, Juliette Baillot, was 'a profession for which I don't think I was specially suited.'

Aldous's brother Julian was meanwhile serving in Italy. He had gone back to Houston in the autumn of 1914 with J. I. Davies, a former laboratory assistant at Eton whom he had spotted as a potential scientist. His judgement was justified; for, having worked in the biological laboratory, Davies studied, took his degree, and eventually gained his professorship.

Life at Rice was radically different from life in Oxford, and back in England Huxley was later to write how 'now and again in London, with its restraints, its class-distinctions, its high pressure, its fog, its artificiality, I see mentally the prairie and feel the soft winds from the Gulf'. Eventually, he and Griffith Evans had joined with Arthur Hughes, Assistant Professor in Physics, in having a three-storeyed house built among the trees about a mile from the institute, Huxley sending home to England for a special wallpaper of flowers-and-bird design for his own rooms. Here the three bachelors lived in comparative luxury, with a man to tend the garden and his wife to cook for them. 'It was an invigorating walk in the morning out to the Institute along the street-car track,' Evans recalls. 'According to the student paper, the street-car service was always delayed by a cow or a professor on the track.'

Huxley had the double task of teaching the first Rice students and, at the same time, of building up the biological department. It was a full life spent in an environment which still had a sniff of the frontier about it, a country which Huxley set about exploring in a model-T Ford. He used it to continue his observations of that process which so strangely combined scientific utility and aesthetic enjoyment, the courting habits of birds, and on one occasion spent some time in the famous bird refuge on the McIlhenny estate in Louisiana. This visit brought him what remained, after half a century, one of his most memorable experiences. He was watching two herons sitting just within physical contact of one another.

> Upon some unascertainable cause the two birds raise their necks and wings, and, with loud cries, intertwine their necks [he reported later]. This is so remarkable a sight that the first time I witnessed it I did not fully credit it, and only after it had happened before my eyes on three or four separate occasions was I forced to admit it as a regular occurrence in their lives. The long necks are so flexible that they can and do make a complete single turn round each other – a real true-lover's knot. This once accomplished, each bird then – most wonderfully of all – runs its beak quickly and amorously through the just raised aigrettes of the other, again and again, nibbling and clappering them from base to tip. Of this I can only say that it seemed to bring such a pitch of emotion that I could have wished to be a Heron that I might experience it. This over, they would untwist their necks and subside once more into their usual quieter sentimentality.

In this part of America, travel was still difficult, and Huxley long remembered how he tried to drive from Houston to Austin, 150 miles away. 'The second day,' he recalled, 'I made twenty-eight miles and was eleven hours about it – and in a Ford, too!' At this time there were no 'stock-laws' in Texas – which meant that if you wanted to keep cattle from eating off your land it was your duty to keep them out, not their owners' duty to fence them in. 'Otherwise,' comments Evans, 'they and Julian's Ford were free to roam. He was likely to startle a companion by turning suddenly off the road, across the ditch and over the prairies to the far horizon.'

On one occasion he abandoned the car for a holiday in distant Wyoming, and spent some time among the Bighorn Mountains in a rich grassy valley which stretched down towards the barren Badlands three thousand feet below. He climbed Long's Peak. And he astonished his cowboy companions by piling three Horned Toad Lizards 'into a grotesque edifice of catalepsy-struck reptilian flesh', whose frozen immobility the cowboys were completely unable to understand. With Professor and Mrs Isanoff, he also went to Estes Park, Colorado, and with the so-called good luck that frequently comes from careful observation, he gained another memorable experience of watching birds.

> Our camp was among a grove of magnificent aspens, close by a

clear mountain river full of trout [he later wrote in *Bird Watching and Bird Behaviour*]; and in one of the aspens a pair of sapsuckers had made their nest. Sapsuckers are a kind of woodpecker, and like other woodpeckers they excavate their nests in the solid wood of tree-trunks and limbs.

The young were well-grown and sometimes used to climb up and peep out of the next hole to see if their parents were coming with food. I rigged up a camera in the tree with a string attached to the shutter, and got one or two photographs of both old and young birds. One morning as I lay there watching and making notes, one of the young birds came to the entrance, pushed his body farther out than he had ever done before, and set up a fearful shrill chirping. I wondered what was the matter; and then, at the end of a couple of minutes, he suddenly precipitated himself out of the nest, spread his wings, and waveringly, but quite adequately, made his way through the air to alight on the trunk of a neighbouring tree. What he had been excited about (and not at all unnaturally) was that he had been plucking up courage to launch himself on his very first flight. . . .

Such experiences confirmed and strengthened Huxley's interest in ornithology. But there were other experiences, other sights which added to his education in the United States. He was at Houston when Galveston Bay was struck by the second so-called tidal wave, and long remembered the almost measureless power of natural forces which the calamity revealed.

It was not an earthquake wave, it was a storm-wave [he later wrote]. It was a south wind which blew the very shallow waters of the Gulf of Mexico far inland, and actually steamers of over a thousand tons were dropped a mile inland and more.

And in the States Huxley felt, for the first time, the primitive promptings of race. It was in central Texas and he had arrived by car on market day in a little town whose streets were crowded almost wholly by negroes; there were hundreds of black men to tens of white.

I am bound to confess [he wrote in 'Racial Class' in the *Cornhill Magazine*] that this first experience of being in a small minority among human beings of another colour and another physical type gave me an emotional jolt; and I began, without any process of ratiocination, to understand why white men living in such circumstances generally took to carrying revolvers and developed a race-complex. One could doubtless get over such feelings; but the point is that they arose unbidden.

Life in the United States thus did more than broaden Huxley's biological experiences. It enabled him to regard the world and its peoples objectively. It made him realize, as he later put it, that

> all the familiar institutions and ideas of [his] own country were not the inevitable and permanent things that they had seemed (and that they seem all along to those who do not make themselves, or are not made to, reflect upon them) but relative, a product of time and place and circumstance interacting with a particular kind of human nature.

And it was while browsing in a library at Colorado Springs, beneath the shadow of Pike's Peak, that he came across an essay in which Lord Morley had written that 'the next great task of science will be to create a religion for humanity'. The words struck home with particular force. While still at Oxford Huxley had, he later wrote in *Essays of a Humanist*, become

> convinced of the necessity of extending the general theory of evolution to cover the manifestations and processes of human nature as well as those of nature in the customary sense; but at the same time of the folly, and indeed danger, of simply extrapolating biological principles into the human sphere.

Now, beneath Pike's Peak, Morley's words acted as a catalyst and Huxley's disparate ideas began to coalesce and to form the substance of what was to become scientific humanism, that religion without revelation which was to provide hope for many and also to bring down on Huxley's head the imprecations of being 'the great anti-Christ'.

These ideas were naturally to develop through the years. He was to expand and qualify. But the basic problem which he set out to solve has rarely been outlined more clearly than in the last of a series of lectures which he gave early in 1916 in the city auditorium at Houston. There were six lectures in all, dealing with various aspects of 'Biology and Man'; they were open to the public, and within a week of their conclusion Huxley had been asked to repeat them as part of what the local papers called a 'municipal lecture course'.

The final lecture dealt with biology and religion. The problem was, as Huxley put it,

> that new ideas, usually classed as scientific, have permeated a large section of the community and prevented them from belonging to any of the established churches, whose belief in miracles, in revelation, in the inspired authority of the Bible, runs counter to the established truth, as the scientifically trained see it. The problem is to make a

> religion for these men and women, whose numbers are bound to increase with the spread of education, and who will otherwise be left without a religion, or with one to which they cannot whole-heartedly give their assent. The conflict between religion and science in the last half-century resulted in the complete defeat of religion's claim to impose its view as authoritative on man's mind, but it did not build up anything for those whom it emancipated. That reconstruction is our problem today.

To that reconstruction Huxley was to devote a considerable part of his life. First, however, there was to be the experience of the war. He had felt it necessary to return to Houston in 1914, and had sailed confidently from a Britain where beliefs about the prevailing war were still of the 'over before Christmas' variety. With the early disasters, the mood changed; Huxley gained a year's leave of absence and came back across the Atlantic with the aim of joining what was then the Royal Hospital Corps.

He left America with memories of a young country basically different from anything he had known before – 'a new country which has no stable upper class, a boiling pie without its crust yet on', as he later described it. 'No one who has lived in the West but will remember with gratitude the raciness, the independence, the young hopefulness which sets off all the disadvantages of an immature civilization.' In Britain he was finally given a cadetship in the Army Service Corps, and in the spring of 1917 was in training at Aldershot where, as he put it in a letter to President Lovett,

> there's not much time to yourself after you have had eight hours' drill, riding, lectures and demonstrations, written up notes, cleaned your boots, buttons and spurs [he had been posted to a horse and not to a motor transport company as he had wanted], mended your clothes and made your bed.

He hoped to pass out with a commission within two months, after which he would be drafted abroad, although there seemed some doubt about seeing action since he expected the war to be over by the autumn. His plans for the future would then arise, and his views on these had swung round since his arrival back in England. When he had gone to Rice early in 1914 Huxley had expected to remain there some eight or ten years – until the new biological department was fully established; when he left the States to join up he fully intended to return. Now, however, he outlined a new position in a revealing letter to Lovett:

> I have at last made up my mind that in the circumstances I owe it

both to myself and Oxford to resign my position at Rice Institute. This sounds abrupt, but it is the result of a long process of thought and reflection. Perhaps before I say anything more I ought to give my bare reason. In the first place, when I was at Oxford (and this must for the present be confidential), Bourne, my old professor, asked me if I would consider the offer, if it were made to me after the War, of poor Geoffrey Smith's job (he was killed on the Somme), which means a Fellowship and Tutorship of New College, and a University appointment in the Museum. I said I would think it over. Now there are only five responsible positions in the Zoology Dept. at Oxford – five years ago those were all filled by good men; one was drowned before the war; two have been killed in France; and one of the few possible Oxford men at other Universities died of Spotted Fever in camp last year. To be plain, it will be hard to fill up the gaps from Oxford men and I am the first choice – I think by a pretty large margin.

From what I can gather, Oxford is apparently in a state of suspended animation, is really liquified – in the melting pot. Everybody wants some reform or other, everybody realizes that this is the time to work for it. . . . Well, if they want me and at this rather critical time, I feel my duty is probably there, apart from any question of inclination. Further, since I landed, I have come more and more to feel an Englishman, if you know what I mean – less of an internationalist. I suppose it is the War combined with the long absence from my country, but I feel an extraordinary sense of fitting in to London and Oxford, in life and work and friends, such as would be impossible in America – however long I lived there – however many friends I made, and if I am to make any contribution to thought, I must be in touch with the currents of thought, and the only current into which I can freely throw myself will be that of England. Curiously enough, since joining up and being thrown with all sorts and conditions of men, even if it be only for a fortnight, I have already a much stronger feeling of the same sort – that I *am* an Englishman, and can only attain to doing anything for the world as an individual by working as a member of the English community – my own particular 'group'.

Then there is the merely personal side – tho' through what I have just said, it dovetails into the other. I do not believe I shall ever do good work, let alone best work in Texas – nor is it the isolation (tho' that counts, as I think I must be one of those people who need much stimulus, and interchange of ideas, as I am more interested in general thought than in particular problems) – for it would be practically the same thing in New York or Boston. Finally comes health – I have been much fitter since I got back – going out at night a good deal, writing, doing a lot of general reading – and now able to stand what is really a very busy day (– tho' not without some effort still!).

The 'general reading' included a good deal of theology, since Huxley wished to see how much of it he could 'grasp in terms of the evolutionary-naturalistic scheme' at which he had arrived. He must therefore have been an unusual recruit, cogitating on religious and philosophical problems as he marched and counter-marched through the warm June nights on military exercises. As so often with the Huxleys, he saw reality as a whole, not boxed into separate compartments, so that religion and biology, philosophy and the day-to-day ordering of life, represented merely different aspects of one problem. Among his books was *Lux Mundi* in whose pages he read the famous essay on 'The Holy Spirit and Inspiration' by Bishop Gore, the Anglo-Catholic who in 1911 had followed Bishop Wilberforce's path to Cuddesdon and had exercised considerable influence over the religious life of the University. Gore had concluded that the humanity of Christ entailed certain limitations of consciousness and Huxley long considered the implications of this.

Such cogitations formed the tenuous background to life. He was eventually commissioned, posted to the Intelligence Corps, and sent to Italy where the Italians and the Austrians were closely locked on a mountain front whose battle-dangers were augmented by those of cold and gravity. Then, in the aftermath of the Armistice, he returned to England, hastening to a different sort of battle, anxious, as he put it, 'to buckle to and refurbish the very rusty equipment of my peace-time profession.'

The Huxleys' Place in Nature

Chapter IX

Julian: The Need to Inform

(i)

During the decade that followed the first world war it became clear that the partial eclipse of the Huxleys during the earlier years of the century had been purely temporary. Fame had skipped the first generation after TH but seemed unlikely to miss the second. This was not merely due to the genes, whose effects might be masked in one generation but which could still bustle along with their biological work in the next. There was also that new evolutionary mechanism of which Julian had written – the speech, books, writings and paintings by which man was 'able to put something of himself beyond death'. TH was in some ways an embodiment of this new mechanism in action. His nearness might have overawed his children but to his grandchildren his influence was decisive. There were rebels who tried to escape. But for most Huxleys who grew into adult life during the first half of the century it seemed natural to speak of 'Gran' pater' as though he might enter the room at any minute. His standards were their standards. 'Never forget you are a Huxley' had a regimental ring. And in most Huxley homes there was at least one portrait of TH in his prime, looking down in benevolent regard from the walls, metaphorically saluted at sun-up and sun-down like the Union flag, the *persona* of a past culture still influencing the present. He might not have believed in a soul but, as with John Brown, something went marching on.

There was much on which his influence could work. All the Huxleys, from Gervas with his three years' experience on the Western Front to Thomas Eckersley with his adventures in the Middle East, had survived the war unscathed. They were also lucky in a different way, for it was part of the family tradition that a Huxley should adapt himself quickly to fresh conditions, and in the new world that the war had created each was to find his own niche more quickly than many men. Each soon concentrated his ambitions and it was natural that Julian should emerge from the war knowing, with a certainty he had not achieved before, that 'for minds like mine in a civilization like ours, the only salvation must include constant work and activity, not by any means necessarily directed to immediate practical ends, but based on the conviction that it is bound up in some way and in the long run with practical results'.

It soon became clear that the purest strain of the essential Huxley spirit was being transmitted through Leonard, to Julian and Aldous Other descendants of that long line of brothers and sisters attained their own ambitions; few indeed failed to make of their careers what in any other family would have been lauded as success. Yet it was in the lives of Julian and his brother Aldous that the Huxley character was to be most clearly revealed and in their achievements that the point counterpoint of science and art, heightened by the contrasting Huxley and Arnold backgrounds, was to be most strikingly displayed.

On his demobilization Julian returned to find his father moved from the pre-war home in Bayswater to Bracknell Gardens, Hampstead, only half a mile or so from North House. These two centres were for years to be the accepted headquarters of the family. In reminiscence, their rulers have survived as rather contrasting characters. Leonard is remembered as quiet, unassuming, almost insubstantial, passing on to the next age what he had received from the one before. His sister Ethel, 'The Dragon' to one generation and 'The Grand-Dragon' to the next, ruled from North House with a firm hand and idiosyncratic charm, keeping at table three small china ornaments – a pig which was placed before anyone undisciplined enough to drop or spill food; a dormouse for those who made unexpectedly pleasing remarks; and an alligator for those who did the reverse. To her last days she kept up a great correspondence with most members of the family, and she financed the education of more than one. She was slightly feared, much loved, something of a family match-maker, and the impressive figure before whom potential brides or bridegrooms were paraded for approval. Her attitude was exemplified when she inspected Elizabeth Powell, engaged to Rupert Crawshay-Williams, the son of her step-daughter Joyce. 'You are marrying into one of the great atheist families,' she is remembered as warning. 'I know you are an atheist now; but will you be able to keep it up until you die?'

Leonard was by this time raising a second family of two sons, David Bruce born in 1915, and Andrew Fielding born in 1917. He was busy, industrious, content. At last he had found his métier. Reginald Smith, who had brought him to Smith, Elder's at the turn of the century, had died in 1916 and when the firm was acquired by John Murray the following year Leonard Huxley succeeded Smith as sole editor of the *Cornhill*. But he was not only editor. He contributed regularly – a brief story, poems, and a number of reminiscent articles on such men as Hooker, Darwin, Tyndall, and the Professor Lewis Campbell whose assistant he had been at St Andrews in the 1880s.

There was other literary work on which he was almost devoutly employed. The life of his father had been followed in 1918 by an equally massive biography of Sir Joseph Hooker – a work of no less quality. Its writing had presented almost the complete range of problems which can face a biographer and the extent of the available material had been not merely considerable but excessive. More than 700 sheets of letters to Darwin alone; the same number to his six next most regular correspondents; scientific essays, of which the first had been written at the age of nineteen, the last at ninety; a huge official correspondence; and regular weekly letters to his family which continued for nearly seventy years – all this was but part of the mountain of paper which Leonard and his wife sifted and collated and worked upon during the evenings and the week-ends at Hampstead. Much help came from the aged Lady Hooker, and on the title-page it is recorded that the book was 'based on the materials collected and arranged by Lady Hooker'. But the widow was a little cautious of allowing letters to pass beyond her personal control. And when these finally reached the Huxleys many of the most potentially important were that nightmare of biographers – letters written in fading ink, both horizontally and vertically, on both sides of thin transparent paper. When decipherment was complete, many letters were found to be undated, and for years Leonard kept on his desk, as he worked, a special form of perpetual calendar from which he could quickly tell the day of the week for any date during the previous half-century.

His life of Hooker, published in 1918, showed that the biography of TH had been no flash in the literary pan. It was clear that Leonard Huxley had that unusual mixture of qualities which enabled him to absorb a vast mass of material, to utilize directly essential letters or reports, to synthesize the rest, and to produce a 'life' which included all the necessary facts and figures without concealing the flavour of a man. And one result of *Hooker* was that Leonard was now approached by Mrs Tyndall. A quarter of a century earlier she and her husband had planned to write what they intended to call *Our Autobiography*, but after his death she felt unable to carry on alone. Helped along with her own drafts by many friends, she was unwilling to allow publication of anything – with the solitary exception of an article for the *Dictionary of National Biography* written mainly by herself. She continued to live on in the gaunt Hindhead house where the fatal dose had been given, and she considered one project after another for further aid with her work. For a while she relied on Dr Heinrich Debus, whom Tyndall had known at Marburg more than half a century earlier, and at one point offered to buy him a house at Hindhead so that he could work on the documents. Debus died in 1915, and after the end of the First World War plans for 'the life' were revived. Then came publication of Leonard's biography of Hooker. Huxley, Hooker and Tyndall had been the three splendid scientific musketeers of the previous century, and it seemed natural that the last of the three widows should now call in the biographer of two of them.

Leonard was distressed at Mrs Tyndall's lack of method. With the knowledge of what was involved, he felt that the biography would be beyond Mrs Tyndall's powers; and he was now persuaded by Sir Francis Darwin, son of Charles, and by other mutual friends, to propose that he himself should tackle the work. At first Mrs Tyndall welcomed the idea. Then difficulties arose. First she insisted that the choice of material should be hers alone. In addition, she harboured a natural if somewhat inflated idea of the danger to which the precious documents would be subjected were they moved from the Hindhead home. It would therefore be necessary for Leonard to work there during the week-ends, deciphering a mass of papers almost as great as those accumulated by Hooker. Discussions and talks spread through the 1920s with Mrs Tyndall obviously anxious that Huxley should write the book, and as obviously insistent on impossible conditions. The matter was still unsettled when Leonard died in 1933. The reason for vacillation only became clear when Mrs Tyndall, in great despair, visited Mrs Huxley. Considerably older, she had expected to die before Leonard, and had hoped that he would then write the book. As it was, she lived on for another seven years, and only then was work started by Professor A. S. Eve and C. H. Creasey on the *Life and Work of John Tyndall* which finally appeared in 1945.

Thus the long and abortive discussions ended in disappointment. It would have been a fine thing to have completed the biographical trilogy of Huxley, Hooker and Tyndall. However, the two set-piece works by which Leonard Huxley is mainly remembered were no more than the background to his other literary interests. He was, in some ways, a practised journeyman writer, producing his able poems; editing without fuss Jane Welsh Carlyle's letters to her family, and Elizabeth Barrett Browning's letters to her sister. He was deft at producing the finished article, in the form required, on time. All this was admirable. Yet it failed in some degree to show that synthesizing ability which was the scientific reflection of Arnold's injunction to see the world steadily and see it whole; that facility which TH had epitomized in his phrase about science and art being not two things but merely different aspects of one. This non-appearance of the native Huxley characteristics may well have been due to the lasting effects of a youth lived within the shadow of the great man himself, an experience during which even the best of work or thought was apt to be set in possibly discouraging perspective.

This was unfortunate since it is quite clear that below the surface there coursed in Leonard's mind the same stream which had been responsible for so much of TH's philosophy. The fact is shown most clearly in a paragraph from the centenary appreciation of Darwin which he wrote for the *Cornhill* and which illustrates in striking form the beliefs which he helped to pass down the Huxley line:

> Unreason in every form is the enemy of scientific method, and the victory of science which we associate with the name of Darwin means the gradual banishment of unnumbered bogeys and fanciful superstitions, offspring of strong sensibilities and false reasoning. With these, also, go many fancies and myths and fairy tales, which survived to form a beautiful if misty background to everyday thought. Is it then true, as the lovers of the day before yesterday deplore, that the march of evolutionary science has robbed the world of its illusions, its beauty, its aspirations, and given in their stead naked fact, mechanical order, pedestrian reason? It is true, rather, that each new ideal, each new generalization, pushes out the old, ruthlessly tearing the fair fabric of imagery and allegory which drapes it round. Man cannot live without some ideal, any more than he can live without some sense of beauty: but it is with the ideal as with beauty, for beauty does not rest in untruth, nor is the loveliness of a landscape less appreciated by reason of a knowledge of perspective. The knowledge which destroys false beauties enthrones new ones, while it brings certain desirable and ideal conditions nearer present realization.

This was the simple essence of TH, but while Leonard merely restated it in persuasive prose, the Huxleys of succeeding generations were to spend much of their lives on developing the central conundrum and in seeking answers to the questions which then arose; after trying to pin down man's place in nature they began asking what man was going to do about it. As scientists, writers, administrators, they became bound up in an almost corporate fashion with the practical applications of the most recently discovered facts of evolution; with the shadowy borderline between mind and matter; with the problem of what man should do with his natural environment and his natural resources; and, over-topping all, with the problem of what basic beliefs should govern his actions. These were the subjects which splayed out across the twentieth century; wherever they were discussed there was sure to be at least one Huxley ready with his specialized knowledge, and there might well be more than one.

Among the most formidable was Julian. For while TH had helped to shrink man into a molecule of cosmic dust, his grandson was now stressing the singularity, indeed the uniqueness, of the molecule.

(ii)

In 1919 Julian Huxley returned to Oxford as he had hoped to do, a Fellow of New College and Senior University Demonstrator in Zoology. He prepared to 'buckle to'. But first of all he married; and in doing so he illustrated what from the time of TH onwards has been a marked trait in the family – an ability to pick the right wife: the woman who would be most suited to share the frustrations of working lives that have rarely been calm and have frequently been tempestuous.

It was at Lady Ottoline Morrell's Garsington Manor, set on the high ground some four miles south of Oxford and looking across a green bowl of country towards Cuddesdon Palace, that Julian first met Marie Juliette Baillot. She came from solid Swiss stock in Neuchâtel, the little town which had been the centre of the watch-making industry since the beginning of the eighteenth century. Her father was a lawyer whose partner had decamped, who had refused to accept bankruptcy as a result, and whose family had thereafter spent a good deal of their lives in wiping out what they considered to be a moral debt. One of her aunts had lived in Britain since the start of the century, and from the age of sixteen Juliette had acted as family courier, accompanying aged relatives across the Channel and then returning alone to Switzerland – a foretaste of the able way in which she was to handle her branch of the Huxley family.

When her father had died in 1914 Juliette, still in her teens, decided to combine part-time studentship with work, and applied to a London agency. The first post she was offered was at Garsington Manor where Lady Ottoline, 'a character of Elizabethan extravagance and force, at once mystical and possessive, quixotic and tempestuous,' as Lord David Cecil has described her, required a governess-companion for her eight-year-old daughter. Somewhat diffident, utterly self-possessed, the fair young Swiss had been seized upon by Lady Ottoline and quickly drawn into the intellectual Garsington circle which included Bertrand Russell, Lytton Strachey, the D. H. Lawrences, Vanessa Bell, Virginia Woolf and Maynard Keynes.

The circle was also to include Aldous Huxley, of whom Juliette quickly became a confidante. And into it there came, on his way to the war in 1916, Aldous's brother Julian.

'I was amazed at their difference,' Juliette has written, '. . . Julian ebullient, forthcoming, putting himself out to entertain; Aldous reticent, gentle, often remote; but both with innate gifts of high-powered intellect and imagination.' Julian followed up this first meeting with letters from Italy. On demobilization and return to England early in 1919 he immediately went north to Callander, where Juliette Baillot was now in charge of the three small daughters of the Ranee of Sarawak, formerly Sylvia Brett, sister of an old Garsington friend. They were engaged at once and married in March. Aldous was best man.

Julian and Juliette – the 'very attractive and sympathetic bride whom we have all taken to our hearts' as Leonard put it – first settled in lodgings at 50 High Street, Oxford. They moved after a term to Postmaster's Hall in Merton Street, and here Juliette did her best to emulate the Garsington furnishing scheme with bright yellow curtains and gaily painted furniture. The results were excellent but short-lived. Merton, the landlords, needed Postmaster's Hall and the Huxleys were forced to move, this time to a house in Holywell Street; a house remembered as one where the door was always open and undergraduates endlessly climbed the stairs for tutorials.

From the autumn of 1919 Julian settled down in Oxford to the work which was to make him famous.

> There are two ways of living [he once wrote]; a man may be casual and simply exist, or constructive and deliberately try to do something with his life. The constructive idea implies constructiveness not only about one's own life, but about that of society, and the future possibilities of humanity.

It was not surprising, therefore, that his work during the next few years was to spill over in numerous directions from the purely biological research to which he devoted so much of his time. This research provided the essential foundation for his reputation as a biologist. But just as TH had found that the championship or evolution led him inexorably on towards a criticism of religion and ethics, so did Julian find that his own study of biology led not only towards a new assessment of religion but also towards a study of the ways in which science might be applied to social problems.

Another similarity between grandfather and grandson lay in their common belief that a scientist's work was part of the world's work, and that it should be explained to laymen whenever this was possible. Julian demonstrated this belief shortly after he had recommenced work at Oxford.

The occasion was produced by experiments on the axolotl, an amphibian somewhat like a salamander which retains for the whole of its life the gills and other residues of its early tadpole state. The axolotl's metamorphosis from aquatic tadpole to terrestrial salamander is never completed and it is therefore true to say that the animal 'never grows up' – although this is not true of the earlier forms from which it has evolved over the millennia. Now it was well-known in 1919 that the metamorphosis of frog tadpoles into froglets could be speeded up by the use of mammalian thyroid gland, or thyroid extract; could thyroid be used, Huxley asked himself, not merely to speed up a process which would take place anyway but to initiate one which, in the case of the axolotl, would not normally take place at all. Would it be possible to make an 'artificial animal' by the use of thyroid – an animal whose physical metamorphosis would have been directly conditioned by the use of a chemical? Work began in the Oxford laboratory on 30 November 1919, with Huxley and a colleague feeding two five-inch-long axolotls on a diet of ox thyroid. Within fifteen days the animals had begun to change in colour, and their gills and fins were already being absorbed into their bodies. Four days later one of them was taken from the water and had no difficulty in walking on dry land. The experiment had quickly shown that thyroid could, in fact, induce artificial metamorphosis.

The experiment had been a success, and Huxley wrote a brief note which was published in *Nature* on 1 January 1920 – a note which was to excite that most imaginative of animals, the British Press in search of a headline. In this case the Press did not have far to search, and Huxley soon found himself the centre of news. 'Young British Scientist Finds Elixir of Life' was the story, and it was with more understanding than is sometimes shown on such occasions that Huxley pointed out that no elixir of life had been discovered, and then went on to explain, in simple terms that the layman could understand, what all the fuss was about.

In the early 1920s it was unusual for the professional scientist, hooked up on a headline, to do more than struggle to escape. Huxley did the reverse. He outlined to reporters the significance of the work within its scientific context. And to the paper which had published the first of the sensational reports he wrote a long explanatory letter, pointing out that the experiments had not yet been worked out in any way which could apply to human beings:

> It cannot be too strongly insisted upon that the phenomena of life are so complicated that no amount of theoretical prediction can take the place of experiment. By experiment, and by experiment alone, can we hope to pierce further into these secrets of life. If the public wants to know the answer to these, and similar questions, if the nation thinks them of importance, they must be prepared to set aside a definite proportion of the country's manpower in the form of research workers, and of its income in the form of research grants for apparatus and upkeep, in order that the problems may be investigated in the patient way which alone can be of permanent value.

There is an interesting footnote to the episode. For after the excitement, while Huxley was making further researches, he found that a similar set of experiments had been carried out some years previously by a Czech biologist; the results, moreover, had been published, but they had been overlooked in the upheavals of the war – a case curiously reminiscent of Gregor Mendel's early experiments on heredity whose results were 'lost' for almost half a century. In this case the outcome was to be wholly good. For had the earlier work been publicized Huxley would have been unlikely to repeat it; and, had the axolotl story never provided the morning newspaper readers with a gasp of surprise, Huxley might not have discovered, so early, his ability to explain the simple facts of science to the layman.

The experiments had barely ended when he was presented with one of those magnificent opportunities which offer scientific research and the tingle of adventure, both intellectual exercise and the physical challenge of living in difficult country. When it was suggested in Oxford that a University scientific expedition should visit Spitsbergen in the summer of 1921, Julian Huxley, Senior Demonstrator in Zoology, was naturally selected as a member of the party; he was also brought on to the executive committee which planned the enterprise from the autumn of 1920 onwards. The members of the expedition, led by the veteran ornithologist, the Reverend F. C. R. Jourdain, included an extraordinary galaxy of talent. Huxley and Carr-Saunders were among the biologists; N. E. Odell and R. W. Segnit were the geologists, while Tom Longstaff came as combined ornithologist and geographer; the expedition also included Charles Elton, later the doyen of animal population studies, and Seton Gordon as bird photographer.

Huxley sailed for Norway in June, leaving to his wife the care not only of his year-old son, Anthony, but also of the axolotls, the frogs and the *Gammarus* which formed some of the raw material of his research. Juliette had begun a part-time course in biology in the University – although forced to give it up when her first child was expected – and was already typing many of her husband's MSS and papers. The new job was very different. 'I still remember having to go down, sometimes at midnight, to the Museum, a large Gothic place, and having to fish about in the tanks to find the frogs, and then to separate them if they were about to mate,' she says.

Julian was by now observing colour mutations in the eyes of little crustacean *Gammarus chevreuxi*, and studying the histology and development of the eye in the various mutant types by comparison with the normal. 'One of the things I had to do while he was away,' says Juliette, 'was to look for the colour in the eyes; I didn't realize then that this developed only after some weeks. If I had, we might have made an important discovery.'

While Juliette was thus minding the biological stock-in-trade, her husband arrived in Tromsö with the ornithological members of the expedition. Shortly afterwards the party left in the *Terningen* for Bear Island where a week was spent on mixed scientific work. Then they sailed to Spitsbergen, landing at Advent Bay, where Huxley was responsible for fixing a number of experimental rafts, to be inspected on their return. Work at the Plymouth Marine Biological Laboratory had shown that some marine vertebrate animals grew mainly in winter, others mainly in summer, and it was believed that in the cold of the Arctic life would be prolonged, growth retarded.

> The method of testing [Huxley explained] is to put out freshly built rafts early in the season, at a time when the minute free-swimming larvae of most common marine animals are abundant. Some of these settle upon the rafts which are then examined at intervals, and specimens removed from them. And so, comparing the rates of growth of common marine invertebrates at Plymouth and in Spitsbergen, it is hoped to arrive at results of very general biological interest.

After the rafts had been built, the party set off up the west coast of Prince Charles Foreland, the sixty-mile-long island to the west of Spitsbergen itself. Here Huxley, Elton, Summerhayes, and R. W. Segnit were landed; they established a camp on the shores of Richard Lagoon and then watched the *Terningen* sail north again, leaving them less than seven hundred miles from the Pole for what was to be eleven days' isolation.

Huxley's work during this major portion of the Spitsbergen expedition was a detailed study of the courtship of the Red-throated Diver which collected for a brief nesting and mating period on a part of the island – a further entry on the subject which he had begun to make his own with the Crested Grebe almost a decade earlier. The observations on what he christened the plesiosaur race, on the beak-dipping ceremony and on the extraordinary dives from which the birds would emerge close to one another in an almost vertical position with 'the whole white undersurface . . . exposed to view, the bird seeming almost to stand on its tail in the water, and then slowly settling down to a sitting position', added fresh details to a corner of the map of bird behaviour. Yet on his return to Britain it was not only his purely scientific work that Huxley wrote about; he also described his impressions of Spitsbergen and, by implication, the effect on him of this land which he had first seen in the thin primrose twilight as he climbed up into the crow's-nest of the *Terningen* with Tom Longstaff. On one occasion he and a companion made a tough fifteen-hour journey, first by heavy open boat and then on foot, to reach the great cliff bastion more than a mile long and 2,000 feet high at the northern end of Prince Charles Foreland.

> When we were still nearly two miles away we began to hear the birds [he wrote in *The Times*]; and by the time we were half a mile off, the noise was like the parrot-house at the Zoo heard from just outside. The chattering and screaming of hundreds of birds blended into one continuous high-pitched roar. Though it was 11 p.m. when we at last reached the foot of the cliff, the midnight sun made bright daylight, and there was no abatement of the birds' activity. Innumerable kittiwakes, guillemots and razor-bills, with a sprinkling of puffins, crowded the cliff-face, and, near the top, colonies of the huge and predaceous glaucous gulls, the robber barons of the Arctic bird-world. Against this background of deafening noise, hundreds of tiny winged specks whirred into the high ledges for food, whirred out again to fish for more. It was an amazing concentration of vital activity . . .

Exhausted by their journey the two men rested and studied the astonishing scene.

> I lay down on the grass and, though less than seven hundred miles from the Pole, was able to rest the better part of an hour in perfect comfort, so windless and balmy was the air, tempered by the midnight sun. The birds' clamour filled the place; their forms shot to and fro at every level, up to nearly half a mile above my head, hundreds

every minute. It was a complete revelation of the abundance of nature and her unconcern with man on this uninhabited Arctic island.

Reading Huxley's articles on Spitsbergen, it is easy to see how natural it was that his biological work, as it developed after his return from the expedition, should cover three separate but overlapping fields. There was first, and scientifically the most important, the 'pure' research whose results he described in *Nature*, in ornithological and other scientific journals and in two major books. There were his writings aimed at the layman, scientific writings which were understandable to the educated minority even though it barely comprehended the language of science. And there was also his advocacy that biology should be considered as a subject whose implications overflowed into most of the activities of mankind. As he said when speaking on 'Biology and Society':

> It is the only link, for instance, between the sciences of matter – that is, physics and chemistry – and the science of mind – that is, psychology. Both aspects are inextricably entangled in biology. Your animal from one point of view is a chemical machine, from another it is a being with a mind. Both views are in their degree true.

Biology as a link not merely between matter and mind but also between the Humanities and Science, was a leading theme in a remarkable but little-known series of three lectures given by Huxley under the general title *The Outlook in Biology* when he visited the Rice Institute in 1924. In these he explained how the subject had outgrown its earlier birds-and-beasts limitations and now provided both the framework within which man could manage or mismanage his planet, and the foundation on which he could build a philosophy. There lay, in the lectures, the seeds of many ideas that Huxley was to develop in later years. They formed a remarkable *tour de force* and added to the impression that by the mid-1920s, Oxford's Senior Demonstrator in Zoology, still under forty, was becoming a force to be reckoned with.

Of Huxley's purely scientific work during this period the most important was that on relative growth. For most of man's life his form changes but little; the same, however, is not true of the majority of living organisms and Huxley first came up against the fact when he found it necessary to establish, in the course of certain experiments, the 'normal' form of the male and the female crab. The male presented no problems; with the female, however, the ratio between the breadth of the abdomen and the breadth of the whole crab becomes constantly larger as the animal grows older. 'In other words,' Huxley has said, 'the female of the common shore-crab has no fixed form, no constant proportion which one can speak of as typical or adult.' When the fact was pushed on to his attention, two questions at once presented themselves. The first was the ubiquitous 'why?'. The second asked whether such relative growth could be expressed quantitatively by an empirical formula. The work involved in arriving at the answers was to occupy much of Huxley's time during the next few years.

One of his first successes came at the Marine Biological Laboratory at Wood's Hole, in the United States. His subject was the curious fiddler crab whose males have one claw which, throughout life, grows progressively larger than the other – until, late in life, the single chela, or claw, may weigh twice as much as the rest of the crab. At Wood's Hole, Huxley weighed 400 of the male crabs and, at the same time, noted the weight of their larger claws. The results were as he had expected and hoped, for there was a constant relationship between the two figures for each specimen.

> I was here able to find [he later said] a definite mathematical expression relating the weights of the claws and the rest of the body. The two behaved like two sums of money put out at two different rates of compound interest; in other words, the *ratio* of their growth rates was a constant.

This was basically different from the methods of dealing with growth-rate evolved by d'Arcy Thompson whose *On Growth and Form* was then the standard work. Thompson's was essentially a 'simple interest' method, and while Huxley's methods were less comprehensive they were, as Thompson's daughter-biographer has said, 'much more usable and informative and . . . were widely taken up from the moment they were described.'

The work at Wood's Hole was merely a beginning. It was followed by comparable investigations on deer, familiar animals whose problems of relative growth are visible to many laymen. For while male deer shed their antlers every year, new antlers grow at a different pace from the rest of the animal. If a 200-pound deer has 4-pound antlers, a doubling of the animal's weight might produce not 8-pound antlers but 12- or 16-pounders. In this case, as in the previous one, Huxley resorted to personal experiment, weighing more than 250 pairs of antlers from the famous herd of Warnham Red Deer in the grounds of Warnham Park near Horsham, Sussex and comparing them, whenever possible, with the weights of the animals concerned. Later he appealed in *The Field* for further information, and eventually obtained figures for a total of more than 500 animals. As with the crabs, the figures could be explained in the simple terms of a constant differential growth-rate.

All this material, and much more, was included in *Problems of Relative Growth*, Huxley's first major scientific treatise. It was to be followed two years later, in 1934, by an equally important volume *The Elements of Experimental Embryology*, written in collaboration with Professor (later Sir) Gavin de Beer and describing the results of experimental attack on that riddle of philosophers and scientists down the ages – how it comes about that a multitudinous assembly of differently formed and differently functioning organs grow from the simple collection of similar cells in the egg.

These two volumes firmly secured Huxley's reputation as an experimental biologist. Both *The Individual in the Animal Kingdom* and his later *Essays of a Biologist* had shown him to be deeply involved in the philosophical implications of his own specialist discipline; now he established what his position was within that discipline. The demonstration came at a fortuitous moment, for by the early 1930s Huxley's fame was steadily becoming that of a popular expositor; the two stout volumes on relative growth and embryology helped to restore the balance.

(*iii*)

In 1925 Julian Huxley was thirty-eight. He was married. He had two sons, Anthony aged five and Francis aged three. The Linacre Professor in the University Museum, E. S. Goodrich, would presumably remain there for years, and the prospects for an ambitious man were slight. In 1925 Huxley therefore accepted the Chair of Zoology at King's College, London. It was to be merely the first of two moves made in quick succession. For in 1927 biologists were, as *Nature* put it, surprised to learn that Huxley was to resign from the Chair after only two years' tenure. He was to retain his laboratory at King's College as an honorary lecturer, but would drop routine day-to-day work and devote himself entirely to writing and research. This implied, *Nature* commented, that an increasing number of those interested both in pursuing knowledge, and in teaching, were now 'able to make a livelihood without lecturing to students in a college or university'. It called Huxley's move a courageous venture, but it pointed out that a new situation was being created 'with regard to the purveyors of knowledge and their relation to the academic institutions, a situation which all who are

Two of the sons of the United States Ambassador, Mr Joseph Kennedy, at the opening of the Children's Zoo in London. Bobby and Professor Huxley watch while Teddy cuts the tape

Julian Huxley defending his policy at the Zoo, 1942

The B.B.C. 'Brains Trust' team discussing the next session over lunch during the Second World War. *Left to right:* question master Donald McCullough, Professor C. E. M. Joad, Julian Huxley and producer Howard Thomas concerned with the spread of knowledge will do well to examine thoroughly'.

This most dangerous of all decisions for a man approaching middle age, the decision to toss security overboard in order to expound his own chosen subjects, marked a change of emphasis in Huxley's work oddly similar to that which had taken place in both his grandfather's and his father's lives. For TH had found himself, in his middle forties, gradually swung out from pure science into the fields of religion and ethics; Leonard had discovered, only at the age of about forty, that his real interests lay beyond schoolmastering. And now Julian realized that biology was merely his main interest around which so many others clustered. Thus the process of evolution, which the Huxleys had always appreciated as so central to existence, was to be strangely illustrated by their own lives in three successive generations.

All such decisions to cut the painter result from many varying forces and those which moved Huxley were no less complex than most. Ambitions, beliefs, ancestry, all played their part, but in this case it would seem difficult to over-emphasize the ancestry. For in the background there stood the towering figure of TH, general on an earlier scientific field, deploying his forces as he wished, commanding many, influencing all. With his working-men's lectures he had sown in a new field an awareness of what science meant. Through the London School Board he had hammered away at the idea that science and the humanities should go forward together rather than waste their energies on unnecessary and artificial battles. And with his books and his essays he had provided ample ammunition for the battles that did have to be fought. What more encouragement could a grandson want were he tempted to embark on a similar course of exposition?

Thus, with the example of his grandfather before him, Julian had by the end of 1927 hoisted himself into a position from which he could devote a great deal of his time to disseminating his own ideas as writer, as lecturer and as a speaker in the expanding field of broadcasting.

The work was demanding, the prospects at times precarious, although Huxley was lucky in having two supports of great aid to any such freelance operator. One was a small academic income, the other was a wife both able and willing to bear with the frustrations of a life in which the contrasting success and disappointment of the writer was mixed with the steady application of the scientist.

Huxley's variety of interests, combined with his inability to resist new and exciting ventures, left little time for family affairs. His sons were to remember every country walk with him as an exhilarating event – during which the elder was to be drawn into his father's botanical field, the younger into the zoological. Yet time was scarce, there was always much to be fitted in, and there was frequently a father who returned home, as TH had so often done, merely to work behind closed doors.

There were to be long-term compensations in this. For almost a century most Huxleys had been reared within the shadow of TH, standard-bearers of a tradition which had, as Julian had outlined it in *Religion Without Revelation*, a

> implications of high but hard thinking, plain but fiery living, wide intellectual interest and constant intellectual achievement, great outspokenness and moral courage, and, back of all, [a] sense of the ultimateness and supreme value of truth and goodness.

In itself this was demanding enough. Yet more than one Huxley father had utilized this tradition as a press to force from each individual the same standards of achievement which TH had attained. Julian's sons escaped the full rigours of this added pressure.

The first of the major popular works on which Huxley had embarked was *The Science of Life*, begun with H. G. Wells and the latter's son in 1925. Five years previously, Wells had published *The Outline of History*, a synoptic look at the rise and fall of civilizations from the earliest times to the twentieth century. There was a great need for the book, even though, as Huxley subsequently said, 'the average man can read history without floundering in technical terms'. How much greater, therefore, was the need for a biological counterpart to the Wellsian history, dealing with sciences whose very vocabulary was almost unknown even to the majority of generally informed readers. There were other reasons which increased the need. Since the early years of the century, when the significance of Mendel's work had been realized, there had been a constantly growing understanding of the mechanisms of heredity – and, with it, a growing appreciation of the biological basis of so many human endeavours. Now, for the first time, it was becoming possible to breed plants or animals which had particular qualities – cattle as milkers rather than stock; pigs which were fat in the right places; corn which was resistant to certain specific diseases. The biochemists, moreover, were now probing farther into what for the nineteenth century had been mere metaphysical speculation – the relationship between mind and matter. In addition, as the authors of *The Science of Life* wrote in their introduction, much new and exciting material being revealed almost monthly was imperfectly accessible to ordinary busy people.

> It is embodied in scientific publications, in a multitude of books; it

> is expressed in technical terms that still have to be translated into ordinary language; it is mixed up with masses of controversial matter, and with unsound and pretentious publications. . . . Obscuring the facts of heredity there are heavy accumulations of prejudice and superstition. In the care of his health and the conduct of his life, the ordinary man, therefore, draws far less confidently upon the resources of science than he might do. He is unavoidably ignorant of much that is established and reasonably suspicious of much that he hears. He seems to need the same clearing up and simplifying of the science of life that 'The Outline of History' and its associates and successors have given to the story of the past.

The Science of Life attempted to meet this need, to describe life, of which the reader was a part; to state what was surely known about it, discuss what was conjectured, and draw from the account as much practical wisdom as could be drawn. In view of its position as to 'popularization', open to technical criticism, the book enjoyed an astonishing reception, the reviewers in *Nature* recording their appreciation of the 'remarkably successful presentation of the essentials of biology' and referring only in passing to the fact that their pleasure in reading it had 'been occasionally interrupted by finding a crumpled rose-leaf'.

However, Huxley's ideas were not concerned solely with biology. They might initially have sprung from his work as a biologist but they were conditioned and directed by the purely religious beliefs which had grown simultaneously with his work. The building of his religious framework had really started on that day beneath Pike's Peak when he had come across Lord Morley's prognostication that 'the next great task of science will be to create a religion for humanity'. Here was fitting work for TH's grandson. For, though there need be no basic conflict between science and religion, it was yet true that the work of Darwin, of TH and of their fellow thinkers, had all helped to release flood-waters which had swept away the contemporary gods. Something was needed to replace them and it was right that the task should fall largely to one who believed that 'while the practical task of science is to provide man with new knowledge and increased powers of control, the practical task of religion is to help man to decide how he shall use that knowledge and those powers'.

This work had been taken up by Huxley two or three years after the war when he had been asked to write a paper on science and religion for a summer school at Woodbrooke. 'I was, through having undertaken the task,' he confesses, 'forced to hammer at my difficulties, to think out conclusions, to find where loose threads would connect, to examine what I really did mean by this or that casually-used term.' The result was a paper which appeared in 1923 in *Essays of a Biologist* and was followed four years later by a full exposition of his views in *Religion Without Revelation.*

The key to this book in which was deployed so much of his humanist faith lay not so much in its emphasis on the situation produced by the Darwinian revolution – a situation in which the theological edifice would no longer bear the weight of the universe – as in its emphasis that the situation held out great opportunities.

> The 19th century [Huxley had already pointed out in what had developed into *Science, Religion and Human Nature*] has shown, or so many of us believe, that a whole spawn of monstrous ideas about religion – verbal inspiration, eternal damnation, magical efficacy of prayer, or formula or rite, miraculous intervention, and the like – have no validity in themselves, and indeed are none of them vital to any true religion.
>
> Religion in the light of science is seen not as a divine revelation, but as a function of human nature. It is a very peculiar and very complicated function of human nature, sometimes noble, sometimes hateful, sometimes intensely valuable, sometimes a bar to individual or social progress. But it is no more and no less a function of human nature than fighting or falling in love, than law or literature.

It was, moreover, now possible to develop as a religion – one defined by Huxley as 'the reaction of the personality as a whole to its experience of the Universe as a whole' – an ideas-system based on humanism, that word which came in the year of the Huxley–Wilberforce encounter to mean 'the religion of humanity'. A humanist as defined in these circumstances was someone.

> who believes that man is just as much a natural phenomenon as an animal or a plant, that his body, his mind, and his soul were not supernaturally created but are all products of evolution, and that he is not under the control or guidance of any supernatural Being or beings, but has to rely on himself and his own powers.

Evolutionary humanism, that specific set of beliefs which Huxley was later to set forth in detail,

> affirms that knowledge and understanding can be increased, that conduct and social organization can be improved, and that more desirable directions for individual and social development can be

found. As the overriding aim of evolving man, it is driven to reject power, or mere numbers of people, or efficiency, or material exploitation, and to envisage greater fulfilment and fuller achievement as his true goal.

This was an optimistic basic creed. It was, moreover, a humble one, akin to that of TH, for whom the ultimate nature of reality was beyond the bounds of philosophical inquiry.

> That the universe is incomprehensible is a ground for humility [his grandson wrote]; that it is mysterious, an occasion for awe; that pain and misfortune can often, perhaps always, be turned to good is one of the great lessons which all should learn. . . . As to the existence of another world or another life at all, I am simply agnostic. I do not know. I find extreme difficulties, in the light of physiological and psychological knowledge, in understanding how a soul could exist apart from a body; but difficulties are never disproof.

The belief that mankind should consider its place in nature as that of a conscious questing animal, and should act accordingly, gave a unity to Huxley's views on a large number of diverse subjects. It helped him in a curiously useful way, 'to see life steadily and see it whole', whether he was working in his laboratory at King's College; lecturing at the Royal Institution (where in 1926 he became, like his grandfather before him, Fullerian Professor); or travelling the five continents to discover what mankind was making of its opportunities in each of them.

His travels were numerous and varied. It is not only generals who are helped by luck, and in 1929 Huxley received an invitation whose results were to affect the rest of his life. It came from the Colonial Office Advisory Committee on Native Education and suggested that he should visit East Africa to advise on certain aspects of native education – an opportunity to visit the country which, as he wrote, had thrilled his boyhood, 'the country of bush and big game, primitive tribes and thorn-scrub and volcanic hill.' He accepted. 'Somehow, I feel he'll dodge through, and the tsetse flies won't bite him,' D. H. Lawrence consoled Juliette, when he heard of the proposed journey.

For more than four months Huxley travelled through four East African territories, including a quick dash to the western part of the Belgian Congo. On his return to Britain the advice was duly given, with the usual wealth of logical reasons and practical suggestions on how particular recommendations might be carried out. Yet this was only one result of the African tour. Huxley's first visit to the continent had triggered off a series of thoughts and speculations. Central Africa was, as he saw it, 'the one continental bulk where the step from barbarism to civilization has not yet been taken; the one major region of the world still free to achieve a new civilization without destroying the old.' And what, he asked in his subsequent book *Africa View*, were the rulers of this vast area to do about it? 'What,' he asked, 'are we really in Africa for? Have we any clear idea as a nation, of what we think or hope the country will be like in fifty or a hundred years? I am not at all sure that we have....' This question was to be pushed into the limelight a decade and a half later as the African peoples began to struggle into independence. The question was to be the focus of heated post-war argument and one in which Huxley, by that time Director-General of Unesco, could not help being involved. And it was to be of great importance that he had, as early as 1929, made direct personal contact with the problems – contact which softened, conditioned and qualified, even if it did not alter, the preconceived ideas which he held.

Contact with the African reality did, however, modify those ideas.

> The traveller in Africa, without indulging either the false sentimentality of jingo imperialism or the false shame of doctrinaire little-Englandism, can simply feel proud of belonging to a nation which does a difficult job, demanding such unselfish devotion, honesty and hard work, and does it on the whole so well [Huxley wrote in *Africa View*]. Undoubtedly, our men have their defects compared with those of other Empires, such as the French or the Dutch. But these defects are perhaps mainly defects of intellectual attitude and limited outlook; in the routine of practical administration, our average performance seems to stand the highest. If a contact with a bit of the British Colonial Empire has not yet made me a full-blooded devotee of *Kiplingismus*, it has certainly shown me the way to a spirit of Liberal Imperialism.

In an entirely different sphere, there was the first-hand experience that Huxley gained of the immense variety of Africa's teeming wildlife.

> Where else [he asked] can you see a hundred great aquatic beasts like hippo in one glance; find creatures, like giraffe, as tall as watch-towers; see herds of a thousand head, zebra, gnu, gazelle, and all the other various buck; or hear the roaring of lions so often so readily? Where else can one still discover big animals new to science, like the okapi, the giant forest-hog, or the strange hyaena-like creature only this year sent back from Uganda? Africa boasts the largest of all living land animals, the largest fresh-water mammal, and two of the

three lone survivors of man's nearest kin, the higher anthropoid apes.

Yet this country so rich with wild-life, where at night the lions roared 'from far and near as nightingales answer each other in Surrey', was already under attack. The camera had hardly begun to replace the rifle as the hunter's weapon, and throughout the breadth of the continent there were only two National Parks, Kruger Park in the Union and the Parc National Albert in the Congo. This discrepancy between the magnificence of Africa's fauna and the scanty measures being taken to preserve it made a deep and lasting impression on Huxley; and it was partly due to his own persistent lobbying that when he visited the continent almost exactly thirty years later to report on wild-life preservation, East Africa alone could claim nearly forty National Parks or their equivalent. This first visit underlined for him the danger of man's accelerating destruction of just those natural features which helped to give life its richness. More than two decades earlier he had shown, in his Brackenbury Essay on the conservation of Britain's coasts, how well he appreciated one aspect of the problem; now, in Africa, he caught a more dramatic glimpse of the need for thought and care and that much-disputed move, intervention by the State.

He was still primarily a biologist, working daily in his laboratory at King's College in his long white jacket; writing regularly to *Nature* on subjects as diverse as the maladaptation of trout spermatozoa to fresh water, the histology of eye mutants in *Gammarus*, and the biological effects of abnormal weather. Yet increasingly there appeared in Huxley's letters to *Nature* or to *The Times*, in the pages of his books and in the lectures and broadcasts for which he was constantly in demand, the signs of a growing belief that man's thoughtless destruction of his environment would only be prevented by government intervention.

He still believed, as he stressed in his Norman Lockyer Lecture in 1926, that 'the man of science pursues knowledge because to him the pursuit of knowledge and the discovery of new truth are the breath of his nostrils'. Yet this was no longer quite enough. Something more became necessary as the men of science increased their ability to control the processes of nature itself. This produced, as the twentieth century moved steadily towards its appointment with nuclear fission, a radically new situation. It was a situation whose significance Huxley was among the first to appreciate. He now began to stress with growing force that the knowledge which gave man ever greater control over natural resources and over the limitations of his own life should be used deliberately for social ends. Science and social needs, science and the cultural background of life, science and the ends for which it should be exploited – these are the phrases which recur in his works throughout the 1930s. They are phrases which are now common coin but which, a third of a century ago, suggested an almost revolutionary break with accepted thought. The mere idea that the scientists should exercise their ability to alter man's environment, should help man to play his own part in controlling his place in nature, had a hint of arrogance if not of blasphemy. In the western world it was, moreover, dangerously against the political climate of the times, since any marshalling of scientific knowledge for the common good rather than for individual benefit presupposed national planning.

Any such organization of resources – at first nationally and then internationally – was still anathema to all except dedicated socialists. Furthermore, of those who did believe in such things, few had in the 1930s any very clear idea of how this could be worked out in practice. Indeed, State planning in peacetime, on the scale that was now creeping into discussion, had been tried on a sizeable scale only in Soviet Russia and by the Tennessee Valley Authority. During the mid-1930s, Huxley became one of the very few men, if not the only one, to investigate both experiments at first hand; he investigated them, moreover, in the spirit of the disinterested inquirer rather than that of the dedicated political enthusiast.

Huxley went to Russia with Juliette in 1931, and as members of a scientific party they spent three weeks visiting research stations. On their return Huxley described the tour to an audience which packed the lecture theatre of the London School of Hygiene and Tropical Medicine – an audience drawn, as the *Manchester Guardian* commented, not only by an interest in Russia, but by 'the interest taken in the doings and opinions of Professor Huxley'. In the early thirties Russia was still a country pulling itself up by its technological boot-straps, still cowed by the violence of the Revolution, only just awaking from its long sleep and starting to lash about with dire effect as it did so. And yet, even then there were the signs of things to come. Huxley noted the vast areas of poverty stretching across the country; but he noted also that the Russians were spending more on their geological survey than the rest of Europe put together. He saw how troops with fixed bayonets still stood guard at the bridges of a country alert for sabotage; but he saw also how in the Institute of Plant Industry several hundred research workers were applying in practical form the latest knowledge of genetics in order to grow special kinds of flax, 'tailor-made' for the linen industry; how the Russians were scientifically testing no fewer than 28,000 different strains of wheat; how they were breeding plants in artificial conditions that simulated long, medium or short days – a matter of significance in a country that stretches from the Arctic to the sub-tropics. Here was a country ruthlessly ignoring the suffering of the present to invest in the future. Huxley was quick to criticize the tyranny which was an essential element of the operation, but he was equally quick to note that the next generation might reap staggering advantages from this nationally planned use of the latest scientific knowledge. Three decades later he was less surprised than most people by the rise of the *sputniks*.

However, Russia was not the only place in the world that provided an example of scientific planning for social ends. There was also the Tennessee Valley. Here in 1933 a public corporation had been set up to plan, develop and control the natural resources of a district which drained an area four-fifths the size of Britain. While on a lecture tour in the States in 1935 Huxley eagerly seized an opportunity of visiting the Tennessee Valley Authority, of which extremely little was then known in Britain.

> At first [he later wrote] I thought it was interested solely in the manufacture and distribution of cheap electric power. Then, as I went deeper into it, I learned that there were other phases to its programme. In England I thought that it was a sort of autocratic organization with a definite plan for a new kind of society which it was forcing upon the people.

He therefore set off in a somewhat critical frame of mind, which steadily changed as he toured the Valley and began to understand what was being done. His final conclusions were presented in two articles in *The Times* which gave many British readers their first picture of the great experiment:

> As I flew eastwards to Virginia across the upper reaches of the Valley [he wrote of his homeward journey] I felt that I had been privileged to see the early growth of a new and hopeful type of social organism. Here, science and vision were combined in a way and on a scale new in human history. It marked the beginning of the large-scale application of the experimental method in social affairs. And my final reflection was a hope that an experiment of comparable scale along the same sort of lines, combining vision and science in the same fruitful way, might be initiated here in Britain.

There was little chance of this as Britain lumbered through the 1930s, lulled first by Mr Baldwin's pipe-smoke and then by Mr Chamberlain's umbrella. The best substitute was P.E.P., or Political and Economic Planning, the organization which was to prepare so many useful blueprints which could be pulled from the pigeon-holes when planning lost its bogy-man image. It was natural that Huxley should be drawn into the discussions from which P.E.P. arose. The organization had originated with the 'National Plan for Britain', prepared by Gerald Barry and Max Nicholson among others, and published in the *Week-End Review* which Barry then edited. Considerable correspondence was stimulated by the plan, and Huxley was among those who met with Nicholson, Barry, Kenneth Lindsay and the Elmhirsts – of Dartington Hall – to start the new organization. As chairman of the Research Group, his special concern was not biology in its narrow sense but its practical applications to everyday life, above all to the problem of over-population, which he had already discerned as threatening not only Britain but the whole world; and to the preservation of natural resources – a concern from which it is possible to trace in an almost unbroken line the setting-up in 1949 of Britain's National Parks Commission and the Nature Conservancy. Huxley's influence on the infant P.E.P. was not only that of biological adviser but also of scientific prodder and awkward questioner. Thus he would often sit quietly through much of a meeting – having prefaced it by recounting the latest funny story, curious limerick or droll occurrence, and would then break in by asking: 'Yes, but what is this argument really about?' Not infrequently, he would provide his own answer.

A great many ideas came from P.E.P.'s early days, but they were, with few exceptions, only to be implemented a decade or more later. The broadsheets issued went, moreover, to a public that was small even if it was already partly informed. Huxley hungered for the wider public and in the mid-1930s eagerly seized the chance which he was given of putting down in print, in popular form, just how he felt the opportunities offered by contemporary scientific knowledge could and should be utilized by the politicians. An added inducement to write *If I Were Dictator*, the book which was to embody these ideas, sprang from the fact that his brother Aldous had only recently written *Brave New World*, an astringent warning of what could happen if misapplied science were carried to its logical conclusion. Now, felt Julian, was the time to show the reverse of the coin.

His proposals, made some thirty years ago, have a strangely contemporary ring, so that the biologist wears the air of a prophet; yet most of them were carried out only under the pressures of war. All of them had but one end:

> That end is that my people shall be healthy and long-lived, inhabiting houses which are clean and roomy and well-furnished, and cities which are beautiful and convenient to dwell in, with opportunities for work and for leisure, for education and enjoyment, for individual development and communal satisfaction.

The structure on which Government was to be organized would be regional, the regions themselves numbering a dozen – as they did during the 1939–45 war – and being based on those which had developed between the departure of the Romans in the fifth century and the establishment of Norman rule six hundred years later. So far as food was concerned, it would be largely handled by Marketing Boards, then still in their infancy. Furthermore, efforts would be made to discover how the State could best ameliorate what were still, in the 1930s, the wretched conditions of the people.

> I should progress towards a community in which profit is no longer the paramount incentive but only one among several, and do so without going through the revolutionary process of nationalizing the means of production and exchange. I should therefore hope to achieve the socialized State without Socialism.

Finally – strange prophecy for the 1930s – he forecast the six-hour day and the looming problem of leisure.

If I Were Dictator emphasized Huxley's role as a social scientist, a role which he had openly taken up the previous year when briefed by the B.B.C. to survey the whole field of scientific research and social needs, and to prepare a dozen talks on the subject. In a preface to the published version of the talks which was prepared with Professor Hyman Levy he stressed the need for a new outlook.

> I became [he wrote of his work] more than ever impressed with the fact that both our existing structure of civilization and our hope of progress are based on science and that the lack of appreciation and understanding among business men, financiers, educational authorities, politicians and administrators, was a serious feature in our present situation . . .

Increasingly, his work swung round to remedying the situation. He talked, lectured, broadcast and wrote on the subject unrepentantly – and to those who claimed that he did too much of each he might reply as he did in the introduction to one of his books by saying: 'We are about to cut the cackle. But cackle, do not forget, plays an integral part in the production of eggs.'

Huxley's versatility was well illustrated by his record as a broadcaster, a role in which his experience as university lecturer gave him a head-and-shoulders advantage over many who were still struggling with the comparatively new medium. The sincerity of his deeply-held beliefs came well over the air; and if at times he betrayed annoyance at anyone not well enough informed to hold his own views, this was no more than the trace of 'character' which attracts listeners. He made himself, moreover, master of the set-piece series, of which 'The Stream of Life' was the first, the series which could deal with a subject in more than snippet fashion, exploring and developing it so that education became inextricably bound in with entertainment. Thus his 'Bird Watching and Bird Behaviour' opened up for thousands of listeners the exciting prospect of an interest on their own front-doorstep. 'Science in the Making' dealt with the subject in a new way while his talks and discussions on 'Scientific Research and Social Needs' linked the two in a pattern commonplace today but excitingly original in the 1930s. All these broadcasts helped to do two things. They helped to spread – especially among younger listeners – the beliefs which Huxley held so strongly; and they helped to transform him into the familiar figure who during and after the war was listened to not only because of what he said but because of who he was. As early as 1930 he had been included in the lists of 'Britain's five best brains' compiled by readers of *The Spectator*. And while he ranked sixteenth in a list headed by Shaw, Sir Oliver Lodge, Lord Birkenhead and Churchill, he no doubt chuckled to find himself followed by, among others, Sir James Jeans, Rutherford and Bertrand Russell.

If there was an almost esoteric variety about Huxley's broadcasts during this period, the same was true of the books which came in a ceaseless flow from the Regency house through whose windows he could look, across green gardens, towards Hampstead Heath appearing over the distant trees. The massive volumes on embryology and on relative growth were balanced by a series on 'Simple Science' which he wrote with Professor Andrade, *What Dare I Think?* and by a slim volume of poems, *The Captive Shrew*, which was to bring in royalties for more than a quarter of a century. Some of these poems, written in Spitsbergen and Texas, Italy, North Wales, Switzerland and New York, showed the viewpoint of the man who could

> . . . sit and look
> In quiet, privileged like Divinity
> To read the roaring world as in a book.

Others underlined the feelings of the scientist concerned with the predicament of man and his inability to do much about it. Of birds, for instance, he wrote:

> But some with deeper and more inward sight
> See them a part of that one Life which streams
> Slow on, towards more mind – a part more light
> Than we; unburdened with regrets or dreams,
> Or thought. A winged emotion of the sky,
> The birds through an eternal Present fly.

His vision was that of the poet, although he was apparently a little shy of the fact, commenting at the time on these poems written over two decades: 'I was letting my brain get lop-sided, so I wrote a volume of poems as a safety valve. I found relief from my laboratory by writing about the beauties of brooks and sunsets.'

Huxley's writing was by the early thirties almost as time-demanding as his science, and in 1933 there came an additional task. Leonard Huxley died on 3 May, and his papers in Bracknell Gardens were found to include the mountain of material from which he had quarried the life of TH. The collection of letters, essays, cuttings and notes was still in disarray, and as Julian later wrote, 'letters from the most eminent Victorians were found cheek by jowl with laundry bills; the original MS of various of my grandfather's essays were piled among miscellaneous press-cuttings. . . .' But among the papers, jostling shoulders with a group of old household account-books, there was a diary written in the comparatively legible hand of TH's younger days, crammed with information and containing the story of four vital years. This was Huxley's original diary of the *Rattlesnake* voyage, a volume of great value as a record of its author's scientific work, as an historical document in its own right, and as a social document of naval life nearly a century before. To Julian there now fell the labour involved in deciphering, editing, and preparing it for the press as *T. H. Huxley's Diary of the Voyage of the Rattlesnake.*

This task was but one more added to a number already exceedingly large. Sieving through the record of Julian's activities during this period it is, at first, difficult to see how he could have survived the work-load. His laboratory research at King's College, his lecturing, his lobbying for a score of causes from eugenics to the organization of scientific workers, his books and pamphlets – all this crowded in upon his waking hours, and it would be easy to envisage him cracking under the sheer weight of it all, under the strain of switching from experimental biology to economic planning, from the practice of bird-watching to the finer points of scientific humanism.

That he did not crack was due largely to two reasons. One was that Huxley had never been the sort of man to draw down a firm line between work and play. To reveal in the laboratory new facts about the astonishing world of nature was surely not work but participation in exciting discovery; to hammer out some way in which science could be used for the benefit of all rather than for the profit of the few, was not only duty but an enjoyable task on which to stretch the intellect. And, whatever the work in hand, it was certain to be of interest to friends with whom one could discuss it on a long country walk – one of those walks whose mixed intellectual and physical content was almost a throw-back to Leslie Stephen and his 'Sunday Tramps'.

There was also, to relieve the pressure, the inspired stage-management of Juliette, deftly helping to order his day, ensuring that the complexities of life were reduced to a minimum, taking as much of the load as she could, advising discreetly and on occasion intuitively knowing which was the better course to take. She combined to a remarkable extent the qualities of wife, companion, mother, part-time secretary and general organizer of victory through the years. She also, like Julian, contrived to arrange her hours so that they left time for creative leisure. Much of this was employed in modelling and carving, begun when her elder son Anthony was, in his late teens, knocked from his bicycle and forced for a while, in the doctor's words, 'to do something which did not exercise his brain.' A young man was brought in to give instruction in modelling. The outcome was that an inborn talent was discovered not in Anthony but in his mother, who later trained at the Central School under John Skeaping, and whose magnificent carving of Schweizer's red river hog, now ornamenting the family hall, is merely one of the fine pieces she has exhibited.

From the days of TH onwards, the Huxleys had always had an appreciation for real country, and Julian's preoccupation with bird-watching helped to balance his sedentary and purely mental activities and to keep him physically trimmed to the bone. He was now rising fifty but in the country his extraordinary keenness of eye and ear was frequently a subject for comment. He could usually hear or see a bird, and identify it by quick appreciation of its features, well in advance of younger men. He noticed plants more quickly and would seize immediately on their unusual forms. Thus on a walk in Pembrokeshire he spotted the small but handsome Newport centaury, a rare plant with larger petals and taller habit than the common centaury – even though he had never before seen a specimen and did not know of the particular variety when he noted its unusual characteristics.

This occurred near the home of R. M. Lockley, one of Huxley's great number of friends. In 1933 Lockley, then a young amateur naturalist, had described in *The Countryman* the rich bird-life of Skokholm, an island off the extreme south-west of Wales where he lived with his wife and three-year-old daughter, and of the neighbouring Grassholm. Huxley, reading the article with interest, saw that the author had a detailed and intimate knowledge of sea-birds in general and of the huge gannetry on Grassholm in particular. Here, dug into two acres of sloping ground, there lived ten thousand of these huge spectacular birds,

> the white head tinged with golden yellow, the bill plumbeous and bayonet-like, the eye pale as silver, the plumage snow-white except for the black wing-tips, and the legs and the toes of the webbed feet black with unreal longitudinal stripes of blue-green,

in Lockley's words – each grown bird nearly six feet from wing-tip to wing-tip. The chance of studying such an assemblage at close hand fascinated Huxley, and in mid-May he visited the Lockleys on their island home.

> The sight as we climbed over the crest of the little islet, took my breath [he said in a broadcast]. Except perhaps for the half-million flamingoes on Lake Nakiri in Kenya I have never seen any spectacle of living nature to rival it. Acres of great white birds sitting on their nests in close and regular array over the rocky slopes – thousands of them, with hundreds more wheeling in the air. As soon as I had taken my fill of looking, I said to Lockley, 'Someone ought to make a film of this. Why shouldn't we do it?'

Lockley himself had long wanted to do so and as they put up hides, photographed the aldermanic puffins, took sample movie shots of the gannetry, and generally talked birds, the idea of a film began to take shape; a film which was to be an artistic creation in its own right, far more than merely 'instructional'.

In London, Huxley began to interest possible film-makers. This was not too difficult. A few years earlier he had edited the controversial *Cosmos, the Story of Evolution*; and he was now working as general supervisor of biological films for G.B. Instructional Ltd for whom he was preparing the Eugenics Society's *Heredity in Man*. Huxley soon induced John Grierson to visit Skokholm and talk over possibilities with Lockley. Then he succeeded in getting London Film Productions Ltd to supply two cameramen. Lockley would provide transport, camping equipment and food, and would contribute his knowledge of the gannetry and of when its inhabitants would be most suitable for filming. Plans were discussed a few days before Christmas, and in the spring of 1934 Huxley came down to Wales to work out final details, bringing with him Juliette and their two sons, who for the first time were taken across to Skokholm.

By the summer all was ready. London Films had just finished *The Private Life of Henry the Eighth* and they now sent down two of their best cameramen, to help Huxley and Lockley film what they were already calling *The Private Life of the Gannets.* On 7 June Huxley, Lockley, his wife, and the two cameramen, steamed across from Skokholm to Grassholm in the tug *Taliesin*, taking with them the assembled camera equipment, camping kit and, since there was no fresh water on Grassholm, seven nine-gallon casks of water and a cask of cider. Having circled the island to get opening shots of the wheeling gannets, the party landed and the tug steamed away – leaving them to share their surroundings with the ten thousand gannets, thousands of other sea-birds, seals, and a school of snorting porpoises. They set up camp, drank tea and shot off some test-lengths of film which development proved to be satisfactory. For Huxley there must have been more than one reminder of that spell in Spitsbergen just thirteen years away.

> The work went smoothly on, and, aided by the perfect weather, we completed four-fifths of the film in a week [Lockley has written in *Island Days*]. Each morning we were at work by six o'clock. When the afternoon sun filled the west-facing gannetry the reflection from the white bodies of the birds added to the light reflected from the sea and made an eye-tingling glare that was far too bright and shadowless for attractive camera-work. We therefore rested in the afternoon, starting work again after tea and continuing for four or five hours in the evening. The sun was then low enough to put a sharp gleam into the pale eyes of the gannets, and throw pleasing shadows through their close ranks.

Grierson volunteered to take the spectacular diving shots that the party had so far failed to get. The whole film was processed and assembled, and Huxley then wrote, and subsequently recorded, the commentary.

The Private Life of the Gannets showed the birds bringing seaweed to make their nests; it showed their elaborate courtship and the hatching of the ugly chicks; its slow-motion sequences revealed the grace of the gannets' flight, and others showed their spectacular vertical dives for fish. It was, moreover, a remarkable success in that it satisfied both the experts and the general public. The specialists had their first sight of the film at a private showing in the London Zoo on the evening of

6 November 1934, and there seems little doubt that that showing was to affect Huxley's future. For the next year Sir Peter Chalmers Mitchell, Secretary of the Zoological Society of London, was due to retire. The Society's Council had been considering a number of possible successors, of whom Huxley was one, and as they watched the film of the gannets they no doubt realized that in him they had, whatever his other qualifications, a biologist who could both get the facts right and make them entertaining to the layman. The latter point was stressed by the public première on Boxing Day at the Leicester Square Theatre, where it provided a curtain-raiser for *The Scarlet Pimpernel* – and raised even more applause than this main film.

Another change was now about to take place in Julian Huxley's fortunes. *The Private Life of the Gannets* was to decide the issue with the Zoological Society. As Secretary he was to venture on to the perilous waters of administration. A change was also approaching for his brother Aldous, by now as well-known as Julian, and attracting the Press-men, at the première of the gannets film, by his gaunt willowy figure, broad-brimmed black hat and promise of quotable remarks.

For while Julian had been cutting out his niche as scientist-philosopher, Aldous had followed his own path in his own way, the most provocative and the most incandescent of the Thomas Huxley grandchildren.

Chapter X

Aldous Emergent

(*i*)

Throughout the first world war, while Julian had been constructing his own view of the universe, Aldous had been passing through a time of testing and self-inquiry, loaded with the memory of his mother's death, the bitter loss of Trev's suicide, and the prospect of near-blindness. Thrice hammered by the Fates, upheld by little more than inherited resilience and the memory of Julian's injunction never to forget the intellectual nobility of his forefathers, he managed to survive.

In his mind there was no doubt that he must become a writer and by the end of 1920 he already had to his credit four volumes of poems. The first, *The Burning Wheel*, was published by Blackwell in 'Adventurers All, A Series of Young Poets Unknown to Fame', whose object it was 'to remove from the work of young poets the reproach of insolvency'. Two years later came *Jonah*, of whose title poem Aldous had fifty or sixty copies printed as a Christmas card; in 1918 there came *The Defeat of Youth* and, two years later, *Leda*. All four might be written off as postgraduate *jeux d'esprit*, and it is certainly true that they give little indication of things to come. Yet in the very title poem of *The Burning Wheel* it is possible to see some hint of that desire for absolute detachment from the world which was to characterize Aldous's later philosophy. And in view of the novels to which he was to turn with such relish only a year or so later, Virginia Woolf's comment on *The Defeat of Youth* is significant:

> The advice that one is inclined to give to an urbane and cultivated writer of his quality, is to cease to use poetry in the serious, traditional manner, and to use it instead to explore those fantastic, amusing or ironical aspects of life which can only be expressed by people of high technical skill and great sensibility.

This was wise advice; Aldous, applying it to the novel rather than to poetry, was to find fame by carrying it out. Yet for the moment it did little to ease the problems of life, problems which were particularly acute for one as anxious to marry as Aldous had by this time become.

He had been a frequent visitor to Garsington soon after Lady Ottoline Morrell had settled there with her husband. Their home had become a haven not only for those with pacifist leanings but also for refugees and among the latter was Maria Nys, the daughter of a Belgian industrialist.

> She was small, rather plump, but lovely beyond words [Juliette Huxley later wrote], with large blue-green eyes matching an Egyptian scarab ring on her long finger, a delicate slightly aquiline profile and a small pointed chin under a full mouth. Her hair, cut short by Philip Morrell (the fashion was just beginning with Slade students), hung like a dark helmet. She had the vulnerable and defenceless look of a child with a mature body.

From the first it was clear that Aldous was becoming absorbed with Maria; by the end of the war it was equally clear that only lack of prospects was preventing their marriage. Prospects were indeed chimerical. Aldous was just twenty-four. He was physically handicapped to an extent which would have crushed a lesser man. His qualifications fitted him for little other than teaching, an occupation he regarded with distaste. And in the climate of the times, with demobilized men anxious for almost any job that came, it was obvious that he would stand towards the end of most employment queues. Nor could much help be expected from the family. Leonard had, it is true, been left £40,000 by his first wife, but he now had a second family to educate, and one that would grow to maturity only in his older age. A loan, to be repaid punctiliously over the years, was the most he would arrange. Ethel Collier alone among the Huxleys could offer much help, the majority of the family belonging, as Aldous himself put it, to

> that impecunious but dignified section of the upper-middle class which is in the habit of putting on dress clothes to eat – with the most studied decorum and out of porcelain and burnished silver – a dinner of dishwater and codfish, mock duck and cabbage.

It was therefore a gloomy Aldous who for a while shared a London flat with Thomas Earp, Russel Green and Roy Campbell. He must have been deep in a mental trough, 'the great Mahatma of all misanthropy', as Campbell described him in a paragraph as revealing of Campbell himself as it is of Huxley:

> As a practical zoologist and botanist and one whose knowledge of

beasts and birds, cereals, grazing, and fodder had a human value; as one who belonged (unlike the other poets around me) to the most essential and necessary type of skilled workers – the provers of meat, fish, corn, leather, wool, oil and fats, I felt ill at ease with this pedant who leeringly gloated over his knowledge of how crayfish copulated (through their third pair of legs) but could never have caught or cooked one; let alone broken in a horse, thrown and branded a steer, flensed a whale, or slaughtered, cut, cured, and cooked anything at all. . . . Huxley was always as lost and bewildered by the very scientific civilization of which he is one of the main prophets, as a wild African giraffe would be if it were suddenly to be dumped in the middle of Piccadilly or Broadway.

It must have been a happy quartet.

By March 1919, when Aldous served as best man at Julian's wedding, Maria had left England for Italy where she was now living with her mother and sisters. Aldous was on the point of taking a poorly paid but interesting lectureship at the Sorbonne when, unexpectedly, there came an offer from Middleton Murry. *The Athenaeum* was being reorganized. Would Aldous join the staff? Aldous accepted by return and was married to Maria within a matter of weeks. 'You will think,' said Ottoline Morrell to Leonard at the wedding, 'that I keep a matrimonial agency at Garsington.'

Aldous and his wife set up home first in Hampstead, the district from which so many Huxleys have looked down and across the metropolis to the North Downs beyond, later in a basement flat in Westbourne Terrace. Each day he descended to work on *The Athenaeum*, doing a good deal of journeyman writing, and reviewing many books each month. Many of these dealt with the aftermath of the war, but it was only rarely that Aldous allowed his own views to obtrude, as when he wrote of one author who had entered the war full of military enthusiasm and come out of it a pacifist. This, Aldous pointed out in his review, was not inconsistent; on the contrary, such were the faithful ones – faithful to 'the ideals with which the war began, and which so soon grew dim and vanished'. After a few months he began to contribute a regular series of light anonymous essays, 'Marginalia,' discussing literature and commenting on the passing world. The less ephemeral were subsequently reprinted in *On the Margin*.

There were soon disagreements with Murry, and while still writing 'Marginalia' Aldous joined the *Westminster Gazette* as dramatic critic.

It was my fate [he later wrote] to go to the theatre some two hundred and fifty times in one year. On business, I need not add; one would hardly do that sort of thing for pleasure. I was paid to go. By the end of the year – and, for that matter, long before our planet had completed its orbit round the sun – I had come to the conclusion that I was not paid enough; that, indeed, I could never be paid enough for this particular job. I gave it up; and nothing would induce me to resume it.

In some ways, the giving up was only a change of load. For Aldous now threw himself into a welter of mixed journalism which within a few years included articles on house decoration and architecture, on the revival of marbling, on royalty and character; reviews of novels; and bibliographical notes. For one year he averaged more than three book-reviews a week, a record remarkable enough even for a reviewer who did not have to read through the thickest of spectacles, in just the right light, and did so then only with difficulty.

Much of this work was done while on the staff of *Vogue*, then a journal as much concerned with art and society as with fashion, run from upper floor offices in Breams Buildings off Fetter Lane. For some while Aldous worked here as art critic; he contributed short notes; and at times he rewrote the advertising copy for the magazine, an effort which, it was subsequently stated, 'improved the literary quality of the text but had disastrous results on the effectiveness of the advertising'. He himself had no illusions:

> I have discovered the most exciting, the most arduous literary form of all, the most difficult to master, the most pregnant in curious possibilities. I mean the advertisement.... It is far easier to write ten passably effective sonnets, good enough to take in the not too enquiring critic, than one effective advertisement that will take in a few thousand of the uncritical buying public.

All this was valuable training.

> What he was proud of [wrote one friend of his later years] was that he could earn his living by his pen, an occupation which he enjoyed and for which he had a craftsman's love and concern. He looked upon himself as a writer who should be able to communicate with all kinds of people, not only the sophisticated or the erudite. He never felt it beneath him to write for the films or the popular magazines . . . He wrote for 'Playboy' and 'Daedalus', for 'Life' and 'Encounter' and considered they were equally acceptable channels of communicating with people.

So, of course, did TH with his lectures to working men.

Yet it was not the journeyman craftsmanship of this emergent Huxley which attracted attention. Instead, it was a figure which made it difficult for the caricaturists to exaggerate the reality. He was now well over six feet, with 'legs twice as long as Lytton Strachey's'. He was still top-heavy and his short-sightedness helped to produce the figure 'like a willow that swayed and bent, not ungracefully, in the middle'. Peering down from on high, he could only with difficulty identify the small boys whose voices wafted up to him the cheeky inquiry: 'Cold up there, Guv'nor?'

His appearance alone would have commanded attention. But he had also developed a careful and unusual mode of walking, lifting his feet so that he would not trip over objects which were in his path but far beyond his range of sight. To this was added a fondness for the broad-brimmed sombrero, partly for the practical reason that it helped to shade his eyes. All this gave him a slightly bizarre look, as did the long black cloak which he habitually wore. These details increased the Huxley mystique. And the short-sight alone produced some memorable mishaps, as when he entered a Hampstead shop, head down, be-cloaked, lifting his feet carefully, and arrived unscathed in a shower of fragments from the glass door through which he had walked.

Huxley's physical characteristics helped to imply an aloof personality cut off from the rest of mankind. Public misunderstanding of much of his early writing reinforced the suggestion. Thus the belief grew that this gangling odd-man-out was mainly concerned with exhibiting his own personal grudge against life. It is true that he was apt to prod humanity in the places where it hurt most. It is true that his near-blindness and the deaths of his mother and brother produced an almost pathological concern with the physical results of death and disease; even the list of artists he studied most deeply – Brueghel, Callot, Piranesi, Goya and Caravaggio – shows, as Sir Kenneth Clark has pointed out, 'a dominating trait of his mind – his sense of horror.' Yet this very sense of horror was motivated by pity, and it was counter-balanced by an inextinguishable marvel at life – an emotion very different from the perverted pleasure in disgust which was often attributed to him. 'Huxley's findings are always the same,' bemoaned the late John Strachey. 'Go where you will, do what you will, you will never escape from the smell of ordure and decay.' This judgement, provoked by Huxley's refusal to paddle an orthodox Left-wing canoe, is not untypical of one opinion of his work which began to form from the early 1920s onwards.

These opinions were founded on a misinterpretation of Huxley's work, but they sprang also from ignorance of what the man himself was really like. 'Aldous Huxley?' commented one lawyer who knew him well and who had few illusions about the human race. 'I never knew a man of letters so close to being a saint.' And almost half a century after the days at *Vogue* one of the staff remembers Aldous Huxley, not as the misogynist enjoying his hatred, but as the young man who would turn the gallant compliment better than most. 'Just to meet him,' she says, 'was to make one's day.'

Much of Aldous's humanity came from the rough-and-tumble of the immediate post-war years. So did much of his craftsmanship. For dousing in the cold water of magazine journalism had an astringent and cleansing effect on the bone-structure of his writing. However deadening the influence of constant theatre-going, however trivial the subjects on which he was ordered to write, there was the rigid requirement that his words should be understood by a mixed bag of brains; that although an allotted 500 words might be allowed to swell by an additional 50 it must not swell by 500. And just as the thought of hanging 'concentrates his mind wonderfully', so does a man with a printer waiting for copy find idle words fading before essentials. Thus, grotesquely enough, the demand for half a column on new wallpapers, some frivolous fashion paragraphs, or a brief account of a jewellery exhibition, provided the disciplines which enabled him to write of the metaphysical mysteries in a prose which at its best was understandable despite its convolutions. When he later held a mirror to experience, creating Francis Chelifer, the poet-editor of 'The Rabbit-Fancier's Gazette', the image is no more extravagant than that of Aldous Huxley, seeker after truth, hacking away at advertising copy for *Vogue*.

In the writers' world he is jack-of-all-trades and master of most, an arch-philosopher who might, one suspects, have delighted in the task of helping a few poor souls with words of counsel in Auntie Pru's advice column. Much of this stemmed from his anxiety to press out on to the world the beliefs which he held so strongly; the ability to do so, to keep men and women listening in large numbers, sprang from the hard frustrating journalism of the immediate post-war years.

(ii)

Aldous Huxley's motives for choice of work were two-fold and accurately revealed in an interview which he gave to a reporter on *The Observer* in the early 1930s:

> My chief motive in writing has been the desire to express a point of view. Or, rather, the desire to clarify a point of view to myself. I do

> not write for my readers; in fact, I don't like thinking about my readers. In addition, I like writing for writing's sake. I am conscious of possessing a certain talent, and I like to exercise it in solving the literary problem I put to myself. But this aspect of my work interests me less than it did. I am chiefly interested in making clear a certain outlook on life.

From this, as well as from the steady evolution of his writing between 1920 and the early 1930s, the main point emerges. He was motivated largely by the nagging desire to understand reality. He was under its influence for nearly half a century. And he could heed it better by presenting the various problems of the universe in print and by then trying to provide tentative answers to the riddles. It follows that each answer was provisional, only a single step or so nearer the ideal solution. And while this ideal solution was being approached, he had to continue writing – not merely to make progress but for a second, more prosaic, reason.

> I must make money in the meantime. That is not the whole reason why I publish, of course, but it is certainly a real and important one. Although I write for myself and not for my readers I must have readers in order to get a living.

He was well equipped for the task. There was first his preoccupation with words in their own right, his experience and comprehension of the varying ways of expressing ordinary events, his knowledge of the shock which unexpected syllables would evoke, so that when he wished he could use words like a blowlamp, burning out whatever he wished to burn out with a success that either delighted or repelled. There was also his hard-won experience in journalism. Before he was launched in full stream on a career as a professional prose writer, he already had a working knowledge of the tricks of the trade.

Finally, there was the encyclopaedic knowledge of esoteric and startling subjects which he had soaked in – and not forgotten – since his childhood. Whether it was the practice of traditional Chinese medicine, the faking of medieval ivories, the mechanism by which grasshoppers hop, or the problems of psychophysical types and their difficulties in understanding one another, he would have the rare facts available, ready to be tipped out and arranged to illustrate the particular point at issue. To this storehouse of secondhand facts, Huxley continuously added from his own firsthand experience. As Gerald Heard has put it:

> Huxley's eye for foibles and his fascination with the grotesque gave him his original impetus. Boredom, as he told his intimates, was his

main terror. In comparison with his own extraordinarily stocked mind and the originality of its arrangements, the information and conversation of most people seemed platitudinous, jejune, banal. He could, then, only entertain himself by studying the irrational quirks, the ludicrous inconsistencies, the absurd reflexes and reactions whereby the average person gives the involuntary lie to his dreary pretensions.

These abilities were to be deployed for more than forty years on a literary career as remarkable for its variety as its output. Julian's achievements, spread across biology and broadcasting, poetry and popular science, were paralleled by those of his brother who first gained fame as a novelist and essayist, wrote plays and poetry, found time to contribute to the popular Sunday papers, and ended as compound of philosopher, mystic and guardian of the public conscience. The greater part of this output was a reflection, in different media, of Aldous Huxley's evolving beliefs, and it is possible to trace over-lapping stages in this evolution. There was first the period of the four novels which came to a breathless climax with *Point Counter Point.* There was the period of growing interest in the philosophy of non-attachment, culminating in *Ends and Means* and the defence of pacifism. And there was, following emigration to the United States, his final acceptance of the mystic's inner beliefs and hopes.

This steady stream of development through the years was independent of such books as *Brave New World* and *Eyeless in Gaza.* There were also essays, travel notes, and more than one play. But between these Huxley's progress as a writer continued to develop from the starting point which had been the novels of the 1920s.

Before embarking on the first of these four novels he had provided in *Limbo*, a collection of short stories, more than a hint of things to come. For 'The Farcical History of Richard Greenow', a long short story, suggests the method to be used and, like many of his later novels, contains almost painful overtones of thinly disguised family history. It was followed by *Crome Yellow*, largely based on Garsington, the first of the four novels which were to be written between 1921 and 1928 as he travelled about Europe living on his literary wits. Each involved him more closely with the battlefront of the bestseller lists. Each revealed a new development in his attitude to life and his concept of reality. Each was to be of greater technical complexity. Yet in some ways the four books – *Crome Yellow*, *Antic Hay*, *Those Barren Leaves* and *Point Counter Point* – were all of a piece, having a resemblance which went beyond the superficial similarity of the characters, the mechanisms by which they were operated and the points of view which they were apt to erect as Aunt Sallys. In *Crome Yellow* and *Those Barren Leaves* events are focused by a house-party, and in the other two books there is an almost comparable to-ing and fro-ing within a small socially restricted circle. In all four novels the men and women are so tailored that despite their eccentricities, despite their individuality as people, despite their attractiveness or repulsiveness, they are yet similarly shaped vehicles, built largely for the exposition of carefully arranged, logically articulated thoughts, theories and attitudes. In all, moreover, the figures argue on Olympus, settling the fate of mankind if not of the universe, by careful, courteous argument and counter-argument, with only a distant glance at the proles on the plains below. Were this all, the quartet of novels would still be remarkable, preserving as it does, a picture, only just too iridescent to suspend belief, of the post-1918 world which had tossed into the discard-tray almost all that was pre-August 4th, pre-Grey, pre-the-lights-going-out-in-Europe.

Yet it was not all. Neither the glittering façade of Lady Tantamount's parties nor the summer palace of the Cybo Malaspina; neither the stately towers of Crome nor the exciting possibilities of Mrs Viveash's boudoir, could even begin to conceal the perennial Huxley concern. The novels which founded Aldous's financial independence and brought a stutter of shocked comments from the literary hinterland did not deal directly with man's place in nature, but they did deal – obliquely, in convoluted form maybe, but nevertheless all-pervadingly – with man's predicament, his relationships with reality, with the awful circumstance which bound aspiring spirit to wretched flesh. For Huxley, this essential of the novels was more important than the trimmings which he hung from it. This was natural enough. That a body such as Julia Arnold's should have been at the mercy of tormenting and malignant growth; that Aldous's own youthful visions should have been corralled back into a world limited, without artificial aid, to less than an arm's length; that Trev, even Trev, had found it impossible to face the awful world – these were the specimens, laid bare on life's operating table, which revealed that the old beliefs had lost both their utility and their credibility. Aldous might, as he did for some while, take it 'for granted that there was no meaning' in the universe; yet once one had taken this for granted, it became more than an intellectual exercise of great fascination to construct a compass for the human voyage. It became a necessity if one were to survive the voyage with mind intact.

Thus the need to struggle and to understand. Thus the developing beliefs through these first four novels. In the first of them, *Crome Yellow*, elderly Scogan, the first of the one-man Greek choruses which Aldous was to use throughout most of his novels, merely declaims that

> We are tied down by the frightful limitations of our human faculties, by the notions which society imposes on us through our fatal suggestibility, by our own personalities. For us a complete holiday is out of the question.

In *Antic Hay* this lamentable position of humanity is not merely stated, but the futility of seeking a solution is suggested – so strongly that one critic could write that as he watched 'the goat-feet of this book's men and women like satyrs dancing the antic hay, we wonder what has happened to cause in Mr. Huxley this reversion to the adolescent'. The mood passed. And at the end of *Those Barren Leaves* one finds Calamy filled with a measure of something which at least looks like hope —

> Perhaps if you spend long enough and your mind is the right sort of mind, perhaps you really do get, in some queer sort of way, beyond the limitations of ordinary existence. And you see that everything that seems real is in fact entirely illusory – *maya*, in fact, the cosmic illusion. Behind it you catch a glimpse of reality.

This mood also passed, and if the next novel, *Point Counter Point*, marked the end of one stage in a journey it marked also a pessimistic, iconoclastic stage at the end of which Spandrell the destroyer is inevitably destroyed.

These four novels showed that Aldous, like most of the Huxleys, had no intention of shirking the central issue; indeed, like more than one member of the family, he seemed to be drawn to it partly because in fact it was the central issue around which all worth-while discussion must hover. It might or might not be true, as J. Donald Adams later claimed in the *New York Times*, that 'Huxley's equipment as a novelist is incomplete. He fails in the final test by which a novelist must prove his right to survive – his ability to create four-dimensional, memorable characters.' Whatever the validity of this claim – and a case can be made for it – the intellectual stratum of novel-readers took little note of it when they bought their books or made their reservations at the circulating libraries. The four books established Huxley as a writer who would be listened to.

Yet listeners do not always understand, and in the case of the early novels, misunderstanding was of several varieties. There was first the doubt expressed in *Nature*'s review of *Point Counter Point*, about the author's real aim:

> He introduces character after character into his pages, psychoanalyses them, and then lays them aside once they have served their purpose whether of explaining their reactions to environmental

stimuli in terms of old or new theories of behaviourism, or as vehicles for the expression of his varied and conflicting thought on different types. His analyses are brutally realistic, although it is probable that, by restricting his field of choice to sex, he loses some of his effect. At the end he leaves us wondering whether he intends to point a moral or merely to record his observations concerning the disastrous effects on some people of the breakdown of tribal authority and the waning influence of the old taboos resulting from the impact of science on society.

Wondering about the moral was bad enough. Even worse, was the ease with which readers got the moral wrong. For some, the most obvious feature of the novels was not the argument but the vehicle used to carry it – the warren-like sexual coming and going of many characters, the mental and moral scrofulousness of others, the grotesqueries which were paraded almost as everyday occurrences. Many readers found it difficult to believe that the creator of Lucy Tantamount or Mrs Viveash could hold acceptable moral views. The reportage was mistaken for approval, the statement for sympathy – even though these stigmata of the post-war order were being held up not for praise but for attack. The author's intent was purely cautionary; he would shock, if shock he must, just as the physician must sometimes switch on the electric current to restore the proper workings of the brain. His aim was only to shake the reader into an awareness of his predicament. Aldous looked at much of the post-war world with as much dislike and dismay as did many of his critics, and it is almost the author himself who, in *Antic Hay* speaks through the mouth of old Lypiatt:

> You disgust me. You disgust – you and your odious little sham eighteenth-century civilization; your piddling little poetry; your art for art's sake instead of for God's sake; your hoggish materialism, your bestial indifference to all that's unhappy and your yelping hatred of all that's great.

For in some ways Aldous was the last of the Victorians, as responsive as any of the nineteenth-century Olympians to what G. M. Young has called 'the peculiar element, what Clough called "an almost animal sensibility of conscience", this super-morality of the nerves and sense, of bodily repulsion and social alarm'.

Quite apart from misunderstanding of the points which the author was trying to make, there were other results of the first Aldous novels. One was a reinforcement of the existing public image. Many readers found it difficult to think in human terms of the author who could discuss the fate of the world with what was called 'a puritanical hatred of life and a bleak cerebral pessimism'. Years later a critic could still claim that 'Huxley the novelist has been hampered . . . by his deficient sympathy with human beings. One cannot read Huxley's fiction without becoming painfully conscious that this is an author who is revolted by the human spectacle . . .'. The comment typifies an attitude. 'Revolted by' suggests a part only of the true feeling; 'appalled by,' 'distressed by' – these convey better the novelist's reaction to the facts of life. Most writers run this occupational risk – that the inner motives which drive them to write will be misunderstood. Huxley's risk was greater than most since his intellectual stature combined with physical disability to widen the gulf between himself and the average reader and critic. Thus he remained in the public imagination as the quintessence of the young, advanced intellectual, aloofly looking down from the heights through his thick glasses. 'Surely,' Gilbert Frankau wrote a few years later, 'even Mr Huxley must yearn, every now and again amidst his snow and ice, for the warm companionship of kindly, ordinary, everyday men and women.'

This was only partially true, although Aldous himself did something to create the picture:

> I belong to that class of unhappy people who are not easily affected by crowd excitement. Too often I find myself sadly unmoved in the midst of multitudinous emotion. Few sensations are more disagreeable. The defect is in part temperamental, and in part due to that intellectual snobbishness, that fastidious rejection of what is easy and obvious, which is one of the melancholy consequences of the acquisition of culture.

Yet even Aldous would have drawn the line at 'ordinary, everyday'; warmth, companionship, kindliness, were essentials to one side of his character, just as those of his grandfather had included, much to the surprise of the Archbishop's wife, the ability to be 'a loving father and husband'.

D. H. Lawrence perhaps said the last words on the subject. 'But, as I say, there's more than one self to everybody,' he wrote to Lady Ottoline Morrell when commenting on *Point Counter Point* and the way in which the death of the child in it had distressed Maria,

> and the Aldous that writes those novels is only one little Aldous among others – probably much nicer – that don't write novels – I mean it's only one of his little selves that writes the book and makes the child die, it's not *all* himself. No, I don't like his books: even if I admire a sort of repulsion and repudiation. . . .

Another result of the early novels sprang from the caste-like structure of the social order of which Huxley wrote. As Philip Quarles says in *Point Counter Point*, 'the chief defect of the novel of ideas is that you must write about people who have ideas to express – which excludes all but about ·01 per cent of the human race.' It was natural that Aldous should write of this ·01 per cent. 'My circle of acquaintance,' he wrote in the *Athenaeum* in the early 1920s,

> includes a certain number of journalists, poets, novelists, dons, editors, painters, upper middle class families, a few domestic servants, peasants and gardeners, a few of the idle and elegant rich – and that is about all. Of the business men, of whom we hear so much in the press, I do not think that I know one; of all the teeming millions who live in the suburbs and come up daily to the City, I am also wholly ignorant. I have never so much as passed a night in any of the great industrial towns of the North. I have never talked to a miner or a steel worker or a cotton operative. Of the more than a million regular readers of the *Daily Mirror* I am acquainted with perhaps two dozen, and I have no reason to suppose that they represent the mental average of that enormous audience.

Thus the experience of the novelist chimed in perfectly with his artistic requirements. But the result laid him open to Left-wing attack. On one level, he could be described by Mirsky in *The Intelligentsia of Great Britain* as the writer who 'with cynical irony . . . describes the world in which the parasitic bourgeois consumers come into contact with bohemian producers'. On another it was concluded that he condoned, even if he did not applaud, a system under which a group of argumentative lay-abouts could run the world. This mattered little during the late 1920s; a decade later, when Huxley's pacifism conflicted with the view that all good men should come to the aid of the party in the fight against Fascism, it mattered a good deal.

The novels of the 1920s made Huxley's name. They also produced more than one tremor of worry among his friends. For the value of the four novels as commentary on a period stems partly from the fact that Huxley's raw material had lain around him. He had merely to listen in order to hear, drolly talking, the human beings who were the physical embodiment of his various ideas. The Huxley world was peopled with artists and scientists and writers and thinkers, and extravagantly sprinkled with a condiment of post-war characters who showed nature apeing art in every grotesque gesture. Once the characters had been chosen they merely had to be manipulated; or, if one were lucky, and Aldous frequently was, one had only to observe the characters at play.

As one watched, the basic material grew and changed before one's eyes, ready for shaping like newly-risen dough. Thus, like all good reporters, he succeeded in pinning down the essentials of the world he saw and understood; he knew – intuitively, in his bones as Snow would say – that this world was passing and he succeeded in getting it into the exhibition case before the colours faded. His success in this was emphasized thirty years later by V. S. Pritchett who in reviewing Huxley's *Collected Short Stories* noted that

> The old educated class is seen breaking with Victorian commitment as it loses its sons or its property, and ascending into that captious island of Laputa which floated in sunny detachment above Western Europe between the wars.

This ascent into Laputa was described through the experiences of those who were not only plausible but also recognizable; and there are dangers, both artistic and legal, in leaving the raw material too raw. This was brought home by Raymond Mortimer in his review of *Antic Hay*:

> The only characters even in his new book which seem at all real are those that I recognize as portraits. These I can clothe with the flesh which I know them to possess, and I suspect that some of the characters whose reality escapes me would take on life if I had the honour to know their originals. But an author cannot rely on his readers to do this part of the work for him.

There were other dangers, although Huxley avoided them by a combination of skill and luck. Lady Ottoline Morrell did not object to the way in which she scandalously dominated some of his pages; nor did J. S. Haldane object to the resemblance that some saw between himself and Lord Edward in *Point Counter Point*. The original of Lord Badgery in *The Tillotson Banquet* no doubt recognized himself but acquiesced, as did J. S. Haldane's son, J.B.S., when he noted the efforts of Shearwater in *Antic Hay*. Philip Heseltine, the composer known as Peter Warlock, was 'positively delighted' when he recognized himself in *Antic Hay* as Coleman, 'a virile, sinister, diabolic monster of vice and iniquity.'

> I can . . . recall quite clearly the occasion on which the central idea of the book presented itself to Huxley [Cecil Gray writes of *Antic Hay*]. One evening in the summer of 1922, after a Promenade Concert at which Philip and I came across Huxley in company with Eugene Goossens, we all went to Verrey's in Regent Street for a drink, and there, in answer to a question asking why he had grown a

beard, Philip made a witty and brilliant speech of which the essence is reproduced in the book. His inveterate propensity, moreover, for making outrageous puns and plays on words has undoubtedly suggested to Huxley many of the most entertaining witticisms in his 'Where the hormones, there moan I. I long for progeny, I live in hopes, I stope against Stopes', and many similar others, are all in the authentic Phillipic tradition. . . .

Not everyone was as detached. D. H. Lawrence did not object to his appearance as Kingham in 'Two or Three Graces', a short story which appeared in 1926, but he rejected his portrait as Rampion in *Point Counter Point*. And almost half a century after the publication of *Crome Yellow*, Bertrand Russell still took a poor view of Mr Scogan. It was not the description to which he took exception —

> like one of those extinct bird-lizards of the Tertiary. His nose was beaked, his dark eyes had the shining quickness of a robin's . . . The skin of his wrinkled brown face had a dry and scaly look; his hands were the hands of a crocodile.

Russell was not the man to object to accurate if cruel portraiture. He did, however, protest that Mr Scogan was made to put forward seriously the very ideas which he, Russell, had discussed as a joke at one of Lady Ottoline's house-parties. Like Proust, Huxley 'changed nothing and altered everything'.

There was, moreover, Burlap of *Point Counter Point*, identifiably Middleton Murry – even to those who did not know that he had employed on the *Adelphi*, and then sacked, the girl to whom he had been engaged after Katherine Mansfield's death. On reading *Point Counter Point*, Murry had at first thought of challenging Huxley to a duel, an occasion to which Murry's biographer, F. A. Lea, remarks, only Max Beerbohm could have done justice. Murry later wrote:

> I couldn't resist looking out the passages about Birlap [sic]. I don't know whether A.H. intends him as a caricature of me; but he's certainly too generally intelligent not to know it would be taken by others as a caricature of me. And that, I supposed, is rather disgusting of him.
>
> But oddly enough it doesn't seem to touch me personally (I may be deluding myself about this, of course; if I am, at some future time I shall surprise myself by feeling an intense hatred of A.H. But it doesn't seem possible). I have been hurt in this way, by D. H. Lawrence, once – made to squirm – by a short-story about myself; but the difference is, I suspect, that I have a pretty deep admiration

for Lawrence, and I haven't for A.H. In other terms: D.H.L. can stick the barb in deep, and A.H. can't.

And that's about all I can say. I think I know myself well enough to be positive that my only valuable reaction is a feeling that A.H. has rather beautifully confirmed my own strong impression that he hasn't very much notion of what I *am* driving at. I have thought that any time during the last six or seven years; and that, rather oddly – here perhaps is some corroboration of the feeling of yourself and others about him – because I have felt that if he really had a notion he would be on my side. . . .

And, one thing more. A.H. has settled it. I must call my blessed book 'God'. It would be monstrous in me to try to safeguard myself against that kind of misinterpretation. One is frightfully tempted to: but it's weakness. So I'm grateful to Birlap for making me realize this clearly.

But more went to the complaint than personalities. For the essential difference between Murry and Huxley – and a good deal of what they stood for – was that they wrote at opposite ends of the argument; both rebelled about the condition of man, social and otherwise, but Huxley was the rebel from within, while Murry was the outsider.

First with *Crome Yellow* and then with *Antic Hay* Huxley had pulled the right lever of the literary machine. The money at last began to flow in. So did contracts. At last he could take the voyage round the world that he had promised himself and Maria, a trip justified by the contract for a book on the journey. India was to be the main objective. The book was to be *Jesting Pilate*. And the result of the journey was to focus an increasing amount of his thought on that mysticism of the East which had attracted him in his Oxford days.

In Lahore, as elsewhere, Huxley and Maria stayed with an Indian family, a circumstance that might have proved an embarrassment. For at Lahore there was stationed Christopher Huxley, Aldous's cousin, who had stayed on in the army as a regular soldier after the war. And there now followed the almost unprecedented situation in which a white family actually living with Indians was invited to an army mess, an event which cut clean across the *mores* of the times. 'The extraordinary thing,' Christopher Huxley recalled, 'was the way in which Aldous made himself liked by everyone – even the more crusty characters for whom his reputation as a writer was no recommendation at all.' His lasting memory is of Aldous watching a ceremonial march-past, standing like a stork on two legs and gradually beginning to sway with the music.

The travels in India – and to a lesser extent his journey across the United States on the last leg of the road home – marked a watershed in Huxley's life.

> I set out on my travels knowing, or thinking that I knew, how men should live, how be governed, how educated, what they should believe [he concluded]. I knew which was the best form of social organization and to what end societies had been created. I had my views on every activity of human life. Now, on my return, I find myself without any of these pleasing certainties. . . . My own losses, as I have said, were numerous. But in compensation for what I had lost, I acquired two important new convictions: that it takes all sorts to make a world, and that the established spiritual values are fundamentally correct and should be maintained. . . . But if travel brings a conviction of human diversity, it brings an equally strong conviction of human unity. It inculcates tolerance, but it also shows what are the limits of possible toleration. Religious and moral codes, forms of government and of society are almost endlessly varied, and each has a right to its separate existence. But a oneness underlies this diversity. All men, whatever their beliefs, their habits, their way of life, have a sense of values. And the values are everywhere and in all kinds of society broadly the same.

Here was a first glimpse of the path which he was to follow, the first sight of the 'oneness' which he was to see as the essential reality and which was throughout the next third of a century to dominate his beliefs. The change had a mixed reception. 'We feel,' the reviewer noted in *The Times Literary Supplement*, 'less surprise than a touch of malicious satisfaction at the spectacle of Saul meekly harping accompaniment to the prophets whose beards he has so often tweaked in the past.'

In one other way the journey to India marked a watershed. Before it, Huxley had been economically tied. Now all could be different. 'Professionally free,' he wrote after his return, 'I have taken care not to encumber myself with the shackles that tie a man down to one particular plot of ground; I own nothing, nothing beyond a few books and the motor-car which enables me to move from one encampment to another.' And so, for the rest of the 1920s, he moved – away from England whose meteorological climate both he and his wife disliked and whose social climate they detested, away to Italy or southern France, to small hill-towns where one could consider life with a gentle civilized consideration; where one could live well and cheaply and think one's own thoughts, at one's own pace, at one's own time, as one wished. It was a life they lived for more than a decade, both determined that the ties of family, house, and domesticity should be as slender as could be. A minor problem had been Matthew, the son born in 1920. But the Huxleys could always be relied upon to come to the aid of the family. Matthew, therefore, was cared for by one relative after another until, in God's good time, he was able to join the caravanserai.

It was, in many ways, a less opulent travelling-party than legend transmits. The story of the special box built to accommodate the *Britannica* itself implies a luxury vehicle to contain it. In fact, most of the early motoring was done in a 10-horse-power Citroën, while the *Britannica* consisted of one volume of the twelfth half-size edition, printed on India paper. 'It was,' says Bertrand Russell, 'the only book that ever influenced Huxley. You could always tell by his conversation which volume he'd been reading. One day it would be Alps, Andes and Appennines, and the next it would be the Himalayas and the Hippocratic Oath.'

There was also, never omitted from a waistcoat pocket, the small sexto-decimo of La Rochefoucauld's *Maxims*, which 'take a minute to read and provide matter upon which thought can ruminate for hours'. In addition there were other essentials – 'A pair of spectacles for reading, a pair for long range, with a couple of monocles in reserve'. To these, in the summer, in the South, there were added, as he put it in *Along the Road*, 'three pairs of coloured glasses – two of light and darker shades of green, and one black. The glare from dusty roads, from white walls and the metalic blue-hot sky is painful and even dangerous. As the summer advances or retreats, as the light of each day waxes or declines, I adjust to my nose the pale green, the dark green or the black spectacles. In this way I am able to temper the illumination of the world to my exact requirements.' All this was still necessary. For Geoffrey Young's mountaineer the constant companion – 'I never see him but his tread Sounds just before my own' – was the dark angel of Death; for Aldous it was blindness.

While the threat remained suspended he and Maria travelled, moving at the bidding of season and spirit to Cortina, to Vence, to Les Diablerets, occasionally back to London, sometimes to Spain, but most frequently to Tuscany. Quite apart from his novels he was producing more poems, numerous essays. He was writing once more for *Vogue*, and for its American stable-companion *Vanity Fair*, but now his contributions were travel articles or essays hung on whatever suitable peg circumstance offered – 'The Spread of Bad Art', 'Socratic Dialogues of the Moment', 'A Plea for Individual Education' or 'Reading, the New Vice'. He wrote now and again for *Harper's Bazaar*, for *The Nation*, keeping the pot busily boiling and producing enough income to cover the family's peripatetic existence from one village to another.

To those who knew him well Aldous already exhibited that quality of detachment which enabled him to look inquiringly at the world that included even such odd creatures as himself. Yet nothing could be commonplace; everything presented innumerable connections with the rest of reality, and each connection helped to transform the reality. It was this that was remembered years later, rather than the details of his talk, his wit, or his ambitious plans for new literary enterprises. Thus a cousin, Renée Tickell, daughter of Oriana Haynes, great-granddaughter of TH, forty years later recalled one memorable visit to the Huxleys' home on the hills above Florence:

> I was very young, and did not enjoy as much as I should now his stimulating talk about the pictures and buildings of Florence itself in the hot light and black shadow of a brilliant June. In fact I longed to go swimming. But I have never forgotten his discussion of a great house we visited with its formal gardens and fountains and cypresses, or the way in which his being there enhanced every moment of a walk in deep-evening dusk through a field of young wheat with the green fireflies rising and falling on either side of the path. One's own enjoyment of the landscape was quickened by his reflection of it. One perceived it as it were 'quivering within the wave's intenser day'.

During these years of travel in the latter half of the 1920s, Huxley was greatly influenced by D. H. Lawrence, whom he had first met during the first world war. His account of the meeting is as informative of himself as it is of Lawrence who was, so they both imagined, about to set off for Florida to found a colony of escape:

> Before tea was over, he asked me if I would join the colony, and although I was an intellectually cautious young man, not at all inclined to enthusiasms, though Lawrence had startled and embarrassed me with sincerities of a kind to which my upbringing had not accustomed me, I answered 'yes'. Fortunately, no doubt, the Florida scheme fell through. . . . It was better that it should have remained, as it always was to remain, a project and a hope. And I knew this even as I said I would join the colony.

Lawrence had no doubts. 'I liked Huxley *very* much,' he wrote to Lady Ottoline. 'He will come to Florida.'

A decade later, while in India, Aldous received a letter from Lawrence who had read and liked some of his essays and who now sought a meeting. Nearly a year passed. Then, in September 1926, Huxley called on Lawrence in London, making a casual visit before leaving for Cortina where he was taking a house for the winter months.

The real friendship began two months later after Aldous and Maria had driven in their new car up the corkscrew road to Lawrence's Villa di Mirenda at Scandicci, lying in the pine-clad hills seven miles from Florence. For the next four years their paths crossed and inter-crossed. At Scandicci, on the glass-enclosed second-floor belvedere of the house, overlooking Florence and the silver curves of the Arno, they began the first long discussions in which they dissected the problems of the writer and the ways in which he should tackle them.

From the first it was Lawrence who influenced Aldous.

> D.H.L. in admirable form, talking wonderfully [Aldous noted in his diary on one occasion]. He is one of the few people I feel real respect and admiration for. Of most other eminent people I have met I feel that at any rate I belong to the same species as they do. But this man has something different and superior in kind, not degree.

Lawrence's feelings about Aldous were mixed. He read the first seventy pages of *Proper Studies*, Huxley's first attempt to give man a political context, 'with a little astonishment that you are so serious and professional. You are not your grandfather's *Enkel* for nothing —' he added, 'that funny dry-mindedness and underneath social morality.' But the following year, with the appearance of *Point Counter Point*, and himself as Mark Rampion, he commented on Huxley's preponderance of intellect; and of his need for a further scope of instinctive and intuitive awareness – speaking thoughtfully, and commenting '*poor* old Aldous, *poor* old Aldous'. To Huxley himself he wrote in different vein:

> I have read 'Point Counter Point' with a heart sinking through my boot-soles and a rising admiration. I do think you've shown the truth, perhaps the last truth, about you and your generation, with really fine courage. It seems to me it would take ten times the courage to write P. Counter P. that it took to write Lady C., and if the public knew *what* it was reading, it would throw a hundred stones at you, to one at me.

It was natural for Lawrence to use *Lady Chatterley* as a yardstick, since more than one member of the Huxley family had by this time become involved with her fortunes. At the beginning of the year Aldous and Maria had taken a chalet at Les Diablerets where the Lawrences had moved for a few months owing to Lawrence's health. And to the Huxleys' chalet he came to discuss the book, the first half of which was arriving from London in typescript. Maria sat at the head of the table in the immaculate wooden room, Aldous near-by in a pale olive corduroy suit. The Julian Huxleys, making one of their regular Swiss visits, had a chalet close by, and Juliette was also present. The conversation ranged across the universe with Lawrence 'trying to frighten Aldous off his four-square rationalist perch'. One result was that Maria was conscripted to type the second half of *Lady Chatterley's Lover*.

To type but not to utter, as she discovered one day when Lawrence approached her with distress and embarrassment. 'Maria,' he said, 'you must never use that word again.'

'But Lawrence,' she replied, 'you're always using it in *Lady Chatterley*. Besides, it's a very good word.'

'It would shock Aldous,' Lawrence insisted. 'It is not a good word at all, and anyway it would never do.'

According to Humphry Osmond, to whom Maria later recounted the incident, Maria was puzzled since Aldous had not appeared distressed; but as Lawrence obviously was, she dropped the word from her vocabulary.

However, it was not only Aldous and Maria who were drawn into the vicissitudes of *Lady Chatterley*. Juliette also read the manuscript and was, according to Lawrence, '*very* cross, morally so'. What, she contemplated aloud, if her son Anthony were sixteen and the book fell into his hands – a reaction that persisted in spite of her later less critical comments. Should it not, she suggested rather savagely, be called *John Thomas and Lady Jane*? Lawrence noted that many a true word is spoken in spite – and promptly changed the title; something, probably caution, eventually restored the original.

Two months later, when Secker's had refused to print the book, Lawrence wrote despairingly to Aldous, saying that he had to sell a thousand copies. 'So you must help me,' he added. 'I'll send you a little batch of order-forms, and I'm sure you and Maria will make a few folks buy.' And the following month it was to either Aldous or Maria that he instructed his agent to hand the manuscript, trusting them to ensure that it would not be impounded. Eventually, in Italy, he was successful in arranging publication and commented to Aldous:

> I've corrected forty-one pages of proofs and it was *almost* Maria's typing over again. Dear Maria, all those little mistakes you made, and I followed like Wenceslas's page so patiently in your footsteps: now it's a Florentine printer. He writes dind't, dnid't, din't, din'dt, didn't like a Bach fugue.

The Huxleys helped to buttress Lawrence as the contemporary gales swept round his head, and they were with him at the end, staying at a near-by hotel in Vence when they knew that he was dying, and helping him through his final hours. Some of his vital spirit had flashed across to Aldous, influencing him, possibly in spite of himself, throughout the later 1920s when his reputation was being confirmed. Now, by one of those coincidences that infect history, another influence began to make itself felt as the old one passed away.

(*iii*)

The Realist, a literary magazine whose editorial board included H. G. Wells, Arnold Bennett, Harold Laski, Rebecca West and the two Huxley brothers, had been started in London in the spring of 1929. The magazine 'carried no advertisement, paid no salaries, and delayed on all bills and author's remittances' according to its editor. Yet it had for a while 'like the primitive Montgolfier balloons, buoyed up by the hot air of literary reputations, held its inflated course'. It had been able to do so since those running it thought they had been underwritten for at least two years by Lord Melchett, Chairman of I.C.I., a happy circumstance which they believed gave them, among other things, immunity from advertisers. However, the backing was not forthcoming; there were financial difficulties after four issues, and the magazine ceased publication after ten. Before this, however, it had published, spread across its first three issues, Aldous Huxley's illuminating study of Blaise Pascal. In January 1930, as *The Realist* died, Aldous met the editor, apparently for the first time. This was Gerald Heard, writer-cum-philosopher-cum-journalist, whose future works were to range from *The Creed of Christ* to *The Riddle of the Flying Saucers (Is Another World Watching?)*, and whose literary awards were to include the Henrietta Herz Prize administered by the British Academy and First Prize in an Ellery Queen Mystery Magazine contest.

> Huxley was worth study as a presence quite as much as in his works: six feet four inches tall, eyes dilated through high-magnification lenses, broad, lofty forehead and, on the top of that, an outsize-brimmed felt that [he has written of their introduction at a mutual friend's]. Before listening, one needed to take in. And his approach, his 'port', had about it something of a galleon's. He came in, as it were, under full sail, a long coat billowing around him. The voice, however, was as neat as a seamstress's stitching. And, indeed, the

long fingers made the precise movements of a needlewoman handling thread and seam. One would have expected from that leonine head (for the hat doffed showed the ancestral, Thomas Henry Huxley mane) at least an echo of the grandfather's roar.

The two men talked until the early hours. Huxley accompanied Heard to his doorstep, then made off for a two-mile walk home through deserted London streets.

They met again: they met frequently. By January 1932, Heard and Aldous were discussing on the radio 'Is Cruelty Out of Date?' And throughout the next few years it became clear that Huxley's developing views were being influenced by those of Heard. Initially he had merely regarded man's predicament and had insisted that his readers, also, regarded it. This largely negative attitude was slowly transformed by a growing interest in the changes which might be made in man's political and social organizations; by a deepening awareness of the perils, as well as the possibilities, presented by a science which gave man increasing control over his environment; and finally by a mounting belief that all problems might be solved by a spiritual intuition which rose triumphantly from that borderland between mind and matter which had so intrigued his grandfather half a century earlier.

Some hint of these developments which were to condition his thoughts might have been seen in his early poems, in more than one story from *Limbo*, and in the closing pages of *Jesting Pilate*. Yet the first intimation of what they might become was given in *Proper Studies*, in which he ruminates on political democracy, on the idea of equality, on the essence of religion, and on the ways in which education might best cope with the biological inequality of mankind. The first of his books with an openly serious intent, it tended to confuse both critics and public, who now found themselves considering a literary animal certainly different in form from the novelist, and possibly very different in power; an animal which was now apparently changing, chameleon-like, into the teacher, the professional philosopher, the writer who had ceased merely to regard his curious fellows and was now telling them how they might better their intellectual selves and their physical condition.

This new attitude revealed by *Proper Studies* had developed into a focal point of Huxley's beliefs by 1936, when *The Olive Tree* was published. The nine years between the two books took him from the heart of dedicated intellectualism to the verge of mysticism. Much of the journey was taken in the company of Heard, and some at least of the steps were influenced by Matthias Alexander, the Australian physiologist-philosopher who, in Aldous's words, was to reveal 'a totally new type of education affecting the entire range of human activity, from the physiological, through the intellectual, moral and practical, to the spiritual. . . .' During these years the journalistic flood did not abate, but it was significant that the first of a series of feature-page articles which Aldous contributed to *The Sunday Referee* was on 'The Problem of Faith'. He wrote more than 150 pieces for *The Chicago Herald and Examiner*, many of them syndicated across the United States; and in these, too, there were many indications of the direction in which his beliefs were moving. Like his grandfather and his brother, he had no objection to proclaiming these beliefs in the market-place, where he could find the largest audience, and by 1936 he was possibly the best-known Huxley of them all, already the subject of critical studies, the first of the flood which was to rise round him during the next two decades.

His output is all the more remarkable in view of the fact that he wrote neither easily nor quickly. His manuscripts, first typed then hand-corrected, were partly re-written, amended, and then in part written again. Looking at the be-mazed page one is reminded of Huxley's own comment in 'Joyce, the Artificer' on the way that James Joyce worked:

> His discovery of what he wished to say was like the conquest of Mexico. It began with the islands, touched the mainland, climbed to an astounding vision of pyramids and feathered warriors and ended in the triumphant capture of Tenochtitlan. Shakespeare would have landed on the roof of Montezuma's palace by helicopter. Joyce has to take the long, hard road. However, he got there in the end. And that, after all, is the only thing that matters.

Huxley also got there, and his progress can be clearly followed through the eighteen books and plays which he wrote during these years between 1927 and 1936. Some are naturally of more significance than others. There was, for instance, *The World of Light* whose central character was the tender-hearted, methodical Mr Wenham, who had 'never taken a risk, never strayed off the asphalt path of duty, in his whole life; never, though he was made for intimacy, come close to children, friends or wife'. Here, as in *Limbo*, Huxley laid himself open to a family complaint that he had unduly allowed autobiographical over-tones to intrude. More than a trace of Leonard Huxley, some felt, was concealed in Mr Wenham.

The choice of spiritualism as the vehicle upon which to load the ideas expressed in *The World of Light* was symptomatic of the direction in which Aldous's mind was by this time moving. Spiritualism itself might be largely the province of charlatans, but he had been drawn to consider it as he broke away from his quizzical contemplation of man's lot and began to wonder what man might do about it. The question of what happened after death, the riddle of the connection between mind and matter, the difficulty of discovering some framework into which the apparent answers to these conundrums could be fitted with any semblance of intellectual honesty – these were the subjects to which Aldous now began to devote increasing thought, and it is fortunate that his position at this period, cut free from his previous beliefs and not yet safely anchored up to the new ones, should have been held and fixed by a long newspaper interview in the London *Observer*. It is significant that it was one of a series held mainly with scientists, including Sir James Jeans and Max Planck.

Huxley said that he would like to think that life on earth was not by accident, but that he could see no evidence to support the happy thought; however, he was not certain. There was also the question of suffering – that question which runs like a dark line through so much of his work. He found it 'at present quite inexplicable', and he had 'read no explanation of it which seems at all plausible', he told J. W. N. Sullivan.

> Of all the explanations I have been offered I find the Indian notion of Karma the most satisfactory; I mean the notion that our past lives condition our present life. But the Indians suppose that the final end of the whole thing is Nirvana, and that prospect does not seem to me very pleasing.
>
> No, I am afraid there is no solution. Evil is an absolute thing. It is not an aspect of good. It cannot be explained away. If there is a scheme I think it must be something of which we would approve. That is to say, if there is a universal mind, I do not think it can be indifferent to human values and aspirations. It must be a mind something like ours. And I expect the whole problem arises because of our undeveloped consciousness. Very likely the problem does not really exist at all. It is a pseudo-problem, and originates merely from the way we think about things. Of course, if there is a scheme of things, something that we could call ultimate reality, then it is possible that our values, that I have called purely human, really refer to this reality. But I confess that I am a pragmatist by temperament. My tendency is to believe that everything is purely human, and that nothing in our experience points beyond itself to some ultimate reality. . . . I don't believe that a man's personality survives his death, but I think there is very good evidence that something survives.

Huxley was, in fact, already moving towards the position he outlined two years later.

> My own belief is that in a pessimistic Humanism . . . man will be able to find a philosophy at once sufficiently realistic and sufficiently noble, an ideal sufficiently high, a faith sufficiently inspiring. One great obstacle, however, stands in the way of the immediate acceptance of Humanism. The philosophy of reason has not yet been interpreted in those terms of picturesque and exciting unreason which alone have power to move the minds of men. Not until it is so interpreted can it become a power in the world.

This was, it is intriguing to note, the very task which his brother Julian was already taking up; and it is equally intriguing to realize that as his brother carried out the interpretation Aldous himself moved away from the concept of humanism into the fields of eastern mysticism which he was already contemplating.

Before this move was to be complete, he was to produce two books which are among the most remarkable items of his remarkable output: *Brave New World* and *Eyeless in Gaza*. The first, an anti-Utopian novel on the grand scale, has become the more famous of the two, partly because it is easier to read, telling a simpler story in a simpler way; partly because it had the initial publicity of numerous public library bannings – 'if people choose to do ridiculous things, let them', said Aldous – and the widespread benefit of attacks such as Dr Hensley Henson's condemnation of it as 'a gross book, grossly written'.

In it, Huxley carries to its logical conclusion the misapplication of science which he feared would inevitably come about in a democratic world, a world where the ideal of the greatest good for the greatest number would cause standards to slip slowly down from precedent to precedent. The dehumanized sterilized existence of *Brave New World*, with babies born in bottles, 'the feelies' on tap for simulated pleasure, and mind-control a working proposition, was extraordinary in its foresight. There had been able prophets before, but Huxley was one of the few who lived to the verge of their own prophecies. 'The general outlines of the book are true today,' he said a few months before his death, roughly a third of a century after *Brave New World* was written; 'the drugs, the organization of society, the problems of leisure. Everyone knows now that a scientific dictatorship would not use terror because terror is very inefficient. The manipulation of minds is better than clubs or concentration camps.' Yet another feature of *Brave New World*, obvious when it was published, was its almost guileful plausibility, the ease with which it suspended disbelief, so that one puts the book down to meet a shock of relief that the world, after all, is not really like that. This quality no doubt stemmed from Huxley's rough years of journalism, since all that was necessary was for him to contemplate the landscape of his imagination and then carry out on it a thorough reporting job.

So far as the story and its machinery are concerned, therefore, *Brave New World* was a successful *tour de force*. When it came to the moral of the tale, there was a niggling unsatisfying quality which made the book something less than a masterpiece. This chink in the armour has been noted by two writers as dissimilar as Frank Swinnerton in *The Georgian Literary Scene* and Charlotte Haldane who reviewed the book in *Nature*. What Huxley does in the book, Swinnerton claims with some reason,

> is to cry for the old simple earth, the old simplicities of relation, motherhood, mother-tended babies, the unsullied countryside, as if having scorned the Chestertons and Bellocs, he had mysteriously found himself in their army and on the staff with these two stout generals.

Yet the Noble Savage who provides the book with a hero plays an unsatisfactory role, and is as much the figment of the Arnold inheritance as of literary necessity.

> Dr Jekyll and Mr Hyde are nothing to Dr Huxley and Mr Arnold [Charlotte Haldane commented]. Mr Arnold is always doing it. He did it in 'Point Counter Point'; he does it in 'Brave New World'. Dr Huxley who knows and cares about biology and music, science and art, is once again ousted by this double of his, morbid, masochistic, medieval Christian. Mr Arnold takes charge of the last chapter of 'Brave New World'. The result is distressing. Nevertheless, this is a very good book.

It is a very good book almost because of its failure rather than in spite of it. For Huxley knew, when he wrote it, that the Noble Savage, for all his literary usefulness, could not provide an answer to the problem he had posed. He was still, in the early 1930s, searching round for the answer.

The account of that search, as it had been made since his early days, came four years later and was explained in fictional guise in *Eyeless in Gaza*, a novel with which any student of the Huxley family can play an intriguing game. Aldous wanted to clarify his own thoughts and to explain how and why he had taken one particular path. He wanted to explain his position in the situation presented by the growth of the Axis powers, a situation which for thousands of men and women was bringing the problems of right and wrong from the impersonal debating chamber to the personal gas chamber. And now that his father was dead he felt able to clear his mind of the bottled-back reactions of the years. What a novel it would be! And what an intellectual exercise to satisfy both self and reader as one looked back through the arches of two decades!

Eyeless in Gaza is the story of Anthony Beavis, who is met in the early pages travelling through the countryside to his mother's funeral on just such a winter's day as Aldous himself remembered. Carefully cut sections of reality are disguised and utilized throughout the book, their private significance just deftly concealed from public understanding – so that the young Aldous, waiting in the great entrance cavity of the Natural History Museum as TH's statue is unveiled, valiantly fighting down the sickness and quietly asking for an Etonian topper in case the worst happened, becomes the young Anthony, equally queasy at his mother's funeral. The unfortunate father in *The World of Light* might have been discerned as a portrait in which some traits of Leonard Huxley could be seen, yet this was a pallid comparison when matched against the deeply etched figure of Mr Beavis in *Eyeless in Gaza*. It is not only the widower who is here; while later in the book there follow other incidents in the Huxley progress. Here, in almost photographic detail, is a transmuted record of the pre-war holiday below the Scheidegg, complete with incidents long remembered. Here also – shown as Dr Miller, the 'elderly little man, short and spare', who had 'a mouth like an inquisitor's. But the inquisitor had forgotten himself and learned to smile' – is Matthias Alexander, the Australian who, in searching for a system of muscular control, devised a method used by Archbishop Temple, Shaw and the Crippses, as well as by Aldous Huxley.

The portrayal of living people in forms far less carefully disguised than the novelist's caution usually demands, was not the only notable feature of *Eyeless in Gaza*. While the juggling with reality produced three-dimensional characters more living and personal than those of Huxley's earlier novels, a juggling with time was used in presenting their story. For the narrative does not flow forward in chronological progress. Instead, it plays tricks with time and shuffles, without immediately obvious reason, the events during four widely separated periods of Anthony Beavis's life. Thus Miller's instruction 'in use of the self' comes before the first casual contact with Miller, the flight of Helen from Anthony Beavis comes before their first adult meeting. Superficially the method has failings. The most painstaking writer can make slips and in this case Edward Thomas's poetry is read before its publication, while Brewer's Temperance Movement is accidentally referred to some years before it came into existence. For the reader there are other difficulties and, as Phyllis Bentley has noted, in analysing not only the book but its reconstruction in chronological sequence, 'a card index should not be necessary for the understanding of a work of art.' Yet in an odd way the method succeeds – quite apart from its value in obfuscating any chance of a libel action. For what at first appears to have been the haphazard over-printing and re-over-printing of mental negatives is finally seen to be a process of enforcing the book's impact. The extraordinary shock which the story produces at times may be the result of a complicated intellectual exercise on the part of the author, but the result is there, a result which would have been deadened or lost completely had Huxley followed the Churchillian dictum that the whole art of story-telling lies in chronology.

There was some family feeling about the book, even some hint that it was a betrayal of the recently dead. Aldous touched on this very question two years later when an interviewer from the *Saturday Review of Literature* hypothesized that heartlessness was one of the three main criticisms of his writing.

> I don't feel myself to be extremely heartless [Huxley replied]. But the impression is partly my fault. I have a literary theory that I must have a two-angled vision of all my characters. You know how closely farce and tragedy are related. That's because the comic and the tragic are the same thing seen from different angles. I try to get a stereoscopic vision, to show my characters from two angles simultaneously. Either I try to show them both as they feel themselves to be, and as others feel them to be; or else I try to give them rather similar characters who throw light on each other, two characters who share the same element, but in one it is made grotesque.

It was significant that he agreed that father and son in *Eyeless in Gaza* were examples of this.

Eyeless in Gaza was a full fleshy novel in the way that the earlier quartet was not. Even for those who did not know the details of Aldous's personal involvement with his characters, it was obvious that he felt as strongly about them as about the ideas they put forward. It was here, when it came to the ideas, that many critics parted company with him. David Garnett, for instance, described the book as Huxley's finest novel. However, he felt forced to write of Beavis, the mouthpiece for the author's philosophy, that

> his real trouble seems to be that he is a victim of words; that he can never stop pinning out the facts and ideas like an entomologist arranging a collection of dead butterflies. The trouble is that there are a terrible lot of cabbage whites and meadow browns among them.

The widespread criticism of the ideas, as distinct from criticism of the vehicle used to carry them, was partly due to the climate of the times. When *Eyeless in Gaza* appeared in the summer of 1936, Europe was already looking upwards towards the watershed of the war, a barrier which seemed with increasing clarity to cut off the way ahead. Hitler had already been in power for five years, and England was about to be split down the middle on the subject of intervention in Spain, where Franco's forces were on the point of rebellion against the legally elected Government. Even in the creative world, where Picasso was awaiting Guernica and Hemingway preparing to hear the bell toll, one might agree or disagree but one did not stand aside. At least, that was the normal reaction. Yet the end of the philosophical journey described by Huxley brought him to the verge of the mystic's non-attachment which he was to pin down in detail two years later:

> Non-attached to his bodily sensations and lusts. Non-attached to his craving for power and possessions. Non-attached to his anger and hatred; non-attached to his exclusive loves. Non-attached to wealth, fame, social position. Non-attached even to science, art, speculation, philanthropy. Yes, non-attached even to these for, like patriotism, in Nurse Cavell's phrase, 'they are not enough.'

However, there was one great exception: by the summer of 1936 Huxley was firmly and resolutely attached to the pacifist cause.

It is easy to consider this pacifism as a combination of good intentions and a divorce from the real world which sprang from physical disability and intellectual superiority. Yet this was not quite the case. In Italy he had found that the Fascist authorities were opening his mail. His political opinions were known and resented, and in the early 1930s he had moved into France, buying a rambling house on the coast at Sanary near Toulon. He was aware of the evil and he was also strangely aware, in at least one respect, of how the dictators might have been penned away from war. This is revealed by Gerald Heard, who has explained how Huxley

> had apt, practical and immediate proposals as to how by foresight the cataclysm could be postponed, time gained; how by skilled economic pressure the mechanized military monster that Germany was undisguisedly building could have its growth seriously embarrassed. For instance, he and I found out (it was easy to discover) how anxious the Nazi armament engineers were to get nickel, of which Germany was desperately short. The next thing was to see where the vital stocks lay – and that was in Canada. The price to corner the whole Canadian load was not much more than that of one of those

floating steel anachronisms still then called 'Dreadnoughts'. Through relatives we were able to get our brief but enormously important statement to the fatal Chamberlain. He sent back verbally the pet word of the purblind, 'Impractical'.

Looking back today, with all the accumulated advantages of hindsight, it is easy to see that such schemes, set against the dedicated aggressiveness of the German leaders, may indeed have been impractical. Yet they also suggest that Aldous, shut off though he was from the cut-and-thrust of the ordinary world, nevertheless held a strongly realist view of what made wars practicable.

Yet this proposal for peacetime economic warfare was at variance with the methods proposed by Aldous in his espousal of the pacifist cause. On 16 October 1934 Canon Dick Sheppard had proposed that a positive pacifist movement should be started in Britain. Among those who agreed to support him in the foundation of what became the Peace Pledge Union there was General Crozier, Rose Macaulay, Siegfried Sassoon, Donald Soper, Arthur Wragg and Bertrand Russell. There was also Aldous Huxley, who overcame his resistance to public speaking in order to lecture on 'Peace and Internationalism', and who now began to throw the weight of his name and the vigour of his dialectic behind the pacifist cause.

There were three strands in the reasoning which led him to support the movement which, however good its intentions, fed Hitler's belief that he could wage aggression with impunity so far as Britain was concerned. The first was the conviction that bad means invariably produce bad ends; there was his basic leaning towards non-attachment and its corollary, wartime non-resistance; and there was, more simple yet perhaps more important, his difficulty in realizing that men would not, when it came to the crunch, be swayed by logical, reasonable, responsible, commonsense arguments. This difficulty is easy to understand. Basically, Aldous did not believe that human nature could be so unrealistic as to follow, in that day and age, the road that led to war. Reason, surely, must come uppermost if only it were put forward by enough strong, logical voices? This misapprehension arose from the basic goodness which prevented him from realizing that a minority of men could be as bad as they were; from his abnormal intellectual fibre which prevented him from realizing that the majority of men could be as stupid as they were; and from his physical incapacities and personal fastidiousness which shielded him from a full knowledge of the way the wicked world turned. Thus he did more than believe in the moral purpose of pacifism. At times he actually believed it would work.

This hope is made clear in *What Are You Going to Do About It? The Case for Constructive Peace*, which appeared in 1936. Here Huxley starts by raising the objections of the heckler who claims that 'war is a law of nature'; and he then successfully shows that this is not so. He proves that man is not, in fact, 'a fighting animal.' He disproves the theory that war selects the fittest human beings. He rightly claims that war 'is only one, and that the worst, of schools in which men can learn the military virtues'. And he has the courage to admit that in modern war non-violence itself will inevitably be ineffective and that once war has broken out pacifists are almost helpless. Thus far, one follows the argument without reason dissenting. But there then comes his proposal for dealing with Germany, Italy and Japan:

> Over against these three hungry and thwarted powers, stand four satiated powers, possessing between them the greater part of the world's surface and most of the raw materials indispensable to modern industry. These four powers are the British Empire, the United States, France, and Russia

– a quartet to which he adds Holland, Belgium and Portugal. The answer to the problem is clear.

> The great monopolistic powers should immediately summon a conference at which the unsatisfied powers, great and small, should be invited to state their grievances and claims. When this had been done it would be possible, given intelligence and goodwill, to work out a scheme of territorial, economic and monetary readjustments for the benefit of all.

The weakness lay in deciding what to do if, as many suspected, there were no goodwill. The good cause for suspicion has been shown by the publication, during the last two decades, of the Germans' and Italians' own documents. These make it clear that, even at the time of the Rhineland occupation in 1936, a show of force would have nipped off aggression firmly in the bud. The contemporary reaction to the Huxley pamphlet was well put by Cecil Day Lewis in his reply wherein he argued that the

> . . . Case for Constructive Peace constructs nothing more solid than a great big, beautiful idealist bubble – lovely to look at, no doubt; charming to live in, perhaps; but with little reference to the real facts, and inadequate protection against a four-engined bomber.

This criticism from the Left, which was to swell up a few years later with the publication of *Ends and Means*, may well have been fanned by the atmosphere of isolation from the lower orders which had grown up around Aldous. He was not only able and willing to lacerate society with his criticisms but he appeared with his wife and son as the full-page frontispiece to *The Tatler*. He might be poverty-stricken judged by the standards of those who tried to entice him into the social round, yet he could live for a while in Albany – whose great advantage, his wife pointed out, was that they could do all their household shopping at Fortnum's. All this put added sting into the Left-wing attack.

Yet events have confirmed the view that, while at its best the pacifist argument had an undeniable moral strength, belief in its effectiveness was in the 1930s grotesquely unjustified. The fairest as well as the kindest judgement on the Aldous of this period has been given by Dennis Gabor, the physicist who came to Britain from Berlin in 1934, the year after Hitler's rise to power:

> Between 1931 and 1937 Huxley's spirit soared above all practical considerations, in a tragic epoch in which evil won all the battles in preparation for the great, final blow. The Huxley of this time was a little less than the earlier or the later Huxley – the Huxley who could understand a greater slice of human life than any of his contemporaries. *Satyagraha*, which he advocated, brought Gandhi triumph ten years later, against a mellow, somewhat weary Britain. It would have led to nothing but a catastrophe against a mad Germany and Japan. It was not Huxley at his best who under the influence of Dick Sheppard recommended absolutes; so simple that a child could grasp them but only an angel could follow them.

The essential goodness which induced Huxley to believe that pacifism would actually work also prevented him from apprehending that even for him, a semi-blind man, a journey to the States in 1937, and a continued existence there throughout the war, would affect the reception, and criticism, of his work. Thus he did not hesitate when in the spring of 1937, moved partly by a wish to settle his son in an American university, partly by his wife's horror of involvement in another war, he decided to visit the United States with his family and Gerald Heard.

It is, as we shall see, quite clear from the evidence that when Huxley left Britain he had no firm intention of remaining in the United States. Yet it was rather bitterly remarked by his critics that in *What Are You Going to Do About It?* crossing the Atlantic was not among the recommended answers. And it was unfortunate that he was quoted as saying, as he left, that 'Europe is no place for a Pacifist'

Chapter XI

A Diaspora of Huxleys

By the 1930s, the name of Huxley had once again become as well-known as it had been at the height of TH's fame. But while the renown of the previous century had been borne on one man's shoulders, now it was borne mainly by two. Julian and Aldous – or Aldous and Julian if tastes went that way – dominated the scene, and it was easy to overlook the fact that TH had begotten a large family, that its members had in turn flourished, and that the two Huxley brothers around whom controversy so often swept were by no means the only grandchildren of 'Darwin's bulldog'.

Not all the lesser-known Huxleys relished the notoriety of their name. For half a century it had usually brought the inquiry 'one of *the* Huxleys?', even though there was the occasional episode to demonstrate that even the fame of TH was merely relative. Thus Trev, seated in the chair of his new dentist, was greeted with the comment: 'Ah, Mr Huxley, your name is very familiar to me.' The follow-up was unexpected: 'There is a well-known member of our profession of that name in Birmingham.'

Usually, however, the name summoned up visions of academic brilliance to which not all members of the family wished, or were able, to aspire. It was not only Roger Eckersley who bemoaned the fact that scholarships and Firsts always seemed to be expected of Huxleys. There were others who preferred a different intellectual climate. One Huxley father was heard to plead for his new-born child: 'Please God, *don't* make her brilliant' and decades later one of Julian's granddaughters pointed out: 'It's not that I'm not proud of my family – some of them have done wonderful things – but being a Huxley in England can be a bit of a bore.' It could also be something of a burden. One might prefer a quiet life, free of the Huxley demon; yet from whichever branch of the family one sprang, it was sure to contain at least one senior member ready to emphasize the great family past, an intellectual colonel of the regiment forever insistent that standards should be maintained.

Against this background the ancillary Huxleys prospered. None reached the eminence of TH; even so, they were more numerous, and more influential, than is usually realized.

What qualities would one expect to find permeating these strata of lesser-known Huxleys? First of all, no doubt, dedicated devotion to truth, however disagreeable the ensuing arguments, however surely mere money-grubbing was thus relegated to a secondary place. One might also expect to find at least some reflection of that central belief of TH that science and art are but two aspects of the same thing; and thus there would be scientists appreciative of the humanities, philosophers with a leaning towards science, men or women in that border country between technology and entertainment. One might also expect to find, permeating the Huxley atmosphere, a conspective approach to the world and its problems; with at times the unspoken assumption that Huxleys were rather better fitted than the rest of mankind to carry the burden of solving these problems. TH had never been arrogant; but he had rarely been less than confident.

The record runs up to expectations. Few Huxleys fall completely by the wayside, and it is notable that in almost all the families descending from the family tree which spreads across the page there is at least one member whose activities have a striking link with the scientific-philosophical activities of TH.

On the far left of the line, the younger of Jessie Waller's two children, Noel, had succeeded his father as diocesan architect of Gloucester, winning the Military Cross in the Gloucester Regiment in the First World War and subsequently becoming Colonel of the Fifth Gloucesters, a Territorial Battalion of the Regiment. It was through his sister, Oriana, that the Huxley strain was to be most obviously transmitted. While it has always been a trait of the Huxley men to marry capable women, competently equipped to help organize their lives, Oriana epitomized the female trait of bringing into the family fresh injections of ability, provided by professional men who worked in different fields from most of the Huxleys. Her husband was E. S. P. Haynes, like Julian Huxley both a Scholar at Eton and a Brackenbury Scholar at Balliol; 'an atheist with Catholic prejudices,' as he described himself; a dedicated divorce law reformer, and the original of the lawyer in A. P. Herbert's *Holy Deadlock*.

A man of wide interests and regular routine, Haynes worked for more than thirty years in the Lincoln's Inn chambers from which his father had practised, catching the same train morning after morning, lunching in the same oyster bar, returning to consult with his clerks at the same hour each day and returning home for the punctual meal which he enjoyed. The routine of his Sunday walk was equally fixed, starting from his Hampstead house at 11.00 and following a route which took him past the White Stone Pond, across the Heath to the Leg of Mutton Pond, and back past the Spaniards to arrive home exactly at 1.20. What results might not be expected from a union which would combine the Huxley tradition with that of a thoughtful lawyer who considered the ultimate problems with the same logical precision he gave to the intricacies of his profession?

There were three Haynes children, Renée, Celia and Elvira, and it was soon apparent that the first and eldest was drawn towards that borderland between mind and matter which had so attracted TH from the central years of his life. As a child Renée Haynes had read Sinel's study of telepathy in animals and men, *The Sixth Sense.* Ever afterwards she was interested in psychical research, devoting a good deal of thought and writing to it, and finally reaching a point where she believed

> that spontaneous telepathy probably occurs among most living creatures, and certainly in human beings . . . that will telepathy can occur, among both sophisticated and unsophisticated peoples . . . that experiences of time-displacement occur . . . that cumulative evidence . . . seems to warrant the assumption that telekinesis (or psycho-kinesis) may occur . . . that the success of dowsing or water-divining cannot always be explained by coincidence, fraud, imagination or a shrewd assessment of 'the lie of the land'.

This preoccupation with the para-normal, revealed in her remarkable book, *The Hidden Springs*, was only one side of the Renée Haynes who during the years between the wars studied at the Lycée in South Kensington, went up to St Hugh's, Oxford, and embarked on a writing career with three successful novels in a row – *Neapolitan Ice*, *Immortal John*, and *The Holy Hunger*. All gave hints of the way in which her mind was working, and the Huxley imprint became apparent soon afterwards with her *Pan, Caesar and God*, a study of comparative religion, and a lengthy essay on the life and work of Hilaire Belloc. In the 1930s she married Jerrard Tickell, a young Irish writer, and, following the example of Rachel Eckersley and Julia Huxley, began the production of three exceptional sons.

The next branch of the family was represented by Joyce, issue of John Collier's first marriage, born in his Tite Street home, and barely able to remember her mother, the dark-haired Marian Collier who had died so tragically in Paris. This was the extraordinarily attractive girl 'after whose entrances and exits', it was written of one Swiss holiday before the first world war, 'all the heads of the young men in the hotel seemed to turn as if by clockwork.' In 1906 Joyce Collier married Leslie Crawshay-Williams, linking the family with the South Wales ironmasters; of their two children, Rupert and Gillian, the first showed the Huxley traits most clearly. During this period between the wars, however, he followed the conventional path that took him to Oxford, successfully evaded a proposed career as accountant and, as the 1930s were about to end, was starting life as a freelance writer.

The next branch of the family was during the same inter-war period providing the best-known Huxleys, Julian and Aldous; while their half-brother Andrew, the younger of Leonard's two sons by his second wife, had already begun the physiological work which was to make him the first Huxley winner of a Nobel Prize. Julian's two sons Anthony and Francis, and Aldous's son Matthew, were preparing for things to come, while their aunt Margaret had already started her own successful girls' school at Bexhill. It was still Leonard Huxley's offspring that forced the pace.

Yet blood is thicker than surnames, and after Aldous and Julian the Huxley grandsons best-known to the public – though rarely known as such – were the three Eckersley brothers, the children of Rachel Huxley's first marriage. Roger, the eldest, demonstrated the Huxley charm; Peter, the youngest, typified the Huxley outspokenness; and the third brother, Thomas Lydwell, carried on the Huxley tradition by being elected to the Royal Society on the treble qualifications of mathematics, physics and engineering. At the end of the first world war both Peter and Thomas Eckersley joined the firm of Marconi, the first confidently experienced from his work as a wireless engineer with the R.A.F., the second already immersed in the short-wave research which was to bring him fame. Both were for the next decade to be directly concerned with the impact of wireless on the British public, while their elder brother Roger was to be involved, although in a non-technical capacity, a few years later. From the early 1920s onwards, therefore, the stories of these three grandsons of TH are inextricably merged in the development of radio.

Marconi had played a considerable part in producing radio equipment for the armed forces and the firm was now determined to provide a post-war civilian service. As a start, there appeared '2MT Writtle', a transmitting station in the attractive village of Writtle six miles west of the company's works in Chelmsford. Peter Eckersley directed the building and equipping of the station – whose transmissions were improved by the special earth screens designed by his brother Thomas – and was responsible for the nightly broadcasts, each one consisting of a string of three-minute transmissions broken by the three-minute gaps on which the Post Office insisted.

The contents of the programmes, as well as the technical work, fell within Eckersley's province, and one evening he decided to play only a few records and then to start talking. 'A certain ebullience, which often overcomes me when I have an audience, prompted a less formal attitude towards the microphone than was customary,' he said later. The listeners liked the performance, and a fan-mail of more than fifty post-cards asked him to repeat it. Eckersley's programme from 2MT Writtle quickly became famous. One evening he provided a one-man 'night of grand opera', not only singing all the arias but also providing mock interruptions. On occasion he would take over the microphone for an hour or more at a time, continuing a long flow of stories which were broken only by the compulsory G.P.O. breaks. As he wrote:

> We were pioneers. We performed the first radio play, an excerpt from Cyrano de Bergerac. The actors sat round a table; the microphone, similar to that used today for the household telephone, was passed from hand to hand, our lines lay beside us, typed out with instructions – voice raised, voice discreet, voice passionate.

There was also a theme song, sung at the end of each night's programme by Peter Eckersley in a high tenor and ending: 'Dearest, the concert's ended, sad wails the heterodyne. You must soon switch off your valves, I must soon switch off mine.' All this was too good to last. The very success of 2MT Writtle and the work of other enthusiasts made their transformation into a single Government-blessed British Broadcasting Company – as it then was – almost inevitable. After Writtle had made its final broadcast Peter Eckersley moved, almost in the natural order of things, to an appointment as Chief Engineer of the B.B.C.

His independent and somewhat uproarious character failed to fit in either with the public image of what had become, by its transformation in 1926 into the British Broadcasting Corporation, a quasi-Government body, or with the stern Covenanting spirit of Sir John Reith, its Director-General. In 1929, Eckersley was, as he himself has said, 'forced to send in my resignation because I was about to become what is called the "guilty party" in an action for divorce.'

Meanwhile, his eldest brother Roger had also been helping to guide a part of the corporation – 'Gentleman Roger', as his brother described him, 'never expressing an opinion, seeing both sides of every question and with these safe supports, floating upwards to a resting-place near, but never too near, the top.' Roger Eckersley had been brought in during September 1925 as Organizer of Programmes, a post which he held for five years before being promoted to Assistant Controller. The Huxley blood came out in his reluctance not to have a finger in any pie likely to come under discussion, in the pertinacity with which he pushed his ideas. Thus he did not merely organize programmes, he laid down the lines along which they should be organized; he did not merely administer but, wherever possible, created policy. He stayed with the corporation for two decades – and he not only became its Chief Censor for the whole of the war but composed 'Here's to the Next Time', known throughout Britain as the signature tune of Henry Hall.

While Roger was continuing to carry the Eckersley flag in the corporation, his younger brother Thomas was becoming one of the country's leading experts on short-wave radio-propagation, a subject with which the corporation became more concerned as the needs of Empire broadcasting grew.

At the Colliers' North House in Hampstead, Thomas Lydwell Eckersley had met Eva Pain, daughter of Barry Pain the humorous writer. They were married in 1920 and settled a few miles from the Chelmsford headquarters of Marconi. Like many with Huxley blood in his veins, he combined an intuitive understanding of natural phenomena with appreciation of the arts; his wife was an able pianist and composer, and from the 1920s onwards their home at Danbury was constantly visited by distinguished musical friends.

As early as 1927 T. L. Eckersley had become one of that small band of scientists whose work had produced a genuinely 'classic paper' – in this case an analysis, read before the Institution of Electrical Engineers, of data on long-wave propagation collected by a Marconi expedition in Australia. Then, with the advent of short-wave propagation as a serious competitor with the long waves for long-distance commercial working, Marconi's realized the potentialities of the subject. Early in 1925, therefore, Eckersley was put in charge of a special team at Great Baddow, on the outskirts of Chelmsford. Here, for the fourteen years until the outbreak of war, he planned and supervised a whole series of investigations and experiments. Several stations had to be listened to regularly – by 1926 no fewer than seventy short-wave transmissions could be heard in Britain, including some from Australia – and the passage of the waves and their reflections from the ionosphere had to be estimated or calculated. It was in this, as well as in the design of the experimental work, that Eckersley showed his power, using his considerable mathematical ability to deduce, from what was sometimes very sparse experimental data, the major phenomena which produced them. He worked out a basis for predicting the performance of short-wave long-distance services that was of immense use when war broke out and, in addition, he exercised a major influence on the engineering development of radio systems throughout the world.

All this produced a series of learned papers. It raised Eckersley, a non-self-seeking man who had 'something of the absent-mindedness associated with genius', into the scientific limelight. And by a pleasing coincidence it brought him election to the Royal Society at the same time as his cousin, Julian Huxley, in March 1938. *The Times* devoted a short leader to the double election, noting that the members of the Darwin family, which had provided four successive generations of Royal Society Fellows, would 'doubtless join with the general public in thinking that the choice of the Society could not have fallen on two more admirable men'.

This simultaneous election of Julian Huxley and T. L. Eckersley, one produced by the first Leonard Huxley's branch of the family, the other by Rachel's, was a good example of continuing tradition. This could also be discerned among Henry's children.

Of his three sons the eldest, Gervas, was demobilized in 1919, and was about to enter the Foreign Office when an old friend, George Booth, took him into the family firm of Alfred Booth, the ship-owners and bankers. He married in 1919 Lindsey Kathleen Foot, and then spent some six years – in Liverpool, London, and elsewhere – occupying himself in the distinctly un-Huxleyan business of commerce. He had the physical build of the family, six foot four, with the slim and slightly wavering physique which disguised the steel beneath. The one family characteristic which he appeared to lack was a certain flamboyance; instead, there was a diffidence, so that he had a facility for dissolving in the crowd as surely as he stood physically above it. Yet in one way he epitomized the contradictions of the Huxleys; for while hesitating to push himself, Gervas soon revealed an extraordinary facility for pushing ideas.

In the summer of 1926 he had received a letter from Stephen Tallents, an old family friend and then secretary of the newly created Empire Marketing Board. Tallents explained how it was essential to increase the sale of Empire goods and asked whether Huxley would handle the publicity side. Huxley agreed, and until the axing of the Board in 1933 helped to direct a series of famous advertising campaigns. This was the first time that a peacetime Government had embarked on publicity in a major way, and progress was made by trial and error. With various committees handled by Frank Pick of the Underground – the first man to commission artists for major poster campaigns – and

Sir William Crawford of the advertising agency, the errors were relatively small. Through the late 1920s and early 1930s the public became aware for the first time of what was being grown in the huge production unit on which the sun never set. As a progressive in outlook, Huxley had a leaning towards the less conventional artists, and still remembers how Frank Pick and he commissioned a series of posters by Stanley Spencer. These were, he recalls, acutely Spencerish, and when the originals were finally displayed for approval before the overriding political committee they were quickly consigned to the storeroom, unused. Some years later the Treasury raised an anguished protest about the fees that had been paid for unused art-work. Determined not to be beaten, Pick and Huxley decided that the originals should be sold. Sold they were – at a profit to the Government of about 900 per cent.

In the autumn of 1932, when it was clear that the Empire Marketing Board would last only a little longer, Huxley was offered, and quickly accepted, the task of handling the overseas promotion work of the Ceylon Tea Propaganda Board – the start of thirty years' work in encouraging the spread of tea-drinking, not only in Britain but in the United States.

Long before he had become tea's Director of Propaganda in London, Gervas had remarried. His wife was Elspeth Grant, whose father had been one of the early Kenya settlers. She had been brought up in the tough but invigorating climate of colonial life and had been fascinated – much as Julian Huxley was fascinated – by the human and zoological problems of an emerging continent. In 1933, two years after her marriage to Gervas, Elspeth Huxley published *White Man's Country: Lord Delamere and the Making of Kenya*. This was a remarkable and evocative book from which there still rises up an almost three-dimensional picture of the days before yesterday, an age in which Delamere had hopefully envisaged an East African dominion. It was the first, and in some ways the most important, of a long series of books with which Gervas's wife was to build up her reputation not only as an expert on Africa, but also as novelist and critic. These activities were in the main Huxley stream, and it was natural that to the world at large Elspeth was soon regarded not as a Huxley by marriage, but as the genuine article, for whom the puzzled inquirer could discover no place on the genealogical tree.

Gervas's younger brother had, meanwhile, been successfully launching *The Geographical Magazine*. Michael Heathorn Huxley joined the Diplomatic Service in 1922 and served in Tehran, in Washington and at the Foreign Office. While in Washington he was deeply impressed by that part of the 'American way of life' which consists in conveying to the widest possible public what elsewhere is too often regarded as information suitable only for the few. One example of this was the *National Geographic Magazine*, published by the National Geographic Society of Washington, D.C., and with 1,250,000 annual subscribers of whom well over 170,000 were in English-speaking countries outside the United States.

At that time there was in Britain no comparable periodical. The Royal Geographical Society's quarterly *Journal* was intended for a mainly academic readership which was expected to be familiar with geographical concepts and terms. Michael Huxley became convinced of the need for a publication designed to provide British readers with a substitute for the *National Geographic Magazine*; but, also, of the need to avoid the situation existing in the United States, where the body serving the many (the National Geographic Society of Washington) functioned quite separately from that serving the few (the American Geographical Society of New York). Between 1931 and 1934, therefore, he launched *The Geographical Magazine*, fully illustrated, appealing to a wide public, but with indissoluble links with the Royal Geographical Society.

By comparison with Michael and Gervas, their brother Christopher was the odd man out. In training at Sandhurst when the first world war ended, he had remained in the army as a regular, the first of the Huxleys to adopt one of the armed services as a career. He had served in Ireland during the Troubles, been posted to India for seven years, and back in England had 'passed Staff College', that qualification which is an essential requirement for higher appointment.

Both Henry's daughters married during the inter-war years, the elder, Marjorie, to E. J. (later Sir Edward) Harding, Permanent Under-Secretary of State in the Dominions Office, and the younger, Anne Heathorn, to Geoffrey Cooke.

On the far right of the Huxley line there lived the Colliers, descendants of John Collier's marriage with Ethel, the youngest of TH's daughters. John Collier himself died in 1934. Crippled by a mysterious form of paralysis in his later years, he had installed a lift in North House to carry him to his studio. Moving before his easel in a wheel-chair and using brushes tied to long bamboo staves so that he could 'stand back' from the easel, he had painted on to the end, continuing with his portraits of the Huxleys – Aldous in 1926; a replica of the famous TH 'skull' portrait for Down House in 1928; Leonard in his St Andrews robes three years later; two of the Buzzards and one of the Haynes daughters the following year; and, only a few months before his death, a remarkably modern head and shoulders of John Huxley Buzzard in

1933. Ethel continued to live on for another seven years in the great red-brick building with its distant view of London to the south, its massive Collier portraits lining the walls, and its tall french windows which at the back of the house seemed to open not only on to a green garden but on to another century.

Here the younger members of the family still came during the Christmas holidays, using the house as a base for their parties and their visits to the theatre, a relic of the days before the war when a whole row of seats at the pantomime would be reserved for Huxleys. Here more than one of the rising young men came for advice or aid, here the prospective brides and bridegrooms were still kindly but conscientiously interrogated by Ethel Collier. And here more than one impecunious young Huxley lived while establishing himself in London.

Of Ethel's two children, Laurence had prospered in the Foreign Service, where he had survived one curious wartime incident which had involved his aunt, Nettie Roller. This most eccentric of TH's daughters had continued to wander about the Continent with her daughter Marian during the early 1900s, had made friends with Madame Destini, the Czech opera-singer, and had followed her to Prague, where both had been caught by the outbreak of war. 'In 1915,' Laurence Collier subsequently wrote,

> the Austrian Government used her as a channel for some tentative peace overtures which brought me into a rather embarrassing prominence in the Foreign Office and prompted Duff Cooper who was then working with me there, and had discovered that I had had aunts in Mexico and in Italy as well as in Austria, to write a poem beginning:
>
> Collier has an Aunt in Prague
> And an uncle in the Hague,
>
> and ending, with a reference to Count de Salis, then British Minister at the Vatican,
>
> Though the King of Italy,
> Frowns upon the Collieri
> Count de Salis has a hope
> Of a future Collier Pope.'

At the end of the war Collier had been sent to Tokyo as Secretary of the Embassy, had returned to Britain two years later and had climbed up the ladder until, a few months after the outbreak of the second world war, he was about to be appointed Minister to Norway. Then, as the appointment was about to be made, the Germans invaded.

Finally, at the far right of the line, there was Laurence Collier's sister Joan, youngest of TH's grandchildren, mother of two sons and one daughter and as the wife of a regular officer somewhat outside the main Huxley stream. Of her two sons the eldest, John Huxley Buzzard, followed his great-grandfather, the first Lord Monkswell, who had been Attorney-General under Gladstone, and after having won an Open Classical Scholarship at Oxford in 1931, was called to the Bar in 1937. His younger brother Richard showed the Huxley strain, qualifying as a doctor like TH and, like him, never actually practising. Instead he had started, by the outbreak of war in 1939, a career in industrial medicine where, also like TH, he was to use a scientific tool to help shape the social scene.

By the late 1930s Julian and Aldous might form the crest of the Huxley wave; the rest of TH's twenty grandchildren provided a considerable groundswell.

Chapter XII

Inheriting the Animal Kingdom

In February 1934 Sir Peter Chalmers Mitchell, Secretary of the Zoological Society of London, informed its Council of twenty-one Fellows that he was nearing the age of seventy; that he had much enjoyed his long spell of work as Secretary of the society; but that he now felt he should give way to a younger man and would relinquish his post at the annual general meeting in the spring of 1935. It had indeed been a long spell. Sir Peter had grown up during the tempestuous years which followed the Darwinian revolution in biology; he had known the Victorian giants at first hand, and had written a brief biography of TH which had appeared in 1900. University demonstrator at Oxford, then hospital lecturer, he had become Secretary of the Zoological Society soon after the turn of the century. And from 1903 it had been Mitchell who had been chiefly responsible for making it the finest institution of its kind in the world. He had moved the Zoo from its archaic quarters in Hanover Square to the broader bounds of Regent's Park; and had later created his own personal monument with the concept of Whipsnade, the 'Open Zoo' on the Bedfordshire Downs where animals could be seen not behind bars but in something at least resembling a natural habitat.

Now Mitchell was going and the Fellows had to find a new Secretary. A special committee was set up to find one, and after much deliberation, cautious questioning and delicate probing, two possible candidates were interviewed. One of them was the son of a former Zoo official. The other was Julian Huxley. The results of the interviews were circulated, and there was renewed discussion. Finally Huxley was unanimously chosen, and agreed to take up the post when Mitchell retired at the end of April 1935.

In some ways 'the Zoo' was the most fitting body over which Huxley could have exercised his talents. His life-long interest in the animal kingdom was buttressed by a deep personal knowledge of this particular Zoo, built up over the years and begun in the days when TH was still alive. He had been taken there frequently as a boy by relatives and friends, and his cousin E. S. P. Haynes, husband of TH's eldest granddaughter Oriana, once wrote that he would 'never forget taking [Julian] there in the days of his youth and asking a keeper to produce an enterprising female inhabitant who lays eggs but suckles her young. This keeper did on receiving my assurance that Julian was "a family man".' For years the grounds which stretch gradually up northwards from Regent's Park towards the Hampstead heights had been Huxley territory, and slipping down to the Zoo had become almost a commonplace of everyday life.

There may have been some men as academically equipped for the post as Julian Huxley. Yet for the Zoo something more than a purely scientific qualification was needed. When the society was set up in 1826 its aims laid down in its royal charter were not merely scientific but also educational – one being the fostering of popular interest in all matters concerning animals. Thus the Secretary had to operate like a circus rider with one foot on each of two horses, initiating and supervising the serious scientific work of the society's laboratories but also spreading, at a popular level, an understanding of animals' place in the natural world, of how and where they live, and of the complex causes which have made them what they are. He therefore required not only biological knowledge but also enthusiasm for popular exposition, as well as a diplomatic ability to satisfy, if not to control, three kinds of Fellows – the genuinely scientific; those who took only a superficial interest in zoology; and those who were content merely to stroll in the sunshine, on the privileged Sunday morning, looking at the animals. To the first, biological, third of this task Huxley brought more than was needed; as a popularizer in the best sense of the word, the man who could excite the imagination and give answers that were not merely correct but also understandable, he was unsurpassed in his own particular field. As a diplomat, forced to handle the diverse and sometimes contradictory interests of the Fellows, and to suffer the occasional fool if not gladly, at least with a pleasant word, he found his powers strained.

Together with his wife and two sons, Huxley moved into the Secretary's flat at the Zoo in the spring of 1935. There was much to be done, since his predecessor's tastes had been settled in the early years of the century. In the home, both refurnishing and redecorating brought the quarters into line with the 1930s, and the long balcony looking south across Regent's Park was glassed in to provide an additional room. In the offices much the same process was gone through and within a few weeks visitors were being received in a re-equipped room whose black carpet and red and black steel-frame chairs were an augury of the new era that had begun. As a link between new and old, almost as a symbol of continuity, there hung above the new Secretary's mantelpiece one of the famous portraits of his grandfather. 'What an agreeable destiny,' wrote Wyndham Lewis, who saw it shortly after Huxley had moved in, '– to inherit, as it were, the animal kingdom.'

The change from Mitchell's day was considerable. Sir Peter had dominated the Council by his very presence, by the authority he had built up over the years – and also by the fact that he had outlived most of the potential trouble-makers. Huxley had to start from scratch. Nor was this all. Sir Peter had been an autocrat, even though a benign one, a Secretary of slightly feudal outlook, although of extremely left-wing politics, who regarded the Zoo staff as his own personal responsibility, and who felt it part of his duty to concern himself with every detail of their work. Huxley took a totally different view, giving the staff instructions but frequently leaving to them the manner in which these were carried out. The men of verve and imagination appreciated the new policy; but to some of the older ones, unused to acting on their own initiative, the change was a cause for head-shaking and regret that times were not what they were.

Innovations were numerous. Within a short while, Huxley had appointed a team of assistant curators, bringing in to fill the newly created post able young men such as James Fisher. From now onwards all curators were encouraged to give lectures to young people – at Christmas time, for instance. And, possibly the most revolutionary move, a completely fresh approach was made to relations between the Zoo and the general public. This was accomplished by the appointment of G. R. Doubleday, the Zoo's chief Administration Officer, as the society's first Public Relations Officer – a move in itself somewhat shaking in the mid-1930s. This was, moreover, no mere paper-move. A press conference was now held in the Zoo every morning and there were few days when the newspapers – particularly the London evening papers – were not given some choice titbit which reached the news columns. One result was that from 1935 onwards the Zoo became, without the expenditure of much money, one of the most publicized of British institutions. Another result, possibly inevitable in the circumstances, was that many Fellows began to fear that the public was being encouraged to take too much interest in 'their' Zoo. Huxley did his best to explain the advantages of the change – 'let Doubleday play to the gallery so that it can subsidize our scientific work', was the gist of his appeal. It was not always listened to.

There was a reverse to this particular coin. It was salutary that the Secretary should influence the policy of the society by his personal actions. Yet with Huxley's extraordinary ability to seize the nub of an argument, with his great expository powers, there went an inability to grasp simple mechanical principles, a handicap which occasionally obtruded on his efficiency as an administrator. It was said of him, with some truth, that when his car stopped he just sat with his finger on the starter-button hoping the problem would solve itself. And when it came to approving publicity material he could never grasp the essential difference between three-colour or six-colour printing and would disclaim all interest in anything but the finished result. Again, when Eric Hosking, the noted bird photographer, attempted to describe how to get the best results from a camera, he was taken aback at the reaction. 'I remember trying to explain the why and wherefore of different kinds of filter,' Hosking says. 'And the man with one of the finest brains in the world astounded me by saying "Yes, yes, but I can't understand all that; it's far too complicated for me".' This is interesting, since from early days Huxley had realized not only the scientific but what might be called the moral value of photography.

> Bird-photography is a splendid sport [he wrote after his Spitsbergen journey]. In so far as it is a sport, it is an end in itself. Looked at objectively, it has the further great advantage that it does not destroy but helps to preserve; those who have watched a bird for days together from a hiding-tent will never wish to kill the creature whose inmost life has been displayed before their eyes.

Partly in this spirit, partly with the resolve to overcome difficulties, he did in fact learn the technicalities of the craft – as those who study the colour plates in *From an Antique Land* will realize.

From the first Huxley broadened the scope of the Zoo's scientific work encouraging an outlook which considered the animals neither as items in a menagerie, nor as zoological specimens, but as living illustrations of evolution. Much of the research was along expected lines, but some of it branched out into new fields, as when Huxley and two colleagues tested all the captive chimpanzees in England for their sensitivity to the bitter-tasting PTC (phenylthiocarbamide).

> We found, to our delight [he later recorded], that within the limits of statistical error they had the same proportion of non-tasters as human beings. People asked: 'How did you find out?' Actually it was quite simple; we offered them a sugar solution containing PTC. If they were non-tasters, they drank it up and put the cup out for more; if they were tasters, they spat it in our faces: it was an all-or-nothing reaction.

He encouraged the new disciplines of statistical analysis and the use of the latest equipment – and it is significant that he reorganized the photographic department so that what had been a slightly haphazard collection of photographs by members of the staff, taken as opportunity offered, became a scientifically planned record.

Yet it was to be the Zoo's public image on which Huxley was to leave his greatest mark – and which was to cause the greatest controversy. His aim, he stated, was to make it

> more than a menagerie. . . . It might become the centre and focus of popular interest in every aspect of animals and animal life – scientific, artistic, literary; the preservation and protection of wild animals and birds; pet-keeping and animal-breeding; animal welfare; animal health; animals in the service of man like guide-dogs for the blind, canaries in mines, carrier pigeons and so on.

This was a bold conception, in the true Huxley tradition, and it was a conception which he began to nourish within a short time of his appointment.

Rebuilding was an important item among his ambitious plans – starting with the elephant house which dated from 1869, and which he envisaged as an entirely new structure in which the animals would be seen in some of their natural majesty. Even more imaginative was the studio of animal art, an entirely new idea, in which a building that would accommodate animals as large and as restless as lions or tigers would also allow up to twenty-five students to sketch or paint. After complex negotiations with the authorities, the studio was finally opened in 1937. It was the first of its kind in the world, and as many as 200 students were soon using it every week. At Whipsnade, which had been opened only four years earlier, a major building programme was already being carried out, and to Whipsnade Julian Huxley and his family journeyed most week-ends. Here, 800 feet up on the edge of the 500 acres across which animals roamed almost at will, lay the Secretary's flat. Near by was a large field in which the Huxley boys camped, and here were kept two Iceland ponies which they rode regularly. A new elephant house, in which the public were separated from the animals not by bars but by only a water barrier, was nearing completion; so was the cheetah enclosure and the giant tortoise pit, originally a quarry and now converted into a home for the huge specimens from the Galapagos. All this formed a playground which any growing family might envy, replete not only with strange sights but with the chance of stranger experiences – so that Anthony, the elder son, can claim to be the only horseman ever unseated in England by a charging rhinoceros.

While these major operations were in progress, Huxley was thinking up still more schemes for expanding the Zoo's influence. He himself was now at the zenith of his numerous activities – or so it might seem – and the visitor to the Zoo would find him bursting with ideas, pacing up and down his room as he talked, sitting to put his feet on the desk for a few moments, then pacing off once again, his body apparently filled with inexhaustible nervous energy and his brain packed with ideas which tumbled out in startling profusion. So far as the Zoo was concerned, one thread ran through most of them – that here, under Huxley's control, were the multifarious, diverse, contrasted, extraordinary creatures which the passing millennia had produced, a living illustration of how evolution works.

It was natural, therefore, that when he decided to hold two special exhibitions during the Christmas holidays of 1935 both should be linked with evolution. One, illustrating colour-changes in animals, presented a collection of chameleons, tree frogs, toads and other animals which changed colour according to the background against which they were seen – a protective ability evolved through millions of years. The second exhibition was an ingenious display of Mendelian heredity, in which mice, budgerigars and rabbits were used to show how such characteristics as colour were inherited on predictable lines.

These exhibitions, which were visited by thousands of children during the school holidays, exemplified the new role which Huxley felt the Zoo could play in the life of the country. The point was emphasized in a brief but illuminating book, *At the Zoo*, which he wrote during this period:

> The most far-reaching demonstration of evolution in action comes from the study of comparative anatomy and classification. . . . For instance, what could look more different than the foot of an antelope, the hand of a man, the wing of a bat and the flipper of a sea-lion? Yet the skeleton of all of them can be reduced to a common plan – one bone in the upper arm, two in the lower, a number in the wrist, and five fingers. The variations are brought about by the enlargement of some parts, as with the bat's fingers, the reduction or loss of others, as in the side toes of the antelope, or the joining of originally separate parts into one, as in the antelope's cannon bone. The plan is the same, though one is used for running, one for grasping, one for flying, and one for swimming. This only has any meaning if the different creatures are all descended from a common original ancestor possessing this plan for fore-limb structure in a simple and primitive form,

and that then, in the course of evolution, they specialized in different directions.

The vital thing, so far as Huxley was now concerned, was that all these animals could be observed and studied during a short stroll round the Regent's Park Zoo.

It was thus largely due to his secretaryship of the Zoological Society that Huxley was now able to develop one of his favourite pursuits – educating the young in the facts of evolution and the need to conserve the world's rapidly disappearing fauna. The opportunity came with the invitation to give the Christmas lectures at the Royal Institution, the 'one hundred and twelfth course of six lectures adapted to a juvenile auditory', as they were rather pontifically described. Three quarters of a century earlier, TH had been lecturing here to his working men and injecting into them an almost revolutionary interest in the living world. Now his grandson was to extend the mission. His subject was 'Rare Animals and the Disappearance of Wild Life', and just as TH had captured the attention of his audiences by an attack that was in advance of its time, so did Julian Huxley bring an immediacy to his descriptions of the world's wild life and the threats to it. At his first lecture he produced Mac, an eight-month-old lion cub that the children could stroke as they learned how the spots, which would disappear as Mac grew up, were a sign that lions had once lived in forests where the spots would merge with the dappled shadows and help to conceal them from their enemies. Throughout the lectures he produced a series of animals – parrots, a wallaby, a king crab, two freak gophers – which he used to illustrate little-known or exciting facts about wild creatures. He explained how many species had become rare and then extinct. He suggested how those that remained might be preserved, and he carried the argument to its logical conclusion by proposing that not only rare types of animals, but also rare types of human beings should be protected.

This sort of education should begin early, and one of Huxley's first innovations was Pets' Corner. Soon after his appointment he had made a tour of the more important European Zoos, and in Berlin he had seen how children were frequently lifted over the railings to touch and stroke some of the animals. Back in London he heard of a recent book, *Friends at the Zoo*, written and illustrated by a young photographer, Eric Hosking, who had taken a small girl to Regent's Park and photographed her beside the more attractive animals. As Huxley talked with Hosking, enthused over the prints in front of him, and remembered his recent experiences on the Continent, the idea began to take shape.

Later that year a part of what had been the Fellows' Lawn, a sacrosanct area in front of the society's headquarters, was railed off. Here, during good weather, there mixed together a young chimpanzee, a lion cub, a Shetland pony, a small python, a baby yak, a young eland, rabbits, a giant tortoise and, from time to time, other animals. Here, too, the chimpanzees' tea party was held every day, the chimps cavorting before the enthralled onlookers. The attraction of Pets' Corner was that children could stroke and handle the animals. They could, in addition, be photographed with their favourites, an innovation which at one simple stroke created a link between child and animal on which all manner of education might be hung. The opening of both Pets' Corner and of its extension received considerable publicity – partly because the members of the Russian Ballet were present at the first event, and the extension was opened by the children of the American Ambassador in London, Joseph Kennedy, among them Edward and Robert. During the first year nearly 7,000 children came to mix with the animals. The following year the number rose to more than 55,000; in 1937 it reached 97,000 – a measure of the enthusiasm which the idea had aroused.

This was by no means the only method which Huxley introduced of edging the Zoo's work into the public mind. At his suggestion *Zoo Magazine* was started by a commercial publishing house and, combining education with entertainment, was soon selling 100,000 copies a month. The guide to the Zoo was rewritten by Huxley himself, *Nature* noting that it formed 'a sharp and striking contrast with the stereotyped form which had done duty for so many generations of visitors', and that it would 'open up an entirely new conception of the part the gardens play as a source of information concerning the animals . . .'. Modern post-cards were put on sale at kiosks in the ground, as well as distribution maps, models of animals, and a pictorial 'animal wheel'.

The fortunes of this last device well illustrate both the strength and the weakness of Huxley's attitude. The wheel was a simple cardboard circle on which a moving pointer could be adjusted to indicate any one of a number of animals whose names were printed round its circumference. As this was done, facts and figures emerged beneath a number of openings. By turning the pointer to 'Elephant' – or to any of the other animals named – the user could learn where that animal was found in nature, what its normal life-span was, and the kind and amount of food which it ate. There was also its 'period of gestation', and it was this that caused the trouble. When the prototype of the wheel was shown to Doubleday he shook his head and warned that mothers would never buy their children anything with that piece of knowledge on it. Huxley was unbelieving. Children, he argued, have got to be told the facts of life: what better way than this? Ignorance was the cause of much unhappiness in the world: here, surely, was one way of lessening it – and so on. There seemed no way of convincing him that the British mother still preferred the gooseberry bush, and the Zoo wheels were put on sale. The result was a shocking failure; thousands of unsold wheels were eventually disposed of at less than cost price.

All these novel schemes were aimed at helping the Zoo perform one of its functions: that of informing the general public about the animal world. Yet at the same time they provoked a strong reaction amongst the more conservative Fellows, many of whom believed that a serious interest in zoology must, in the natural order of things, be left to the professional classes. There was also something perhaps more basic, a different attitude of mind which is well illustrated by one otherwise unimportant incident. Eric Kennington was privately commissioned to paint the two Huxley sons, and mentioned that in his yard he had Eric Gill's 'Humanity', a fine piece of sculpture which Gill was ready to sell very cheaply. Huxley inspected the work, was greatly impressed, and conceived the notion of mounting it at the entrance to Whipsnade. The council refused. 'Just like them,' Huxley later commented. 'They said that they were only concerned with animals; but of course they really turned it down because it was a nude.'

What can only be described as an anti-Huxley movement had began slowly to form during 1936. Its leaders bided their time, however, and struck only in the spring of 1937, when an opportunity was brought about by the dismissal of two curators in a reorganization of Zoo duties. The annual general meeting of the society was held on 29 April. After the case of the curators had been raised, one of the Fellows moved the rejection of the society's annual report, an unheard-of thing, and a move which represented a call for a vote of No Confidence in the Secretary. A somewhat heated discussion followed, at the end of which the members raised their hands to vote. When the tally was made the numbers were equal. Only the casting vote of the President, Lord Onslow, saved the day for Huxley.

But the argument had only in part revolved around the two dismissed curators, and it was quite clear what the turmoil was really about. The Zoo, complained one Fellow, was becoming 'a glorified fun fair'. It was claimed that 'the Fellows are being squeezed out'. An air of farce had earlier been introduced when a member of the Council had produced a number of photographs taken in Pets' Corner and showing a chimpanzee in a state described as of suggestive nudity. 'In fact,' summed up the offended Fellow, 'dirty postcards – just like Cairo.' There was scant chance of Huxley winning this battle with aggrieved propriety. He could, however, appeal to the pocket; and, as he said, 'as long as we rely on the public for the sixpences and shillings we must provide some entertainment.' He was supported by a good deal of the Press. *The Nottingham Guardian* wafts up from three decades ago a trace of a vanished world with its complaint about the Fellows who, alone, were admitted to the Zoo on Sundays. 'And what is the result?' it asked. 'So far from using these exclusive passes themselves, the Fellows give them to their butlers and servant maids. They do not even avail themselves of their exclusive opportunity.'

Huxley survived this first attack by the Old Guard, and went calmly on with his plans for popularization and modernization, plans which were to be brusquely interrupted by preparations for war and then by war itself. The repercussion of events in Europe had made itself felt soon after his appointment when Dr Hans Honigmann, former Director of the Breslau Zoological Gardens, had begun working at the Zoo with the aid of the Academic Assistance Council. Soon afterwards there arrived in England another refugee from Hitler's Germany – Ludwig Koch, who was already building up his library of bird-recordings. Huxley invited Koch to the Zoo, listened in amazement to his records, wrote out the addresses of a number of publishers, and insisted that Koch should carry on with his work. This was to be the beginning of a fruitful partnership. Koch was invited to record animal noises at the Zoo; he was invited to the Huxley flat at Whipsnade where he could record the night noises of the animals in their quasi-natural habitat. And some while later there appeared *Animal Language*, written and prepared by Huxley and Koch – a 'talking book' whose records presented the listener with such sounds as the wolves' chorus at Whipsnade, the birdlike chatter of the panda, the 'talk' of camels, the explosive grunts of the gnu, and the extraordinary outbursts of the hyaena's laughter.

Animal Language appeared in the autumn of 1938 and by this time the Zoo had already begun to prepare for what everyone called the 'emergency' but what everyone knew was war – an event which presented special problems to an organization which controlled many hundreds of potentially wild animals in the heart of the capital. During the Munich crisis of September 1938, plans were put in hand for converting the basements of the society's buildings into air raid shelters. Whipsnade, it was decided, provided an ideal evacuation centre for books, documents and wives, although the more valuable of the society's archives were in fact cared for at Woburn Abbey by the Duke of Bedford, a former President of the society. A few months later, in

April 1939, an official War Emergency Committee was appointed and detailed arrangements were made as to what was to happen if war broke out.

In September, as the German troops crossed the frontier into Poland, Huxley was attending the annual meeting of the British Association in Dundee. The meeting was abandoned, and he hurried back to London where the Zoo had already been closed, and where the first emergency steps were already being taken. The great problem, naturally enough, concerned the larger, the more valuable, and the more potentially dangerous animals. Some of them, including the giant panda which during the previous few months had become the most famous of all the Zoo's favourites, were taken to improvised quarters at Whipsnade. The rest had to remain in the middle of the biggest city in Britain, a city which was, moreover, expected to be heavily bombed by the enemy at any moment. The thought of lions, tigers and elephants marauding central London after their cages had been broken open by bombing must have given Huxley a good deal of worry, but the Council of the society had wisely decided to keep a sense of proportion about the threat. The poisonous snakes were decapitated and burned. So far as the other animals were concerned the society relied on the expertise of its special air raid precautions squad which included a number of crack shots armed with rifles – the only civilian A.R.P. staff to be thus equipped – and instructions to shoot any dangerous escaped animal.

These details had been given by Huxley to Mr Churchill a few days before the outbreak of war when the man who was soon to become First Lord of the Admiralty had visited the Zoo to see the giant panda. Churchill listened as the safety precautions were outlined.

> You could almost hear the mental wheels going round inside that magnificent head [Huxley later wrote in *The Times*]. Then he said: 'That sounds very efficient. . . . But it's rather a pity, isn't it?' To which all I could reply was 'A *pity*, Mr Churchill?' And then again silence, with the mental wheels working away for what seemed a very long time but was actually, I suppose, about a minute. When he broke silence again it was clear that he had utilized that minute to compose a chapter of the history he was going to write of the war that had not yet broken out. I wish I had had a tape recorder, or at least tape recorder memory, for it was magnificent Churchillian prose. But the potted version which is all I can give is better than nothing. The gist of it was something like this:
>
> 'Imagine a great air raid over London – squadron after squadron of enemy planes flying in – Dropping their explosive bombs on the

people and the buildings of this great capital city – Houses smashed into ruins – Fires breaking out everywhere – The ruins crumbling into ashes – The corpses lying about in the smoking ashes – and the lions and tigers roaming the ruins in search of the corpses. And you're going to shoot them – What a pity, what a pity!'

As it happened, there was almost a year's respite. No raids came with the outbreak of war on 3 September, and on 14 September most of the Zoo was reopened. The only exception was the aquarium, the occupants of which were removed. The water-tanks were then emptied, the danger from fractured glass propelled by high-pressure water being considered too great a risk. Thus prepared, the Zoo and its staff settled down to deal with their problems.

On the outbreak of war Huxley had immediately suggested that he should be put on half pay, provided that he could find additional part-time work of national importance. As we shall see, this was soon found. However, the problems with which the Secretary had to cope were numerous and tricky enough; prominent among them was the task of feeding animals in what was to be a severely rationed wartime Britain. To cope with this difficulty, an ingenious 'adoption' system was devised since it was the cost of food, almost as much as its availability, which created problems during a period when the Zoo's income from visitors had slumped. Under the adoption system, any member of the public, or group of members, could provide the cost of a particular animal's food – and in return would have an 'adoption' notice attached to its cage or compound. Ten shillings a week would provide for a leopard, five shillings for a llama, half a crown for a flamingo, and so on. Scores of animals were eventually adopted; ships became responsible for some animals, the famous *Punch* Round Table adopted a lion, while one family alone provided for a giraffe, a bear and two camels. Financially, the idea was straightforward and obvious enough; from the human point of view it was a stroke of genius.

Other methods of sustaining public interest in the Zoo were used on Huxley's suggestion. Thus, at a time when on account of security regulations very few things in the whole of Britain could be photographed, an 'animal photo contest' was launched; for in the Zoo enthusiasts could snap away to their hearts' content. There was also the War Utility Exhibition, ingeniously planned with poultry, goats, bees, and rabbits – which were being bred in large numbers in what had once been the reptile house; all these could be conscripted to provide food – and, of course, to show yet another aspect of animals' place in nature.

With the autumn of 1940 there came the blitz, the long series of nightly raids during which bombs showered down on London. The Zoo was remarkably lucky. Although more than fifty high explosive and oil bombs dropped on its grounds, as well as scores of incendiaries, losses were limited to some birds which failed to return after an incendiary bomb had dropped through the roof of the crowded bird house and skidded out through a wall without causing a single casualty. There was a direct hit on Monkey Hill, the artificial erection of stone and concrete, but the monkeys, secure in their artificial caves, appeared to take little interest.

The most famous incident occurred at the height of one raid when the zebra house was seriously damaged by a bomb. None of the animals was touched, but three escaped. It was midnight and A.R.P. watchers soon reported that one of the animals had been seen by the light of a burning kiosk near the main society offices. A number of fire engines were working in the grounds, there was the continuous drone of bombers overhead, and no one knew what would happen next. Meanwhile the zebra, according to Huxley,

> disappeared into the darkness and must have made its way through the Tunnel into the Main Gardens, where it emerged through the stores gate, which was open for use of the Auxiliary Fire Service. A zebra in Camden Town, though not a dangerous animal, might have created surprise and even alarm, though probably not despondency; it was also a valuable animal (Grevy Zebras are rare, and the London Zoo has one of the few good breeding stocks in captivity); so half-a-dozen of us set off in pursuit, leaving another group to block the animal's retreat. With some driving and coaxing, and generalship in disposition of the man-power available, the beast was got back into the stores-yard and the doors shut. But he did not like the shed invitingly opened for his reception, and his jibbing was accentuated every time the neighbouring A.A. guns went off – which was very frequently. At one moment I confess to having been scared, when he backed until his hindquarters came within a couple of yards of myself, securely wedged in a corner.

The animal was eventually induced back into quarters, and the next day Huxley confessed his fear to the keeper. 'Oh, you needn't have worried, sir,' was the reply. 'He's a biter, not a kicker.'

In a very typical way Huxley utilized the experiences of the blitz to find out more about animals. This he did by making as accurate a record as possible of their reactions under fire, a record that showed many of them to be far less disturbed by noise, blinding flashes, or bomb-blast than might have been expected. He collected information from correspondents in many parts of Britain, and he was able to arrive at some general conclusions as to why animals behaved as they did under certain specific wartime conditions.

This work was sandwiched in between much else, for Huxley had taken on a good deal of war-work unconnected with his post as Secretary of the Zoo. At the end of November 1941, he was given three months' leave of absence without pay and soon afterwards left for the United States on a lecture tour organized by the Central Office of Information. Then, in mid-February, within a few weeks of returning to England and to his work as Secretary, he was awakened by a telephone call from a reporter who asked for his comments on 'the news from London'. Huxley asked what the news was, and was briefly told: 'You've been sacked from the Zoo.'

He had not, in fact, been sacked. But the members of the Council had decided, for reasons which were later explained by the comprehensive word 'economy', to suspend the post of Secretary, an action which they were allowed to take by the society's constitution, laid down more than a century previously. It was necessary for them to seek approval of the Privy Council for their step and, this done, it was officially announced that the Secretary had been suspended.

The shock of the announcement was considerable and the informal committee which sprang up almost overnight issued a formal statement dissociating its members from the Council's action. They had, moreover, discovered that the members of the Council had made a curious mistake, possibly having been baffled by the complexity of their own constitution. For this laid it down that an appeal to the Privy Council, such as had been made, must follow a formal resolution; and the Council had, by an oversight, failed to move such a resolution.

At this stage, with the ball firmly at their feet, the informal committee of protesting Fellows complained to the Privy Council. The Zoological Society's Council countered by passing the necessary formal resolution and re-applying to the Privy Council for permission to suspend the Secretary. By this time, however, the game was being played in public view; and the Privy Council decided that the suspension should only be carried out with the 'support of a substantial majority of the Fellows'. The contest now appeared to have moved back to square one, with Huxley still formally Secretary but with the Fellows divided into two opposing forces.

By this time it was early May, and there now followed a lull during which the society's Treasurer made a statement to the Press about Huxley's reaction on hearing of his suspension. Huxley issued a denial. The Council itself remained quiet.

Then, on 15 May, the informal committee stated that the society's Council had told them that no fresh approach would be made to the Privy Council; furthermore, the society's Council would not nominate their own candidate for the secretaryship when this came up for re-election at the annual general meeting.

The skill of the Council's play became evident at the meeting on 19 August. It was suggested that 'a more representative body might be elected'. There were criticisms of Huxley's suspension and of the way in which the business had been handled. But although Huxley himself was re-elected as Secretary – inevitably, since no other candidate was put forward – candidates for the other offices put up by the informal committee were rejected, leaving Huxley isolated. The sequel was almost inevitable, and on 26 August he resigned, leaving the field to the Council.

There are two revealing footnotes to the dispute. One was provided by H. G. Maurice, the Chairman of the Council and later President of the society. Relations between Huxley and the Council had always been good, he blandly asserted, but he regretted that 'a man of such brilliant parts as Dr Huxley should be of such restless genius as not really to fit in with the routine drudgery of an institution of this character'.

The other footnote was provided by the society's annual report. This merely stated, as though it were part of the natural order of things, that the Secretary had resigned and another one had been elected. If explanation were needed for the complete ignoring of the bitter struggle which had taken place, it was conveniently provided by the paper control of the Ministry of Supply which, the report added, imposed restrictions. 'Consequently,' it went on, 'there are many matters which it has not been possible to include or which have been dealt with only very briefly. If any Fellow requires further information, will he please apply in writing to the Secretary.'

On this curious note the matter ended. Huxley had been beaten by an enemy deeply entrenched in good positions – and by travelling abroad on war work had let his attention stray from the battlefield at what he might well have realized would be a vital moment. Yet in other ways the Council had acted too late. The move forward which Huxley started had by this time gained too much momentum to be easily stopped. The transformation which he had begun was to continue after the war. And if the London Zoo is still the leader in its field, one reason is the prod forward which it was given under Huxley's secretaryship between 1935 and 1942.

Chapter XIII

The War Years - Europe

(*i*)

The outbreak of the second world war had been regarded with mixed feelings by most members of the Huxley family. More than half a century earlier TH, inspecting Pitt-Rivers's famous collection illustrating the development of weapons, had described it as a witness to man's ignorance and stupidity. During the 1930s Julian had more than once warned that the preservation of peace was now a main objective for men of good-will, while Aldous had rejected war as a solution to international problems. On the surface all seemed strangely different from the comparative certainties of 1914 when most members of the family had joined those leaping to arms unbidden, and Julian had returned from across the Atlantic to do the same.

Yet when it came to a decision the position cleared. Beneath the new disguise there remained the same unavoidable ultimatum, regarded by most men as having even fewer qualifications than in 1914. Aldous, who had tried so hard to serve a quarter of a century previously, now thought differently. Yet most other members of the family, whatever their qualifications, whatever their regrets, agreed with Julian.

> British science [he wrote in *Argument of Blood: The Advancement of Science*] now stands far above German, but unless its forces can be gathered to withstand the Germans, our science will become as that of Poland and Czechoslovakia, our universities will go the way of Cracow and of Prague, and our art, our learning, and our letters, along with our whole civilization, will be brought down by a world catastrophe and will be forgotten in a new Dark Age.

When it came to the point, one had to fight.

The family effort in the second world war was unexpectedly diverse. It included conventional soldiering; it included service in a number of scientific units, one so confidential that in 1945 its activities were considered too secret to be detailed even in official records; it included work in the diplomatic service; and, as might be expected, it included much work of a miscellaneous propaganda character concerned not only with the war itself but with the nature of the peace. Thus the Huxley activities fall into occupational categories rather than family groups.

The purely Service element was mainly represented by the Wallers who carried on their long connection with the Gloucestershire Regiment. Colonel Noel Huxley Waller who had commanded the 5th Battalion until his retirement in 1929, and who subsequently became the Battalion's Honorary Colonel, was now appointed Army Welfare Officer for the Gloucester district. His son, Anthony, left his architect's practice in Bristol on the outbreak of war to join the Battalion and was killed some nine months later during the evacuation from Dunkirk; while one of his three sisters was attached to the Battalion as a clerk in the A.T.S. From the other side of the family tree there came Christopher Huxley, the youngest of Henry Huxley's three sons, by this time a brigadier, who also took part in the Dunkirk operation. 'Being a typical Huxley,' he later commented, 'that is, standing six feet three or so, I was able to wade out farther than most people.' He returned for a while to Staff College, becoming Assistant Commandant before returning to regimental duties, first in the western desert and then in Italy and North-West Europe. Those who served in uniform also included Julian's elder half-brother, David Bruce Huxley, and Julian's younger son, Francis, an Ordinary Seaman in the R.N.V.R. in 1942, who served in H.M. destroyers before being commissioned and joining first H.M.S. *Ramillies* and later H.M. Light Carrier *Vengeance*.

The most important of the family's civilian activities in the scientific war were concentrated in the complexities of radio and radar, the 'Wizard War' as Churchill called it. It was here that Thomas Eckersley was to affect events in two vital ways. On the outbreak of war, Eckersley's team of short-wave experts at Great Baddow was automatically ear-marked for official employment. Within a few months it had been incorporated into the Air Ministry as Air Intelligence 4, and in 1942 it was enlarged to become the Inter-Services Ionosphere Bureau. Its work was largely concerned with short-wave radio transmissions – those sent out by the Allies, and the enemy transmissions which were picked up and, if possible, decoded. Eckersley himself, however, was also deeply concerned with radar, whose apparatus and techniques were by now in a state of wild proliferation. The problems presented to the radar experts were extraordinarily varied, and among them was that of finding submarines by radar in rough weather. Heavy seas were found to mask the returning pulses, and the need for eliminating this stumbling-block in the way of submarine-detection became of increasing urgency. Eckersley was, very largely, the man who eliminated it.

This success, crucial though it was in the Battle of the Atlantic, was of less significance than Eckersley's part in the 'Battle of the Beams' which was fought out in the summer and autumn of 1940 when Britain was under heavy air attack. Preparations for the battle had begun the previous spring, when Intelligence authorities in the Air Ministry, led by R. V. Jones, a young scientist brought in to study the enemy's scientific work, began to suspect that the Germans might be planning to use radio-navigation over Britain – a frightening possibility a quarter of a century ago when all but the largest of targets were still concealed by the blanket of the dark except on moonlit nights. However two question-marks still hung over radio-navigation. One involved the spread of the beams, a factor which would decisively affect accuracy. The other concerned the range at which such beams could effectively be used, and it was here that Eckersley became involved in a remarkable way. Some while earlier he had prepared, but not published, a paper dealing with the propagation of radio waves such as might be used by the Germans, and had argued that there was nothing to rule out their use at ranges as great as the distance between Germany and Britain.

It was the argument outlined in this paper of which Jones made great use when, early in June 1940, he convinced Churchill's scientific adviser, Professor Lindemann (later Lord Cherwell), that the threat from the German beams was real. As a result of Jones's determined intervention, plans were made for discovering whether the beams did really exist. Churchill decreed that the search should be given top priority and that all reports should come to him personally. And it was then, on returning to the Air Ministry from the conference at Downing Street at which these vital decisions had been made, that Jones met Eckersley and recounted what was being done. Eckersley's reaction was disconcerting. His paper, he said, had been prepared largely as an academic exercise; in his opinion there seemed only a slight chance of the threat being a real one. Jones, relying on the Intelligence material which had been collected over the preceding few weeks, insisted on the search being made. This was just as well, for the beams were found that very night, 'set' across Derby where Rolls-Royce aero engines were being made. Counter-measures were immediately put in hand to distort, camouflage and confuse the complete German system. Eckersley's 'theoretical' paper, in whose practical applications he had little faith, had helped to give the counter-measures a month-long start that was to be of decisive importance in the campaign ahead.

There is something intriguing about the fact that Thomas Eckersley was engaged throughout the war on this most secret of work – and that his elder brother Roger was the Chief Censor of the B.B.C. For when his younger brother Peter had returned from Germany before the outbreak of war, his second wife had remained in that country. Her pro-Nazi sympathies had become dominant and before the end of the war she was broadcasting on the German radio; and her husband, though transparently patriotic and personally above all suspicion, was naturally a marked man. So the technical talent of Peter Eckersley, brother of two men who knew some of the country's most closely guarded secrets, remained only partially used for the whole of the war.

Apart from Thomas Eckersley, no fewer than four Huxleys were involved in radar or Operational Research, that science which grew directly out of the need to calibrate and work at their greatest efficiency the special radar sets designed for use with anti-aircraft guns. Three of them – a distant cousin Leonard Huxley from the department of physics, University College, Leicester; Julian's elder son Anthony; and John Huxley Buzzard, General Buzzard's eldest son – were working during the early years of the war at Fighter Command headquarters, Stanmore. The eldest of the three was Leonard, a descendant of one of TH's uncles. His family had emigrated to Australia at the turn of the century, he had returned as a Rhodes Scholar and at the outbreak of war had been head of the Department of Physics at University College, Leicester. He had first gone from Leicester to the Telecommunications Research Establishment, the unique T.R.E. which had started as the Bawdsey Research Station under Watson-Watt in 1935 and which under Dr A. P. Rowe was to play such a significant part in winning the war. Then he had been seconded to Fighter Command, and with two colleagues had prepared a report on the working of the radar chain which had saved Britain during the second half of 1940 – a report so good that it was circulated as a guide to NATO countries some fifteen years later and has been officially described as 'a landmark in the history of operational research'. From Fighter Command Leonard returned to T.R.E., where he ran the station's famous radar school through which thousands of civilians and servicemen passed through the war. At first he was the sole lecturer, working in a single small hut, but as the demands of radar grew so did demands on the school, and a considerable staff was eventually involved. Its importance can be gauged by Rowe's comment: 'A lasting impression I have of the school in its later years is a picture of a front row of Air Vice-Marshals and Air Commodores sitting at the feet of a succession of flannel-bagged lecturers.'

The second member of the Huxley family to arrive at Fighter Command was John Huxley Buzzard, who a few months after the outbreak of war had heard that the Air Force was recruiting barristers for what turned out to be the Stanmore filter room. He was accepted, was subsequently regarded as an outstanding filter officer, and was subsequently attached to the Americans in Iceland to instruct them for a short time. Then, in the spring of 1941, he was sent to take charge of filter rooms and allied work in India and such of the Far East as was left.

The third Huxley at Fighter Command was Anthony, Julian's elder son who in the autumn of 1939 had left Dauntsey's for Cambridge. Shying away from science, he had spent two years on English literature at Trinity; after graduation he had become a civilian Operational Research worker and was soon posted to Stanmore.

The fourth Huxley involved in radar and Operational Research was Andrew, the earlier Leonard's younger son by his second marriage. He had taken part two of his tripos at Cambridge in the summer of 1939 and in the Long Vacation had begun research work at the Marine Biological Laboratory at Plymouth with A. L. Hodgkin, also based on Cambridge. He had then worked as a medical student, first in Cambridge and then at University College Hospital, and it at first seems strange that a man with such training should be drawn into operational research. Yet those accustomed to the biological disciplines were frequently at home with its problems – partly because they normally worked in fields where, contrary to those of physics, variations were great and exact results unlikely; partly, no doubt, as one physiologist has explained it, because 'they were more accustomed to making the best of very imperfect and inadequate data and drawing some sort of conclusions from them'. Initially, Andrew was recruited from University College into what became known as 'Blackett's Circus', the team led by Professor P. M. S. Blackett and consisting of three physiologists, two mathematical physicists, representatives from three firms making radar equipment, and an astrophysicist. This assorted bag was responsible during the late summer and autumn of 1940 for making radar-control of anti-aircraft guns a working proposition – and, at the same time, for laying the foundations of what was to be Operational Research (Operations Research in the United States). Andrew Huxley remained with Anti-Aircraft Command for two years and then joined the Directorate of Operational Research which Blackett had by this time set up in the Admiralty.

Two other Huxleys had meanwhile become implicated in wartime diplomacy. One of them, Laurence Collier, had suffered the wry experience of having been earmarked as new British Ambassador to Norway only shortly before the German invasion of that country in 1940. As the Norwegian Government was re-established in London, Collier became first Minister and then, as the Governments in exile were put on a different basis, Ambassador – but took up his appointment in Oslo only three years later when, in 1945, the returning Government sailed up Oslo Fiord.

On the outbreak of war, Michael Huxley had been recalled by the Foreign Office. He served in various capacities, notably as Lord Lothian's liaison officer with the American Press in Washington during the spring and summer of 1940; and then, in 1940–41, as organizer of the Inter-Allied Information Committee and Centre in New York. This was supported by the representatives of nine European countries, all subjected to Nazi domination and all contributors to the American melting-pot – common factors which permitted joint action in impressing on their officially neutral American relatives the truth of what that domination implied.

Diplomacy is sometimes regarded as the practice of propaganda with the gloves on. The less inhibited kind was to involve both Gervas and Julian for a great deal of the war – naturally so, since Gervas had by this time acquired great expertise in official and quasi-official publicity work, while Julian's intuitive understanding of the principles underlying the need for this particular war made him an ideal lecturer in countries like the United States during the years before they were drawn into the conflict.

Gervas had been recruited into preparations for propaganda well before the outbreak of war, having joined a group set up under Sir Ivison Macadam, Secretary and Director-General of the Royal Institution of International Affairs, to prepare plans for a wartime Ministry of Information. 'All through 1939 I attended regular meetings of the group, growing increasingly horrified at the folly of making any large-scale and detailed preparations for a completely unknown contingency,' he says. When war broke out, he found himself a member of an advisory 'brains trust' but the outlook for this group was as bleak as for the earlier one. 'No one ever discovered what we were supposed to do,' says Gervas, 'and, with the phoney war being all that was occurring, the whole vast structure set up was merely revolving frustratingly on its own axis.' Early in 1940 he resigned, and later joined the National Savings Movement as a part-time adviser on publicity.

In 1943 he returned to the M.O.I. as Director of the Empire Division and of the American Forces Liaison Division.

This second organization was formed as U.S. troops began to arrive in force. Relations between Allied troops and the civilians in whose countries they are stationed are at the best delicate and at the worst explosive. On this occasion the role of trouble-evader had first been handed to the Foreign Office, which had formally set up a committee whose members appealed for the names of British people willing to act as hosts to the Americans. The replies arrived in thousands but virtually no Americans applied for the hospitality, and the hot potato was hurriedly passed over to the M.O.I. Gervas, instead of suggesting that Americans should accept 'blind dates' through a central organization, set up regional committees which could encourage informal and local get-togethers – 'a kind of gigantic Paul Jones', as he described it. This he now organized, using a central committee of representatives from the Y.W.C.A., the W.V.S., the Church Army, Salvation Army and Women's Institutes to start the operation at local level.

All this worked well. So much so that when, during the months before D-Day, the number of U.S. troops in Britain rose dramatically, it was the new organization, rather than the Foreign Office, which was given the task of dealing with any major problems. Gervas Huxley became chairman of the small working committee that was set up: it had little real trouble to deal with.

(*ii*)

While Gervas was thus performing diplomatic services behind the scenes, hardly known even as a name to the general public, his cousin Julian was becoming a well-known national figure. This was partly due to involvement in one of Britain's most popular wartime radio programmes, but it was by no means solely due to it, since his activities through the war ranged across an astonishingly wide field. For the first two and a half years he was still Secretary of the Zoological Society. In addition he wrote; he lectured; he produced his greatest feat of scholarship – *Evolution: The Modern Synthesis*; and the war saw him for the first time drawn on to official bodies where his concern with planning the future could be translated from paper schemes to reality. In all these ways Julian helped to form the climate of opinion that was to exist in the post-war years. He was able to exercise greater influence than his position would seem to warrant, partly because he had a foot in two camps. Julian in his black hat, once the friend of the iconoclastic D. H. Lawrence, pulling at the pillars of the Established Church and suggesting that scientists should actually help in planning the future, was a typical figure of the Left. Yet as an old Etonian and a Balliol man, he had, like so many Huxleys, the entrée to a totally different kind of society, and in the universities, in the Civil Service and in the professions, his opinions were not only given but listened to.

Within a few days of the outbreak of war, Julian was trying to discover whether any specific war aims had been decided upon, and before the end of September 1939, *The Times* published a lengthy and significant letter from him on this still unpopular subject. In view of Germany's present division, and of the numerous international agencies which have come into existence during the last two decades, this letter was remarkably prophetic, pointing out that the dismemberment of Germany could only postpone the emergence of a new anarchic crisis:

> Long-term war aims envisaging an incipient federalization of Western Europe should therefore include the setting up of international economic agencies, designed to promote the increased consumption and better distribution of raw materials; of unified transport institutions, notably pooled civil aviation; of educational and cultural machinery (including provision for large-scale educational and research interchange, inter-availability of medical and other professional qualification, facilitation of travel); of health organizations (based presumably on the health action of the League, but with much greater powers, notably for improving nutrition); of a population section, to deal with migration, including refugee settlement; the pooling of tropical colonial possessions, with the eventual establishment of an international administrative staff; and, of course, the strengthening of existing arrangements for settling international disputes (Hague Court), as well as the establishment of a political federal centre, with powers of federal taxation and with control over some international armed force (accompanied by some considerable measure of purely national disarmament).

If ends were to be at least affected by means, it was essential that some such plans should be made. But public reaction was summed up by the correspondent who wrote to *The Times* suggesting that people should 'not waste over-much time pondering on this subject when the war has scarcely begun'.

Huxley's insistence that a war without war-aims was rather stupid helped to make him an ideal semi-official propagandist in such uncommitted countries as the United States, and he was lecturing there on behalf of the Government before the end of 1939. He spent two months in America, meeting politicians, churchmen, scientists, film stars, business men, artists and journalists. And he found much preoccupation with 'the supposedly imperialist and therefore anti-democratic aims of my own country and the danger to democracy involved in waging war in the modern totalitarian way'.

This first wartime visit was notable for Huxley's address to the American Association for the Advancement of Science, then meeting in Ohio. The first address in the U.S. under a scheme in which Britain and the U.S. were to supply guest lecturers in alternate years, it was boldly entitled 'Science, War and Reconstruction' – a forward-looking subject in which Americans might have had little interest and about which the British might well have been too preoccupied to speak. Yet Huxley ranged across the whole subject of war and its consequences. World-wide conflict was not inevitable; but conflict existed if not here and now, at least only one ocean away, and it was necessary to consider 'this war and the problem of war in general in the long-range perspective of science'. For war was a vehicle for change, that intrinsic element in living organisms; and if men only began in time to formulate a plan more workable than that of the League of Nations, the catastrophe might even be turned to advantage. In the United States as in Britain, Huxley was anxious to stress that one could not wait for victory before laying plans:

> The end of the war will face the world with a task for which it is ill-prepared. It is urgent that every country, and perhaps most of all those countries which are not actually immersed in the struggle, should begin thinking out the plan of the new world order in detail, designing machinery which will work, as well as defining the limits of their own participation. It is equally urgent that the world, perhaps again chiefly through those countries like the U.S.A. which are already best equipped technically for the task and are not being diverted from it by the needs of war, should begin constructing planning organizations on a large enough scale to function as a social brain and not a mere ganglion, in order to ensure that any first step which we may be able to take directly after the war will be a step in the right direction.

America was to be 'diverted' before two years were out. Huxley was perhaps optimistic in his statements. Yet it is difficult to over-estimate the effect of his address on a wide and influential section of potential U.S. decision-makers.

The difficult war years saw the deaths of both Ethel and Nettie, TH's two surviving daughters, both in their seventies and both affected by the heavy German bombing of London. They saw also Julian's involvement in the first of the innumerable radio and TV 'quizzes', question-forums, and party performances which have since proliferated. A good deal of Britain was spending much of most evenings behind the black-out, either in air raid shelters or in their own homes, with the choice of sounds limited mainly to the drone of bombers passing overhead, A.A. fire, the explosion of bombs, or whatever the B.B.C. chose to provide. Why not, someone asked, gather round the microphone three or four men who had not only high intelligence but the facility for talking to ordinary people? Why not present them with a series of provocative, interesting, amusing or socially significant questions – preferably sent in by listeners – and then let them argue out the answers amongst themselves, unscripted, off-the-cuff, and not knowing what the next question would be?

Howard Thomas was instructed to find three men who 'were well known, were potential radio personalities and who could speak knowledgeably, wittily and briefly'. Eventually he picked his trio – Commander Campbell, who had sailed the seven seas and survived a wide variety of extraordinary experiences; Professor C. E. M. Joad, the well-known philosopher and author; and Julian Huxley – 'I wanted a keen brain and Julian was the best bet,' Thomas said later. Huxley contributed his own extraordinarily wide zoologist's knowledge. He also contributed just that touch of the irascible scientist, irritated that lay minds should move more slowly than his own, which gave the programme a threat of the slumbering volcano. As a result, Huxley became a national figure, known not only to the literate layers of the public, but to the vast mass for whom he now represented the Voice of Science. Once again, the public image became a subtle distortion. Irascibility was translated as bad temper, the expert became the know-all, confidence became arrogance. Stories were gleefully circulated about Huxley, of which the best known was that after he had entered a cab the driver turned to him and asked: 'You wouldn't be connected with the B.B.C.?' At the first stop he turned round to ask: 'You wouldn't be part of the Brains Trust, would you?' Then, as Huxley got out at the end of the journey there came the awe-stricken question: 'You wouldn't be Professor Joad, would you, sir?' One fact of which most people were ignorant was that the person who recounted the story with most delight was Huxley himself.

The programme – at first known as 'Any Questions?' but soon to become 'The Brains Trust' – was moved to a peak listening hour and within a few months had become almost a feature of Britain's wartime life. Between them Campbell, Joad and Huxley found from their personal knowledge or experiences the answers to the most abstruse queries; they did not often agree on the answers, and the arguments which spluttered across the radio were the high spot of many a dreary evening. Huxley naturally handled the questions dealing with biology and was able to answer many of them not only from personal experience but with just the right touch of the born explainer. Thus when someone wanted to know how a kangaroo kept its pouch clean, he replied that he himself had seen the process being carried out by a tree kangaroo in his own Zoo. 'She was cleaning out the inside with her hands, much as a lady might clean out the inside of her handbag, except that here the bag was attached to the lady, so to speak,' he added. He also fielded what became the most famous of all questions, raised by a bomber pilot who wanted to know how a fly landed on the ceiling. But even Huxley did not know the answer to that one, and for seven days a large number of Britons at war anxiously debated among themselves the possible ways in which the fly might be able to do the trick. Only at the following week's session was Huxley able to explain that the fly began by making a half-loop which brought the ceiling within its sight. The apparent movement of the ceiling, he went on, triggered off a reflex action which extended the fly's forelegs, which thereupon came into contact as the insect reached the top of the loop.

There were questions scientific, technical, and moral. The Queen sent a question from Sandringham which completely stumped the team. And at times there were questions which inevitably laid themselves open to endless discussion – as when the panel was asked what eight half-crown classics a man could best take with him on active service. 'I think it is good to have some good, long novel to get your teeth into and I should have thought that (especially for a soldier) Tolstoy's *War and Peace* was unrivalled,' said Huxley. 'You should take a book of poetry and it should be a selection. If the *Oxford Book of English Verse* is in a cheap edition, that would be ideal; if not, *The Golden Treasury*.'

Huxley was a regular member of the Brains Trust panel until the late autumn of 1941. Then, early in December, he left for another lecture tour of the United States, arriving in New York three days after Pearl Harbor. He still attracted trouble, and Sir Patrick Hannon gave notice that he was to ask the Minister of Information 'if his attention has been called to the interview given by Professor Julian Huxley on his arrival in the U.S.A. to isolationist newspapers, in which he had expressed opinions tending seriously to affect the good relations between the U.S. of America and the British Commonwealth of Nations; and if he will take immediate steps for the recall of this lecturer'. Huxley's lecture tour went on unchecked. He met many groups concerned with post-war planning. He revisited the Tennessee Valley, lecturing there on the twin tasks that now lay before both the United States and Britain – winning the war and ensuring that the inevitable transformations of society which war would bring about took place within a democratic framework. He covered a vast amount of ground, both physically and in his lectures. He drew extensively on his earlier contacts with America, managing to gain the confidence of his hosts yet remaining the figure from across the Atlantic that was to American minds the quintessential Englishman. 'Tweed suit and herring-bone topcoat,' ran one description by a journalist in the Tennessee Valley, 'slouch hat and Scotch plaid muffler, beetling brows accenting a keen face above a bright plaid necktie; businesslike stride, quick and sure; someone you have to run to keep up with!'

It was on this tour that Huxley received the news that he had been 'sacked' from the Zoological Society. And following his return to Britain – and to the Brains Trust – he found himself back in the position he had occupied for so much of his life – a free-lance scientist and writer, and one whose long-term aims were now linked to the immediate task of helping to win the war. He was also without a home, since the ending of his work with the society meant a move from the Regent's Park flat. He was lucky in finding an ideal house in Pond Street, only a few hundred yards from Hampstead Heath and lying in the heart of the Huxley country. To this new base he moved in the summer of 1942 and here he continued to produce throughout the next two decades and more his impressive succession of books, pamphlets, lectures and miscellaneous papers.

Huxley's wartime writings fall fairly clearly into two groups – those which were produced as part of the war effort, even though it would be misleading to describe them as 'propaganda', such is the weight of mud still clinging to the word; and those which were produced as a natural part of the Huxley organism. In the first category came *Race in Europe*, one of the Oxford pamphlets on World Affairs, a brief summary of the matters outlined in an important book which Huxley had written with A. C. Haddon before the war. This was *We Europeans*, a survey of 'racial' problems which refuted the old conceptions of 'race' and suggested that the reader might conceive of a typical Teuton 'as blond as Hitler, as dolichocephalic as Rosenberg, as tall as Goebbels, as slender as Goering and as manly as Streicher'. *We Europeans* had made a considerable impact. It was significant that the basis of this sober piece of scientific writing made, without 'slanting' of any sort, such effective propaganda. *Race in Europe* was followed by *Argument of Blood: the Advance of Science*, published as one of the Macmillan War

Pamphlets and outlining in extraordinary detail how the Nazi theories of a superior *Herrenvolk* had already crippled German scientific prospects. *Reconstruction and Peace* – written under the pseudonym of 'Balbus' – came next, while in 1944 Huxley produced *The Future of the Colonies*, one of a series of 'Targets for Tomorrow' booklets in which eminent men outlined what they felt the post-war world should be like.

More solid meat was *The Freedom of Necessity*, a lengthy survey of the way ahead written under the pseudonym of 'Archimedes' and published in four issues of *Horizon*. A curious mixture of propaganda and world-appraisal, it began by underlining that 'The war we are now fighting is not only the greatest but the most important war that has ever been fought. It is the most terrible and at the same time the most hopeful of wars . . .' – hopeful because it would enable men to take the big strides forward which would otherwise have been blocked by ignorance and vested interests. Huxley's cross-heads indicated clearly what these strides should be – 'Planned Economy', 'The Best Human Environment: Biological and Social', 'Human Needs' and 'Use of Natural Resources'.

All this, good stuff though it might be, was slight when ranged against his other work. He produced two volumes of essays, *The Uniqueness of Man* and *On Living in a Revolution*, each of which contained some of his best prose. He wrote *TVA: Adventure in Planning*, an account of the Tennessee Valley Authority in which he emphasized that the long-term planning, of which it is such an admirable example, was also needed in Europe. And he completed what was by far the most important item of his wartime output, *Evolution: The Modern Synthesis* – 'the first comprehensive post-Mendelian analysis of biological evolution as a process'. This was begun in his Zoo study, working late and lonely. It was rewritten three times, and while its content was a tribute to the author's mastery of the whole subject, the sheer labour of its production was an indication of the Huxley stamina. This massive book, more than 600 pages long, reviewed the progress of ideas about evolution which had been put forward during the preceding half-century; it explained how new discoveries in a jigsaw puzzle that included the whole world of living things each fitted into place; and as *Nature* said, it accomplished the very difficult feat of 'placing before the non-specialist scientific reader concise understandable accounts of recent important researches which were often difficult to follow in the original publications'. In other words, Huxley was in this case doing for the scientist the synthesizing and explanatory task which he had so often done for the layman.

Evolution was published in 1942, and the following year Huxley brought the family wheel full circle by giving the Romanes Lecture at Oxford. His grandfather, half a century earlier, had spoken on 'Evolution and Ethics', of which the essential statement was that ethics formed no part of the cosmic evolution and that man, to be man, must fight against nature. His grandson, speaking in 1943 on 'Evolutionary Ethics', regarded what were substantially the same facts from a different viewpoint, one which was farther out, and which offered certainly a fresh and possibly a wider sight of the process. From this vantage-point it seemed clear that TH's contradiction could be resolved –

> on the one hand by extending the concept of evolution both backward into the inorganic and forward into the human domain, and on the other by considering ethics not as a body of fixed principles, but as a product of evolution, and itself evolving.

Ethics were thus seen as merely one product of the long climb upwards from the mud. Man was now able, in Julian Huxley's words, to 'inject his ethics into the heart of evolution'.

Throughout the war, he continued to become a more substantial figure in this border country between science and moral philosophy, He himself began to realize that his own particular experience and background, his work as a biologist and the life he had lived in the invigorating air of the Huxley tradition, made it right for him to focus his attentions and to concentrate his energies on one subject above all others: man's place in the cosmos and what he should do about it. To this subject and its ramifications he therefore began to devote increasing time and thought. And from now onwards it is possible to trace a link back to this subject, tenuous at places but nevertheless existent, from almost all his work and activities.

Before the end of the war Huxley was again caught up in the official machinery. First he agreed to serve on the Elliott Commission, set up to recommend what should be done about Higher Education in West Africa. The result was a three-month tour in which he covered fifteen thousand miles of West Africa by plane, train, car, cycle and on foot – and picked up an amoeba germ which on return to Britain had the unusual distinction of putting him out of action.

It was typical that while he was away Juliette should be drawn into the running of the Visiting Scientists' Club; quite as typical that her initially part-time help should so develop that many years later she was widely credited with having started it.

Then, as the war was ending, Huxley was officially drawn into the subject on which he was to lavish so much of his energy, enthusiasm and knowledge – the preservation of the country's animals and flowers and of its landscape, two aspects of the same problem that are summed up in Britain by the phrases 'Nature conservancy' and 'National Parks'. Huxley was suited both by temperament and experience to play the influential part that he did play in such matters. TH had had a feeling for natural scenery that showed itself in his love for the Alps and his attachment to the downland heights of Beachy Head. Leonard Huxley had revealed, in more than one quiet contribution to the *Cornhill*, the same awareness and appreciation of the scene around him. Julian, however, had not only inherited all this. In the matter of nature conservation, and all that it implied, he united aesthetic concern with scientific interest to a degree remarkable even for the Huxleys. Thus a delight in fine scenery ran in double harness with the scientific knowledge that unless action was quickly taken many species might die out – and, what was worse, many habitats be destroyed – overwhelmed by the advancing tide of industrial man. The result of this Huxleyan combination had been epitomized when, almost a decade previously, he had warned that:

> Man does not live by bread alone nor by machines alone. Some men at least need the beauty of nature, the interest of nature, even the wildness of nature, the contact with wild animals living their own lives in their own surroundings, the temporary release from civilized routine and elaboration into the immediacy of camp and travel.

In 1943 the Nature Reserves Investigation Committee of the C.P.R.E. proposed setting up statutory reserves, and the British Ecological Society suggested much the same thing. In 1945, the Biological Committee of the Royal Society made similar recommendations, and later in the year a Government committee under John Dower recommended setting up both National Parks and 'a permanent organ of Government . . . called the Wild Life Conservation Council'. Two subsidiary committees were thereupon formed to discover how these recommendations might best be carried out. Of the first, set up under Sir Arthur Hobhouse to deal with National Parks, Huxley was a member. But in addition he knew Hobhouse well. Leonard Elmhirst, another member of the Hobhouse Committee and the founder of Dartington Hall, was also an old friend; so was Clough Williams-Ellis, who also served on the committee. The second committee, officially the Special Committee on Wild Life Conservation, was set up under Huxley's chairmanship, and from the autumn of 1945 onwards he became increasingly involved in its work – until, after only a few months he was diverted to full-time work for Unesco. But by that time the committee was on its feet and its path forward had clearly been set out. Huxley had, moreover, brought on to the committee the members who were to provide the first Chairman and the first two Directors-General of what was to become the Nature Conservancy – Sir Arthur Tansley, Captain C. R. P. Diver and Max Nicholson. When the Conservancy and the National Parks Commission were brought into existence by the Town and Country Planning Act 1949, Huxley's official connection with both organizations lay in the past. Yet it would be unwise to underestimate his influence behind the scenes, his exercise of the continuing Huxley facility for dropping the right word into the right ear at the right time.

By 1949 Huxley was also directly involved in a new scheme for presenting the post-war public with accurate and understandable information on the multitudinous aspects of natural history they could see about them. This was the 'New Naturalist' series, a range of books soon to be numbered by the dozen, each written by a specialist and each dealing with one aspect of natural history in Britain – either by regions or by subject. From the start of the series in 1944 Huxley was one of its general editors, and although he himself did not contribute a single volume he could, and did, exercise a powerful influence on what subjects were chosen and how they were treated. 'The remarkable thing about him,' says Eric Hosking, the photographic editor of the series,

> was that whatever subject came up he would be certain to know something about it. If for instance someone mentioned the subject of pollination, Huxley would be sure to perk up with: 'Then we mustn't leave out that fascinating example. . . .!' Even when it came to land usage, geology and such subjects really outside the scope of the biologist he would be able to talk knowledgeably on them with such a man as Stamp.

The new eager post-war public which created the demand for such books was an encouraging illustration of the changes that the war had brought about. In the bright light of the peace, opportunity beckoned – even though from some positions its finger had a slightly grisly aspect. For just as men were learning that they must collaborate in their control of the natural world, just as even the most obdurate were beginning to see what advantages there were in using the scientific method to improve man's lot, just as the lesson appeared to be sinking in, the nuclear genie was let out of the bottle.

Five years previously, as Huxley had sat in the Zoo's basement shelter, listening to Sibelius against the chorus of anti-aircraft guns outside, he had realized how the very outbreak of war had, as he put it, 'tied up the threads' and had underlined that the post-war civilization must be created on the basis of a social outlook:

> The essential economic and mechanistic ideals of the great era of *laisser-faire* no longer either satisfy or convince. . . . The new belief must be a social one, based on the concept of society as an organic whole, in which rights and duties are balanced deliberately, as they are automatically balanced in the tissues of the animal body. Economic values must lose their primacy, and become subordinated to social values.

All this still held good. But now, in the second half of 1945, the entire human prospect became overshadowed by the release of nuclear energy.

Huxley, almost inevitably, was drawn into the nuclear argument. His position was best shown in a speech which he made in New York after flying out to address a rally organized by the Independent Citizens' Committee of the Arts and Sciences. Henry Wallace, Helen Keller and Harold Urey were among the others who spoke, and who heard Huxley tell a packed Madison Square Garden:

> The best thing would be if we could agree not to manufacture any atomic bombs. But if we fail in this, the irreducible minimum for man's future safety is that no bombs should be in the possession of separate nations as such. If bombs are made, they must be by and for UNO.

This attitude undervalued the deterrent effect that nuclear weapons would have when held by both the major world powers, and it assumed that the United Nations would be able to operate on a far higher level of human wisdom than individual countries. Less disputable was Huxley's prescient view of what nuclear power might mean to man's adaptation, or even control, of nature. The polar ice-caps might be melted to help govern the climate. At a lesser level, dams might be built in a fraction of the time, while a whole range of exciting projects were now within man's range:

> To mention only the Sahara, atomic power could be used to distil sea-water, leaving the salts behind as sources of magnesium and other valuable elements, and to pump fresh water into numerous depressions in its vast area until they again blossom into the fertility they had in the Ice Age.

The future, there could be no doubt, would be a future of great opportunity. It would, moreover, be a future in which men would be forced to think for themselves, more generally, more often, and more deeply, than they had thought before. This would seem to make it a future into which the Huxleys would step with greater influence. And in the post-war years there was to be a proliferation of Huxleys, with the family producing its first Nobel Prize-winner, more than one fresh writer, and both men and women devoted to the study of man and his environment. Yet the scene was still to be dominated, as it had been between the wars, by the two remarkable brothers – Julian who had now developed into the prototype polymath, practising science and art, epitomising the twentieth-century version of the Elizabethan's 'compleat man'; and Aldous, who in the United States had grown to new stature in his search for some philosophy which would reconcile mortal coils and mental aspirations.

Chapter XIV

The War Years - America

Aldous Huxley's journey to the United States in the spring of 1937 was in Britain the subject of much comment at the time and has often been misrepresented during the past thirty years. It is certainly true that his call to action *What Are You Going to Do About It?* had evoked little response, and that his arguments were being brushed aside for events. This was doubly discomforting, for it was not only that he firmly believed pacifism to be humanity's only hope; he himself had struggled long before deciding that he should take a part in trying to direct the affairs of the world. Now he realized not only that the pacifist plea was being largely ignored but that he himself was, as he put it, 'completely unsuited to political life,' with 'no power to organize things and very bad on committees'. In future he would leave such things to the movers and shakers, and get on with his less directly implicated writing. He had never been quick to send down emotional roots in any one country, let alone any one place; and it was, of course, just as easy to write, for a while, away from the Europe of which sane men could only despair. He looked westward across the Atlantic and decided to spend a few months in the United States.

It was easy for a myth to grow upon such foundations – the myth that Huxley had emigrated to avoid the war which he so clearly saw was coming. The legend – which swiftly took hold in Europe even though, in the nature of things, it fell on less fertile ground in the United States – was helped along by Huxley's own ingenuousness as well as by the very honesty of his pacifist beliefs; and it was to be further swollen by the feelings of a wartime British public who looked with inquiring eyes from the storm centre towards the comparative calm of North America.

However, a cool look at the evidence shows beyond any doubt that when Huxley left Britain for America he had no firm intention of settling there. His motives for making what was in fact a largely speculative journey were mixed. There was Maria's horror of involvement in another war; there was Aldous's wish that his son should finish his education in the United States; and there may well have been the hope that the American climate would help his sight – although it was actually in California that, as he put it, his 'capacity to see' was realized to be 'steadily and quite rapidly failing'. Some of these factors at least combined; but they did not combine to drive Huxley from Britain irrevocably intent on emigration. Indeed, on arrival in New York he implied that he was making a three-month visit during which he would finish another book – *Ends and Means* – for which he as yet had no title. The visit was later extended, and extended more than once. After giving a series of lectures in New York in December he held a Press conference at which he let it be assumed that he would be returning to England for Christmas; furthermore, on the following day, 11 December, he wrote to a friend saying that he would 'return to Europe if nothing doing in Hollywood'. The truth of the matter is that he was driven on by a multiplicity of urges, and that motives which now appear simple and firm were at the time complex and changing. 'It is very hard,' as Maitland has said, 'to remember that events now long in the past were once in the future.'

Huxley left Britain early in April 1937, sailing from Southampton on the *Normandie* with Maria, his seventeen-year-old son Matthew, and his friend Gerald Heard, whose plans were as unsettled as his own. The party made a brief stop in New York where Aldous bought a car, and in this the quartet set off westwards. They stayed with friends at Denver, then moved on to visit the Huxleys' old friend Frieda Lawrence, now living on her ranch some seventeen miles from Taos, 9,000 feet up. And here, almost isolated in the desert, Aldous stopped to tie up the loose ends of reasoning, to dot the i's and cross the t's of his philosophy, and to make quite clear how he had arrived at it. The result was *Ends and Means*, now completed in the desert in a matter of weeks in virtual isolation from the worries of the external world.

In this, among the most important of his books, Aldous tried, as he put it, 'to relate the problems of domestic and international politics, of war and economics, of education, religion and ethics, to a theory of the ultimate nature of reality.' On those who were with him as he was finishing the book, his taut objective honesty made a lasting impression. Gerald Heard wrote nearly thirty years later:

> With spare and even bald plainness Huxley argued out his austere view of life. There must, he felt, be no more shade of possibly ambiguous emotion than in a legal testament. And the rules of conduct are as precise, the goal as rigorous. Not a hint of eloquence

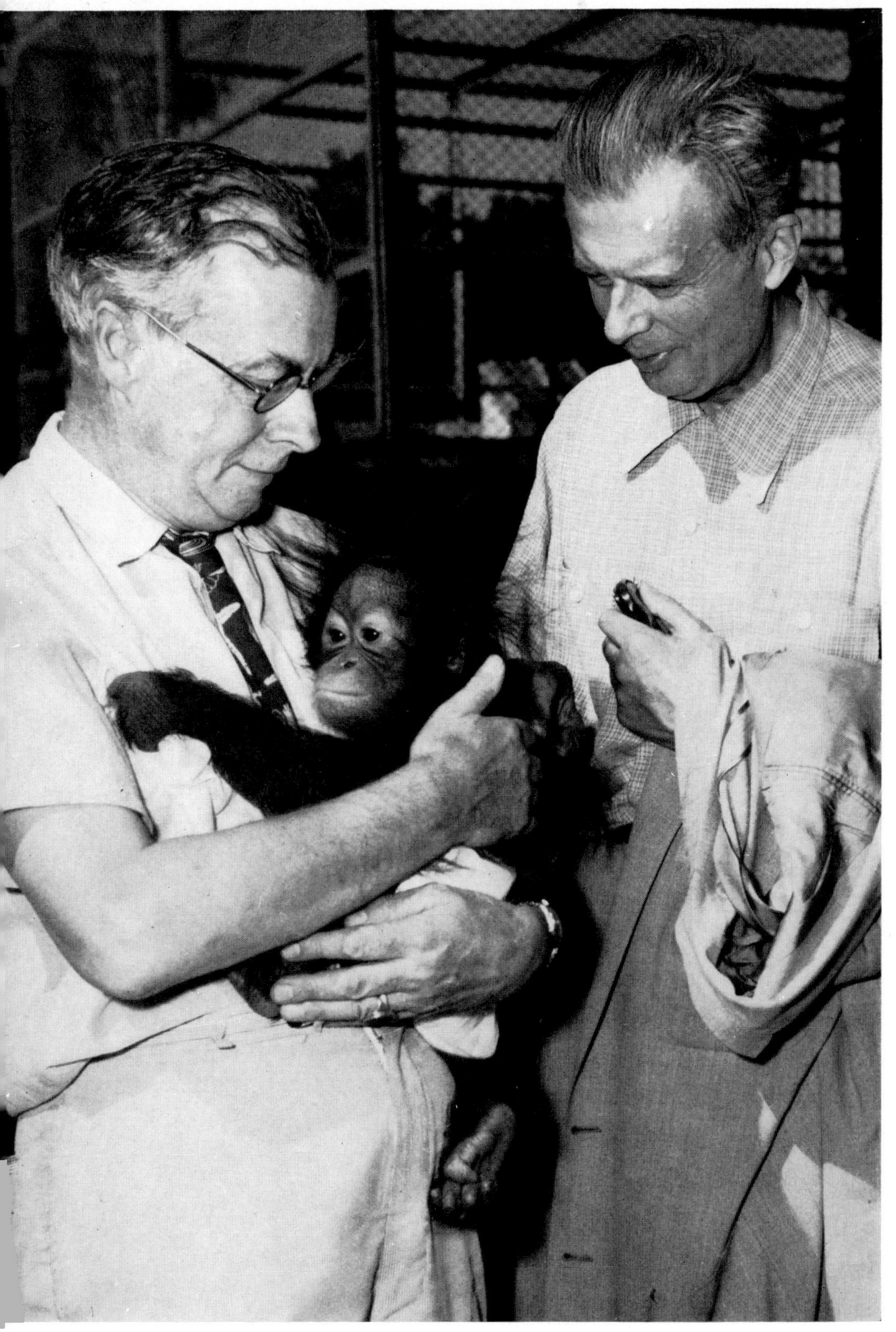

Julian and Aldous Huxley at San Diego Zoo

Julian Huxley at Unesco House after receiving the 1953 Kalinga Prize. With him is Mr Shri Sarvepalli Radhakrishnan, later to become President of the Republic of India
(Unesco Copyright)

must risk lifting the heart from the exact instructions. The body-mind must be informed in detail how it is to perform if it is to survive. Even the way the spine carries the neck and head is treated as being of cardinal importance.

This was one opinion. There were others. For while Aldous was not yet the active proponent of Eastern mysticism that he was to become a few years later, although he was not yet immersed, he had waded in deeply enough. And for most practical purposes his philosophy of non-attachment meant, in the contemporary situation, non-involvement in the struggle against Fascism already flaring into the first main battles of the Spanish Civil War.

Aldous was no more worried about practical politics than his Arnold ancestors would have been. He was worried, first, second and all the time, about moral principles. But it was natural enough that those who had to translate principles into action should demur; and it was thus natural that Huxley's philosophy should be badly received on the Left, which felt that one of its more important potential supporters was engaged in pulling the rug smartly from beneath its feet at a crucial moment. In fact, Aldous had spelt out his attitude years earlier. When he had begun a popular weekly column in *The Sunday Referee* one of his first contributions had been a blistering attack on war which could have only come from a pacifist unlikely to change his views for political expediency:

> Our world is lousy with armaments and we are so utterly lost to all reason and decency that we complacently accept our verminous state. A couple of pennyworth of commonsense and insecticide would rid us for ever of all our loathsome parasites. But we prefer to remain verminous. We prefer to run the risk of being killed by the party insects we ourselves have fashioned.

This might have been acceptable enough in the early 1930s, when it was written, but the idea began to lose its cogency for the Left when the alternative to arms was seen to be the concentration camp.

The Left was naturally unwilling to forgive Huxley for sticking to his lack of guns, and much of the reaction was exemplified by K. S. Shelvanker in what has rightly been described as a rather ill-tempered little book, *Ends* are *Means*:

> Stripped of its fine phrases, its pretensions to eternal truth and its ostentatious rectitude, the philosophy of idealism is seen once more, as in every past age, to safeguard the interests of the ruling classes and paralyse the energies of its opponents, to defend the lords of the

money bags and the machine-guns who are driving us all towards death and unspeakable degradation.

However, comment was not limited to such brash overstatements. The more unanswerable criticism came from such thoughtful reviewers as Kingsley Martin, who in 'The Pacifist's Dilemma Today', published in *The Political Quarterly*, stated his opinion clearly – and that of many other men who admired Aldous's ends even if they felt his means to be unworkable:

> I approve his [Huxley's] argument with the more sympathy because my own values, phobias and preferences are much the same as his. I recognize in 'Ends and Means' the valiant effort of a sincere and brilliant writer to find an objective justification for exactly that attitude to life which for at least one day in each week I long to take myself.

But the book was an unsuccessful effort:

> It is merely tautological to argue that we cannot do ill that good may come; the problem is to decide in view of the doubtful nature of the consequences whether an action is good or bad.

Life, after all, is merely a choice between evils, and if ends never justified means, then no reforms would ever take place since each inevitably carries the threat of violent opposition.

> For myself [Martin concluded] whatever compromise I may accept as the best available political expedient, I regard myself as on the same side as the pacifists, because I share their belief that it is the non-attached individual life that matters. I therefore look to them as allies in the struggle for freedom against the Totalitarian monster that threatens us all.

But Huxley, in this particular case, was no ally, and it says an immense amount for his personal qualities that the standard-bearers of the Left, about to enter battle, regarded him more in sorrow than in anger, admiringly, and acknowledging that if only all men could be like that then the world would be a better place. Much of Huxley's weakness did in fact lie in his simple belief that a majority of men might be induced to act in his own unselfish way. *Nature*, which has a record of strikingly perceptive comment on his works, said in the course of a review that spread to more than a full page, that Huxley had applied himself to his task 'with a certainty which belongs far more to the mystical world of religious reformers than to the world of reality in which the book was written.' Like almost every other critic, the writer had an underlying respect for Huxley's integrity and for the logic of his argument. There was only one awkward point. 'It is plain,' the reviewer pointed out,

> that to enter Mr Huxley's kingdom of man, man must completely stop being the mammal we now know him to be. . . . Retreat to mysticism is a poor prescription for the millions who already through the turn of political fortune, have to face violent death.

The *Hibbert Journal*, lining up its philosophical wisdom with the verdict of *Nature*'s scientific scrutiny and Kingsley Martin's political opinions, gave much the same verdict, praising the book's intellectual honesty but observing that 'the category of ends and means in his case, as in Aristotle's, breaks down as soon as he attempts to apply it sensibly to the problems of human life.' However, writers are not compared with Aristotle every day of the week.

It would probably be unfair to say that Huxley was disappointed with the reception accorded *Ends and Means*. It was, in fact, widely praised for the closely reasoned work that it was. But it is difficult not to feel that he had unrealistically hoped, even if he had not gone on record as hoping, that readers would not merely read but would also be converted. There was little sign of this in a world in which Germany was preparing for the *Anschluss* and in which the first British radar stations were already turning their metal antennae towards the quarter from which attack was expected.

Huxley's attitude was later underlined by a letter which he wrote to Jake Zeitlin, a Los Angeles bookseller who had quickly become a good friend. Zeitlin had passed on to Huxley a request for a contribution to protests against Nazi terrorism being prepared for the Hearst papers. Huxley declined.

> I used at one time to do a lot of writing letters to the papers and signing statements [he wrote], but it is better not to do these things unless there is some specific and concrete piece of good to be gained by doing so – as there was, for example, in the case of the Spanish Children, where my preface might serve to raise a little extra money.

He then, referring to *Ends and Means*, went on to elaborate his reasons.

> If one confines oneself to denouncing or expressing horror, one is merely indulging and permitting others to indulge in the pleasures (very considerable, admittedly) of using intemperate language. It took me about three hundred pages to elaborate the kind of theory I

have been talking about; and I see now that there are considerable additions and modifications that ought to be made. This being so, I don't see that any good would be done by my writing even two or three thousand words on the subject. The persecution of the Jews in Germany is horrible in the extreme; but it is not by proclaiming the fact in a loud voice that this particular persecution will be stopped or that human beings will discontinue the habit of persecution, which is immensely old and which is bound up with habits of thought, feeling, action and belief, with traditional methods of social and economic organization such that, if the latter persist, the former must inevitably manifest itself. It is useless to treat small-pox by cutting out the individual pustules and stitching up the wounds.

By this time, Aldous was almost settling down in the United States. He had certainly not crossed the Atlantic to 'avoid the war' which he felt was coming. Yet soon after his arrival on the far side of the Atlantic he had begun to feel that here, beyond the barrier of the ocean, a nation of sane men might be able to build their lives in peace. 'The thing that strikes me most about this country is its hopefulness,' he said at the time:

> In spite of the depression, in spite of everything, I find an extraordinary hopefulness running through people. It is this quality which distinguishes your Continent from Europe, where there is a hopeless depression and fear. It makes for a comfortable atmosphere, and, from a practicable point of view, it is sound.

With certain qualifications, Huxley liked the United States. He would remain, temporarily at least. And he might, moreover, even try to write for the films, a suggestion which had been made by Frieda Lawrence, who was corresponding with Jake Zeitlin, a man of perceptive taste who was to have a considerable influence on Huxley's life.

Aldous had written to him, inquiring of the prospects in Hollywood. Zeitlin replied and followed up the reply by a visit to New Mexico the following month. He agreed to represent Aldous discreetly in Hollywood and three months later Huxley arrived in the film city, commissioned to write his first script – a scenario entitled 'Success' that was never used.

The relations between Aldous and Zeitlin were cordial at the start and were to become more so.

> Conversation with him [the bookseller later said] was always a memorable experience because, by lifting you up to his level, he gave you the feeling that you too were brilliant, and also because

you were conscious that profound and witty things were being said, yet said as if they were commonplace. One could not be trivial with him or talk of trivialities.

When Zeitlin opened a new bookshop in 1938, Aldous wrote for him an eight-page essay on book-buying, some 500 copies of which were printed for the occasion. It was at Zeitlin's suggestion that a few years later Aldous wrote a foreword to Ashley Montagu's *Man's Most Dangerous Myth: The Fallacy of Race*. It was at his request that in 1949 Aldous produced the essay on the *carceri* etchings of Piranesi which were published in a limited edition by Zeitlin and Ver Brugge. And it was Zeitlin who by producing a Latin–French dictionary with marginal notes by Toulouse-Lautrec sparked off 'Doodles in the Dictionary', which Aldous introduced into a series he was contributing to *Esquire*.

All this, however, was trivial compared with the fact that it was Zeitlin who introduced Aldous to Hollywood. Huxley and the film city were mutually interested and mutually suspicious. To most Americans at this time he was the arch-intellectual, although in many ways different from the legend which had already been built up.

He is a kind, gentle-spoken, thoughtful man – entirely free from a sort of intellectual arrogance I expected to find [wrote Ross Parmenter, who interviewed him for the *Saturday Review of Literature* at this period]. With his thick, heavy glasses on, Mr Huxley looks exactly like an intellectual as caricatured in one of Mr Hearst's papers – tall, thin and dressed in ill-assorted, loose, shapeless clothes. The impression is deepened when he reads, for he holds the book almost touching his nose. But when he takes his glasses off, as he does in conversation, there is a transformation; the intellectual becomes the Byronic poet. . . . His body is a thing of two parts. From the waist up he is a man of average size, but his enormously long legs bend out in front of him grotesquely; and he keeps shifting them, sometimes crossing them at the knees, sometimes twining them round each other and sometimes unwinding them and resting one ankle on the knee of the other leg.

This figure from the old world was soon a 'sight' even in a city of sights, and during his first visit to a Hollywood film studio Aldous was stopped by the guard on the gate with the words: 'Wish I had a copy of "Crome Yellow" for you to autograph.' Inside, Huxley discussed Brueghel prints with the producer, Albert Lewin, and whether or not *Manon Lescaut* would make a good film. He watched Anna May Wong on the set in *Daughter of Shanghai* and after looking on while Mr Chang Wah-Lee was 'shot dead', commented: 'Sir, you acted well, I thought. You looked very dead and very preoccupied.' He was greeted by Frank Lloyd with the words: 'Huxley, eh. Sir, your grandfather wrote a good book on "A Piece of Chalk". Will you be seated a while?' And Aldous then watched through a hand-binocular the filming of *Wells Fargo*, commenting of the location scenes: 'Beautiful. Very wonderful indeed! It's there. I know that country.'

From Hollywood, Huxley went east to lecture, but it was to Los Angeles that he returned after deciding, at the end of 1937, to remain in the United States. With Maria and Matthew he settled down early in 1938, first taking an apartment in Pacific Palisades and later moving out to Santa Monica. He had got *Ends and Means* out of his system. He had moved on. He was now searching about for something more. Meanwhile, he had to live; meanwhile, therefore, he would travel regularly to those extraordinary hives, the film studios, and make money by deploying his talents on their amazing projects – how often he must have thanked that journalistic run-of-the-mill training of two decades earlier!

There were a number of projects over the years. One of the first was a treatment for *Madame Curie*, a film to be made by Metro-Goldwyn-Mayer starring Greta Garbo. Huxley's work consisted of a 145-page manuscript which is in some ways one of his most revealing pieces of writing. He knew enough about science to feel the drama of the discovery of radium and enough about medicine to understand its potentialities and its dangers. Moreover, he knew so much about people that he understood both the majesty and the pathos of Madame Curie's life. Perhaps all this was to be expected. Yet the surprising thing was that he also showed in his treatment an astonishing grasp of the visual, cinematic, tricks-of-the-trade. The result – a blue-foldered file copy that Aldous delivered on 26 August 1938 – is a minor masterpiece.

What saw the light of day was a film starring Greer Garson.

> A great many writers worked on this [says M.G.M.], two having been employed before Mr Huxley's employment on it, and the company [which had acquired rights in Eve Curie's biography of her mother] also undertook considerable independent research on the life of this remarkable woman. While Paul Osborn and Paul H. Rameau received credit for the screenplay in accordance with the procedures for determining this credit, it is possible that the final screenplay relied on the earlier material to some extent, so that it may well be that Mr Huxley's efforts were used.

Aldous continued to work for M.G.M., and by 6 September 1939 had produced with Jane Murfin the first of two treatments for *Pride and Prejudice*, the forerunner of a script finally shot a few years later.

According to Anita Loos, Aldous was unhappy with the initial idea of taking on this assignment.

'I wanted to know why,' she has written.

'"Because it pays twenty-five hundred dollars a week," he answered in deep distress. "I simply cannot accept all that money to work in a pleasant studio while my family and friends are starving and being bombed in England."

'But Aldous, why can't you accept that twenty-five hundred and send the larger part of it to England?' was her suggestion.

This proved to be the solution, and Aldous continued as a familiar part of the Hollywood scene, later helping to adapt *Jane Eyre* for 20th-Century Fox and turning his own *The Gioconda Smile*, published years earlier in *Mortal Coils*, into Universal's *A Woman's Vengeance*. He became a subject for the gossip columns, and high enough in the Hollywood hierarchy to appear in the *Variety* feature 'Ill in Pix' as 'Al Huxley'.

The ways of Hollywood and of Aldous were at times very different. Sam Goldwyn is reputed to have met him for the first time with the comment: 'I'm delighted to meet you, Mr Huxley, I understand you're practically a genius.' But Hollywood was not always the place for the species. 'I hired Mr Huxley to write a part for the character of Lewis Carroll and to supervise some of the touchier intellectual aspects of the story,' said Walt Disney who had been about to produce *Alice*. 'But he was brainy. The second day he handed me a ten-page outline of what should be done. It was so literary I could understand only every third word. If you want to work in Hollywood it is not good to have brains.'

It was good, however, to have an observant eye, and from 1938 onwards Aldous observed with due care the exotic fauna of the film city in its natural habitat. From this observation there came his next novel, one in which he balanced his natural ability as a story-teller with his desire to make the story a vehicle for the counterpoint of good and evil, illusion and reality. *After Many a Summer*, his first novel to utilize the Californian scene, reflected to a high degree the novelist's practice of taking and transforming personal experience. Just as his aunt, Mrs Humphry Ward, had woven the life of her own Buckinghamshire village into the texture of *Marcella*, even to the details of incidents that were still in living memory; just as she had awaited from Julia Arnold the news of young Julian's exploits to be incorporated into *David Grieve* – so did Aldous survey the Hollywood grotesquerie and describe it as he had described Lady Ottoline Morrell's house-parties of the 1920s.

He described it, moreover, with a gusto which lifted the book on to a plane quite different from that of most of his novels, and he thus rose above what he himself frequently recognized as an insufficiency.

> I think quite frankly that a good novelist has to be in some sense larger than life [he once said when being interviewed on the radio]. I don't feel that I am larger than life. I mean, you look at a figure like Balzac or Dickens or Tolstoy; they were much larger than life. To start with they had colossal physical energy which, alas, I don't have. You can get, I think, quite a good minor novelist being life-size, even a little smaller than life-size, but the big novelist has to have this gargantuan capacity for experience and enjoyment, and unfortunately I don't feel I have that.

Whatever the general truth of this self-criticism, it was belied by the wild extravagances of this novel with its central problem of rejuvenation. The subject had been inspired by Julian who, when discussing the irregular longevity of certain species with his brother, had mentioned that carp tagged in Scottish waters more than a century earlier were still flourishing. From this starting-point there grew the story of the American tycoon in search of eternal life, a story which came as near to the literary knuckle as the law allowed, one part of the tale being, as Gerald Heard has written, 'dangerously close to the facts of a scandal which only mighty money had kept from breaking'. It was also of interest that Aldous, settling down beyond the Atlantic, rootless and unattached, continued to draw on the recollections and scenes of his youth. Thus some of the more bizarre incidents in the book take place in the Hog's Back country where he had been happy as a boy. Today one can still discover, by the banks of the River Wey, the original of that 'circular chamber cut out of the yellow sandstone' where the apelike Fifth Earl of Gonister plays with his Order of the Garter at the age of two hundred and one.

In one respect *After Many a Summer* was more than a partial reversion to the novels of the 1920s, to fiction used as the vehicle for a multiplicity of different viewpoints and ideas. It was primarily a vehicle for a single idea, for the philosophy of non-attachment which was increasingly to govern Huxley's beliefs and which was to create a widening gulf between those who admired his literary ability but detested his ideas and those for whom ability and ideas were complementary parts of an admirable packet. In *After Many a Summer* Huxley's personal Greek chorus, Mr Propter, claims that: 'It's a matter of experience and observation, that most idealism leads to war, persecution and mass insanity.' To a Europe falling over into war this might be an objectionable truth but it was objectionable just the same. Typically the book was, to one British critic, 'Mr Huxley's petition in moral bankruptcy'.

After Many A Summer appeared almost as the 1939 war broke out, the war that Aldous had so feared, not for himself but for others.

He realized as surely as anyone the evils being spread across the world by Nazi power; even so, few deplored more than he did that war was at last arriving. For him, this final solution was hardly less evil than Hitler's Final Solution. 'I am at the studio all day and too much preoccupied with the war and its implications to want to do anything at night but meditate in solitude,' he wrote early in September. His fear that war would in any case abolish democracy had in his opinion been more than justified by the news of the preceding few weeks. And it was typical of his despairing feelings that he should write a few years later, while the war was still being waged, that in England honesty, morals and civic liberties, had all gone as a result of it. The feeling that a part of the world was at last turning to confront evil things, however late and however inadequately, was relatively absent from the Huxley home at Pacific Palisades.

To Aldous's mental distress there was now added an increased physical problem. For here in California he once again found that reading was becoming more and more difficult.

> There could be no doubt about it; my capacity to see was steadily and quite rapidly failing [he later wrote in *The Art of Seeing*]. But just as I was wondering apprehensively what on earth I should do, if reading were to become impossible, I happened to hear of a method of visual re-education and of a teacher who was said to make use of this method with conspicuous success. Education sounded harmless enough and, since optical glass was no longer doing me any good, I decided to take the plunge.

The method had been evolved by the late W. H. Bates, an unorthodox system depending largely on eye-exercises which has undoubtedly achieved notable successes but which is still the subject of criticism. The teacher was Dr Margaret D. Corbett of New York, to whom Huxley now went for advice. The results were remarkable: Within a couple of months

> I was reading without spectacles and, what was better still, without strain or fatigue. The chronic tensions, and the occasional spells

of complete exhaustion, were things of the past. Moreover, there were definite signs that the opacity in the cornea, which had remained unchanged for upwards of twenty-five years, was beginning to clear up.

Five years later his vision was, as he put it,

> about twice as good as it used to be when I wore spectacles, and before I had learnt the art of seeing, and the opacity had cleared sufficiently to permit the worse eye, which for years could do no more than distinguish light from darkness, to recognize the ten-foot line on the chart at one foot.

There are still friends and relatives of Aldous who doubt whether the Bates method was the reason for improvement in his sight. He himself was quite certain of the fact, and in *The Art of Seeing* he explained the method, and his own experiences, for the benefit of others. A good deal of scepticism showed itself in the book's reception, and even today it is still not quite clear how much of this scepticism sprang from informed knowledge and how much from distrust of the unorthodox. Aldous remained convinced, and when an attempt was made to pass through the Californian State Legislature a law curbing unorthodox eye practitioners, he visited the State capital at Sacramento to make a – successful – protest.

In such matters Aldous was surprisingly practical. He knew the power of the orthodox; he knew also the difficulty of making people carry out the regular exercises demanded by the Bates method. And it was quite in keeping that he should write to Lawrence Clark Powell of University of California, Los Angeles two years later, saying that an archery instructor in a mid-West army camp had found that eyesight was improved by archery. The sport was carried on at U.C.L.A., and Huxley knew that many men there wished to improve their sight.

> The thing I would like to see happen is this [he wrote], to get a few of the fundamental principles of visual education incorporated into an accredited sport, so that boys and girls could learn the art of seeing while at play and without the necessity of doing a lot of tiresome exercises, which they would always be tempted to neglect. This would have the further advantage of completely by-passing the oculists and optometrists, who could not then have anything to say on the matter.

This practicality with which Aldous treated the physical everyday aspects of life was matched, from the early months of the war, by his deepening concern with the problem of good and evil, not as it might be theorized upon, but as it might be solved, in the real world, by the men of decision. This was essentially the problem of power, that arbiter of ends and means, and the manner in which it was exercised. He had constantly discussed this, during the previous few years, with Heard, who has written:

> It was clear that Jefferson's famous solution, 'break power up into little pieces', was no solution now. Huxley, therefore, was hunting for a story that would make the issue plain. By 1938 he had found the time and place and the hero. And this, in brief, was the riddle he was now to pose; can power be used purely? Can coercion operate aseptically? Conversely, if all violence is doing evil that good may come, and so self-defeating, is there obtainable any non-violent force that can control violence?
>
> He had to find an actual, well-documented character who exhibited several improbable characteristics. In the first place, while the hero must possess full power he must be without any of its trappings and should be generally regarded as an innocuous figure in the shadow. And he must honestly be more than scornful of recognition. Beside the goal *he* sees, the climb he is set upon, conventional human success and public recognition are slight. Secondly, this person must be the player of a game so vital and far reaching that, while none of the rulers with whom he deals as pieces on his board conceive the compass of his secret strategy, the moves he makes, the motives that inspire him, we must deal with today – or perish.
>
> In short the hero must be possessed of all the heroic virtues that go to make a saint. And he must persistently and unwaveringly practise all of these extreme denials, austerities, vigils, and mortifications which the heroic virtues exact.

Such a man was François Leclerc du Tremblay, known as Le Père Joseph, the original 'grey eminence' whose intricate machinations had through Richelieu controlled the destiny not merely of France but of Europe throughout a decisive generation. Huxley's account of Father Joseph's convoluted operations, half Machiavellian, half mystic, was more than a remarkable literary achievement. He wished to make people think about the inter-relationships between ends and means as they were laid bare by the actions of men in high places. This time he used neither the philosophical essay nor the novel which provided a platform for exposition and counter-exposition; instead he used biography, and used it to describe, in extraordinarily readable detail, the development of Father Joseph's influence on policy. The result, *Grey Eminence*, was a remarkable success. It was biography at a new level and it reinforced the existing opinion that Aldous Huxley could turn with success to whatever literary form he chose.

Yet it was not to provide yet another feather in a literary cap that the book had been written. Huxley wished to make people think, and he had done so. Whether or not he had moved them in the intended way was more doubtful. The moral of the tale was intended to be that while Father Joseph's ends were initially noble if misguided, these ends became first endangered, and eventually controlled, by the means that were used. Yet it did not look like this to all readers.

> At the end of Mr Huxley's book [wrote Raymond Mortimer] I felt that there was, after all, something to be said for Father Joseph. Having decided, however mistakenly, that a particular end was desirable, he was not so spiritually self-centred as to leave the dirty work to other people.

Frank Pakenham, writing in the *Political Quarterly*, voiced much the same complaint, pointing out that

> Mr Huxley looks always to the individual soul, and trembles lest the world corrupt it. But the world, too, has its claims. He never reaches the point of denying that somehow it must be governed.

Grey Eminence – whose manuscript Aldous gave 'to one of the Civil Liberties organizations to be sold on behalf of a fund to defend those unfortunate booksellers who were arrested in Oklahoma for carrying copies of Marx's "Capital" and similar light reading' – was more than a *tour de force* written at white heat. It was a book whose production had driven Aldous to probe, even more deeply than before, into the lives, the motivations, the transforming experiences, of many holy fathers, of many mystics. Until the writing of *Ends and Means* he had been forced along the road of non-attachment by a logical reasoning which he explained in terms of the physical world and the moral principles which might help men through it. An overriding belief was that the world could genuinely be made a better place by the practice of what in political terms was non-violence and in terms of everyday life was the goodness that leaves self out of the equation and is frequently called 'saintliness'. Now he began to believe that non-attachment was merely the first step away from one level of reality, from the world as most people saw and experienced it. A long step farther forward, on a totally different level, lay the world of direct communication with the divine into which the dreamers of the day were apparently able to enter, a world which appeared to have been entered by those who saw visions and heard voices, by those in trance, by the Catholic mystics and, above all, by the devotees of various Buddhist and Hindu sects. If this were in fact the case, surely it was right that one should try to discover more about experience on this higher level of reality, experience in which mind and matter seemed to be curiously and inexplicably intertwined? Thus on to such religious experiences Aldous now turned his own high-powered intellectual searchlight. In common with most others who have carried out this particular exercise, he sought solitude for the operation.

Both Maria and Aldous were happy to leave Los Angeles. Maria, writing to Frieda Lawrence, later explained how coming to the ranch outside Taos in 1937 had changed her life. She now wanted some similar home equally isolated by the wilderness. So, too, did Aldous. In the autumn of 1941 they left Los Angeles and bought a ranch at Llano some 60 miles from Los Angeles; here, on the edge of the desert, both came to terms with a life strangely different from that which either of them had known. They remodelled the six-room ranch house and built a studio. They bought shares in water stock for irrigation, and with the help of a single hired man Aldous began to cultivate five acres of vegetables and fruits. Maria, according to her letter to Frieda, found her 'peace and silence'. Aldous, giving time each day to prayer – 'I couldn't get on without it now,' he told one visitor – studying St John of the Cross in his book-lined study, was now deeply engaged in a pursuit of the mystic's understanding. He became a questioning but enthusiastic member of the local Vedanta Society. In September 1942 he founded, with Gerald Heard and others, Trabuco College in the belief 'that only through change of individual character can there be any real apprehension of God's nature and will, and a lasting change in civilization or humanity'. And, as always, the latest development in Huxley's thought was soon presented in public, an open avowal of his beliefs which helped as usual to clarify the thoughts in his own mind.

In this case the results were twofold. First there came *Time Must Have a Stop*, the presentation in novel form of a Buddhist solution to injustice in the life here and now – a solution in which he included a detailed account of the after-death experiences of one of the main characters. More than a decade later, in November 1961, when Huxley was asked what he considered his best book, he replied, 'I suppose *Time Must Have a Stop* is the most satisfying. It is the book into which I put the most feeling; and this gives it a strength which I did not always achieve.' Even so, it had a mixed reception – as with *Grey Eminence* not because of any technical failing but because, once again, many reviewers failed to agree with the basic premiss. This might have created only disinterested surprise had it come from some writers; coming from Aldous Huxley it produced astonishment. 'What,' it was asked by one typical reviewer, 'has happened to turn Huxley the clear-headed objective intellectual into Huxley the symbolist-mystic with a bias towards Yoga and occultism?' Biological evolution had by this time gained acceptance but intellectual evolution was still rarely considered as a possibility.

The novel was merely the curtain-raiser to the exposition. This came in 1945, *The Perennial Philosophy* that was

> the metaphysic that recognizes a divine Reality substantial to the world of things and lives and minds; the psychology that finds in the soul something similar to, or even identical with, divine Reality; the ethic that places man's final end in the knowledge of the immanent and transcendent Ground of all being – the thing is immemorial and universal.

Huxley explained his own concept of this philosophy by assembling in the book a massive anthology of passages from those saints or prophets who appeared to have approached a direct spiritual knowledge of the Divine. The extracts – from St John of the Cross and the Chinese Taoist philosophers, the authors of the Brahmin scriptures and the followers of Buddha and Mohammed – were linked by a commentary from Huxley which elucidated and developed them.

These open avowals of Huxley's conversion to mysticism brought the wheel full circle from those early days at Oxford when he had, as he subsequently wrote, 'read a good deal of Western and Eastern (mystic) writings, always with intense interest, but always with a wish to "debunk" them.' A change of mind had begun to set in during the 1930s, and then in Hollywood he had met Swami Prabhavananda, who had founded there a centre for the study and practice of Vedantic philosophy. The meetings between the two men had coincided with the deep self-questioning triggered off by the research for *Grey Eminence*, and by September 1942, at the founding of Trabuco College, Aldous was able to say this of the relationship between his concern with mystical religion and his art:

> I came to this thing in a rather curious way, as a *reductio ad absurdum*. I have mainly lived in the world of intellectual life and art. But the world of knowing-about-things is unsatisfactory. It's no good knowing about the taste of strawberries out of a book. The more I think of art I realize that, though artists do establish some contact with spiritual reality, they establish it unconsciously. Beauty is imprisoned, as it were, within the white spaces between the lines

of a poem, between the notes of music, in the apertures between groups of sculpture. This function or talent is unconscious. They throw a net and catch something, though the net is trivial. . . . But one wants to go further. One wants to have a conscious taste of these holes between the strings of the net.

From now onwards it was Aldous's belief that only by attaining the transcendental state of the mystic was it possible to have such consciousness; and from now onwards his search was to be for some method of attaining that state.

As Christopher Isherwood has put it, Huxley's development was 'widely represented as the selling-out of a once-brilliant intellect'. This was especially so when the development was viewed from across the Atlantic. 'The new Californian religion appears to have an eclectic faith which combines elements of Quakerism, Jansenism, Catholic Mysticism, Yoga Mysticism and orthodox Brahminism,' Cyril Connolly pungently noted in reviewing *Time Must Have a Stop*. Raymond Mortimer commented that 'It is possible that [Huxley] and Mr Heard have discovered facts about mystical technique and experience hitherto hidden from the Western world, but the tone in which he propounds his views does not conciliate the still unconvinced inquirer'. And Joad noted of *The Perennial Philosophy* that apparently no one could 'understand what it was all about unless they have already experienced it'. The volume, and sometimes deeply felt bitterness, of much criticism, was occasioned not so much by the views of the Californian mystics as by the artificiality of their world as seen from Europe. To the most committed fighter, the sight of a pacifist or a mystic preaching his beliefs as the bombs came down would have been an inspiring sight; the argument had less force when it came from California. It was no doubt unjust to equate the spiritual withdrawal preached by the mystics with their physical withdrawal to the United States. Human nature being what it is, the equation was sometimes inevitable.

A more objective criticism was made, interestingly enough, by another Huxley. For in 1944 that ardent rationalist, Laurence Collier, the son of John Collier and TH's youngest daughter Ethel, produced *Flight from Conflict*, a small, pungent and closely reasoned book written, as the author put it, to outline 'in as clear and concise a form as I can, the reasons why, in my opinion, we should not accept certain views about morality recently propounded by Mr Aldous Huxley and Mr Gerald Heard and, in another form, by Mr Walter Lippmann'.

As far as Aldous was concerned, his cousin's book dealt mainly with the philosophy of non-attachment as outlined in *Ends and Means*. It pointed out that during the long reign of Hindu and Buddhist mysticism in Asia 'there has been no attempt at political or social reform, no organized humanitarian effort, no belief even in the possibility of ever changing the miserable conditions of ordinary human life'. When his book was republished a few years later, Collier saw no reason to alter his judgement:

> Mr Huxley still preaches his Asiatic quietism; he has collected disciples around him at Hollywood; and his voice has lately been joined by those of Mr Isherwood and Mr Somerset Maugham. The state of the world, too, still offers the same temptation to withdraw from the struggle to improve it: the nightmare of Fascism and Nazism has been succeeded by the nightmare of Soviet Communism.

Collier's little book did in fact summarize one European view of the Californian mystics: that their philosophy involved not merely turning the other cheek but turning someone else's.

It is unlikely that criticism would have been so considerable had Aldous raised the standard in England. For quite apart from the greater weight which would have been given by exterior circumstance, it would have been possible to see that he had not retreated permanently and entirely into the scallop-shell of quiet. One part of Huxley certainly did remain engaged in a search for some gateway into the mystic garden. Yet there was another Aldous about which less was known in Britain, a man very knowledgeable about the practical problems of life, a human fellow who would – and did – join a picket line when necessary, who planned his work on a business-like basis and who still sparkled with an essentially worldly-wise glitter as he deplored the droll follies of the human race.

This dichotomy, this living on two levels of experience, was expressed not only by the contrast of reflective essay and popular novel through which he continued to express his views, but also by the matters which claimed his interests. As a background there was the deepening problem of how the mystical experiences which he felt to be Reality were linked with the physical mechanisms of life; as a foreground there remained the growing problem of contemporary existence compounded as it soon was to be by man's release of nuclear energy.

As to the war, he remained as profoundly depressed as ever. In 1943 Maria's mother and her youngest sister had arrived in the United States from Europe. They had escaped from Brussels three years earlier, arrived in America when Allied fortunes were only just rising from their lowest ebb, and helped reinforce Aldous's view that no ends justified the means of war.

It looks as though at least the European misery might be over pretty soon [he wrote to his cousin-in-law, E. S. P. Haynes on 25 March 1945], and then, let us hope, things may be slightly better in England and on the Continent – though how long it will take to put Humpty Dumpty together again, or whether he will ever be put together in anything but nightmarishly totalitarian and pauperized form is another question. Even the minor problems seem to be quite insoluble. For example, the statisticians say that, when this is over, there will be at least fifteen million more women than men in Europe. What will be the effect of this on family life and sexual morality? Echo answers What – or perhaps the word is also of four letters and even more Anglo-Saxon.

Five months later the prospects of peace looked brighter only by comparison:

I confess that I find a peace with atomic bombs hanging overhead a rather disquieting prospect [he told Victoria Ocampo]. National states armed by science with superhuman military power always remind me of Swift's description of Gulliver being carried up to the roof of the King of Brobdingnag's palace by a gigantic monkey: reason, human decency and spirituality, which are strictly individual matters, find themselves in the clutches of the collective will, which has the mentality of a delinquent boy of fourteen in conjunction with the physical power of God.

Chapter XV

The Chance to Plan

(*i*)

The development of Unesco, where education, science and culture helped to transform into a less insecure peace the equilibrium that Aldous found so disquieting, is sometimes divided into historical ages. There is the Contemporary Age; there was the earlier Middle Ages; and there was first the Heroic Age, the period of genesis and birth that is also called the Huxley Age. The connection seems natural enough. Few organizations follow more closely the Huxley line of thought than one linking the sciences and the humanities, adopting an international stance, taking a synoptic view, pledged to help all mankind 'without distinction of race, sex, language or religion'. Even so, only a prophet would have linked Huxley's name with the venture during its unlikely wartime beginnings.

In October 1942 the Germans were hammering at the gates of Stalingrad; General Montgomery's Eighth Army, backs to the Nile Delta, was preparing for the battle of Alamein; and in the same month Mr R. A. Butler, Britain's Minister for Education, called a conference in London of the Allied Ministers of Education in exile, who met with fine faith to consider the pattern which education would take when Europe was liberated. The meeting was primarily designed to discuss post-war problems, and during the following months it was proposed that a special organization should be set up to deal with them. The scope of the body changed as peace came nearer, as the plans for a United Nations Organization gathered detail: and as the discussions were joined by a representative of the United States, Senator Estes Kefauver.

In the spring of 1944 Mr Butler, by now President of the Board of Trade, suggested that the body might be set up under the United Nations as an organization for educational and cultural reconstruction. 'Reconstruction' was soon dropped as being worthy of a separate body;

'development' and 'co-operation' were alternatives that were put forward and dropped in turn. Some teachers wanted the word 'cultural' omitted on the grounds that its inclusion implied education to be non-cultural. The proposal that 'science' should be added was met by the demand that if this was specifically mentioned, the Humanities must also be included, while there were those in high places who felt wary of the whole proposal. 'We are trying to do these things too hurriedly after a war,' wrote Sir Henry Tizard, drawn into the matter through his position as Foreign Secretary of the Royal Society. 'We may get an elaborate organization which is of very little value. Nevertheless, if we are going to have a Uneco, science must take a very important part.'

The inclusion of science was still under discussion when the United Nations Organization was formed during the spring and summer of 1945, and when it decided to set up a 'special' agency, with headquarters in Paris, to deal with education and culture. The following November a conference was held in London at which the details of the new agency were hammered out. And it was here, partly as a result of the constant lobbying of the scientists, partly due to an outline of the need for international scientific collaboration prepared by Dr Joseph Needham, that science was formally added to the title of the new organization and that the proposed Uneco became Unesco.

The London conference established a preparatory commission to work out a plan for the way ahead, a plan which it was agreed would be formally discussed at the inauguration of Unesco in Paris the following autumn. It also established various committees and sub-committees which together were to erect a framework for the new body. And it elected Sir Alfred Zimmern, a noted internationalist who numbered the deputy directorship of the League of Nations Institute of Intellectual Co-operation among his previous appointments, as Executive Secretary of the new commission. The structure of this preparatory commission, and the still slightly intangible task which it had been set, combined to give the Executive Secretary considerable latitude and considerable power. It must have been clear that the shape of Unesco could, and possibly would, be moulded very largely by his personality and experience.

Then Sir Alfred fell ill. The trouble was serious, and for a while it was thought unlikely that he would recover. His resignation from the post followed automatically, and the British Government which had succeeded in getting a U.K. representative in the key post was now faced with a problem. It was a problem which fell into the lap of Sir John Maud, the recently appointed Permanent Secretary to the Ministry of Education. And Sir John, meeting Julian Huxley by accident a short while afterwards, suddenly realized that here was the man for the post.

Huxley, rather strangely perhaps, was not at first attracted by the offer that Sir John made.

> Quite frankly [he said later], at the time I was busy, had other things to do, and was reluctant to accept. However, I was told it was my duty to accept and little by little I became interested and seized with the urgency and importance of the work to be done.

First, however, he had to meet Ellen Wilkinson, Britain's Minister of Education and President of the preparatory commission.

> She invited me to dine with her and Sir John in the House of Commons [Sir Julian has said since]. We had a discussion on the whole matter, but the most impressive thing about the meal was not anything we said, but, to my mind, the example of democracy in action. As the Minister of Education sat down a waitress came up and in a Cockney accent said: 'What will you have tonight, dearie? There's a nice bit of steak on the menu.'

The following day Huxley met the vice-presidents of the preparatory commission, agreed to become Executive Secretary, and arranged to take up his duties on 1 March. 'I took them over,' he says, 'feeling very much like the small boy on the first day he goes to boarding school, knowing nothing about the job of running an international organization.'

In the spring of 1946 the motive power of Unesco was slight. Its offices consisted of a few rooms in an empty house near Grosvenor Square, and its staff numbered about twenty. Thus it was not merely the policy of Unesco which had to be worked out and then approved by a Commission consisting of men and women of different backgrounds and beliefs; the machinery for actually carrying out the work had to be built up from scratch, work which was inevitably made more difficult by the need to satisfy the various Governments concerned. For it was soon apparent to Huxley that while Unesco might in theory be the least political of organizations, Governments who supplied funds realized clearly enough that in education, science, culture, there lay the seeds of future influence. If any dangerous thoughts were to be involved, each country wanted a hand in directing them; thus appointments, compositions of committees, and all the other executive paraphernalia, had to be delicately balanced.

In this work, Huxley's success or failure can only be fairly judged by drawing up a profit-and-loss account of his record. On the debit side it must be said that he had neither love nor ability for the niceties of administration. A description of the Heroic Age in which Huxley is seen as 'writing papers, and contracts, on the backs of old envelopes and quickly losing them', has the ring of truth. His personal feelings, enthusiasm and prejudices were all apt to run on in happy unrestraint. And the imaginative scale of some schemes was apt both to attract his support and to blind him to practical difficulties. To all this there was added the streak of ingrained naughtiness which TH had noted half a century earlier, a delight in tweaking pomposity's nose that pleased all those who were not involved in the consequences.

These drawbacks were balanced – and, in the opinion of most impartial observers, more than balanced – by three outstanding Huxley characteristics. One was the perpetually surprising range of his knowledge and interests.

> I must confess it has been rather bewildering [he said on one occasion when reporting early progress], especially for the deputies and myself, who find ourselves jumping from fine arts to applied science, from applied science to architecture, from architecture to rural education, from rural education to literature and philosophy – all in the space of a few hours.

Bewildering maybe, but far less bewildering than it would have been to most men. For there seemed to be few subjects of which Huxley did not have a working knowledge, and fewer still in which he could not name the best man to consult.

There was also the strong personal loyalty which he inspired in men and women at all levels. Just as the public image of his brother Aldous was belied by those who met him, so was the picture of a slightly cantankerous and always impatient Julian found to be false by those who worked for him. The respect which he inspired was to be expected; the affection was more surprising. Yet as one of his colleagues put it years later: 'You went out of your way not to let Huxley down.'

Finally there was his enthusiasm, an enthusiasm without which the new organization might well have become bogged down in the mud of apathy and difficulty and political obfuscation which bedevilled its birth and early years. Like an armoured division, he needed a lot of stopping once he got under way, battering down minor opposition, by-passing the strong-points provided by religion or politics, never running out of energy, the fuel which kept him going, confident that if just that little extra effort could be summoned up, one would be through the difficulties and out into the green fields beyond.

As Executive Secretary, Huxley was not only responsible for creating the new international machine, and for indicating the directions in which it should move. He was also responsible for the high-level negotiations in which Unesco was involved, and one of his first tasks was to negotiate in New York the working relationship agreement between the United Nations and its latest offspring. He went as the guest of the U.S. State Department, stayed at Blair House, and after some three weeks of discussions in Hunter College, signed on 21 June, 1946, the formal document drawn up between Unesco and the U.N. Economic and Social Council. In some ways this document underlined the change in the position of scientists which had been brought about by the war. Until its outbreak, the majority of scientists had lived, as it has been put, 'in a little world of their own, with their own hierarchy, their own levels and even their own honours list, which took the form of elections to the Royal Society, medals, and special lectures'. Huxley had for years been one of those who had demanded that they should have more, and stronger, links with the larger world. Now he was able to carry this ideal into practice.

So far as Huxley was concerned, science was going to affect the world, and on his return from the United States he threw all his energy into Unesco's preparatory work. During his stay on the far side of the Atlantic he had made a sixteen-day, twenty thousand-mile information-giving tour of Central and Southern America, visiting Mexico, Cuba, Brazil and Venezuela among other countries to expound the virtues of the new organization. Now, back in London, he began to integrate the results of his campaigning into the mushrooming work of committees, sub-committees and demi-semi-sub-committees.

To start with, however, he had to face the consequences of a major error – an error which could have been made only by a man of his own political innocence. This was the publication of a slim, closely reasoned document which was to have all the impact of a suitcase-bomb. Its title was *Unesco: Its Purpose and Its Philosophy*, and it had been written by Huxley himself with a fine fervour and no thought for passing it through whatever the tyro Civil Servant would have known to be the inevitable proper channels. 'The Unesco Philosophy', as it came to be known, was a carefully-written argument for adopting the humanist viewpoint in the running of Unesco's affairs. It was one man's argument, and however much one may agree with it, there is difficulty in understanding how Huxley came to overlook the fact that it would inevitably blow up in his face. In order to carry out its aims, Unesco needed, Huxley argued, not only a set of general aims and objects but also a working philosophy. It could not, he went on, base its outlook on one religion. It could not specifically support any politico-economic doctrine such as Marxist Communism or free enterprise. It could not be racial and, in view of its practical tasks, it could not adopt an 'other-worldly' outlook. To Huxley there seemed to be one obvious solution, one unexceptionable method by which the new organization could satisfy the diverse demands of its member-countries. For evolution enfolded all mankind, and humanism gave it a direction to which, surely, no reasonable man could object. In general therefore, Huxley proposed,

> Unesco must constantly be testing its policies against the touchstone of evolutionary progress. A central conflict of our times is that between nationalism and internationalism, between the concept of many national sovereignties and one world sovereignty. Here the evolutionary touchstone gives an unequivocal answer. The key to man's advance, the distinctive method which has made evolutionary progress in the human sector so much more rapid than in the biological and has given it higher and more satisfying goals, is the fact of cumulative tradition, the existence of a common pool of ideas which is self-perpetuating and itself capable of evolving. And this fact has had the immediate consequence of making the type of social organization the main factor in social progress or at least its limiting frame-work.

It was not only this central idea which sharply diverged from the views held by many of the delegations from the member-states. Edward Carter, first head of the Libraries Division in Unesco, has written:

> The implication, even, that man as a thinking animal was in control of his own destiny, shocked the religious. A casual reference to dialectical materialism as 'the first radical attempt at an evolutionary philosophy' led the Americans, and no doubt some others, to bring out their pre-McCarthy guns; a reference to the value of contraception as of assistance in planning man's social destiny angered the Catholics, and the fact that an attempt was made to define a Unesco philosophy at all made a spokesman for the communist states ask whether acceptance of Unesco required the abandonment of *their* philosophy in favour of Dr Huxley's.

Rarely can more groups have been ruffled by fewer paragraphs.

The trouble, moreover, was not merely that Huxley had put down his own views but that they had been broadcast under the imprint of the new organization, since the booklet was issued as a publication of the Preparatory Commission of the United Nations Educational, Scientific and Cultural Organization. The author had hoped to form a bridge linking East and West, between whom the gulf was already opening wide. Instead, he had united his potential enemies. That the outcome was not worse is a measure of Huxley's persuasive powers and of the affection which he personally inspired. For the Unesco philosophy was not withdrawn. Instead, a slip was inserted in all available copies, reading:

> The Executive Committee of the Preparatory Commission of Unesco gave instructions in August that this Essay by the Executive Secretary should be published in the form of a separate signed document, as a statement of his personal attitude. It is in no way an official expression of the views of the Preparatory Commission.

Huxley's first dangerous corner had been skidded round with no more than a warning shake-up.

Throughout the summer and early autumn the plenary meetings of the commission continued, and as one reads their minutes it is quite clear that the shape of the growing organization was very largely moulded by Huxley. He was rarely out of his depth, and on the few occasions when he was uncertain of what to do next he showed an unexpected ability to improvise. What is more, his authority as a scientist, as distinct from his success as a popularizer, now stood him in good stead. So did the outspokenness which had marked all his life. He had, for instance, been among the first to protest against the proliferation of nuclear weapons. He was thus in a strong position now to insist that nuclear research itself should have a high priority:

> It is in this field that we wish to dispel some of the misunderstanding about the bearing of scientific work on human life. If we can make people understand that this affords a great possibility of adding to our knowledge in general, and of peacetime applications in engineering and other fields – and especially in the biological field – I think it will be very worth while giving it a high priority.

Towards the end of the summer of 1946 preparations were being completed for the move to Paris, where the first general conference of the new organization was to open in November. In September Huxley, his wife, and the future Unesco secretariat moved to France, the headquarters going in two trainloads and being met at the Gare du Nord with the full panoply of the Garde Nationale, tribute from a France which was still proud at having won the international contest for the seat of the new organization.

Huxley and his wife moved into a flat. The headquarters of what was to become Unesco but was still formally the Preparatory Commission were set up in the Hôtel Majestic, a structure that had experienced a short but troubled history. Built as the Hôtel de Castille by the ex-Queen Isabella II of Spain, it had been converted into a plush Edwardian hotel that had subsequently fallen on hard times. It had been occupied at the outbreak of war by the French Air Ministry, later by General Stulpnagel, the Military Governor of France during the German Occupation, then by the Americans. Now it came to Unesco, Huxley taking over Stulpnagel's former office and finding that his staff had inherited the ingenious switchboard which had allowed the Germans to eavesdrop on half the telephone conversations of Paris. Here preparations went on for Unesco's first general conference, due to open on 20 November.

At least, it was hoped that this would be Unesco's first general conference. But, although 44 countries had attended the London conference in 1945, less than the 20 needed to bring the organization into existence had so far ratified the agreement they had signed. Constant lobbying went on as the deadline approached, and on 4 November the necessary score of signatures was gained.

One of the most important tasks of the conference which opened in the Majestic – soon to be known as Unesco House – was election of a Director-General. In the negotiations which led up to this there had been a good deal of political balancing, horse-trading and general market-bargaining, as the delegations of the various countries received instructions or suggestions as to whom they were to support. In the autumn of 1946 the American presence was still strong in Europe and there was at first a tacit assumption that an American would be voted into power at Unesco. Archibald MacLeish, the American ex-Assistant Secretary of State, poet and man of letters, who had led the American delegation to the London conference, was an early and favoured candidate but declined with the words: 'I prefer to be a poet.'

It was then that President Truman personally proposed that the U.S. delegation should nominate Francis Biddle, the U.S. lawyer who had been a member of the International Military Tribunal at Nuremberg. Admirable as Biddle no doubt was in many ways, he seemed to many of the delegations to be totally unsuited for running Unesco, and it was soon clear that he stood little chance of election. In the subsequent discussions Huxley's name came to the top. There was some feeling against him, partly on account of his humanist views, partly because of his generally liberal leanings that could so easily be distorted to justify a charge of being 'pro-Communist'. And *Unesco: It's Purpose and Its Philosophy* could always be flourished in your face.

It says much for Huxley's scientific standing that his name stayed at the top, and that when voting for the Director-Generalship took place on 6 December he was elected by 22 votes to 3, with only two abstentions. But there was one proviso to his success. The Americans agreed, if reluctantly, to his election. What they would not agree to was that he should hold the post for the full six years allowed under the Unesco charter. Instead, the term was to be two years. Even a Huxley, it may well have been felt, would be unable to stamp his personality on such a complex body in such a short time. This was not to be the case.

(*ii*)

When Huxley began work as Director-General of Unesco at the end of 1946 the organization had ready to hand the ambitious plans which had been prepared during the previous months; it had the nucleus of an international executive. But while it carried the hopes of many peoples it carried also the suspicions of many Governments. Few observers can have expected that a man of Huxley's volatile individuality would succeed in keeping it from disaster during its critical first years of existence. Yet when he retired from the scene in 1948 the Unesco he handed over to his successor was a fully working machine whose teething-troubles had been overcome by a combination of ability, luck and personal enthusiasm, and which was already operating a large number – too large a number, many felt – of separate and ambitious projects.

There were no circumstances under which this achievement could have been easy, and it was made more difficult by the political astigmatism of some member-countries. The *Saturday Evening Post* later recalled how the Majestic had once been described as 'the biggest centre of anti-American propaganda in France' – although the Communists with equal exaggeration claimed that Huxley's deputy, Walter Laves, had 'turned the Majestic into an annexe of the U.S. State Department'. *Life* noted that Huxley was a 'tall, bespectacled, bony-faced scholar who looks placid but erupts in fits of temper or kinetic conversation. Some who know his temperament,' it added, 'think him a risky choice for the job' – a judgement with which many of his best friends would no doubt have agreed. 'Huxley's Zoo' and 'Huxley's Circus' were too much-used descriptions of Unesco headquarters. And it was remarked that the Director-General could 'discuss any subject under the sun with great knowledge and even greater confidence'. There were many spectators watching for a slip in the delicate operations that now began.

Objections were also elaborated as to the ways in which Huxley sometimes brought in staff. It is certainly true that his one criterion was whether the man or woman concerned was the best for the job. Race, colour or religious views counted for nothing. That intellectual ability mattered more than rank in the Establishment was shown when Huxley interviewed one man for a post as head of a department and felt that he was probably the best for the job. At a second meeting the candidate mentioned one point that Huxley might not have known. 'When you get the reports from back home,' he said, 'you'll find that I'm a chap who's always been in opposition, and always had rows with the Government.'

'Fine,' said Huxley. 'You're hired.'

Recruiting staff was in fact one way in which the Director-General moulded the shape of things to come. During the early days of its conception Unesco had been predominantly European; later it had become Americo–European. Yet if it was to become a genuinely world-wide organization it was essential that Africa and India should be represented at all levels, that China and the other countries of the Far East should realize that they were genuinely being invited to play their parts. Huxley therefore started the kaleidoscopic mixing of nationalities which is today such a marked feature of Unesco, demonstrating that he had a genuine feeling for what an international body should really be.

During his years of office he started Unesco on the multifarious activities whose details can be read in the record. But his achievement was more than the sum of these parts, and it was so in two different ways. First, under Huxley's guidance Unesco was prevented from becoming a mere post office for the educational and cultural attachés of the major nations; it did not pass on ideas but created them, and if there were some poor specimens sprinkled among the better, this was no less than could be expected.

Secondly, under Huxley, Unesco achieved an intellectual standing that it might never otherwise have had. Other Director-Generals could perhaps have produced a tidier administrative machine; almost any other director-general would have created an organization more certain of Government good-will, and many might have succeeded in squeezing more money from the exchequers of the world. What Huxley did was to create an inter-Governmental organization with an academic standing that would be trusted by the scientists, the artists and the other specialists who instinctively distrusted Governmental bodies and the constant threat of control by the purse-strings. Thus the International Council of Scientific Unions, a body particularly wary of being tied to any inter-Governmental organization, was at the outset successfully brought into relationship with Unesco; so, at a later date, was the International Council of Museums, the Union of International Organizations, and many others. At the same time, Unesco helped to fill gaps by facilitating the creation of needed bodies such as the International Association of Universities, the International Council for Philosophy and Humanistic Studies and the International Social Science Council. And it was largely at Huxley's instigation that Unesco was directly responsible for the creation of the European Centre for Nuclear Research, C.E.R.N., which later became autonomous.

A good deal of this success sprang from his personal ebullience. He might, as he did on one occasion, play havoc with an official dinner and reception, changing the name-cards so that suitable people might be put together. He might occasionally make his opinions plain with a shattering honesty. He might work non-office hours with a Churchillian irregularity and intensity – years later his colleagues would comment that Unesco had become less exciting with his departure but that it had also become less nerve-racking. Yet the fact remained that the early days of 1947 and 1948 were stimulating and that a recognizable Unesco spirit was generated – perhaps the first faint flickerings of the international loyalty which will be needed if mankind is to survive.

This loyalty to an ideal as well as to Huxley personally was produced by his own stark sincerity. He was completely out of his depth in the inevitable struggles for power that swayed back and forth inside the organization, and his back would be turned towards the dagger with an innocence that alarmed his friends and at times almost unnerved his enemies. But if he was never the politician, he was always, transparently, Julian Huxley, the man who genuinely believed that by spreading knowledge of the sciences and the arts across frontiers one could help to make the world a better place. Thus he was, it was remarked years afterwards, the only Director-General whose entry into the building always remained the same. Others might slowly realize that they were now influential men and might pause, at just the right moment, for the respectful salutations of their staff. Others, involved in the intricate machinery of internecine survival, might hurry into their offices, avoiding all personal contact. Huxley remained himself, as willing to chat with the lift-boy as with a visiting scientist or the head of a department.

The administrative machinery was helped through its running-in stages by two institutions which Huxley inaugurated and which were dropped when he left. The first had a striking similarity to the wartime 'Sunday Soviets' of the Telecommunications Research Establishment at which air marshals and civilians, scientists such as Tizard and Cherwell, and the most lowly of airmen, would all put their ideas frankly forward on the basis that they could 'say anything'. Huxley's version of the Sunday Soviets was a monthly dinner party for a dozen or so of Unesco's staff, which he held in the elaborate dining-room of the Majestic. Here, as at T.R.E., those present might be of any rank or of none. They discussed their projects and their difficulties, almost thinking aloud, putting forward their own plans, shooting down other people's, producing a cross-fertilization of ideas from which Unesco still benefits. Secondly, there was a monthly cocktail party to which staff of all ranks were invited. Here men and women from half a hundred countries found the barriers between them disintegrating – and learned, too, something of their Director-General and, equally important, his wife. When a bust of Huxley by Jo Davidson was placed in the entrance hall of Unesco House, as the Majestic had now formally become, the staff noticed that the left eyebrow had been abnormally accentuated. It was quite in keeping that many of them should touch it for luck as they came into the building each morning.

Throughout 1947 the plans which had been made the previous year were slowly transformed into teams of Unesco workers actually doing things. Multi-national groups began to use fresh methods in what was called basic education – since, as Huxley put it, 'Unesco cannot contemplate a world half literate and half illiterate'. In the field of mass communication attempts were made to implement that ancient hope of the B.B.C. that 'nation shall speak peace unto nation'. Exchange and co-operation between museums and libraries was pushed on, while in the realm of the natural sciences specialist field teams studied the problems of nutritional science and food technology on which rested the future of India, Brazil, China and Africa. In the social sciences and arts and letters there was a coming and going, an intellectual ferment and interchange on quite a new scale. All this helped along Unesco's aim which was 'to contribute to peace and security by promoting collaboration'. Years earlier, Huxley had noted that 'those who have watched a bird for days together from a hiding-place will never wish to kill the creature'. Now, at the human level, there were being created fresh barriers against going to war with the people you were at least getting to know culturally.

By June 1947, it had been decided to hold the next conference in Mexico City and Huxley left Paris for a month's tour of the Americas, during which he visited a dozen countries, completed plans for the autumn's conference and left memories of a voluble, persistent, constantly-inquiring Director-General. He returned to Paris to find that in at least one quarter his resignation was being demanded – by the Texas Branch of the American Legion, a powerful lobbying body, on the grounds that he was an atheist. He publicly replied that the branch seemed to have confused the meaning of 'atheist' and to be using it as a term of abuse meaning a person who was against religion.

> I consider myself a religious man [he replied], though I do not subscribe to a theistic interpretation of the religious spirit. Religion can perfectly well be non-theistic. Take, for example, Buddhism. No one, surely, would deny the rights of the Buddhists to be called religious. I will cheerfully welcome in Paris any Texas member of the American Legion who would like to discuss the finer points of the question with me.

So far as is known, the offer was not taken up.

During the summer preparations were completed for the coming meeting in Mexico City and here, in November, Huxley presented his report of the first year's work. It says a lot for his frequently criticized political ability that he was able to win almost universal praise. Half a hundred countries each had to be persuaded that they were getting their fair share of this particular international cake; enthusiasts from a myriad of specialist subjects had to be convinced that their own particular disciplines were being given due weight. Most were satisfied.

At Mexico City, as elsewhere, Huxley swam through a sea of official committee-work yet still found opportunities to visit whatever he wished, and at the same time kept his eyes customarily alert. There was, for instance, the morning when the conference was in full session and a long and somewhat tedious discussion was in progress. The panoply of international meetings, with the delegates tucked beneath the headphones of their multilingual translation equipment, looked impressive. All minds were on the gently rumbling arguments. And it was now that Huxley beckoned to one of the uniformed messengers standing at the ready and handed him a brief note addressed to a member of the French delegation. The messenger delivered the note which said: 'Please come here. I have something important to ask you.' The Frenchman circumambulated the large chamber, closed up to Huxley, and bent down beside him to hear the inquiry.

'When I was driving here this morning,' said the Director-General, 'do you know what I saw? Of all things a hoopoe. . . .' He looked up as the debate continued to rumble on. 'Did you see it, too?'

The Mexico City meeting proved that Unesco had not been still-born and Huxley's concluding claim to the general conference was more than justified:

> We have planted here the hope of a new spirit in universal col-

laboration – although it may be that Unesco will not reap all the fruit, we hope that it has enabled men from all countries to know each other and to meet in bonds of friendship.

He went back to Paris knowing that Unesco was over its first serious hump.

As its activities continued to expand, Huxley's personal control over them became lighter. He was now more able to follow the course he had followed as Secretary of the Zoological Society, delegating jobs and then allowing his staff to carry on without interference. Yet his mark remained on most things, and there were at least two for which he was very largely responsible, even though they came into existence after he had left Unesco. One of these was the International Union for the Protection of Nature, a body in which more than 200 organizations from 45 counties were soon banded together with the aims of conserving renewable natural resources and areas of outstanding natural interest and of protecting flora and fauna having particular scientific, historic or aesthetic significance. Huxley not only helped to bring the union into being, but fought for a number of specific conservation projects – the most notable, perhaps, being the scheme to save the Galapagos giant tortoises, those creatures of the distant past which had so interested Darwin when he visited the islands in 1835. Huxley, honorary President of the society making the effort, wrote, spoke and lobbied in support of the scheme with his usual intense concentration.

The second innovation was the International Commission for a History of the Scientific and Cultural Development of Mankind, a body which sprang from a proposal in Huxley's 'Unesco Philosophy' for 'a history of the development of the human mind, notably in its highest cultural achievements'. The commission was finally set up in 1950, a body specifically made independent of Unesco – and of any other body – so that the writing of this world history would be free from direct Government pressures. Huxley was an original member of the commission and has remained on it ever since; and it is symptomatic that when, a decade and a half later, discussion ranged across the way in which the second half of the twentieth century was to be treated, it was Huxley who prepared, almost as a casual offshoot from his other work, a memorandum outlining the way in which the job should be tackled – an extraordinary document deftly jumping from Christian theology to cybernetics, from mystical experience to education in emergent countries, and recommending in each case the specialist to consult.

In the summer of 1948 Huxley set off on another of his prospecting journeys to make arrangements for the General Conference which was to be held in Beirut. Unesco already had a special interest in the Middle East since the Arid Zone programme had been the first to apply science to the needs of the under-developed countries and had led the way for many other schemes. As usual, Huxley squeezed in an immense amount of work, made possible partly by his ability to take a cat-nap whenever opportunity offered. In the towns and cities where he met those concerned with Unesco's work, the time would be fully taken up with meetings. Only in the air, as he and his staff flew from country to country, was there time to talk over what action should be taken on the last batch of interviews. Work finished, Huxley would lean back, see from his watch that they still had thirty minutes' flying time ahead of them, and would comment: 'I'm going to sleep for half an hour.' Within a few seconds he would have dropped off.

In Turkey, the Lebanon, Syria, Jordan, Iraq, Iran and Egypt, he met heads of state, leading educationalists, scientists and artists. He also saw many places he had for years been anxious to see. One of these was Petra, Burgon's 'rose-red city', in 1948 still an oasis of the past, remote in the desert and untouched by the tourist trade.

As soon as Huxley entered Jordan he made it clear that he was intent on visiting Petra. King Abdullah was equally intent on occupying every spare minute of the Unesco party's time with conducted tours of the modern schools and other buildings which were going up under his auspices. It was soon clear that a good-natured private tussle was developing between the King's plans and Huxley's insistent: 'Fix Petra.'

Huxley won. After a day of conferences, Huxley and three colleagues were woken at 3 a.m. for a 4 a.m. take-off from Amman airport. At the end of the flight south into the desert the party drove to the fort nearest to Petra – a journey interrupted more than once by a wild shout from Huxley of 'Stop the car' as he spotted one of the rare desert flowers which had sprouted after a recent rain-storm.

From the fort the party went ahead on horseback for a couple of miles. Then, at the head of the little ravine leading down into the valley, the place where, according to tradition, Moses had hit the rock and struck water, they dismounted.

After inspecting the ruins Huxley proposed lunch at a viewpoint high above the valley. The guide objected, adding that he was an old man – that he was aged 57. 'Well, I'm sixty,' said Huxley, bounding off like a mountain goat.

After a long day of inspection and photography the party touched down in Amman as dusk was falling. 'We then,' said one of Huxley's

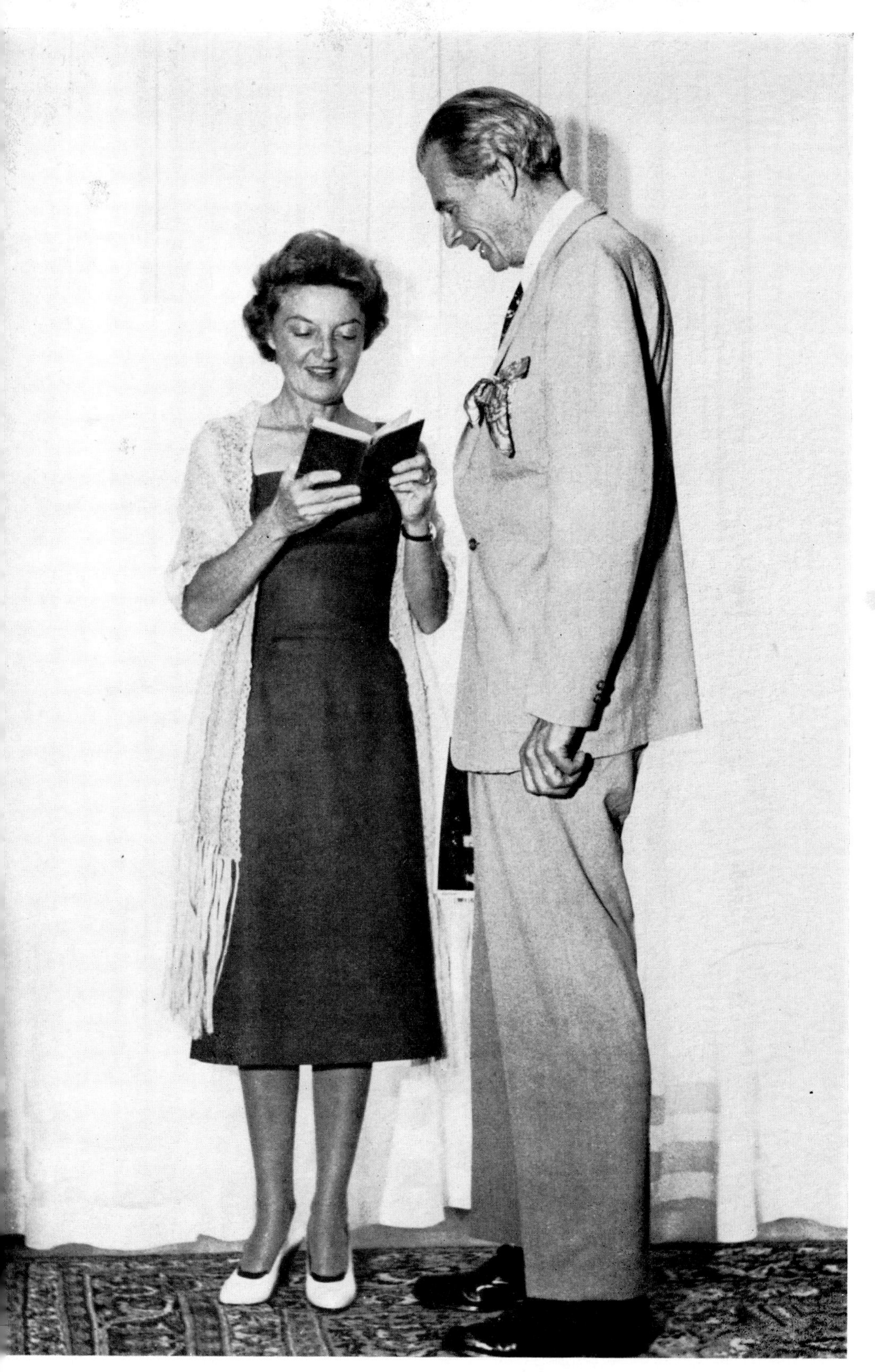

Aldous Huxley and his second wife, Laura

Francis Huxley

Anthony Huxley

Sir Julian and Lady Huxley in the Coto Doñana, Southern Spain, May 1957, with *(centre)* Max Nicholson

companions, 'got on with a bout of Unesco business that went on almost until midnight.'

The general conference which was held at Beirut later in the year marked the end of Huxley's work as Director-General. The Americans were unwilling to move from their initial insistence that while they would accept Huxley for two years, he should not be allowed to run the full six years of office. Huxley himself, seized as he was by the work, had been counting on only the two-year term of office and was already making his plans for the future. There was the inevitable problem of finding for a difficult job the right man who would be acceptable to a working majority of parties. For a while decision hovered near disaster. Then, on Huxley's suggestion, a suitable candidate was found in Don Jaime Torres-Bodet, the former Mexican Minister of Education, later of Foreign Affairs and now again of Education, who was duly elected successor.

What Huxley was now able to hand over was a flourishing international organization, a machine which had an unconventional look but which actually worked. What is more, it was a machine which had already been given its head of steam. By the end of 1948 Unesco was well set on a course which might be altered by the odd few degrees but which could not now be seriously diverted. It was Huxley who had been, as Charles Asher had underlined in *Programme-Making in Unesco, 1946–1951*, 'largely responsible for charting the broad course to which the organization became committed during its early years'.

Chapter XVI

Julian: Creating the Reality

(*i*)

When Julian left Unesco for London at the end of 1948, he returned to a Britain in which the intellectual climate was considerably more favourable to the Huxley ethos than it had been.

The family had become a force during the last half of the nineteenth century, and had been quiescent during the first two decades of the twentieth. Later, between the wars, the two surviving sons of Leonard's first marriage had worked their way into an importance illustrated by Ashley Montagu's jingle:

> Whenever Aldous Huxley writes
> A novel that delights
> His followers,
> His brother Julian
> At once indites
> A learned work
> On Coprolites
> For scholars.

Other members of the family climbed steadily up the rungs of Civil Service or business ladders. During the 1930s, the younger members naturally provided anticipations rather than achievements. Moreover, for the ingrained Huxley practice of critical objective assessment followed by fiery exposition, the 1930s were out of joint, although P.E.P. was started during this decade.

This situation was transformed by the second world war. 'The bomb' – quite apart from its promise of worse to come – had posed in a unique form the choice of co-operation or chaos and had made necessary an international appraisal of the world's problems. Air travel, it was clear to many, would soon be providing the people of far-separated continents with the personal links and associations which only a few centuries back had been those of the small city-state. Television, already beginning to reach round the world, was about to show a power beside which Caxton's twenty-six soldiers of lead could fight merely local battles. These changes, underlined by the advances being made almost monthly in so many branches of natural science, all made it increasingly necessary for men to reconsider both their relations with their fellow men, and mankind's relation with the rest of nature. In a new way, anything less than a world view became parochial. This urgency was not, of course, universally appreciated. The sheer dead weight of ignorance combined with biological conservatism in its age-old task of tugging at the reins: 'Kings crept out again to feel the sun.' It could be claimed that there had been wars before and that nothing had been fundamentally changed. Yet in spite of the overtones, men and women were at last being forced to realize that the world was one, that they must look clearly, argue rationally, decide what their place in the natural world really was and then act accordingly. Their numbers were still small, but they were growing.

In this encouraging climate, Julian returned from Paris and took up life once again in his Hampstead home. He was just 61, at the height of his powers. His knowledge of world problems had been immensely broadened by his experience at Unesco. His prestige, moreover, had been heightened by his conduct under the continuous sniping of Unesco critics and it now gave him an authority which was in strong contrast to the fact that he held no official posts or appointments and was merely a free-lance biologist and writer.

His position in the scientific world had been assured for years, but it was now buttressed by the clear and unmistakable stance which he took up and doggedly maintained in the post-war clash between science shackled to the state and science free to follow its own path, a clash which developed on the international stage after the war, and which rose to its explosive climax in the Lysenko controversy. It is as well to deal with this before describing his post-war work; for at Unesco he had been under regular fire for alleged Communist sympathies, and the Lysenko affair fortuitously gave him an opportunity for nailing his own flag to the mast for both specialist and general public to see.

For more than a quarter of a century he had been stressing that humanity could be helped by the organized application of science. Through more than a quarter of a century it had slowly been appreciated by the world that such organized application was being carried out in Russia as nowhere else. The *non sequitur* was that Huxley approved of the Communist system, a belief sometimes increased by the dispassionate way in which he would carefully point out the benefits as well as the iniquities of the system.

In the summer of 1945 he had been among the nine hundred scientists from eighteen countries who had visited Russia for the 220th anniversary celebrations of the Academy of Sciences of the U.S.S.R. – a curious anniversary to celebrate and one not unconnected with the fact that a triumphant Red Army had captured Berlin in May. In Leningrad Huxley heard how Vavilov's famous collection of cereal seeds had been eaten during the siege. In Moscow he heard how the Russians had been stimulated by the news that at the height of the war Britain had been able to publish the great *Handbook of British Birds* – and were now preparing a Russian equivalent. Wherever he went he saw not only the effects of the war but signs that the Russians had already elevated their scientists and their research institutes into a fifth estate. The implications – more than a decade before the *sputniks* – were clear. Huxley noted:

> The U.S.S.R. is taking its place as one of the foremost countries in biological research, and I anticipate that they will soon be leading the world in some fields, notably in the relation between ecology, field study, taxonomy, genetics and evolution, where their vast continuous territory, with its extremes of environmental conditions, provides them with unrivalled opportunities.

Much the same could be expected in other sciences, and all this was encouraging. Yet though it was right that the state should aid the discovery and marshalling of the information with which its people might march forward, this was the extent of its brief. At the frontier where the collection of evidence became less important than interpretation, it should no longer be necessary to render anything unto either Caesar or the pundits of the ruling party. Here Huxley, together with many other scientists who could follow the Communist experiment so far and no farther, dug in his heels. Had he not, after all, asserted in his Romanes lecture that

> All claims that the State has an intrinsically higher value than the individual are false. They turn out, on closer scrutiny, to be rationalizations or myths aimed at securing greater power or privilege for a limited group which controls the machinery of the state.

Like many others who had for two decades or more been under fire from the Right, Huxley realized that the shot might soon be coming from a different quarter. The first sign of the storm that was to make his stubborn independence clear – just as it was to sweep away a number of scientists from their Communist positions – came in 1948 with the holding at Wroclaw in Poland of the World Congress of Intellectuals. Huxley, then Director-General of Unesco, was invited to become one of the congress's five presidents or chairmen. He had hoped, as he later said, that the congress would devote itself on the non-governmental level to the same tasks, of international co-operation for peace in the fields of science and culture, to which Unesco was devoting itself on the inter-governmental level. He accordingly accepted the invitation and agreed to attend the congress. He was, however, allowed to do so only in his private capacity; and he accepted only on the assurance that the meeting would be purely cultural in its scope.

From the first it was clear that this was not to be the case. As day followed day and the mainly political purpose of the meeting became apparent, Huxley found it more and more difficult to conceal his distaste. Finally, after a somewhat strained closing session, he travelled back to Paris and issued a personal statement that in spite of its reasonable wording had a calculatedly explosive effect:

> The Congress from the outset took a political turn; there was no real discussion, and the great majority of the speeches were either strictly Marxist analyses of current trends, or else polemical attacks on American or Western policy and culture. Purely political, or politico-economic matters, such as the Marshall Plan, Western Union, and imperial and colonial policy, were frequently brought in. No or negligible references were made to the United Nations or to the possibility of cultural, scientific and technical collaboration made possible through the U.N. specialized agencies, such as Unesco, F.A.O. and W.H.O.
>
> I did not sign the final resolution presented to the Congress. It omits all references to many important causes of or predispositions to war, and places the blame for the present state of tension almost entirely on a handful of self-interested men in America and Europe, who had inherited fascist ideas of racial superiority and the denial of progress, who have adopted fascist methods of solving all problems by force of arms. In these and other ways it appears to me to be tendentious and unfortunate. This gathering of scientists, writers and artists from many countries could have provided an opportunity for reconciling, in the intellectual and cultural sphere, what may broadly be called the Eastern and Western points of view. I can only express my regret that that opportunity was not taken.

It was, in fact, something deeper than regret that Huxley felt. For it was more than a cultural failure to bridge the widening gulf between East and West which was shown up by the Wroclaw conference.

More central to the problem of man in the modern world was the failure to draw an acceptable boundary between the dominion of the state and that of the free individual. This age-old dispute, debatable since men first began to form themselves into organized groups, enlarged and underlined by the growing power of the state, was now strengthened physically by post-war weapon-power and intellectually by control of mass-communication. It was about to be illuminated, diamond-sharp, by a battle in Huxley's own particular field, that of biology. The subject was 'Lysenko-ism', and as in so many previous controversies Huxley was to reveal himself as the expositor, the clarifier, the presenter of facts which were both scientifically correct and understandable to the layman. This time, moreover, he had influence; and the stand which he took in this famous debate did a great deal to sway opinion, to create a new questioning climate in which even the most devout Communist was forced to face, if not answer, a hard factual challenge.

The Lysenko controversy was a biological argument with obvious political implications; it was also basically, a simple argument. For while geneticists believed that living organisms could transmit only the attributes locked up in the genes they acquired at conception, the Russian agricultural biologist Lysenko maintained that characteristics acquired during an organism's lifetime could also be passed on to future generations. Lysenko had carried out his main experiments on wheat and other plant species; but if his theory were correct for plants it could well be – in fact it might be expected to be – correct for other living organisms. And here, dramatically it seemed, there might lie a chance of correcting the awkward fact of life that all men are not born biologically equal. For given enough time it might be possible to 'breed men equal' – taking children with mediocre brains, suitably sharpening them, and then allowing them to transmit the acquired brightness to succeeding generations. Here, the devout Russian Communists quickly saw, was the chance of an immensely powerful new weapon, and in their speed to acquire it they overlooked the 'mights', the 'possibles', all the qualifications and doubts with which the objective scientist normally considers the evidence for new theories. While the geneticists were therefore inquiring into Lysenko's experimental results – and finding them open to grave doubt – the Russian authorities were treating his work as revealed truth. They were, indeed, doing more. They were stifling criticism of Lysenko's conclusions, dismissing from positions of authority those who persisted in applying scientific standards to the argument, and raising support for 'Lysenkoism' to a matter of state policy.

This really would not do. It would not do for a great many eminent men, including Sir Henry Dale, one of the great names in English science who in his letter of resignation from the Academy of Sciences of the U.S.S.R. stated: 'The whole great fabric of exact knowledge, still growing at the hands of those who have followed Mendel, Bateson and Morgan, is to be repudiated and denounced.' Yet the development went farther than the rightness or wrongness of Lysenko's claims; the danger would have been as great had his work been scientifically vindicated. And it was in this wider context that Huxley took up cudgels in the argument, first in a seventeen-thousand-word review of the whole situation in *Nature* and later in his book *Soviet Genetics and World Science*. The nub of the matter was summed up in his *Nature* article after he had detailed the various reports which had triggered off the Lysenko explosion:

> These reports, together with the documents already cited, constitute a melancholy landmark in the history of science. They demonstrate that science is no longer regarded in the U.S.S.R. as an international activity of free workers whose prime interest it is to discover new truth and new facts, but as an activity subordinated to a particular ideology and designed only to secure practical results in the interests of a particular national and political system. Consequently the unity of science is denied, and various brands of 'good' science – Marxist, Soviet, or materialist – are distinguished from various brands of 'bad' science – bourgeois, reactionary, idealist and the like.

To those who knew Huxley it must have been inevitable that he would take the stand that he did take on this controversy that was to split the scientific world down the middle. Yet in a subtle way it strengthened his position. It made it less easy for the critics to deride his alleged political tendencies. And it thus helped him during the following years during which his standing carried him as a semi-official negotiator into the arena in which science and government tried to cope together with the problems of the world.

(ii)

From the start of this post-war period, Huxley was immersed in a formidable number of projects. He wrote, he advised, he lectured, he chaired meetings; he still travelled the world with an untiring energy that often exhausted his companions. The mere chronological record of his diary appointments presents a kaleidoscopic series of activities, from cancer research and fauna preservation to eugenics, the latest refinements of Darwinism, and the need to press home the essentials of scientific humanism. Paper succeeds lecture, book succeeds the chairing or organization of a congress, while for years there is kept up the regular fusillade of shots at public opinion represented by letters to *The Times*. Yet if one stands back and regards the record objectively, it is possible to see order beyond the apparent confusion. For these multiple occupations represent specific spheres of interest, each interlocking and resting one within another like a series of Chinese boxes so that each concern is enveloped by a greater.

At the centre of Huxley's world lay biology, and throughout the 1950s and 1960s he continued to exercise himself on the endlessly unfolding problems which living organisms present – and particularly on those problems affecting birds and their insubstantial world. Soon after the end of the war in Europe he revisited Grassholm and found that the island with its unique gannet colony had almost surreptitiously been used as a bombing target, a 'deplorable lapse of judgement on the part of the authorities' as *The Times* called it, and one which Huxley was instrumental in reversing. After leaving Unesco he had repeated with James Fisher a gannet census taken off Iceland before the war, cruising round the great stack of Eldey, some fifteen miles from the coast. On 2 June 1953, when the columns of the papers were largely occupied by accounts of the Coronation and the conquest of Everest, and little else seemed to matter, he had the satisfaction of seeing his letter in *The Times* recording that a great crested grebe in full plumage had been seen in Hampstead on two successive days. And four years later he was a member of the expedition which visited the Coto Doñana in southern Spain to investigate its wild life, an expedition on which Juliette acted as botanical collector, gathering some 250 species.

This was all a spur to work of a very different kind, for in the post-war world the very raw material of zoology itself was coming under heavier attack. Twenty years previously Huxley had seen in Africa the first signs of the threat to come; now one species after another was dying out there, while from the other continents there came almost equally disturbing evidence that animals which had evolved through millennia were being wiped out in a few decades. This destruction of the world's splendid wild-life was a subject on which he felt strongly and about which he had protested much over the years. Before the war he had urged that even in Britain, where the threat was not so great, the general protection of wild life should be an essential part of any scheme for National Parks. At Unesco he had included the preservation of wild life within 'culture' and had helped to set up the International Union for the Protection of Nature, as it then was.

Throughout the post-war years he kept up the pressure, and in 1960 was given an assignment tailor-made for his special qualifications: a survey for Unesco of the wild life and natural habitats of Central and East Africa, and the preparation of a report on what might be done to conserve them. To those unacquainted with the Huxleys it might have seemed strange that the task should be given to a man in his seventy-fourth year, however impressive his qualifications. For the rigours of the survey were clear from the start, and eventually involved a three-month journey by jeep, Land Rover, plane and foot through ten countries, into twenty-five National Parks or similar areas, as well as meetings with more than a hundred administrators, experts, scientists and politicians, both black and white. Huxley swept along on the itinerary with astonishing vitality, filling notebooks, taking photographs, and exhibiting an almost uncanny acquaintance with relevant facts, the men in charge, and the various proposals which had been put forward since he had first viewed the African scene thirty years previously. He was accompanied throughout by his wife, who on their return to Britain showed that she had been far more than the usual good manager and smoother-out of personal problems. For while Julian was preparing his report for Unesco, Juliette was putting on record her own perceptive views of the expedition. The result was *Wild Lives of Africa*, a book which to an extraordinary degree gives the 'feel' of the country and its all-pervading wild life. Julian Huxley's report was discussed at length at the Arusha Conference on Conservation in Modern African States, held in September the following year. Huxley himself attended, and must have been pleased at the results, for here it was possible to sense for the first time genuine stirrings of belief among the new rulers of Africa that they themselves should do something to preserve their unique fauna.

The need to conserve the natural resources of a country was one outcome of the scientific and technological revolution which during the twentieth century enabled man to control – and to destroy – his natural habitat at a rate which was entirely new. But it was not the only result. Another, partly due to medical advances which had been urged on by the demands of two world wars, was the frightening explosion in the numbers of man himself.

Huxley had first become impressed with this problem – 'the problem of our age' as he later described it – when he had read his colleague Carr-Saunders's pioneering work, *The Population Problem* on its publication in 1922. The situation could be viewed in different ways, and it is ironic that one of Huxley's first connections with it was as a member of the Government-blessed Population Investigation Committee, set up between the wars to consider the expected decline in Britain's population. On a larger scale, things were very different and in 1928, a year after attending the international population conference in Geneva, Huxley pointed out that 'Population in many countries is beginning to exert a pressure like gas pent up in a cylinder. We have got to face that problem, which is largely biological, and see how it can best be tackled.' There was, however, opposition to the most obvious way of tackling it. When, in the autumn of 1926, Huxley mentioned the subject of birth-control during a radio debate on: 'Is Science Bad for the World?', there was an almost national outcry. Huxley himself was reprimanded by Sir John Reith, Managing Director of the British Broadcasting Company as it then was; while, through the columns of *The Times*, the company protested humbly that 'this reference was entirely inadvertent and was at variance with our policy. The necessary action has been taken to prevent its recurrence.'

Huxley became increasingly aware of the threat from the population explosion while working with P.E.P. during the 1930s. However, it was only during his work for Unesco, as he saw at first hand the existing problems of the swarming millions of Asia that he fully realized the threat presented by a situation in which the population of a town of more than 90,000 was being added to the world every day.

When, early in 1949, the United Nations began to plan a U.N. Conference on World Resources Huxley, as Director-General of Unesco, was asked to co-operate. He did more than this. He pointed out that a conference on resources would lose half its value were it not supplemented by a survey of the people who consumed the resources. There were difficulties, religious and political, perhaps to be expected in an age in which the Catholics claim that contraception is against the will of God and their strange bed-fellows the Communists claim that it is against the will of the state. Only in 1954 did his proposal finally come to fruition in the U.N. Conference on World Population which was held in Rome – 'a milestone in history', as he has described it, 'as being the first occasion when the subject of human population was surveyed as a whole, and under the aegis of an official international organization'.

Huxley was thus largely responsible for pressing the attention of a reluctant world on to a problem that he could see looming in fearful proportion towards the end of the century. He kept up the pressure – in lectures, in essays, in general advocacy, stressing always that some damping down of the population explosion was an essential if man were to control and direct the resources of his planet with any hope of bettering the human lot. His realization of the way in which this key piece in the jigsaw of international planning fitted in with others was well brought out in an article which he wrote for the *Scientific American* on 'Population and Human Fulfilment'. Pointing out that twentieth-century man cannot easily avoid the problem being thrust at him, he says:

> The traveller is struck by sheer numbers in China, high density as in Java, attempts to control increase as in India, the effects of immigration as in Ceylon or Fiji, large vacant spaces in Australia, and erosion, deforestation and destruction of wild life almost everywhere.

This physical predicament of mid-twentieth-century man would only be tractable to international effort – Julian, like his grandfather, realized how far-seeing Tennyson had been with his 'Parliament of man, the Federation of the world'. Yet the physical predicament, one result of the speed with which medical, technological and scientific advances had suddenly spun a network round the world, was only one of many. There was also 'the question of questions' – 'the ascertainment of the place which Man occupies in nature and of his relation to the universe of things'.

Since that day in America, almost half a century back, when Julian had read Morley's prophecy that 'the next great task of science will be to create a religion for humanity', the vision of man's place in Nature and the creation of just such a religion had occupied much of his thought. Like TH, he had found the revealed religions literally incredible. Like TH he was, 'on the basis of our knowledge of history and comparative religion, ... convinced that the idea of a god as a supernatural but somehow personal being, capable of influencing nature and human life, is a hypothesis, set up to account for various awe-inspiring and mysterious phenomena in man's experience which do not seem to have any natural explanation'. Like TH he had tried to discern some pattern of belief that would be consonant with existing knowledge. This knowledge had been subtly extended and transformed since his grandfather had stood in the Sheldonian and proclaimed in his Romanes Lecture that man must for ever be fighting the cosmic process, erecting his ethical principles not as guide-lines forward but as barriers against the attacks of what TH, with Tennyson, had seen as 'Nature, red in tooth and claw'. Now, more than half a century later, it was possible to see things differently. From inanimate matter, through animate matter to fully conscious mind, evolution had continued, with man and his attempts to erect an ethical structure merely one of the steps in an evolving process.

And now man, presented with ever-expanding possibilities, should really set up for himself a set of principles more in accordance with the station to which evolution had called him. As Julian was to put it in a long letter to *Fortune*,

> We, the human species, through no merit of our own, have become responsible for the entire future of ourselves and the planet we inhabit, through periods of time undreamt of by Comte or Christian theologians, by orthodox Marxists or American believers in the idea that material or technological improvement is synonymous with 'progress'.
>
> It can only discharge this responsibility by a faith in the vast and as yet almost untapped resources of human nature, a determination to explore them and to realize more of man's possibilities so as to achieve greater fulfilment and flowering for more individual human beings, and fuller achievement and satisfaction by more human groups and societies.

This faith was to be the new religion without revelation; it was also, in some ways, the 'philosophy of reason ... interpreted in those terms of picturesque and exciting unreason which alone have power to move the minds of men', for which Aldous had called years earlier, before he had been drawn through the gate into the mystic's garden. Julian had always disliked labels, but at various times he has described his faith as that of an evolutionary humanist. All rests on the second word.

> I use the word 'Humanist' [he has written] to mean someone who believes that man is just as much a natural phenomenon as an animal or a plant: that his body, mind and soul were not supernaturally created but are all products of evolution, and that he is not under the control or guidance of any supernatural being or beings, but has to rely on himself and his own powers.

With this stark fact before him, man must attempt to erect an ethical structure which will help him to realize his great potentialities. And these, Julian has always been fond of stressing, are vastly greater than most of mankind appreciates. In his first book, dealing with individuality in the animal kingdom and writing of personality in human beings, he had said:

> Personality, as we know it, is free compared with the individuality of the lower animals; but it is still weighted with a body. There may be personalities which have not merely transcended substance, but are rid of it altogether: in all ages the theologian and the mystic have

told of such 'disembodied spirits', postulated by the one, felt by the other, and now the physical investigator with his automatic writing and his cross-correspondences is seeking to give us rigorous demonstration of them.

If such actually exist, they crown Life's progress; she has started as mere substance without individuality, has next gained an individuality co-extensive with her substance, then an individuality still tied to substance but transcending it in all directions, and finally become an individuality without substance, free and untrammelled.

That for the present must be mere speculation. . . .

Half a century later it still remains speculation. Even so, Huxley's consideration of inexplicable manifestations has two corollaries. One is the high-lighting of a central belief of his humanism that science has not abolished mystery and left only logic and reason. Secondly, the belief that evolution may have gone even farther across the border separating matter and mind than is yet fully understood. This second belief was to draw Julian in his later years to a deeper study of the paranormal – the range of experiences for which there is as yet merely patchy evidence, as though mankind were only now acquiring the sensitive mental instruments to see through small gaps in a thick curtain. Thus in the 1950s he began to take a greater interest in such phenomena as extra-sensory perception and telekinesis, phenomena in which his brother Aldous already had an unqualified belief. Curiously, therefore, the paths of the two brothers became convergent; scientist and mystic began to find common ground in that borderland between mind and matter which T H had viewed with some wonder almost a century earlier.

The exposition and advocacy of scientific humanism – on the radio, in books, at the First International Congress of Humanism and Ethical Culture which he chaired in Amsterdam in 1952, as President of the British Humanist Association – was by the 1950s becoming one of the most important of Julian's activities. It certainly had a greater impact, and will probably have a more lasting one, than that of the other matters with which he concerned himself – the conservation of wildlife, the world's population explosion, the multiple scientific interests into which he was drawn. His work in all these fields ploughed through the years on lines that were usually parallel; but occasionally they would cross and intercross so that at times there seemed to be but a single broad track along which the head of the Huxleys was attempting to drive a unified policy involving a world faith, an international population plan and world-wide conservation of natural resources.

Energy, involvement, a wide spread of knowledge across a broad target, a memory capable of retrieving the needed name, date or address from across half a century or an entire continent, an incalculable array of contacts – these were the most obvious traits shown by Huxley as he went about his work during the two decades that followed the war. Books, broadcasts, lectures and papers were written in his first-floor library at Pond Street, with the portrait of TH looking down from the fireplace. He would write in fits and starts, checking references as he went along, unwilling to leave more than was necessary for correction or amendment in his own spidery hand and for incorporation in the final draft to be typed by his secretary. He usually wrote in the mornings, trying to get a solid stretch of creative work finished before the meetings and conversations, the interviews and the attendances, of the afternoon and evening; desperately seeking refuge from the telephone, constantly in demand and as constantly ejecting ideas, making fresh propositions, perpetually interested in new discoveries.

His ability to train all intellectual guns on a single subject, to ignore diversions, and to produce in a few months what would demand as many years from most men, was typified by *Biological Aspects of Cancer*, a biologist's-eye view of the subject and a remarkable *tour de force*. It was in 1955 that Dr Rhoads of the Sloan-Kettering Foundation for Cancer Research in New York invited Huxley to deliver the first Alfred P. Sloan Lecture, whose subject had to be some aspect of the cancer problem. Huxley at first declined, on the grounds that he had never been a doctor and had never really studied the cancer question. These very facts, Rhoads replied, made him the ideal man, since he would be able to look at the subject with a fresh mind, unaffected by any conscious prejudices picked up during years of research. The lecture was given with success, and was then expanded by Huxley into what was initially intended to be a paper for *Biological Reviews*; but the result was so long that the paper had to be published in two parts. Once again Huxley felt the need to augment the work, and this time the manuscript was published in book form.

> I can truthfully say [he wrote in the introduction] that the preparation of these two reviews involved me in more hard labour than anything I have attempted since I took my Final Honours examination in Zoology at Oxford more years ago than I care to remember. I could never have finished them if I had been occupied with teaching, administration, or the need to produce a stream of research papers. Indeed, it may be a good thing to have a few elderly scientists quit

of all such professional obligations and free to devote themselves now and again to general survey.

Through the 1950s, honours descended – from the Kalinga Prize 'for distinguished popular writing in science' in 1953, to the Darwin Medal of the Royal Society 'for his distinguished contributions to the study and theory of evolution', and the Darwin-Wallace Commemorative Medal of the Linnean Society in the following year. Knighthood followed in 1958. His success as a popularizer of science, his instinct for reaching the headlines, his use of shock-treatment for making the reader think – 'Is the Bible Fit for Children to Read?' he once asked in a newspaper article; replying, with some qualifications, 'Yes' – had all helped to draw attention away from his solid achievements on the genuine battlefields of science. The extent of these was made clear with the award of the Darwin Medal. In presenting it, the President of the Royal Society, Sir Cyril Hinshelwood, recalled Huxley's classical work on courtship behaviour and on relative growth, his genetical investigations of Gammarus. He recalled that it was Huxley who had both conceived and christened the cline, that gradation of measurable characteristics within a group which had 'proved of such value . . . that it passed almost immediately into very wide use'. Yet Huxley's greatest work might well have been his development of the neo-Darwinian theory of evolution, to which he had contributed by experiment, by mathematical analysis and by theoretical discussion. As a result he had, Hinshelwood concluded,

> a place all to himself in that his wide interests, encyclopaedic knowledge, and ability to see the connection between widely separated fields, have enabled him to bring together and bind into a single evolutionary thesis the findings of the most diverse branches of biology.

Julian therefore had a double claim to attention as 1959 approached and preparations were made to celebrate the centenary of *The Origin.* It was both as an exponent of neo-Darwinism and as the grandson of Darwin's Bulldog that he delivered the Darwin-Wallace centenary lecture at the International Congress of Zoology in the Royal Albert Hall in 1958 – 'when I had to decide who was the most appropriate and competent person to deliver it, my task was easy', commented the congress President, Sir Gavin de Beer, an old pupil of Julian's. And it was in the dual role that he was invited to guide the Darwin centennial celebrations organized by the University of Chicago. Early in 1956 the university began to plan a gathering at which specialists would read papers on different aspects of evolution and at which discussion groups would consider the questions raised. Some shape and coherence had to be given to the disparate contributions. Julian was therefore formally appointed Visiting Professor for the autumn quarter of 1959, and was able, as he put it, 'to look at the evolution problem as a whole, in the light of all the various disciplines involved', as well as to review and arrange the contributions so as to give the conference a unity it might otherwise have lacked.

A massive volume of work had to be completed before the symposium opened and Julian's imprint could be seen on a great deal of it. When it came to naming the various discussion panels he significantly suggested that one should deal not with 'Social and Cultural Evolution' but with 'Man in the Human Phase', since the latter stressed that 'although there is continuity of evolution from animals to man, it changes its mechanism and its character once the initial point of man has been passed.' He proposed authors and subjects for the various papers; he considered the outlines, and he commented in detail on the papers themselves with a freedom which was not always appreciated by the authors. Thus Sir Charles Darwin, grandson of the first Charles and a noted physicist, agreed rather reluctantly to Julian's suggestions and commented that 'It still seems to me that he gives a very mystical colour to his psycho-social evolution, implying it will lead man upwards and on into a millennium.'

Early in the autumn, Julian and Juliette flew to Chicago. The news that Huxley was to spend some time there had become common property and he had been inundated with requests to lecture – from colleges, universities, and from the Third Unitarian Church, Chicago, whose leaders asked whether he would be their 'featured speaker at the ninety-first anniversary celebrations of the founding of our church.' Huxley fitted in as much as he could. He exhibited his usual bewildering ability to take punishment, illustrated by a note in which he informed a colleague that he intended to fly direct from Chicago to Tucson on the morning of Tuesday, 27 October, spend the night there, and return on Wednesday by plane. From Chicago they would then be able to fly down to Phoenix, Arizona, and 'could go on to the Grand Canyon on Saturday morning and sleep there at night and return on Sunday afternoon or night, flying back to Chicago on Monday the 2nd. I ought,' he noted, 'to be there for one of their seminars at 3.30 p.m. on that date.'

The Centennial opened on 24 November, a celebration that included not only symposia, lectures and debates but the presentation of *Time Will Tell*, a musical play based on the life and times of Darwin. In this, the great debate of 1860 formed a high spot in which TH sang that

> I don't see that the Bishop has reason to sneer,
> And I have no wish to abuse him;
> But taking his line,
> If I had to incline,
> Towards ape or divine,
> Would I choose him?

The play was merely the froth on a great event that had begun with the convocation address given by Julian in the university chapel. It was a notable occasion, and one to which Huxley rose splendidly. In some ways it could be compared to the afternoon on which TH had given his Romanes Lecture. Then, two-thirds of a century earlier, the founder of the Huxley dynasty had been summing up the lessons of his life; now his grandson was summing up the way ahead. The title of the address was 'The Evolutionary Vision', its contents an outline of the opportunities which the new understanding of evolution made possible. This was not all, for Huxley was now clear as to the aims to which the opportunities should be directed:

> The important ends of man's life include the creation and enjoyment of beauty, both natural and man-made; increased comprehension and a more assured sense of significance; the preservation of all sources of pure wonder and delight, like fine scenery, wild animals in freedom, or unspoiled nature; the attainment of inner peace and harmony; the feeling of active participation in embracing and enduring projects, including the cosmic project of evolution. It is through such things that individuals attain greater fulfilment.

The idea that man might be in control of his own destiny raised protests from the religious lobby. One paper stated that Huxley's prediction had been that 'a new order of thinking will doom all religions.' One of the organizers of the Centennial referred to the 'flurry on the theological front' that Huxley's convocation address had created, and it was subsequently agreed that this had been proposed 'without any thought to the content of what he would say, only to his position in the field and in the Centennial.'

This position was as central in Britain as it was in the United States, for by the later 1950s Huxley had concluded that typical progress of the successful British intellectual who must first traverse a long ravine of criticism, sniped at from all sides, before emerging to find himself unexpectedly clasped to the bosom of the kirk. He was now the grand old man, the final collective court of appeal on many subjects, one of the rough-hewn pillars of the Athenaeum, wearing his aureole lightly no doubt, but wearing it nevertheless. Of evolution he had become the interpreter and of humanism the prophet. All except the most prognathous of the bishops might even be forced to admit that he was a good man.

By this time Julian was, moreover, the head of a family more than one of whose members were now exhibiting typically Huxleyan traits. Laurence Collier – by this time Sir Laurence – had produced his philosophical criticism of the mystic's creed. Rupert Crawshay-Williams, whose *The Comforts of Unreason* had been a challenge to many accepted concepts, was now devoting himself almost entirely to philosophy. His mother, now re-married, had become, as Joyce Kilburn, a miniature-painter of note. While Gervas Huxley, who had thus far confined his interests very largely to business and trade, had become a member of the National Parks Commission and of the Executive Committee of the British Council. Moreover he had, from the age of sixty-five, revealed the Huxley facility for writing. This had been triggered off by Vandyke's picture of Endymion Porter, favourite courtier of Charles I and an ancestor of his wife Elspeth. The result, after three years of research, was the definitive 'life' – to be followed by three other successful biographies; *Lady Denman*, *Lady Elizabeth and the Grosvenors*, and *Victorian Duke*. 'Even in one's old age, whatever one's other work has been,' says Gervas, 'a Huxley seems compelled to write books.'

Many of the younger Huxleys were already making their marks. Of Julian's half-brothers, David Bruce – the elder of Leonard's two sons by his second marriage – had become Attorney-General of Bermuda. David's daughter Angela was, in 1964, to make the first direct link with the Darwin family, marrying George Pember Darwin, the great-grandson of TH's contemporary. Some seventeen years earlier his younger brother Andrew had created a less direct link by marrying Jocelyn Pease, granddaughter of the first Lord Wedgwood, whose grandfather was Charles Darwin's brother-in-law.

Andrew had before the war come under the influence of the Cambridge physiologist, A. L. Hodgkin, and in the summer of 1939 the two men had worked together at the Marine Biological Laboratory at Plymouth, using the large nerve fibres of the squid to discover the methods by which nerve impulses were transmitted. Their work was soon interrupted by the war, and both men were drawn into the development of radar. After 1945 they returned to

Cambridge and resumed their work on nerves. It had long been known that there was movement of an electric current between active and resting regions of a nerve, and Hodgkin and Huxley now discovered what ions carried these currents through the membrane of the nerve fibre, and established the factors which turn these components of current on and off. The papers in which the substance of this work was published appeared in 1952 and three years later Huxley joined his colleague as a Fellow of the Royal Society. Five years later he left Cambridge to become Jodrell Professor of Physiology at University College, London – working there at T. H. Huxley's desk which had been shown in at least one famous portrait by John Collier. In 1963 he was, together with Hodgkin and J. C. Eccles, awarded the Nobel Prize for physiology.

Meanwhile Julian's sons, as well as his half-brothers, were also following the familiar pattern of Huxley progress. Anthony, who during the war had married a young W.A.A.F. officer, Ann Taylor, combined writing with the interest in plant life which had sprung from his father's enthusiasm, joined the staff of *Amateur Gardening* and later became editor. It was here, while plodding steadily away at the bread-and-butter work of horticultural and botanical journalism, that he branched out in three individual ways. One was as the author of numerous horticultural and botanical books, the most recent being two authoritative works – *Flowers of the Mediterranean* (written with Oleg Polunin) and *Mountain Flowers*. In addition, he became a superb practitioner in the art of photographing plants in their natural habitats.

In the early 1950s this particular great-grandson of T H, tallish and trimmed to the bone in the usual Huxley way, also became the leader of botanical travel parties, taking them abroad for various agencies to such places as Yugoslavia, Switzerland, Greece, Turkey, Jordan, and Syria on tours designed expressly to provide the maximum botanical interest. Here the knowledge which had filtered in almost unnoticed during the long holidays with his father helped a lot. So did the built-in family assumption that if things went wrong in foreign lands, if transport was late, or the dragoman failed to arrive, then a Huxley would be quite competent to straighten out the tangle. Julian had been known to comment in a casual aside, 'You should have seen the place before the caravan route changed.' Much the same mixture of sophistication and Victorian assurance moved his sons. It was usually justified.

Anthony's younger brother Francis had gone straight from Gordonstoun into the Royal Navy during the war, and went up to Balliol only in 1946, at the age of twenty-three. With a taste for outlandish places he had visited Lapland while still at Gordonstoun; from Oxford he investigated hippos in Gambia and the birds of Jan Mayen Island, and shortly before graduating in zoology had sailed, with his brother, as crew to 'Blondie' Hasler on an ornithological expedition to Sula Sgeir and Rona, those barren outposts fifty miles north-west of Cape Wrath. He had veered from zoology towards anthropology and spent some months living with the Urubu tribe in the Brazilian jungle. His subsequent book, *Affable Savages*, made good reading.

Unwilling to settle, he had gone to the United States, studied social anthropology there on a grant from the Wenner-Gren Foundation and had then applied his experience in a big Canadian mental hospital. He began to travel along that frontier between mind and matter that had attracted his great-grandfather, and produced a penetrating essay on Darwin. After spending some while in Haiti on a study of voodoo, he took a lectureship in social anthropology at St Catherine's College, Oxford and, in his later thirties, settled down to record his Haitian experiences, in *The Invisibles*.

There was no doubt that it was the descendants of Leonard who were following the Huxley pattern most closely. But as Julian looked around in the mid-1950s he saw other sprigs from the family tree which were worthy of note. On the left of the line there was Crispin Tickell, one of TH's great-great-grandsons, later First Secretary in the British Embassy in Paris at the age of thirty-five. Away to the right of the line, Michael's son Thomas, who some people felt bore an astonishing resemblance to the young TH, had followed Francis from Gordonstoun to become the eighth Balliol man in the family and to win a Nature Conservancy research studentship for post-graduate training in ecology. There was Anne Heathorn Cooke's daughter Henrietta, one of the few young women to whom Sir Julian would give unqualified praise for the speed and accuracy with which she could identify a bird. At Oxford, where she had become first Secretary and later Chairman of the Oxford Ornithological Society, as well as an early member of the Oxford Women's Exploration Society, she had taken a degree in English. This dual interest in the arts and the sciences was not the only Huxley trait; for, as one friend was later to put it, she 'found life difficult because she was quite unable to compromise with anything mean or second-rate, either in herself or in the world around her.' On leaving Oxford she had first tried teaching, but was not satisfied and found her vocation working in an approved school. Six weeks after the marriage for which she gave up this career she was to be killed in a road accident while leading her pony home in the dusk. The Henrietta Hutton Fund, administered by the Royal Geographical Society to help Oxford women undergraduates and postgraduates of under twenty-five in travelling abroad for scientific and adventurous purposes, is a memorial to this typical Huxley of the twentieth century.

On the far right of the line there were the two Buzzard brothers, the elder by this time a Crown prosecutor and the younger Director of the National Institute of Industrial Psychology. While distinct from the main family tree there was the collateral line that had produced the second Leonard Huxley – now Sir Leonard, Vice-Chancellor of the Federal University of Australia – and his son George, an archaeologist of distinction, Professor of Greek at the University of Belfast.

Many of the younger Huxleys were themselves to have growing families – Crispin Tickell with his great-great-great-grand-children of TH; Julian's son Anthony with three originally-minded daughters; and other Huxleys and crypto-Huxleys all along the line adding to the numbers. It would have been easy among such a proliferation for Julian to rise to the isolation of the patriarch.

Yet Sir Julian Sorell Huxley, F.R.S., continues to retain his rapture for life, just as his wife still retains her staggering youthfulness. His enthusiasms tumble out in quick succession, broken only by an impatient 'Yes, yes, yes.' For as Wilfrid Ward had written of TH, 'If he heard even a word or two he had the clue to the rest, and seldom failed to follow it successfully' – and at times Julian does not conceal the fact that he has already got there. Perhaps the strongest impression he gives is of unsatiated delight at the beauty and complexity of nature. He will pick up and discuss a photograph of a mouse climbing a ladder for a drink of sherry with as much enjoyment as though it were a unique photograph of a rare specimen. He will expound in great detail on a seventeenth-century coloured print of snails, explaining how their curious sexual habits limit the spread of certain species. And there is an extraordinary innocence in his pleasure as he turns over a pile of old photographs, stops at an unexpected print of two young gibbons dancing together, and gleefully exclaims, 'Aren't they wonderful – absolutely wonderful!'

His multiple interests were epitomized in June 1959, when he and Juliette came to Ronald Lockley's estate in Pembrokeshire for a fortnight during which Skomer Island was to be designated a National Nature Reserve.

In the evenings everyone played the Huxley poetry game, the favourite family pastime, Julian reading out the results at the end of each round. On the 15th they were all taken across to Skomer with its breeding colonies of Manx shearwaters, its puffin colony and its colony of Atlantic grey seals. A week later, on Julian's seventy-second birthday, it was discovered that Ludwig Koch was staying only a few miles away at Tenby. A delighted Koch was brought across as a surprise addition to an equally delighted birthday party at which he sang *lieder* and operatic songs.

A few days later Julian, as persistently energetic as ever, demanded a visit to the nearby island of Skokholm. Juliette followed later; as she walked up from the little landing stage she asked her companion how many people now lived on the island. Eight birdwatchers and four lighthouse keepers, she was told. 'How splendid,' she exclaimed. 'We'll all be able to play the poetry game.'

Chapter XVII

Aldous: Interpreting the Dream

(*i*)

The Europe in which so many Huxleys were active in the late 1940s was a continent still recovering but slowly from the wounds of war, still only half aware that nuclear fission had altered everything, only dimly conscious that politically, economically, as well as in other ways, the only salvation lay in cutting the painter with the past. For Aldous, who returned in 1948, Europe was as depressing as America, where greater power than ever before had been concentrated in fewer hands. He had outlined the position as he saw it in *Science, Liberty and Peace*, implored the scientists to do something about it with the fervour of his pre-war pacifist pamphlet, and was under no illusion about the notice that would be taken of him.

He came back with Maria. Together they nostalgically visited Italy, going to Siena, where a quarter of a century earlier they had watched the *palio*, a city whose St Catherine had long attracted Aldous as a subject for biography. They went to Sanary, through Paris, and on to London where a dramatized version of *The Gioconda Smile* was about to be produced.

This version differed from the long short story from which it was adapted, and the differences do not seem to have been due solely to the demands of drama. There was the conversion of the unjustly condemned Hutton whose excruciating experiences were at first 'the only reality'. But

> then, all at once, the pain stops and, for the first time since it started, you see that there's a sun in the sky, you realize that those shadows out there are real people, you discover that your own wretched body isn't the whole world; there's all the rest of the universe.

This was not all; conversion brought both its own reward and an ending that was most ingeniously contrived sent the public home with happy heart and clear conscience.

After the première at the New Theatre, Aldous and Maria returned to the United States. But this time, unlike the occasion a decade earlier, they crossed the Atlantic without doubts. They returned only temporarily to Llano, then let their house and moved on to a new home. This lay 6,000 feet up in the Sierra Madre Mountains, a white bungalow at Wrightwood, a village of some fifty inhabitants lying in the Swartout Valley, sheltered by pines, and only a few miles from the route taken by the Mormon Battalion which in 1851 came this way to settle San Bernardino Valley.

Here the Huxleys settled, less remote than in their eremitic retreat, exchanging for the desert a new landscape of mountains and canyon. Aldous was an unusual inhabitant, long to be remembered for his amiability, and in some ways unlike the other English expatriates who had settled in the far West before and during the war. He never lost his quintessentially English accent that only just failed to parody the American idea of a British voice. He dressed casually but well, not foppishly but with care, and in spite of the international character of his wardrobe somehow managed to convey an impression of irreproachable Englishness; few men were more truly cosmopolitan or more obviously so, yet in Wrightwood, as elsewhere, he remained for ever Eton and Balliol.

Here, in April 1948, he heard that his old family friend and companion, E. S. P. Haynes, husband of TH's eldest grand-daughter Oriana, had died in London.

> The last time I saw him, in October [he wrote], he remarked that he expected that he would die in the following spring. He was a good prophet. Modern circumstances are such that we shall not look upon his like again; for he belonged to that curious and very delightful species of the English Eccentrics – and there is no place for the Eccentric under a system of Fabian Socialism. Our world is too tidy to admit of marvellous disorder, the Dickensian leisureliness of an office such as Ted's. His death marks the passing not only of a friend, but also of an epoch of history and, one might almost say, a character in fiction.

The Huxleys were at Wrightwood when *Ape and Essence* was published. This was a fantasy of the future described by some European critics as the worst of all Aldous's works, and by the Soviet *Literary Gazette* as a 'dirty, disgusting, evil-smelling book', which 'breathes the stenching pathological hatred of humanity'.

As on earlier occasions, the message had been largely misunderstood. For the grotesque civilization of *Ape and Essence*, discovered in the United States after the first nuclear world war, was described as warning rather than example. The occasional reviewer might suggest that Huxley was merely revealing the California which lay only just beneath the skin, nuclear war or not, and the suggestion did little to mollify Americans; the truth was merely that 'the bomb' represented the culmination of that physical suffering and mutilation with which Aldous had been so obsessively concerned for so much of his life. Here, concentrated in a mere pound or so of a single natural element, was the ultimate potential expression of man's soaring intellect and of his physically vulnerable body. Heredity had helped to make Aldous an inquiring pessimist; environment, as he saw it in the post-war world, had merely driven home the lesson. For a writer with the macabre at his fingertips, the natural expression of opinion was through such a book as *Ape and Essence* with its science controlled by war-minded ape-men, its population clothed from disinterred corpses and its fuel provided by the books of the great libraries.

Such horrified reaction as came to Aldous's knowledge – he no longer read reviews since by the time they appeared he was already absorbed in his next project – was received with pained reasoning and an emphasis on the purely practical commonsense rightness of what he had said. Nuclear warfare, as he pointed out in a radio interview with John Davenport, might not be the worst possibility. There was always biological warfare. The prospect had to be considered calmly, the ensuing panic to be prepared for intelligently:

> If one visits a place like New York, one can imagine the horror of that panic; from Manhattan Island to get on to the mainland you have about three tunnels and then about fifteen miles upstream one bridge, over which several million people will have to go; when they get on to the other side, they will find themselves in an enormous built-up area, extending for hundreds of square miles, and it looks as though you might almost disrupt an entire industrial economy without taking the trouble to drop a single bomb or let loose a single bacterium, merely by this terrible psychological result of years of fear-preparation.

Yet even from this prospect – and one can imagine the slight, despairing shrug of the shoulder when hope in rational argument ran out – man would be unlikely to recoil. 'In a few years,' he later reminisced, 'perhaps another ten countries may have the bomb. Perhaps even Princess Grace of Monaco might be in a position to press a button and launch one in a few years.'

In this pessimistic frame of mind he worked on. His sight was as dependent as ever on external conditions. Thus in a dimly lit restaurant he would need a magnifying glass to see small print. Yet out of doors, in the bright Californian sunlight, 'he got by'. His acute hearing helped him in traffic and his acute memory helped him on his solitary hillside walks, although in later years he suffered from one fall which might have been serious but which caused only a few bruises. He did not always need glasses – a result, he still firmly believed, of having followed the Bates method – and one old friend from England tells how he advanced down his garden to meet her, making for a small stream which separated them, and for a smaller foot-bridge which she felt he could not possibly see; he crossed it without hesitation. Indoors, he still worked without glasses. He would breakfast at 8.30, type all the morning, lunch at 12.30, always take at least an hour's afternoon walk, and then continue with work on his return. It was the regular routine of the professional, of the man who wrote slowly but at the 500 words a day which could provide two 75,000-word novels a year.

His next major book, *The Devils of Loudun*, had in some ways grown out of *Grey Eminence*. For during his earlier researches he had been fascinated by the case of Father Surin, the Jesuit whose fate had become inextricably entangled with the supposed possession of the Ursuline nuns at Loudun in the 1630s.

> Demonology as such doesn't interest me [he explained later], only the particular case of Loudun because it happened to involve a very remarkable man, Father Surin. In itself, the subject is almost infinitely squalid – at once comical and loathsome, like all low-grade 'supernaturalism' that is preoccupied with evil.

Yet it was a subject which enabled him to record, once again, a poignant example from his ceaseless investigation of beliefs and the ends to which they could be turned.

The long research which went into *The Devils of Loudun* emphasized to Aldous the immensity of the interior evil against which the spirit has to fight. It emphasized, yet again, that even in the ecstatic world of the fully evolved mystic, the force raised to the highest level might just as likely be for evil as for good. Even so, this world on a different level was the world to which mankind should aspire. For Aldous himself, aspiration was helped by his ability to relax anywhere, almost at will. Yet even for Aldous problems remained, and their solution was not aided by the stature of his formidable mind. Lesser men would find it easier to slough off their surrounding trappings and to retreat into that silent garden where all might be seen or felt; for Aldous Huxley there was always some titillating absurdity, some immense complexity, some intriguing contradiction which the day-to-day world presented minute by minute for attention. Meditative and contemplative he could be, at a level and of a completeness sufficient for most men; but the world here and now would break in just when the step upwards to a different reality was about to be made. For the life of mid-twentieth-century man was in many ways epitomized in Aldous; the manifold attachments against which he was brushed by circumstance, the mere contiguity with the apparatus of a busy life, tended to create barriers between one reality and the next. While it was part of his talent that these barriers were thinner than they were for most people, they nevertheless existed. This helps to explain why he was, by 1953, so eager to seize the chance which then came of breaking through them.

For years, Aldous's mind had ranged across anthropological territory, taking special notice of the various ceremonies and rites in which, by a variety of stimulating means, primitive people appear to be translated to another level of experience and to become, without death, Tennyson's 'breathers of an ampler day'. Among these rites were those of the native tribes whose territory spread across both sides of the U.S. frontier with Mexico, rites which involved the use of an extract from the *peyotl* cactus which was alleged to produce hallucinations of a unique kind. These hallucinations might have some connection with the other-world of the mystic; they might also, moreover, provide fresh information about the relationship between mind and matter which had so intrigued TH with its apparently unanswerable conundrums nearly three-quarters of a century ago.

It was with great interest, therefore, that Aldous read in 1952 an article on psychological medicine in the *Hibbert Journal.* Of the two authors, one was Humphrey Osmond, an Englishman then working in Canada, and when Osmond attended the Los Angeles meeting of the American Psychiatric Association in the spring of 1953 he was invited to stay with the Huxleys. He brought with him a small quantity of mescalin. And after a good deal of self-inquiry, he decided to ask Aldous to 'take' some.

> I was uneasy [he has written]. Aldous and Maria would be sad if it did not work, but what if it worked too well? Should I cut the dose in half? The setting could hardly have been better, Aldous seemed an ideal subject, Maria eminently sensible, and we had all taken to each other, which was very important for a good experience; but I

did not relish the possibility, however remote, of being the man who drove Aldous Huxley mad.

He stirred the water as the silvery white mescalin crystals dissolved and handed the glass to Aldous, who was sitting with a dictaphone by his side, ready to describe what he hoped would be a new and most extraordinary experience. The mescalin began to work. In Osmond's words, 'it slowly etched away the patina of conceptual thinking; the doors of perception were cleansed, and Aldous perceived things with less interference from his enormous rationalizing brain.'

This first experience was repeated again and yet again, although it was only on the first occasion that the drug was taken under medical supervision. Later Huxley said that to take it thus was the worst way of doing it; the surroundings should be aesthetic rather than scientific; and one's companion in the experience should be an understanding friend, an artist, someone who was not too scientifically implicated, since the nature of the experience was not scientific. From 1953 onwards Aldous took one of the psychedelic materials–usually L.S.D.–sometimes once, sometimes twice, a year; partly so that the potentialities of the drug might be assessed, partly because he believed that its use enabled him to step up to a higher level of consciousness, partly because his rational being believed that he was grasping the key to some new and hitherto unexpected link between mind and matter. The breathing disciplines of yoga, after all, altered the concentrations of carbon dioxide in the blood and these changes were simultaneous with the new view of reality to which the yogi attained; the abstinence of those who fasted produced chemical changes which were apparently concurrent with voices heard and visions seen. What, after all, was so unlikely in the suggestion that chemical compounds might open the door to comparable experiences?

Huxley's first sensations under mescalin were recounted in *The Doors of Perception*, his later ones in *Heaven and Hell*. Both short books were to an extent interim reports and it was only later, when the experiences had been absorbed and cogitated upon, that he gave his more considered opinion. There were two aspects of this, complementary though just faintly at odds with one another. The overwhelmingly more important aspect was summed up in his blunt statement in *Life* that:

> When administered in the right kind of psychological environment, these chemical mind-changers make possible a genuine religious experience. Thus a person who takes L.S.D. or mescalin may suddenly understand – not only intellectually but organically, experientially – the meaning of such tremendous religious affirmations as 'God is Love', or 'Though He slay me, yet will I trust Him'.

> ... My belief is that, though they may start by being something of an embarrassment, these new mind-changers will tend in the long run to deepen the spiritual life of the communities in which they are available.

And again, only a year before his death, he described the results with the same unqualified praise:

> The bodily effects are trifling, but the memory of them persists, and so does the mind's comprehension. I found myself temporarily in a world where everything shone with an inner light and was of boundless significance. Words like 'grace' and 'transfiguration' came to my mind. The splendour and richness of bare existence were revealed to me.

A slightly different account was given in England. Of mescalin, Aldous wrote:

> It permits, under suitable conditions, the exploration of the stranger and odder areas of the human mind. This is one of the things which has emerged in recent years: not only is the material universe incomparably larger and stranger than we used to give it any credit for, but the mental universe is also larger and stranger than we give it credit for; we carry about inside our skulls an extraordinary, visionary, mystical world. The interesting fact about these substances is that they open a door and permit us, without doing any physiological harm to ourselves, to explore this world.

These two comments represent, perhaps, little more than a difference of emphasis, yet the difference was important. For the transcendental transformations of mescalin and its companions might be possible only for takers of the Aldous calibre. It had already been pointed out that

> Huxley's experience under the influence of mescalin corresponds so closely to the mystical transfiguration longingly described in his writings that one can't help wondering to what extent wish-fulfilment was involved. It would be instructive to know the effects of mescalin on, say, a sports car maniac or an acquisitive chorus girl.

The answer to this query was at least implied by Huxley's statement in England; even for those of non-Huxley calibre, the drug might be a tool for mental exploration – although the claim of physiological harmlessness appears ingenuous.

Moreover, however much one may feel that escape through mescalin is a second-best escape, it is impossible to deny that after 1953 Aldous reached another stage in his search for the ultimate reality. In a last golden decade all the affectations and most of the mental inconsistencies now seemed to be cast aside. Fate was to hit him between the eyes thrice more; but now he knew better how to take the blows and the fact was reflected in his writing. The bludgeonings of half a century earlier – his mother's death, blindness, Trev's suicide – had all warned him to think rather than to feel, had warned him of the need for 'accepting the horror of life and saying to oneself that in spite of everything, the universe is good'.

Now in the autumn of 1953, Maria learned that she was suffering from cancer. At first it was not clear how far the disease had spread, and Aldous hoped on. Then, as his wife's condition worsened and orthodox medicine had no effect, he resorted in desperation to the less and less orthodox. Hypnotism, acupuncture, and the psycho-pharmacological 'expanders of consciousness' were all tried. When these failed he flew with Maria to the Lebanon in search of a miracle-worker. They returned to Los Angeles still unsuccessful, and by early 1955 he knew that she was dying. As he sat with her he remembered that spring night in Vence twenty-five years before, when they both had sat by the dying Lawrence. Now he could offer more aid, and taking the Mahayana office for the dying, went with her to the edge of the world they both knew. 'It is difficult,' he wrote later to Frieda Lawrence, 'to know what one can do for someone who is dying, incidentally for oneself. What I did seemed to be of some help to her, as well as for me. The men of the middle ages used to talk of *ars moriendi*, the art of dying.' With the letter he sent some pages which he had written after her death – 'I can't get over it,' Frieda wrote to a friend, 'so moving. How he helped her to die in utter love and compassion. No slop . . .'

At first it seemed that without Maria he was lost. For him, it was, as he later said, 'as if I had been amputated.' She had been more than the eyes of an often near-blind husband, more than a helpmeet, more than a wife, more than the driver of cars, reader of books, typer of letters. In Igor Stravinsky's words she 'knew little but understood everything', and she had been part of him.

He spoke little and showed less, English still in his reticence.

> We worried about him continually [wrote Robert Craft]. How could he bear to go on living in that empty, penumbral house? He would allow me, taking him home at night, to accompany him to the door and fit the key in the lock, but he resisted boy-scouting and would refuse my help in, for example, crossing streets – passages which I could only watch (or not watch) in terror.

Few sensed what had happened. It was not that he had recovered. It was that after Maria's death he had become a different kind of thinking being. 'Her death,' wrote Frieda Lawrence to a friend, 'did something to him. Something burst out of him.' And then, in 1956, he decided to marry again.

(*ii*)

In 1956 Aldous's son Matthew was in his early thirties and had successfully launched himself on a career that had followed three-and-a-half years pre-medical training in the University of Colorado. He had joined the army on America's entry into the second world war but had later contracted an illness – 'due, I feel sure,' his father wrote, 'to his reacting badly to all that horse serum they pump into recruits by way of immunizing them'. He was eventually discharged, worked for a while in the story department of the Warner Brothers Burbank Studios, and then took his B.A. Thence he had evolved into a public health administrator through a series of posts with such bodies as the Health Insurance Plan of Greater New York, the American Public Health Association, the Milbank Memorial Fund and the National Institute of Mental Health.

And in 1961 Matthew Huxley had been drawn into the study which had so fascinated his father, his grandfather, and many assorted Huxleys along the line. A friend had asked whether he could find a young anthropologist to study the Amahuaca Indians, a tribe living deep in the Amazonian jungles of Peru and an example of Stone Age man whose culture had almost miraculously survived unchanged for some 3,500 years. Huxley approached three or four likely people: all had field assignments. Eventually he decided to do the job himself. 'That,' he says, 'was the beginning of my love affair with South America.'

With the photographer Cornell Capa he left New York in the summer of 1961 for Puesto Varadero, a community of only seventeen families living on the Peruvian–Brazilian frontier, and maintained by American linguist-missionaries of the Summer Institute of Linguistics. Here the two lived for three months, photographing, taking notes, watching, and trying to form a picture of the Amahuaca mind. 'It was a passionate mutual exchange of watching,' Huxley says. 'I was trying to tell what their daily lives were like and they were as uninhibited about me.' The result of the three months – and of a good deal of hard work on return to New York – was *Farewell to Eden*. It is unlikely to be his last book.

Living now in Washington, working as assistant chief in the National Institute of Mental Health's Office of Planning, he seems to have been diverted permanently towards subjects which are in the main Huxley stream.

Aldous's family was therefore settled and flourishing as, in the early spring of 1956, he decided to take a second wife.

About ten years previously he had been approached by a young Italian violinist, Laura Archera. She had come to the United States before the war, had returned to Italy in 1947 and in Siena had watched the *palio*, the medieval horse-race still run round the cobbled piazza. Back in America she had conceived the idea of a film which would deal with this event, had read Aldous's account of the race, first published in the *Cornhill Magazine* in 1935. She had written to him suggesting that he might write the script for the film, had met him, had interested M.G.M. The idea had trickled out in the sands of cinematic indifference but her friendship with the Huxleys had flourished. Now, early in May, Aldous proposed to Laura and they decided to marry. To avoid publicity they drove to the nearest point on the State frontier with Arizona, crossed it, and being thus free of the Californian registry regulations, were married in the 'Drive-In Wedding Chapel'. A few days later they were back in Los Angeles.

Outwardly Aldous had changed little, although those who studied him at close range might have noted an increase in intensity, a heightened awareness of the work still to be done. He was busy now with *Brave New World Revisited*, initially a series of articles for a Long Island paper, throwing a backward glance at his awful prophecies of a quarter of a century earlier. In some ways they had not been too awful or too far out. The world had already gone some way towards fulfilling the prophecy, tranquillizers having taken the place of 'Soma', subliminal advertising and television standing in for thought-control, and a growing concentration of ever greater power coming under the control of ever smaller brains.

He was invited to Brazil by the President, who hoped that he would write about the country, and for a few weeks experienced an adulation he had known nowhere else. Whenever he left his hotel he was mobbed for autographs, while in Rio de Janeiro one of the papers published a column headed '*O Sabio*' (the Sage) outlining his views daily. 'It is', he commented, 'the only place in the world where anyone wants to read a literary gent's opinion about things in general day after day.'

He became busy with plans for lecturing, since he had discovered only a few years previously not only that he enjoyed it, but that he could speak well to large audiences and that there was a ready outlet for what he had to say. Thus in the spring of 1960 he was invited to the Menninger Foundation in Topeka, Kansas, as the twelfth Sloan Visiting Professor, and lectured extensively for six weeks, not only as the Sloan lecturer – on 'Who Are We?', 'Psychic or Visionary Experiences', 'The Individual in History' and 'Human Potentialities' – but to numerous other audiences in Kansas. In the autumn he was the M.I.T.'s Visiting Professor for the Humanities. Within these few years after his second marriage it did seem as though, in Frieda Lawrence's words, something 'had burst out of him'. It was almost as if a new awareness of what he had been trying to say all his life had suddenly been born within him. This indeed may well have been so, for throughout this period he had one overwhelming preoccupation – development of the work which had been in his mind for a number of years and which he had at last begun to write about fifteen months after Maria's death: the novel in which he tried to create 'a new society, where the potentialities latent in individual people are realized, thanks to a synthesis of Eastern and Western thinking'.

And now the second blow was coming.

On the afternoon of 12 May 1961 Aldous was taking his usual walk through the scrub-covered hills which rise north of Hollywood. He may well have known that a brush-fire was raging at places across the slopes since they are not uncommon; but he heard with astonishment from a passer-by that his own house was threatened. He returned to find it already burning – although by a capricious turn of the wind the neighbouring building was unscathed – and Laura saving what she could. He himself managed to salvage only three suits and the manuscript of his novel. He did not, contrary to reports, have to be restrained from dashing back into the flaming house; instead, when it was certain that no more could be done, he appeared to take the loss philosophically, and prepared to drive off with Laura. Amid the smoke and the confusion there was a difficulty which was solved by a group of local children:

> The gang warned me about fifteen minutes before the arrival of the TV camera-trucks, which in turn, were half an hour ahead of the fire-engines that could have saved the house. After the boys had guided me to safety, by the one passable street, I noticed that some familiar faces among them were absent. I said I was concerned about them, but the leader told me not to worry, that they were merely out starting more fires.

He was calm enough. But the fire had ravaged him. Lost in the flames there was the first edition of *Candide*, a legacy from his grandfather;

there were forty letters from Lawrence, ten from H. L. Mencken, others from Arnold Bennett, Paul Valéry, H. G. Wells, Virginia Woolf and a host of others. There were the manuscripts of *Those Barren Leaves, Point Counter Point, Eyeless in Gaza* and many another of his works. These losses were difficult enough to bear, yet there was more. For the product of his half-century's reading lay in countless annotations, in miscellaneous jottings, in half-thoughts and suggestions and casually set-down ideas, which he would fuse with the travels of his mind; all these were gone, as well as the innumerable small souvenirs of the human associations which had helped to make his life. Maria's diary, in which she had written every day of their life together, had gone. All these, the professional working materials and the tiny things which had combined to become an extension of himself, were all destroyed, burned back into depersonalized fragments. 'Three-quarters of myself is lost,' was his personal verdict to his family.

To friends, Aldous presented a more resigned front. 'I am evidently intended to learn, a little in advance of the final denudation, that you can't take it with you,' he wrote to one friend; and to Renée Tickell: 'It is hard, but it teaches one detachment. It is easy to think one has achieved it, but this demands the real thing.' To the fact-hungry public he showed the bleak but phrase-turning attitude that he knew was expected of him. The fire, he commented in one interview, could perhaps

> be interpreted as a hint from whatever powers are on high that I should break from my old bookish life. . . . Some 3,000 books were burnt. I had annotated them and indexed them in my fashion; now I shall have to start reading them again. A curious thing about losing everything is that I now have no past. I often picked up my old diaries and letters, and things came back to me that I had completely forgotten. Now I can't do this – so it follows that I have not a past – a very interesting condition. Maybe it is an object lesson that one shouldn't live in the past.

There have been few modern examples of a philosopher taking such a loss so philosophically. Yet it was also a warning. 'I took it,' he wrote of the fire to one medical friend, 'as a sign that the grim reaper was having a good look at me.'

Maybe. For only six months previously he had lain in a Los Angeles hospital and, following tests and observation, had heard the doctors diagnose cancer of the tongue. He called in the doctor who had been consulted when cancer was first diagnosed in Maria, and it was agreed that a course of radium treatment should first be tried. The needles worked. Within a few months the treatment was successful and in 1961 he was able to visit Europe. He met his new wife's relatives in Turin and went south to visit Danilo Dolci in Sicily. At St Paul de Vence he attended the international conference organized by the Parapsychology Foundation, went on to Zurich where he conferred with Dr Albert Hoffman, the chemist who was attempting to control the mind by minute biochemical changes, and then flew on to Copenhagen to attend the International Congress of Applied Psychology.

He returned to Los Angeles in time for the publication of *Island*.

This was to be his last novel, the book whose partly completed manuscript he had snatched from the flames, a book which he had continued in Gerald Heard's home at Santa Monica and on which he had toiled throughout 1960. *Island*, the story of Pala, where men had learned how to live, was to be his final major book. All his years of distress, all his experiences and all his learning, now seemed to contribute to this story of 'a society in which a serious effort is made to help its members to realize their desirable potential.' It was the story of a non-existent but plausible state of life, yet it was strangely different from *Brave New World* and from *Ape and Essence*. The difference was not only that here at last Huxley was describing a society with which he felt personal sympathy. It was not merely that he drew for it on his own experiences, recreating the death of Maria with a tenderness which he normally reserved for real life and tended to keep from his novels. It is possible that he took more trouble over the book, sensing that it might be his last. It is possible that his feeling of personal identification with this picture of life as he felt it should be lived helped to raise his professional ability to a higher level, so that again and again one finds in it what C. E. Montague once called 'a splinter of perfection in the art of letters'. Whatever the cause or causes, *Island* describes a society not merely credible but so real that the reader may wonder when some lone discoverer among the eastern archipelagos will find his vessel swept towards its shores.

Curiously enough, he had worked away at the book, with its deeply conceived solutions to personal problems, while his wife had been solving comparable ones nearby. For Laura Huxley had become a practising psychotherapist, and while Aldous was writing *Island* in one room she was dealing with patients in another – and evolving principles and methods later outlined in *You Are Not the Target*, a book which was to sell no less than 250,000 copies in the United States alone.

This conjunction was paralleled by others. For in *Island* Aldous had taken immense pains to translate his philosophy into fictional practice.

> Nothing is easier, of course, than to enumerate ideals, and to say wouldn't it be nice if everybody were good and kind and loving and so on [he explained later]. Of course, it would be very nice, but how do you implement these ideals? How do you fulfil your good social and psychological intentions? When you come down to this problem you see it is a very complex one, of organizing family life, organizing education, organizing sexual life, organizing social and economic life. There are endless factors involved, and I found it a very interesting job, so far as I was concerned, to try to work out what these factors should be.

It was not only interesting but also hard work, involving, as he himself put it in his introduction to Laura's *You Are Not the Target*, 'the picking of a considerable variety of brains', and a great deal of reading.

> Greek history, Polynesian anthropology, translations from Sanskrit and Chinese or Buddhist texts, scientific papers on pharmacology, neurophysiology, psychology and education, together with novels, poems, critical essays, travel books, political commentaries and conversations with all kinds of people, from philosophers to actresses, from patients in mental hospitals to tycoons in Rolls-Royces – everything went into the hopper and became grist for my Utopian mill.

From the mill came a book in which the philosophical drama was played out by marvellously real people; and a book in which Huxley, stubbornly true to the evidence as he saw it, finally matched the triumph of pessimistic reality – 'the yelling of quietly authoritative hypnotists ... the tribes of buffoons and hucksters, the professional liars, the purveyors of entertaining irrelevancies' – with the everlastingness of another reality. For although the oil-men take over Pala, the armoured cars pass by and

> the fact of enlightenment remained. The roarings of the engines diminished, the squeaking rhetoric lapsed into an inarticulate murmur, and as the intruding noises died away, out came the frogs again, out came the uninterruptable insects, out came the mynah birds.

There was not much hope; but there was at least a little.

It would have been easy for Huxley to regard *Island* as the climax of his life, the setting-down of his final conclusions, for it now became necessary for a cancerous gland to be removed from his neck. He did not appear to be unduly alarmed and led the discussion with his doctor to the theory that the body had an unknown capacity to destroy cancer cells. 'Cancer isn't always the winner,' he commented. 'Perhaps my body is building up its own resistance.'

He decided to visit Europe again. He continued working and he began putting the finishing touches to *Literature and Science*, an essay in which he developed and expanded his grandfather's exposition of 'the great truth that art and literature and science are one'.

He sometimes lectured. And in the spring of 1962 he gave one particular lecture which, because of its subject-matter, its reception, and even the place at which it was delivered, had the uncanny quality of bringing his life to the edge of the cliff.

For some while the Los Alamos Scientific Laboratory had held a series of four or five annual evening lectures, open to all, at which distinguished scholars, mostly in the field of science, spoke on a subject of their own choosing. Aldous was invited to lecture early in May, and travelled with Laura to this high barren plateau of New Mexico which he had described, thirty years previously, as the home of his innocent savage in *Brave New World*. Now New Mexico was known for something else, for while the Los Alamos laboratory was technically a part of the University of California, it was also the brain-centre which had produced the world's first nuclear weapons, and was still busy improving them.

The Huxleys arrived the day before the lecture and Aldous insisted on inspecting the Indian caves and ruins tunnelled from the sheer walls of the nearby Frijoles Canyon. His interests were less archaeological than artistic, being concentrated on the colours of the rocks, of the lichens, and of the blue sky above the enclosing canyon walls. He was in no doubt about the past, and when a companion remarked on the problem of the inhabitants who had had to raise water to the cave-entrances 150 feet above the ground, he merely commented: 'No problem in those days. Indian merely tell squaw: "Go down and fetch water."'

The following evening it was soon clear that the auditorium would be unusually full. At most of the evening lectures only a half to two-thirds of the 650 seats were usually occupied. On this occasion something novel had happened. By the time Aldous entered the auditorium not only were all seats filled, but adults and children were sitting in the aisles and lining the walls. Some had even found places along the edge of the stage. In fact, it was later discovered, many high school pupils had been brought by their teachers – not only from Santa Fé, thirty-five miles away, but also from Albuquerque, one hundred miles off, and Las Vegas at double that distance. A few had even come from El Paso, three hundred miles to the south. In all, about 1,100 people had come to this isolated fastness some 7,000 feet up, in order to hear a single brief lecture.

Aldous spoke on visionary experience. He dealt with the various mental experiences which can be induced by different stimulants. He dealt with impressions and voices and beliefs, and in the territory where his grandfather had walked ill at ease he now walked with more certain tread. Something of his integrity brushed off on to the audience, even on to those for whom much of the talk was inexplicable. There was a quite exceptional ovation.

Aldous returned to Los Angeles already prematurely aged and enfeebled, but rallied through the summer. During the autumn and early winter, he prepared one of his last papers, 'The Politics of Ecology; The Question of Survival'. Written as one of the Occasional Papers on the Free Society published by the Center for the Study of Democratic Institutions, it analysed the world's looming problems and came up with an opinion that might have been echoed by his brother Julian.

> My own view [wrote Aldous] is that only by shifting our collective attention from the merely political to the basic biological aspects of the human situation can we hope to mitigate and shorten the time of troubles into which, it would seem, we are now moving. We cannot do without politics; but we can no longer afford to indulge in bad, unrealistic politics. To work for the survival of the species as a whole and for the actualization in the greatest possible number of individual men and women of their potentialities for good will, intelligence and creativity – this, in the world of today, is good, realistic politics.

Objective, informed, beautifully written and still with the unexpected word thrown suddenly in the face to startle or shock, this brief survey of the world and its problems summed up one facet of Aldous's views in the first months of 1963.

Later in the year he and Laura visited Europe together for the last time. They travelled to Stockholm where he worked hard to persuade the World Academy to study human potential. They stayed for a while with Julian and Juliette in London. Then they visited Laura's family in Italy, as they had done almost every summer since 1957. Yet he was still preparing for future work. This time it was another novel. 'They become more difficult as one gets older,' he commented. 'I've made several false starts on this one. I had the idea, but not the body, but now I think I've got it.' The scene would be not the United States but Devon, since the setting needed historical depth – 'California has space but little time,' he remarked. By October he was back there. And by

October he was becoming weaker, sitting in pyjamas at his typewriter as long as he was able and then writing from his bed, in large block letters on a big yellow pad, the sentences of his last essay, 'Shakespeare and Religion'.

What was he really thinking? Luckily he had gone on record for an inquiring interviewer, less than a year earlier. To the correspondent of *Réalités*, Danielle Hunebelle, he spoke of how he had been drawn to Zen Buddhism. He spoke of how mescalin and later psilocybin had helped him to understand some features of that frontier between the body and the soul. And he came in one paragraph to the ultimate question:

> I think it likely that we are going to survive death, yes. There are certain facts that one can scarcely interpret other than in terms of the after-life. I know people here with unusual perceptive gifts. In New York I have had personal experiences through a woman who has extraordinary mediumistic powers, Mrs Garrett, the director of the Parapsychology Foundation. I have had communications concerning people whom I used to know very well, and who are now dead. There is no conclusive evidence about survival, since it is always possible to explain these phenomena in terms of telepathy. All the same, one of my friends, a Cambridge philosopher, says: 'I should be distinctly more irritated than surprised if I were to find myself surviving after death.' And the thing that he says rather humorously is something which I deeply feel.

Now, in the autumn of 1963, he had one more brief stay in the Cedars of Lebanon hospital. But treatment was no longer having any effect, and he returned to the house of the friend with whom he and Laura had lived since the fire two and a half years previously. On 21 November he was able to dictate the final parts of 'Shakespeare and Religion'.

Throughout the whole of his adult life he had walked into the headlines without intending it; during the long week-end of the years between the wars his name had been one of the relatively few in the literary world always to excite interest; and during his quarter of a century of life in America, as the sensational headlines gave way increasingly to longer and more serious accounts of the lessons he was trying to teach, his importance grew. The passing of Aldous Huxley would certainly stir a sizeable segment of the literate world.

Once again chance stepped in. He died on the afternoon of 22 November a few hours after the death of President Kennedy.

Prospect

The death of Aldous Huxley in the autumn of 1963 raised questions very similar to those posed by the death of TH at the end of the nineteenth century. Were the family's future prospects as glittering as past achievements? Would the disappearance of a dominating figure be the prelude to disintegration of the family's corporate body? In any case – and particularly by the time of Aldous's death – was the genetic inheritance by now so diluted as to make any resemblance to the family prototype merely a combination of hindsight and wishful thinking? Would it be possible for this particular aristocracy to survive down the years, keeping alive a name with the constancy of the Percys, the Salisburys and the Douglases, even though unaided by the gift on birth of hereditary position and hard cash? Could it be done on brains alone?

To this set of questions there was in the 1960s added another. By this time a hundred years had passed since TH had leaped to arms in defence of *The Origin*, almost a century since he had asked for an answer to that question of questions, a definition of man's place in nature. And it was now pertinent to ask whether the Huxley characteristics went beyond a purely scientific interest in evolution and its cognate problems. Were there other broader questions to which they almost inevitably returned at the end of the day; was there a typical intellectual stance which they adopted; were there beliefs, attitudes of mind, certain constancies, recurring regularly so that one could, in spite of human individuality, recognize a Huxley by his talk almost as surely as a man's regiment could be recognized by his shoulder-flashes or his buttons?

Any clear answer to the first set of questions is confused statistically by the wide spread of the family across any one generation, brought about by the length of time which passed between the birth of TH's eldest and youngest children, and by the fact that Leonard Huxley's two marriages produced children whose ages were separated by more than thirty years. Dilution alone also makes it dangerous to be dogmatic about any 'family form', the great-great-grandchildren of TH now pressing successfully upward through life having but one-sixteenth of their genes from him and fifteen-sixteenths from other sources, while the younger Huxleys now entering the lists have but one thirty-second of them.

Even so, the form looks encouraging, the quality still well above average. Andrew Huxley as the family's first Nobel Prize winner, Crispin Tickell, TH's great-great-grandson in the Foreign Office, are only two of the most obvious examples. Sir Julian's two sons in the fields of botany and anthropology would stand well towards the top of any family's achievement lists, while Michael's son Tom and Aldous's son Matthew are in similar positions in the race. There is also, and more especially among the younger members of the family, a stubborn strain of individuality, a knobbly core running through the Huxley lives – typified by Anthony Huxley's eldest daughter Susan, training as a cow-hand on Cyrus Eaton's ranch and revealing an unexpected expertise with steers. Such examples, which seem likely to be supplemented by the succession of Huxleys, Colliers, Tickells and Buzzards knocking at the university gates, all suggest that the family is likely to remain in the mental A-level groups, if not for ever at least for another generation or so.

It seems likely that the strain will run true to type. Physically, the abundant energy and the spare nervous frame repeats itself down the generations. Intellectually the interests are the expected ones – man and his environment, the spread of scientific knowledge, the problem of the world's resources and how to manage them for the common good. All this is expected and, to a more general degree than might be statistically expected, all this is given. Yet there is something more. There is, faint at times it is true but almost always discernible, an underlying groundswell of beliefs. Of these the most expected is the view that, in TH's words, 'science and literature are not two things, but two sides of the same thing'. At a Royal Academy dinner he once underlined that while it was 'the business of the artist and the man of letters to reproduce and fix forms of imagination to which the mind will afterwards recur with pleasure,' so it was 'the business of the man of science to symbolize, and fix, and represent to our mind in some readily recallable shape, the order, and the symmetry, and the beauty that prevail throughout nature'. Julian has pointed out that 'No sensible man of science imagines for a moment that the scientific point of view is the only one. Art and literature, religion and humane studies are other ways of exploring and describing the world, and each yields results unobtainable by other methods.' The last book that Aldous saw through the press set out a somewhat similar argument with the insight of an artist who knew much about science and the polish of a scientist who was also a man of letters. And it was Sir Leonard, the physicist, who as Vice-Chancellor of the Australian National University announced that under his direction writers, painters, musicians and sculptors were to be paid £40 a week 'to free them from economic anxiety and routine tasks for a substantial period'.

This continuing emphasis on the belief that a battle between the two cultures is not so much an age-old struggle as one fought on the wrong ground for the wrong reasons is but one half of a continuing ethos. The other half has been presented in various guises, it has been stressed with varying inflection and it directly confronts the popular image of the Huxleys, the bogy-figure built up of arrogant scientist and confident iconoclast. This other half of the Huxley belief was hinted at in *Nature*, a few weeks after TH's death, by his great friend, the physiologist Michael Foster, who was later to edit his *Scientific Memoirs*:

> Great as he felt science to be, he was aware that science could never lay its hands, could never touch, even with the tip of its finger, that dream with which our little life is rounded, and that unknown dream was a power as dominant over him as was the might of known science.

That power suffused much of TH's work and writings. He wrote of Nature as being 'nowhere inaccessible . . . everywhere unfathomable'. He believed that 'the fundamental doctrines of materialism, like those of spiritualism, and most other 'isms, lie outside the limits of philosophical inquiry'. He once wrote of 'that limited revelation of the nature of things which we call scientific knowledge'; and he wrote of how 'intellectually we stand on an islet in the midst of an illimitable ocean of inexplicability.' TH believed that the ultimate truth must for ever lie beyond us, and that belief has been strengthened by the years. Half a century on, his grandson Julian, having watched the partial unravelling of those inter-relationships between mind and matter which had so intrigued TH, found that each solution merely opened the door to yet further mysteries beyond.

> Science [he said] . . . confronts us with a basic and universal mystery – the mystery of existence in general, and of the existence of mind in particular. Why does the world exist? Why is the world-stuff what it is? Why does it have mental or subjective aspects as well as material or objective ones? We do not know. All we can do is to admit the facts.

And Aldous, moving towards the end, could write a few months before his death that 'the older one gets, the more unutterably mysterious, unlikely and totally implausible one's own life and the universe at large steadily become.'

If humility is a surprising word to use of the Huxleys, it is difficult to find one more adequate for this continuing belief. For their conclusions, written in whatever way they have thought best, have been not only that science and art are mirror-images of one another, at times indistinguishable in effect, but that matter and mind may perhaps be related in much the same elusive manner; that there is no way of measuring the poet's vision against the scientist's fact; and that there is not, because there never can be, a final answer to the problem of what is reality, and what the dream that dies at each opening day.

SELECT BIBLIOGRAPHY

SELECT BIBLIOGRAPHY

The most important manuscript material dealing with the Huxley family consists of the Huxley collection held by the Imperial College of Science and Technology, London; its 4,500 letters to about 850 correspondents have been admirably catalogued by Warren R. Dawson (*The Huxley Papers, a Descriptive Catalogue of the Correspondence, Manuscripts and Miscellaneous Papers of the Rt. Hon. Thomas Henry Huxley, preserved in the Imperial College of Science and Technology, London*, by Warren R. Dawson, Macmillan, 1946). A later bequest of about 2,500 letters, the majority of them between T. H. Huxley and his wife, is being catalogued by the College archivist, Mrs J. Pingree. I have found both collections of very great help, and the same is true of *North House*, the unpublished manuscript written by Sir Laurence Collier.

The published writings of the Huxley family are immense – the bibliography of TH, published in his son's *Life and Letters*, runs to 16 closely-printed pages, the 'Huxley' entries in the British Museum Catalogue fill 25 columns, while the latest bibliography of Aldous (*Aldous Huxley: A Bibliography, 1916–1959* by Claire John Eschelbach and Joyce Lee Shober, University of California Press, 1961) contains nearly 1,300 items. It has, therefore, been possible to include in the following bibliography only a selection of the more important writings by members of the family. A great number of other books have been of use to me in writing *The Huxleys* and I have listed the principal ones at the end of the bibliography.

ALDOUS HUXLEY

Adonis and the Alphabet, and other essays. London: Chatto & Windus, 1956. New York: Harper, 1956, under title *Tomorrow and Tomorrow and Tomorrow, and Other Essays*.

After Many a Summer. London: Chatto & Windus, 1939. New York: Harper, 1939, under title *After Many a Summer Dies the Swan.*

Along the Road; Notes and Essays of a Tourist. London: Chatto & Windus, 1925. New York: George H. Doran, 1926.

Antic Hay. London: Chatto & Windus, 1923. New York: George H. Doran, 1923.

Ape and Essence. New York: Harper, 1948. London: Chatto & Windus 1949.

The Art of Seeing. New York: Harper, 1942. London: Chatto & Windus, 1943.

Beyond the Mexique Bay. London: Chatto & Windus, 1934. New York: Harper, 1934.

Brave New World. London: Chatto & Windus, 1932. Garden City, N.Y.: Doubleday, Doran, 1932.

Brave New World Revisited. New York: Harper, 1958. London: Chatto & Windus, 1959.

Brief Candles (short stories). London: Chatto & Windus, 1930. Garden City, N.Y.: Doubleday, Doran, 1932.

The Burning Wheel (poems). Oxford: Blackwell, 1916.

Crome Yellow. London: Chatto & Windus, 1921. New York: George H. Doran, 1922.

The Defeat of Youth and other poems. Oxford: Blackwell, 1918.

The Devils of Loudun. London: Chatto & Windus, 1952. New York: Harper, 1952.

The Doors of Perception. London: Chatto & Windus, 1954. New York: Harper, 1954.

Do What You Will (essays). London: Chatto & Windus, 1929. Garden City, N.Y.: Doubleday, Doran, 1929.

An Encyclopaedia of Pacifism (edited). London: Chatto & Windus, 1937. New York: Harper, 1937.

Ends and Means. An enquiry into the nature of ideals and into the methods employed for their realization. London: Chatto & Windus, 1937. New York: Harper, 1937.

Eyeless in Gaza. London: Chatto & Windus, 1936. New York: Harper, 1936.

The Genius and the Goddess. London: Chatto & Windus, 1955. New York: Harper, 1955.

Grey Eminence. A study in religion and politics. London: Chatto & Windus, 1941. New York: Harper, 1941.

Heaven and Hell. London: Chatto & Windus, 1956. New York: Harper, 1956.

Island. London: Chatto & Windus, 1962. New York: Harper, 1962.

Jesting Pilate. The diary of a journey. London: Chatto & Windus, 1926. New York: George H. Doran, 1926.

Leda (poems). London: Chatto & Windus, 1920. New York: George H. Doran, 1920.

The Letters of D. H. Lawrence (edited). London: Heinemann, 1932. New York: Viking Press, 1932.
Limbo (short stories). London: Chatto & Windus, 1920. New York: George H. Doran, 1920.
Little Mexican and other stories. London: Chatto & Windus, 1924. New York. George H. Doran, 1924, under title *Young Archimedes, and other Stories.*
Mortal Coils (short stories, etc.). London: Chatto & Windus, 1922. New York: George H. Doran, 1922.
The Olive Tree, and other essays. London: Chatto & Windus, 1936. New York: Harper, 1937.
On the Margin. Notes and essays. London: Chatto & Windus, 1923. New York: George H. Doran, 1923.
The Perennial Philosophy. New York: Harper, 1945. London: Chatto & Windus, 1946.
Point Counter Point. London: Chatto & Windus, 1928. Garden City, N.Y.: Doubleday, Doran, 1928.
Proper Studies (essays). London: Chatto & Windus, 1927. Garden City, N.Y.: Doubleday, Doran, 1927.
Science, Liberty, and Peace. New York: Harper, 1946. London: Chatto & Windus, 1947.
Texts and Pretexts, an anthology with commentaries. London: Chatto & Windus, 1932. New York: Harper, 1933.
Those Barren Leaves. London: Chatto & Windus, 1925. New York: George H. Doran, 1925.
Time Must Have a Stop. New York: Harper, 1944. London: Chatto & Windus, 1945.
Two or Three Graces and other Stories. London: Chatto & Windus, 1926. New York: George H. Doran, 1926.
What Are You Going to Do About It? The case for constructive peace. London: Chatto & Windus, 1936. New York: Harper, 1937.
The World of Light. London: Chatto & Windus, 1931. Garden City, N.Y.: Doubleday, Doran, 1931.

ANTHONY HUXLEY

Flowers of the Mediterranean (with Oleg Polunin). London: Chatto & Windus, 1965. Boston: Houghton Mifflin, 1966.
Mountain Flowers in Colour. London: Blandford Press, 1967.

ELSPETH HUXLEY

Race and Politics in Kenya. A correspondence. London: Faber & Faber, 1944.
White Man's Country: Lord Delamere and the making of Kenya. London: Macmillan, 1935.

FRANCIS HUXLEY

Affable Savages. London: Rupert Hart-Davis, 1956. New York: Viking Press, 1957.
The Invisibles. London: Rupert Hart-Davis, 1966. New York: McGraw-Hill, 1968.

GERVAS HUXLEY

Endymion Porter. London: Chatto & Windus, 1959.
Lady Elizabeth and the Grosvenors. London: Oxford University Press, 1965. New York: Oxford University Press, 1967.
Victorian Duke. London: Oxford University Press, 1967.

HENRIETTA A. HUXLEY

Poems. London: Duckworth, 1913.

JULIAN HUXLEY

Africa View. London: Chatto & Windus, 1931. New York: Harper, 1931.
Animal Biology (with J. B. S. Haldane). London: Oxford University Press, 1927.
Animal Language. London: Country Life, 1938. New York: Grosset, 1964.
Argument of Blood, The Advancement of Science. London: Macmillan War Pamphlets. No. 11, 1941.
At the Zoo. London: Allen & Unwin, 1936.
Biological Aspects of Cancer. London: Allen & Unwin, 1958. New York: Harcourt Brace, 1958.
Bird-watching and Bird Behaviour. London: Chatto & Windus, 1930.
The Captive Shrew, and other poems of a biologist. Oxford: Blackwell, 1932.
Essays of a Biologist. London: Chatto & Windus, 1923. New York: Alfred A. Knopf, 1923.
Evolution: The modern synthesis. London: Allen & Unwin, 1942. New York: Harper, 1942.
Evolutionary Ethics. (The Romanes Lecture, delivered 11 June, 1943). London: Oxford University Press, 1943.
From an Antique Land. London: Max Parrish, 1954.
Holyrood. (The Newdigate Poem, 1908). London: Blackwell, 1908.
If I Were Dictator. London: Methuen, 1934.
The Individual in the Animal Kingdom. Cambridge: Cambridge Manuals of Science and Literature, 1910.
Kingdom of the Beasts (with W. Suschitzky). London: Thames & Hudson, 1956.

The Living Thoughts of Darwin (extracts). London: Cassell, 1939.
New Bottles for New Wine (essays). London: Chatto & Windus, 1957.
On Living in a Revolution (essays). London: Chatto & Windus, 1944. New York: Harper, 1944.
Problems in Experimental Embryology (Robert Boyle Lecture) Oxford: Oxford University Press, 1935.
Problems of Relative Growth. London: Methuen, 1932.
"Race" in Europe (Oxford Pamphlets on World Affairs). Oxford: Clarendon Press, 1939.
Religion Without Revelation. London: Ernest Benn, 1927. New York: Harper, 1927.
The Science of Life (with H. G. and G. P. Wells). London: Cassell, 1929.
A Scientist Among the Soviets. London: Chatto & Windus, 1932.
Soviet Genetics and World Science. Lysenko and the meaning of heredity. London: Chatto & Windus, 1949.
TVA: Adventure in Planning. Cheam, Surrey: Architectural Press, 1943.
Unesco, its Purpose and its Philosophy. London: Preparatory Commission of Unesco, 1946. Washington: Public Affairs Press, 1947.
The Uniqueness of Man. London: Chatto & Windus, 1941.

JULIETTE HUXLEY

Wild Lives of Africa. London: Collins, 1963. New York: Harper, 1964.

LAURA HUXLEY

You Are Not the Target. New York: Farrar, Straus, 1963. London: Heinemann, 1964.

LEONARD HUXLEY

Anniversaries (poems). London: John Murray, 1920.
Charles Darwin. London: John Murray, 1920. New York: Greenberg, 1927.
Life and Letters of Sir Joseph Dalton Hooker. London: John Murray, 1918. New York: Appleton, 1918.
Life and Letters of Thomas Henry Huxley. London: Macmillan, 1900. New York: Appleton, 1900.
Progress and the Unfit (Conway Memorial Lecture). London: Watts & Co., 1926.
Sheaves from the Cornhill (selected). London: John Murray, 1926.

THOMAS HENRY HUXLEY

Collected Essays, 9 vols. London: Macmillan, 1894–1908. New York: Appleton, 1893–1894 (9 vols.).

The Crayfish. London: C. Kegan Paul, 1880. New York: International Science Series, vol. 28, 1880.

T. H. Huxley's Diary of the Voyage of H.M.S. Rattlesnake (edited Julian Huxley). London: Chatto & Windus, 1935.

Evidence as to Man's Place in Nature. London: Williams & Norgate, 1863. New York: Appleton, 1870.

The Evidence of the Miracle of the Resurrection (Paper read before the Metaphysical Society). London: Privately, for the Metaphysical Society, 1876.

Lay Sermons, Addresses, and Reviews. London: Macmillan, 1870. New York: Appleton, 1871.

A Manual of the Anatomy of Invertebrated Animals. London: J. & A. Churchill, 1877. New York: Appleton, 1878.

The Oceanic Hydrozoa etc. London: The Ray Society, 1859.

On our Knowledge of the Causes of the Phenomena of Organic Nature (Six lectures to working men etc.). London: Robert Hardwicke, 1862.

On the Educational Value of the Natural History Sciences. London: John Van Voorst, 1854.

The Scientific Memoirs of T. H. Huxley, (edited by Professor Michael Foster and by Professor E. Ray Lankester). London: Macmillan, 1898–1903.

Other books by members of the Huxley family include the following:

Collier, Laurence: *Flight From Conflict* (1944).

Crawshay-Williams, Rupert: *The Comforts of Unreason* (1947). *Methods and Criteria of Reasoning* (1957).

Eckersley, Peter: *Captain Eckersley Explains* (1924).

Eckersley, Roger Huxley: *The BBC and All That* (1946).

Haynes, Renée: *Pan, Caesar and God* (1938).

Haynes, Renée: *The Hidden Springs* (1961).

The following are also among the books which I have found of use in writing *The Huxleys:*

Ayres, C. E.: *Aldous Huxley* (1932).

Bibby, Cyril: *T. H. Huxley* (1959).

Brown, A. W.: *The Metaphysical Society* (1947).

Campbell, Roy: *Broken Record* (1934).

Chambers, William: *Memoir of Robert Chambers* (1872).

Collier, the Hon. E. C. F. (ed.): *A Victorian Diarist. Extracts from the Journals of Mary, Lady Monkswell, 1873–1895.* (1944).

Collier, the Hon. John: *The Religion of an Artist* (1926).
Day-Lewis, Cecil: *We're Not Going to do Nothing* (1936).
Duncan, David: *Life and Letters of Herbert Spencer* (1908).
Fayrer, Sir Joseph: *Recollections of My Life* (1900).
Haynes, E. S. P.: *A Lawyer's Notebook* (1932).
Hilliard: *The Balliol College Register* (1914).
Irvine, William: *Apes, Angels and Victorians* (1960).
Litchfield, H. E.: *Emma Darwin* (1904).
Lyell, Sir Charles: *Life, Letters and Journals* (1881).
Mack, Marjorie: *The Educated Pin* (1944).
Owen, R. S.: *Life of Sir Richard Owen* (1894).
Pollock, W. H.: *The Art of the Hon. John Collier* (1914).
Smalley, G. W.: *Anglo-American Memories* (1911/12).
Thirkell, Angela: *Three Houses* (1931).
Tuckwell, W.: *Reminiscences* (1905).
Wilberforce, R. G.: *Bishop Wilberforce* (1905).
Wilberforce, Samuel: *Replies to Essays and Reviews* (1862).

In addition, I have found of great help the files of *Nature, The Saturday Review,* the *Fortnightly Review,* the *Contemporary Review,* and the other journals to which T. H. Huxley contributed.

The family tree

showing the first three generations descending from T. H. Huxley

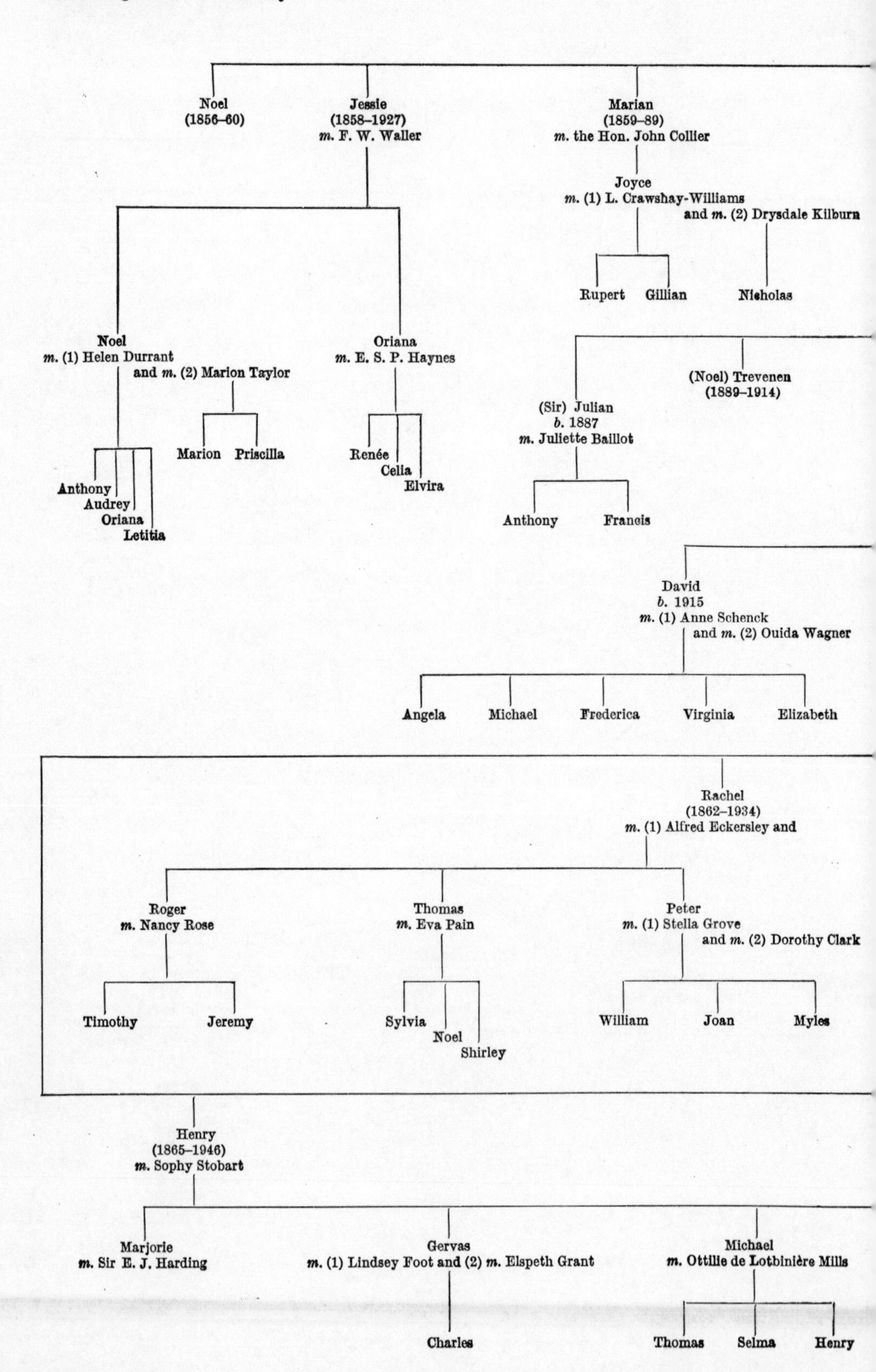

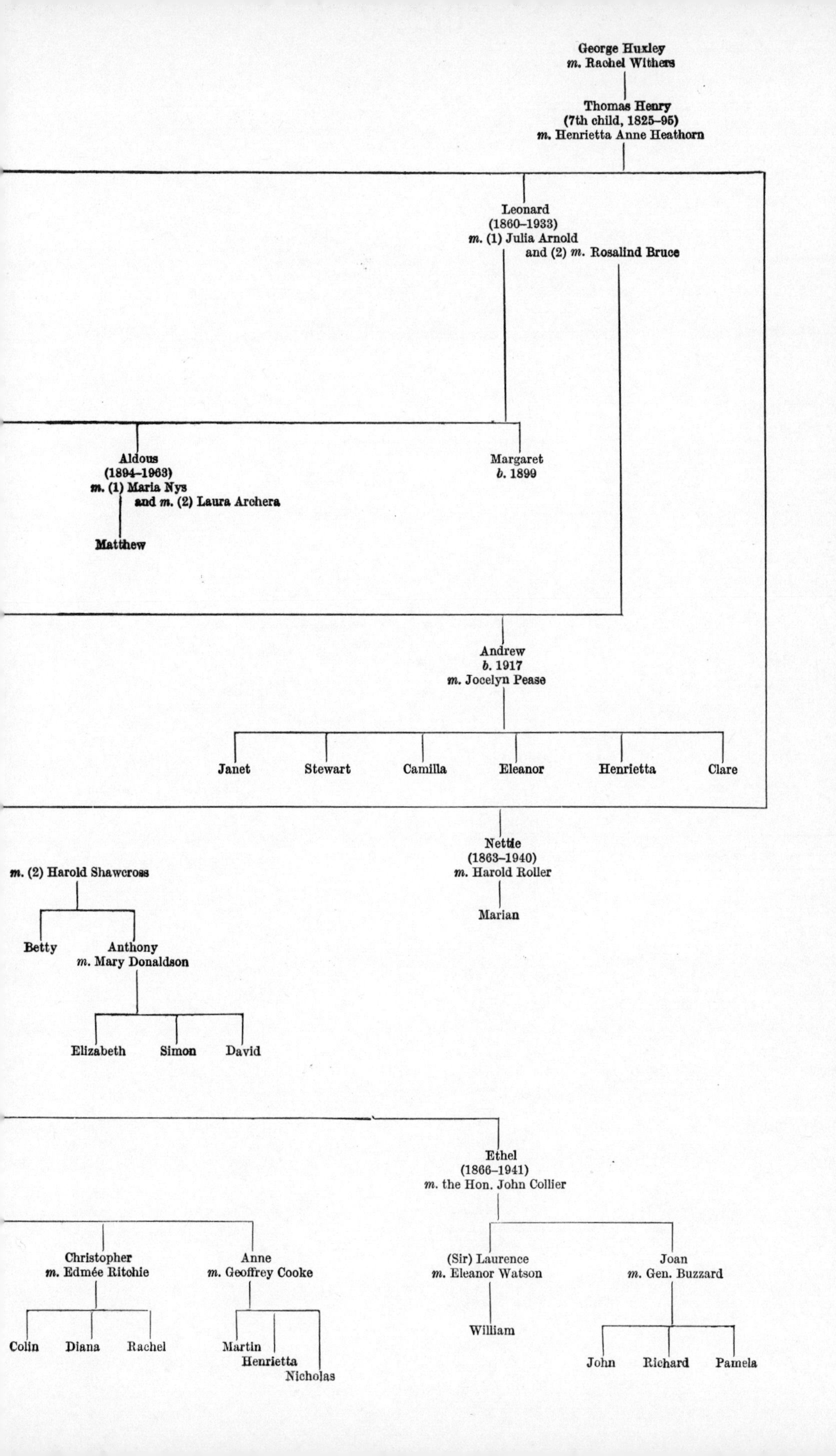
George Huxley
m. Rachel Withers
Thomas Henry
(7th child, 1825–95)
m. Henrietta Anne Heathorn
Leonard
(1860–1933)
m. (1) Julia Arnold
and (2) m. Rosalind Bruce
Aldous
(1894–1963)
m. (1) Maria Nys
and m. (2) Laura Archera
Matthew
Margaret
b. 1899
Andrew
b. 1917
m. Jocelyn Pease
Janet
Stewart
Camilla
Eleanor
Henrietta
Clare
Nettie
(1863–1940)
m. Harold Roller
Marian
m. (2) Harold Shawcross
Betty
Anthony
m. Mary Donaldson
Elizabeth
Simon
David
Ethel
(1866–1941)
m. the Hon. John Collier
Christopher
m. Edmée Ritchie
Anne
m. Geoffrey Cooke
Colin
Diana
Rachel
Martin
Henrietta
Nicholas
(Sir) Laurence
m. Eleanor Watson
William
Joan
m. Gen. Buzzard
John
Richard
Pamela

Index

Index